THE
RESTLESS
REPUBLIC

ALSO BY ANNA KEAY

The Last Royal Rebel: The Life and Death of James Duke of Monmouth

The Magnificent Monarch: Charles II and the Ceremonies of Power

The Crown Jewels: The Official Illustrated History

THE RESTLESS REPUBLIC

Britain Without a Crown

ANNA KEAY

WILLIAM
COLLINS

William Collins
An imprint of HarperCollins*Publishers*
1 London Bridge Street
London SE1 9GF

WilliamCollinsBooks.com

HarperCollins*Publishers*
1st Floor, Watermarque Building, Ringsend Road
Dublin 4, Ireland

First published in Great Britain in 2022 by William Collins

1

A catalogue record for this book is
available from the British Library

ISBN 978-0-00-828202-8

Maps, timeline and family trees by Martin Brown

Typeset in Dante MT Pro
Printed and bound in the UK using 100%
renewable electricity at CPI Group (UK) Ltd

MIX
Paper from
responsible sources
FSC™ C007454

FOR MAUD AND ARTHUR

CONTENTS

MAPS

Atlantic
Ocean

U L S T E R

Coleraine
Londonderry
Strabane
Antrim
Belfast
L. Neagh
Lisburn
Enniskillen
Armagh
Sligo
Newry
Dundalk
Drogheda

C O N N A C H T

Roscommon
Athlone
Liffey
Dublin
Galway
L E I N S T E R
Shannon
Birr

Carlow
Kilkenny
Limerick
Cashel
Tipperary
Clonmel
Liscarroll
Wexford
Fermoy
Lismore
Waterford
M U N S T E R
Cork
Youghal
Bandon

Irish
Sea

N

0   kilometres   50
0   miles   50

FOREWORD

This book was born of ignorance. Studies of the seventeenth century tend to deal either with some aspect of the kingdoms of the Stuart monarchy or with the world of the civil wars and the Revolution. There are lots of good reasons for dividing an entire century into manageable chunks, but it was not, of course, how it was. Those who walked the streets of Lincoln or London, shared a bottle of wine in the inns of Exeter or Edinburgh, in the 1630s often did so still in the 1650s and 1670s. Their dress and the style of their hair might have changed, and age would have weathered their skin and blurred their sight, but this was nothing to how the environment around them had shifted over that time. Few, if any, other generations of British people can have experienced such a period of national political and social change. Many of those I knew from both the earlier and later seventeenth century lived through these republican years and I wanted to know more of what they had experienced. Very few people tuck neatly into one historical 'age' or another, or live only in the years with which they are most closely associated. Samuel Pepys and Christopher Wren, quintessential figures of the age of Charles II, were respectively a naval secretary and a pioneering mathematician during the 1650s. Oliver Cromwell's daughter, Mary, and her husband Lord Fauconberg, whose boisterous wedding party Oliver himself had hosted, were popular figures at the late Stuart courts;

the Earl was ambassador to Venice, a friend of the Duke of Monmouth and, later, a prominent supporter of the Glorious Revolution. Well into the reign of Queen Anne the residents of Cheshunt in Hertfordshire would see an elderly man out riding with his dogs, or sketching landscapes, who was none other than Richard Cromwell, one-time Lord Protector of the Commonwealth of England, Scotland and Ireland.

This book attempts to inhabit Britain in the only period in its history when it was a republic and to try, by seeking to stand at the shoulder of a number of contemporaries, to understand what it was like and why. It is not a book about the civil war, which was largely over by the time it begins. But it is a book about life in a post-war land scarred by conflict and its monumental cost – human, material and financial. The nine men and women taken as protagonists are not representative of British society – the sources make this impossible – but they do represent different experiences. Some, such as John Bradshaw, President of the first Commonwealth Council of State, stood at the centre of events, others, the young visionary Anna Trapnel or the Norfolk gentlewoman Alice L'Estrange, at the periphery. Some, most notably Oliver Cromwell, are household names, others, such as the irrepressible newspaperman Marchamont Nedham, are unknown to all but academics. Through the surviving primary sources I have tried to piece together a picture of what their lives were in these years and to do so in a way which also tells the story of the age. The men and women of the 1650s were not two-dimensional woodcuts or joyless caricatures but real people, with friends and enemies, anxieties and aspirations, desires and disappointments like any person alive today. My hope is that through them the age in which they lived – which was at times as unfamiliar to them as it is to us today – might become more real and make more sense to we who, after all, walk in their footsteps still.

❧ ❧ ❧

There is a risk in writing about a decade sometimes called 'the Interregnum' that it becomes defined in the negative. Given our knowledge of what came next, it is easy to imagine that the return of the monarchy, the House of Lords and the episcopacy was inevitable and that these years were always destined to be a historical blind alley. This is not my contention. The 1650s was a time of extraordinarily ambitious political, social, economic and intellectual innovation, and it was not a foregone conclusion that the British republic would fail. But it was also a time about which a characterisation in the negative, 'Britain without a Crown', is relevant. The decade was defined to a significant degree by what was being rejected. Indeed part of the reason for the fall of the republic was that its protagonists agreed far more on what they did not want than what they sought in its place. Furthermore one of the republic of Britain's enduring legacies has been as a historical cautionary tale, a ghoul summoned up at times of turmoil to deter later generations from a course of radicalism. That the United Kingdom remains a monarchy to this day is due in no small part to the events and experiences described in this book.

❦ ❦ ❦

While the book has 'Britain' in its title, it is fully acknowledged that Britain here – rather as was the case with the first 'British' parliaments of 1656–9 – is weighted towards England.

Dates follow the 'Old Style' Julian Calendar used in England at the time, but with the new year taken as starting on 1 January. Quotations are given with the original spelling unless otherwise stated. Readers who find this hard to understand are encouraged to say the words aloud.

One

The Forced Revolution

T here could hardly have been a more apposite place in which to
make the decision to execute Charles I than the Painted Chamber
at Westminster. When the clouds broke during the numerous morning
meetings here in January 1649, elongated lancets of sunlight streamed
through the tall Gothic windows onto the matted floor and down the
table where the men who brought the King to trial gathered. Created
for Henry III four centuries before, this was once the Great Chamber
of the medieval Palace of Westminster. Outside a terrace of royal
gardens lay between the massive stone building and the wide River
Thames, while inside the high walls had once been painted with the
vivid royal and biblical scenes to which it owed its name. This was the
chamber where medieval kings had slept and dined, and where they
had taken counsel. The building works had been completed just in
time for the meeting of Henry III's Great Council of January 1237.
Here the Plantagenet king had secured agreement to the taxes he
wished to levy by promising various concessions to his subjects.
During this, the first gathering in English history to be called a 'parliament', he had pledged to reissue the famous undertaking which his
father King John had signed, and then repudiated, Magna Carta. With
it was established the principle that everybody, even the King, was
subject to the law.[1]

Whether the men who milled about the Painted Chamber on the morning of 20 January 1649 spared much thought for the room's significance is doubtful. They had the future, not the past, in their sights. In their intense preoccupation none of them noticed the slight figure concealed behind one of the tapestries that now covered the wall paintings – a young royalist interloper, Purbeck Temple, who would later bear witness to what he heard. The discussion was of the final arrangements for the trial of Charles I, which was to commence that afternoon. The tension was almost suffocating. Deliberations turned to prayer, earnest invoking of God's support for the momentous task they had taken upon themselves. Then came a messenger with the news. The King had arrived. One of their number, Lieutenant General Oliver Cromwell, dashed to the window. Here he watched the small, cloaked figure of Charles I disembark from a boat and walk steadily across the wintry garden into the adjacent building. Cromwell's nerve suddenly faltered. When he turned away from the window he was 'as white as the wall'. Speaking only to his closest colleagues he asked them wildly 'how ... they had concluded on such a business'. But almost as quickly as it had risen, his doubt subsided. When he addressed the table a minute or two later he radiated confidence: 'My masters, he is come, he is come and now we are doing that great work that the whole nation will be full of'.[2]

The man to whom Cromwell turned in his moment of doubt was John Bradshaw. A few hours earlier Bradshaw had awoken in unaccustomed splendour. His home was tucked in behind the Guildhall in the heart of the City of London. As a lawyer and City of London judge his professional life was focused on the ancient metropolis.[3] But this morning he had risen and dressed in one of the finest addresses in the royal enclave of Westminster, two miles upstream. Sir Abraham Williams's House stood on Old Palace Yard at right angles to the main north entrance of Westminster Hall. It was from an upstairs room here, twenty-four years earlier, that the Queen, Henrietta Maria, and her ladies had watched her husband's coronation procession. For the past decade or so the house had been rented by the state to house visiting diplomats. Occupants had included the ambassadors from the Dutch Republic who came to negotiate the marriage of Charles I's daughter Mary to the young Prince of Orange just before the outbreak of civil war. Williams's house had comfortably accommodated the three Dutch noblemen, their numerous servants and their luggage (which for just a short visit had filled six barges), so it was a capacious lodging for its single occupant. But while he was no royal prince or European aristocrat, Bradshaw's status required such a house, for he was the man who was to try the King.[4]

In these unfamiliar surroundings Bradshaw dressed in unfamiliar clothes. Though the trial was to open that day, its members had actually been meeting daily for almost a fortnight. During the preparatory discussions a great deal of time had been devoted not only to matters of law, but also to questions of appearance. Heralds from the College of Arms were called in to advise. Accordingly, when Bradshaw walked across the Yard to join his colleagues in the Painted Chamber he was dressed in a long black gown edged with tassels, preceded by a sword bearer and a mace bearer and flanked by sixteen scarlet-clad officers each carrying a gleaming partizan.[5]

The procession formed again as the morning meeting in the Painted Chamber concluded and Bradshaw, Cromwell and their fellow 'commissioners' fell into formation and trooped through a sequence of ever larger medieval chambers towards Westminster Hall. The palace had

New Palace Yard and the entrance to Westminster Hall where Charles I was tried in January 1649. The building on the far side of the yard, to the left of the fountain cover, is probably Sir Abraham Williams's house where John Bradshaw lodged during the trial.

not been used as a royal residence since a serious fire in 1512, but many activities associated with the crown had continued there after the royal family had left: the national accountancy of the exchequer, the periodic gathering of the two houses of Parliament and the dispensing of justice through the royal courts of law. Taking up his seat in a scarlet velvet chair, and with his fellow commissioners sitting on raked benches behind him, Bradshaw turned to one of the officers of the court and issued his instruction: 'Serjeant Dendy, send for your prisoner.'[6]

🜲 🜲 🜲

In January 1649 John Bradshaw was 46. Handsome in a pale, intelligent way, he had reddish-brown hair, dark eyes and a sandy moustache above a cleft chin (Colour plate 1). Before the outbreak of the civil war he had lived a different life in the lush landscape of Cheshire, a county famous for salt, cheese and the Roman city of Chester – the main embarkation point for Ireland. How he came to summon the King to trial beneath the magnificent timber roof of Westminster Hall was far from straightforward or inevitable. The Bradshaws were not outlandish radicals, or dispossessed revolutionaries, but solid gentry. Like hundreds of families up and down the land, they owned property, employed servants, gave generously to the church collection plate and paid substantial sums to educate their children. But while he sprang from this stock, John Bradshaw was intensely his own man.[7]

The last of the Tudors, the elderly Queen Elizabeth had been visibly fading in December 1602, when 200 miles north of the capital the infant John Bradshaw had been held to the font in the medieval parish church of Stockport.[8] Four months later she was dead and the King of Scots, the unpolished but politically astute James VI, set off from Edinburgh to assume his cousin's throne. He travelled south not through the Bradshaws' Cheshire, but by the quicker great north road down England's eastern flank. He began, as he did so, to acquaint himself with the wealthy kingdom he had chanced to inherit. He made excursions to view the great houses and hunting parks, inspecting the mighty royal castles of Pontefract and Newark, little knowing that these would be the scenes of such devastation in the wars that were to come.

Much about the life of the young John Bradshaw would be determined by the chance of birth. His brother was not quite two years his senior, but with age went the family's wealth and Henry would go on to manage, and in time inherit, the Bradshaws' extensive but scattered property holdings across the county. John knew he would have no such inheritance.[9] His mother died when he was just 2 years old and his father developed a dislike for his second son that he did not trouble to hide. In the absence of parental affection or a valuable inheritance, education and a fine brain spurred John Bradshaw on. He attended two grammar schools, one in Cheshire and one in Lancashire, and would be forever grateful for the experience: leaving each a hefty £500 to increase the wages of their schoolmasters 'return[ing] this as part of my thankfull acknowledgement'. He would bequeath a further £700 to establish a new school in his birthplace of Marple.[10]

Bradshaw's model in making these bequests may have been Thomas Aldersey, the wealthy Elizabethan cloth merchant who had endowed the grammar school he attended in Bunbury, 15 miles southwest of Chester. A committed adherent of the reformed, Protestant religion, Aldersey personally appointed John Glover as first schoolmaster. Glover oversaw a rigorous educational regime from the former chantry priest's house, combining classical excellence with Protestant purity. The lessons ran from 6 a.m. to 6.30 p.m., interspersed with 'Godly prayers'. To ensure 'purity of the Latin tongue' classical prose and poetry were to be studied alongside the Bible, with the rider that 'no matter be taught of any author which may hinder godliness and learning'. On this substantial educational diet, Glover reared a flock of talented young men equipped to attend the universities and Inns of Court. On Sundays pupils were sent to St Boniface's church, furnished with pencil and paper to take notes. Here they heard the powerful sermons of another of Aldersey's nominees, the outspoken Puritan minister William Hinde whose salary he also funded. Like many others, Hinde had become seized with the urgent necessity of reinforcing the Protestant reformation and saving England from the influence of Catholicism and spiritual decadence which were felt to be dangerously on the rise. In Hinde's passionate sermons the young John Bradshaw imbibed a strong Puritan draught and developed a lifelong belief in the value of powerful and instructive preaching.[11]

For many in the seventeenth century, God's disapproval was not an abstract concept, or something to be encountered only in the afterlife, but was starkly real and visible daily in acts of divine justice. Among the perils Hinde saw around him were 'those Disorders, which were usually at Bunbury Wakes, & ... threatened God's Judgement against the same'. Wakes or ales were the festivities loosely connected to the church year that periodically took place in English villages and towns. The plays and games, maypole and Morris dancing, animal baiting and drinking they involved were rooted in medieval customs, but sometimes dissolved into drunkenness and violence – and were disapproved of by many in positions of authority.[12]

John Bradshaw's contemporary at Bunbury grammar school Edward Burghall kept a diary in which he recorded the numerous instances of God's intervention in the life of their own parish. When spectators of the bear baiting at the village ales had leaned against the churchyard wall, he noted knowingly, it collapsed on top of them and the bear later gorged his owner. One Mr Lee, 'coming home drunk, as he went to water his Horse, was drowned in his Mote', while 'divers Drunkards [were] taken away suddenly by the just Hand of God, some being drowned, one hard by Hampton post, others by untimely deaths'. As it was within the village, so it was within the kingdom, and the lynching of a 'debauched conjurer' leaving a London playhouse was also confidently ascribed to God's displeasure. No wonder that Burghall bemoaned, 'Oh! that Men would learn at last to be wise, before the heavy Wrath of God fall upon them'.[13]

Bradshaw had both ability and application, and flourished under Glover's tutelage. In 1620 at barely 18, he was admitted to Gray's Inn in London to study to be a barrister. Gray's Inn was one of a clutch of legal colleges, or inns, clustered around Holborn, between London and Westminster, where all those who wished to practise law learned their trade. The profession was a respectable one, and the sons of many wealthy families enrolled without any expectation that they would actually complete the lengthy legal apprenticeship. Of the nine young gentlemen admitted on the same day as Bradshaw four were the sons of knights. One of these was Henry Cromwell of Ramsey in Huntingdonshire, first cousin of Bradshaw's future ally – and adversary – Oliver Cromwell.

To move to London and train for the bar required money and influence. Bradshaw had both through his Cheshire connections. The Leghs of Lyme Park acted as sponsors and supporters; Peter Brereton, son of William Brereton of Ashley and a distant cousin, also entered Gray's Inn that year and would become Bradshaw's lifelong friend. Away from home and rubbing shoulders with a well-heeled and connected tribe of young men, he was now in a different world. The Inns of Court were woven into civic ceremonial life and even participated in court pageantry – only a few years before the men of Gray's Inn had donned exotic outfits to perform in a masque before the royal family at Whitehall celebrating the marriage of James VI/I's daughter to the Elector Palatine. The Inn itself had provided the costumes, with young lawyers playing the roles of the Knights of Olympus, statues, cupids and even a 'He and She Baboon'. The Attorney-General, and august pillar of the law, Francis Bacon, had orchestrated the entire occasion.

While some might see everything through the lens of divine displeasure, Bradshaw's view was broader. As his friend John Milton would later say of him, unlike some other Puritans 'there was no forbidding austerity, no moroseness in his manner'. The Bradshaws were not a family of killjoys; his brother's account book shows that the elder Bradshaw shopped for colourful silk suits, drank alcohol, played cards and made an annual contribution to the local May Day festivities. Immersed in the metropolitan world, with all its grime and glamour, John relayed political gossip to Cheshire friends, asking them 'not to miscensure my forwardnes in takyng notice of theise things, for it agrees w[i]th my genius [character] to have some smattering herein'. He viewed the high jinks of student life with detached amusement, recounting the armed rescue of one of their Inn from the gaol to which he had been committed for debt as a 'mad prancke'.[14]

Bradshaw would remain at Gray's Inn for seven years. As he studied his books and honed his skills of advocacy from his rooms on Holborn he witnessed the comings and goings of court and government. The premature death of James VI/I's eldest son, Henry Prince of Wales, and the marriage of his daughter, Elizabeth, left the King lonely and his family fractured. Into the gap had stepped the gorgeous, peacock figure of George Villiers, and soon both James I and his reserved second son, Charles, were in intense thrall to this powerfully attractive courtier who rose from obscurity to become Duke of Buckingham. The more important he became, the more Buckingham was reviled by those outside his inner circle. Bradshaw described the Duke as 'the high swolne ffavoryte', who secured title after title for his friends and relations, verging even on incest to safeguard his family's wealth, drily noting 'but we are so used to wonders that this is none at all'.

Whatever the troubles of the court, Bradshaw had his own battles to fight. The cost of studying for the bar was considerable and his ever-critical father missed no opportunity to have a dig at his talented son. Henry Bradshaw senior wrote accusing him of not applying himself, having heard that John had delayed one of the moots at which students argued hypothetical cases. Young Bradshaw explained that he did so only to accelerate the moment when he could plead cases alone. Writing to Sir Peter Legh, he lamented: 'It seemeth, how prone he is to take exception agaynst me, when fynding nothing blameworthy, he returned that for a fault w[hi]ch deserveth allowance and prayse.' But John Bradshaw was used to it, and was fast developing emotional fortitude: 'he shall soon[e]r be wearie of afflicting, then I will be of suffering, & by the grace of God I will shew my self a Sonne, though he cease to be my ffather.'

In 1627 John Bradshaw qualified as a barrister and returned to Cheshire, taking up residence not at the family home at Marple Hall but in the town of Congleton 20 miles south. As he became part of the administrative fabric of his own locality, the new King, Charles I, was trying his hands at the ropes of monarchy, with mixed success.[15]

❦ ❦ ❦

In 1625 James VI/I had died, and was succeeded by the 25-year-old Charles I. Shy and fastidious, Charles shared with his Tudor and Stuart predecessors a conviction that he ruled by divine right, but he lacked the political instinct that was necessary in a system in which, in reality, monarchs could do little of substance without the cooperation of at least some of their subjects. He loved beauty and splendour, order and ceremony, was devoted to his family and loyal to his friends, but he was also proud, authoritarian, defensive and jealously protective of his regal dignity. It would be a dangerous compound.

At his accession Charles I promised to send an army to the Continent to help his sister and brother-in-law regain the throne of Bohemia (from which they had been ejected in 1620). The agreement of Parliament's two houses was required to raise the necessary taxes, and Charles called it in 1625. MPs saw this as an excellent opportunity for the shortcomings of the previous reign to be properly addressed. Charles saw it as formality. When Parliament put forward a list of grievances about the rise of 'Popery' and corruption of various sorts, the young King had bristled. The military expeditions he went on to launch with Buckingham's encouragement ended in a series of embarrassing catastrophes, causing the bad-tempered relationship between King and Parliament to deteriorate further. When Buckingham was stabbed to death in a Portsmouth alehouse in 1628, many nodded knowingly, sensing divine justice at work once again. On 10 March 1629 Charles I decided he had had enough and announced that, until such time as they 'come to a better understanding of Us', he would govern without the aid of Parliament.[16]

For an English sovereign to rule without Parliament was not of itself particularly unusual. James I had done so for all but two months of an entire decade and no national crisis had resulted. But to do so successfully required certain things of a king. These included forgoing expensive projects that could not be funded out of ordinary crown income, and operating with political sensitivity in the absence of the release valve that parliamentary sessions provided. On both counts Charles I failed woefully. His determination to build a glorious royal navy, without the additional tax income that needed parliamentary approval, involved using a series of roundabout routes to raise money which were unpopular with his subjects. These included extending to the whole kingdom the levy traditionally applied only to coastal counties known as 'ship money'. Meanwhile, his belief in the need for strict religious uniformity, and his own taste for high church forms of worship (which with their incense and ornaments, bowing and kneeling, appeared more Catholic than Calvinist), fuelled popular alarm about the perceived rise of 'Popery'. The fact that his young wife, the daughter of the King of France, was a Catholic only added to the conspiracy theories.

Without the mechanism of Parliament, which allowed such concerns to be aired, pressure mounted. Matters would come to a head in the late 1630s when, in a crass and catastrophic misjudgement, Charles decided that it was high time his Scottish subjects adopted his preferred form of worship. A new Book of Common Prayer was issued designed to bring the spare Calvinism of the church in Scotland into line with the more ceremonial form of worship favoured by the King and his Archbishop of Canterbury, William Laud. Fiercely independent – their ancient kingdom being still quite separate in laws and traditions – the Scots were furious. They considered 'Laudian' churchmanship to be heretical, a fiendish and essentially Catholic distortion of the proper purity of devotion based on preaching and the word of God, and bitterly resented having their own nation treated as an adjunct to England. A document affirming their commitment to their own traditions was issued: the National Covenant. An indignant Charles then dangerously, and entirely unnecessarily, escalated matters by declaring any protest against the new Prayer Book treason. By the end of 1638 all the bishops in the Scottish church had fled to England fearing for their lives and the King began to organize an armed intervention to force the Scots to submit.

As soon as Charles had decided to use force to compel the Scots to comply with his demands, it was inevitable he would have to call Parliament sooner or later. Ship money and other levies had raised enough to build up the navy, but in an age when there was no permanent army it was virtually impossible to raise men to fight a war without money that only Parliament could grant. In April 1640 Parliament gathered in Westminster. Charles sought the funds for his campaign; the House of Commons seized the chance to articulate their pent-up grievances. It took just three weeks for the King to lose patience and dissolve this 'Short Parliament'. But he could not stave it off for long, especially given that in the summer of 1640 the Scots marched into England. A new assembly, known to posterity as the 'Long Parliament', met in November 1640, clear that a regime that was losing control must now be brought to order.

❦ ❦ ❦

Watching these national events unfold from a distance was John Bradshaw. In the ten years after he qualified as a lawyer he enjoyed professional and financial success, enabling him to take a large timber-framed house in the centre of Congleton where he employed five household servants. Generous and hospitable, and sympathetic to those in need, he was soon supporting his extended family and other hard-up friends with liberal loans of money that he was slow to retrieve. Even people he had never met were to benefit from his kindness, among them an impoverished gentlewoman, Mrs Warren, whose intermediary knew that mention of 'her want of clothinge against this cold tyme' was likely to move the young lawyer. When he married in 1638 his wife was horrified to discover just how much her husband had lent his relations. Bradshaw's sister Dorothy, who had had £100 from her brother and had repeatedly extended the loan, received a stern letter from her new sister-in-law rebuking her: 'if you and some others of your [family] that had land could managed your Affairs no better, howe can you expect that hee which hath no land should pay your depts?' Bradshaw was 36 when he married Mary Marbury, the daughter of one of his Cheshire legal clients. She was 42, and, despite her sharp manner and their childlessness, it seems to have been a happy marriage – in his will he would speak of the bequests he made 'out of my love to her'. Bradshaw himself was a catch. He amassed a clutch of lucrative legal roles, became the lawyer to the Congleton corporation and rose to be mayor in 1637.

Bradshaw, like his schoolmate Edward Burghall, had been brought up to believe that unexplained calamities were expressions of God's displeasure. The winter of 1634–5 was famously, furiously cold. In London the Thames froze over while in Cheshire there was 'exceeding great frost and Snow and grevious tempests so that many lost their lives'. Bradshaw and his fellow aldermen struggled to manage affairs in Congleton. The town records offer glimpses of the human cost, such as the bill for 'cloth to make a winding sheet for a child that perished in the great snow'. If the cruel winter of 1635 made him wonder whether God was indeed making his displeasure known, worse was yet to come.[17]

The risk of plague was ever present in early seventeenth-century England. Both James I and Charles I's coronation processions were postponed for fear of it, and periodic outbreaks occurred across the country. It was a matter of real concern to John Bradshaw and shortly after his election as mayor of Congleton a whole series of policies were instituted to prevent it taking hold. Anyone returning with goods from an infected area was to be immediately isolated for at least twenty days, with a permanent guard stationed outside his or her house at the mayor's charge. But these careful precautions were unable to prevent the catastrophe that befell the town in the spring of 1641. In January life was going on as usual. John Bradshaw had his brother Henry to stay. The two men must have discussed national affairs, as it was while in Congleton that Henry added his support to a petition to Parliament, probably that calling for wholesale reform of the church. Then, suddenly, plague struck. The source, it was said, a box of clothes sent from London. Come the first week of March, Bradshaw's anti-plague measures were in full operation. But no amount of preparation could stem the spread and, in spite of mayoral edicts for the burial of the effects of those who had died, the infection engulfed the town and for months held Congleton in its terrifying clutches.

The town officials tried everything: victims were immediately confined, prevented from escaping by a round-the-clock watchman, or placed in special quarantine cabins where they were ministered to by the tragic figure of 'little Bess', a child whose young mother had already died from the disease. The contaminated corpses were dragged to mass graves in the churchyard by richly paid gravediggers, and the possessions of the dead boiled or burned. Houses were fumigated with smouldering pitch and frankincense, and all means of transmission were destroyed. A payment 'for Killing W[illia]m Newtons Catt at the death of his sonn fearing the infeccon' was one of many for the extermination of animals. The consequences were devastating: more than half the townspeople died and the social and economic life of the town almost ceased. There was 'so little travelling in the streets, that grass grew all over them to the degree that the pavement could hardly be seen', while the town officials began paying to feed the starving poor from their own pockets. Those who did not die fared only slightly better than those whose miserable deaths they were forced to witness.

Bradshaw's friend John Milton saw a two-year-old girl, probably his niece, killed by the plague in these years. In *On the Death of a Fair Infant Dying of a Cough* he railed, 'Yet can I not persuade me thou art dead / Or that thy corse corrupts in earth's dark womb, / Or that thy beauties lie in wormy bed, / Hid from the world in a low-delved tombe / Could Heav'n for pity thee so strictly doom?' The death of such innocents demanded explanation. John Milton's masterpiece, *Paradise Lost*, would be his attempt 'to justify the ways of God to men'. John Bradshaw would have to find his own way.

Amid all this, the instruction came that Congleton was to provide food and lodgings for 500 soldiers marching north on the King's service. The order was met with disbelief and the colonel of the regiment was desperately petitioned to spare the devastated town. It took two years for Congleton to be free of plague. When the time came John Bradshaw had made a decision: he would live on the political periphery no longer. London called.[18]

※ ※ ※

The Long Parliament met for the first time in November 1640 and wasted no time in attacking royal policies, though care was taken to direct criticism towards malevolent 'councillors' rather than the King himself. By Christmas two of the King's closest allies were in prison accused of treason, the Archbishop of Canterbury, William Laud, and the King's lieutenant in Ireland, Thomas Wentworth, Earl of Strafford.

But matters did not stop there. More committed English Puritans, emboldened by the Scots' steely rejection of the English Prayer Book, began pushing for far-reaching reform of the English church, including of the episcopacy itself – on the basis both that bishops were agents of the despised Laudian innovations, and that the office, nowhere mentioned in the Bible, was a Catholic hang-over. Charles was forced into a series of major concessions: agreeing to call Parliament at least every three years and to the closure of the 'prerogative courts', including Star Chamber, which were associated with harsh justice against critics of the regime. As the King conceded these points, and as the radicals began to push harder, including for the abolition of bishops altogether, the political world began to polarize. Instead of more or less universal disapproval of royal policies, moderates, shocked by the aspirations of the radicals, began to distance themselves, and migrated back towards the King. Two camps were emerging.

In the midst of this smouldering political turmoil, Ireland suddenly burst into flames. The Earl of Strafford had, like others before him, maintained the dominance of a tiny Protestant minority over the over-whelmingly Catholic Irish population. Taxed hard, and anxious about the rising power of the Puritans in England, Irish Catholics watched the impeachment, and then execution, of Strafford with rising blood. A plan was hatched to seize the seat of government, Dublin Castle, and from there to compel the English government to soften its approach. Hugh MacMahon and Connor Maguire, Baron of Enniskillen, promi-nent Catholic landowners, were to lead the attack, but just the day before were betrayed and arrested. The news of the failed plot sparked a conflagration, on the one hand fuelling Protestant fears about Catholics' tendency to rebellion and violence, and on the other setting in motion a series of brutal sectarian attacks and counter-attacks. The pent-up grievances of the Catholic majority exploded in a series of violent incidents, in which several thousand Protestants, including numerous women and children, died. The trial of MacMahon and Maguire would be the first of a series of highly political legal cases in which John Bradshaw would act, which turned him from an onlooker to a participant in the great struggle that was taking shape.[19]

On 3 January 1642 Charles I ordered the arrest of those Members of Parliament who had been most vociferous in their criticism of royal policy. Arriving at Westminster in person with the armed guard who were to seize them, the King found the men, known as the 'five members', had already slipped away. He was left to suffer the humiliation of standing, powerless, in the Commons Chamber. It would prove the straw that broke the back of the King's authority. The powerful City of London protected the five fugitives, the King was accused of breaking the ancient privilege that protected MPs from arrest when Parliament was sitting and within days the royal family had abandoned London. On 22 August the King raised the royal standard at Nottingham and war between King and Parliament was declared.

※ ※ ※

Two years into Bradshaw's studies at Gray's Inn a younger cousin of his friend Peter had entered the college: William Brereton of Handforth, heir to one of Cheshire's wealthier families. Energetic and cultured, Brereton became both an active member of the Cheshire gentry – serving as an MP and a JP – and a firm religious Puritan. It was he who ensured that the county produced a petition advocating urgent and extensive church reform, probably that signed by Henry Bradshaw, and when unrest broke out in Ireland in 1641 Brereton, now a baronet, was put in charge of transporting the soldiers and supplies necessary to suppress it. Brereton would go on to be commander in chief of the parliamentary forces in Cheshire, while Bradshaw, to whom he was fiercely loyal, acted as his agent and advocate in the volatile politics of the metropolis.[20]

As there was no permanent, professional army, King and Parliament each had to build up a fighting force almost from scratch. The navy, enlarged at such cost by Charles I, came out for Parliament, who also gained control of the central store of arms and ordnance in the Tower of London. But as the localities experienced the growing parliamentary army at close quarters – both its destructive attitude to Laudian churches and the challenge its cause represented to tradition and order – the ranks of the royalists also swelled. But despite their difference both sides fought, in name at least, for the King. This was never a war between royalists and republicans; there was no question of there not being a king, just of where the limits of his authority lay. When in July 1642 the 3rd Earl of Essex was appointed general of the parliamentary army, his commission described it as having been assembled for 'for the Safety of the King's Person, the Defence of both Houses of Parliament ... and for the Preservation of the true Religion, the Laws, Liberties and Peace of the Kingdom'.[21]

For the first year or so of the war the royalists, who sorely lacked London but were strong in the North, Midlands and West Country, looked to be gaining the upper hand. But in September 1643 the parliamentary cause received a significant boost when their leaders signed a treaty with the Scots. The 'Solemn League and Covenant' saw the Scots pledge to fight with the English Parliament, providing a colossal 20,000 soldiers towards the war effort. But it was much more than this, committing Parliament to far-reaching religious reform, including the removal of bishops and the abolition of the Book of Common Prayer as a condition of military support.

While the Scottish army was massing, in Cheshire a large royalist force under Lord Byron was on the offensive, swelled by English soldiers returning from Ireland – where the political situation had temporarily stabilized. The Cheshire royalists had their headquarters in the ancient city of Chester, still protected by its Roman walls, while Brereton and the parliamentary troops were based 20 miles southeast in the county's second city, Nantwich. Byron's progress was swift and by the new year, 1644, only Nantwich remained of Parliament's Cheshire strongholds. On 12 January Byron began a series of coordinated attacks on the town. Within, William Brereton and his 2,000 men were utterly surrounded. As the besiegers attacked the snow fell hard. The Scots army was still 200 miles away busy with royalist forces near Newcastle. Any hope of reinforcements seemed lost.

Then, after almost two weeks' siege, in which it looked certain the parliamentary army in Cheshire would be crushed completely, came an almost miraculous deliverance. Through the icy sleet appeared a striking black-haired figure, at the head of a relieving force of some 6,000.

Sir Thomas Fairfax, the 36-year-old son of Yorkshire's leading parliamentary officer, had led his men on a gruelling 100-mile march across the breadth of England in appalling conditions to relieve the siege. As he would tell his beloved wife the following day 'Dear Heart', 'I have endured some hardship ... being forced to march and watch night and day this frost and snowy weather', but 'a great victory it hath pleased Him [God] to give us'. The utter routing of the royalists at the battle of Nantwich that day would be the first major parliamentary victory of the war. The bravery and fortitude of Thomas Fairfax, and the growing strength of the parliamentary forces, would offer glimpses of what was to come.[22]

Sir Thomas Fairfax.

From a Miniature in the hands of Brian Fairfax, Esq.

Sir Thomas Fairfax, Lord Fairfax from 1648, a brilliant parliamentary soldier and first Commander in Chief of the New Model Army. Like many senior parliamentarians he was from a well-established gentry family. Fairfax was never reconciled to the radical revolution his army's victory made possible.

Disaster averted, Brereton spent much of the following two years trying to bring down the heavily fortified royal stronghold of Chester. This would be a prolonged task, and one in which John Bradshaw offered crucial support from London, where he was now becoming known as a lawyer thoroughly devoted to the parliamentary cause. In between his work on the prosecution of the Irish lords and other legal cases, Bradshaw was lobbying for supplies and money for the parliamentary army in Cheshire. If Parliament did not act on the entreaties, other means could be found. He struck a deal with two London grocers who had chartered a vessel to collect 30 tonnes of Cheshire's celebrated cheese from Liverpool. Rather than travelling north empty, the *Sarah Bonaventer* sailed heavy with gunpowder and other ammunition for Brereton's army, which were discreetly unloaded on the docks. Money for military supplies – boots and horses, powder and shot – was carried north from Bradshaw to Brereton, while anxious letters were brought south. The ill-discipline of his own men terrified Brereton, as he told Bradshaw: 'If you were but an eye-witness of the outrageous plundering and spoils committed by the soldiers for want of pay and necessaries, it would much afflict and grieve your spirit.' Bradshaw returned measured replies, counselling patience and forbearance: 'What is wanting in present payment must be supplied in good words and promises. More you cannot for the present do. You encounter great difficulties as you have long done.' But behind Bradshaw's soothing words, his concern for the safety of the soldiers ran deep, not least as his brother Henry was now fighting at Brereton's side. When in May 1645 Bradshaw read the news of the royal army's approach to Chester, expected to result in 'a sudden storm [that] is like to blast them all', he sent a courier thundering north to find Henry amid the tents and siege works to give him the steel breastplate that he hoped would keep his brother alive.[23]

🦁 🦁 🦁

After Brereton and Fairfax's unexpected victory at Nantwich other successes followed. The Scots' support together with their command of supplies and the navy put Parliament in an increasingly powerful position. They triumphed in Yorkshire at Marston Moor, the largest battle ever fought on English soil, on 2 July 1644. Marston Moor broke the back of royalist power in the North, but it would be the comprehensive parliamentary victory at Naseby, in Northamptonshire, a year later, that decided the military outcome of the war. As Parliament was gaining the upper hand, the prospect of peace discussions with the King came into view, and the question of what sort of settlement might be acceptable began to divide them. Those who were for a swift negotiated peace with the King to end the war, to include a reformed but strong national church, were known as 'Presbyterians'; those who were for pushing for a complete military victory to realize their aspirations for greater religious reform, potentially including freedom of worship without a national church, were the 'Independents'. The latter prevailed and the removal of the Earl of Essex and those around him from the leadership of the army followed, together with the forging of an integrated, centralized, meritocratic 'New Model Army', staffed by senior officers fired up with reforming zeal. Command was given to the hero of the northern campaigns, the fearless Sir Thomas Fairfax, under whom the far more political Cambridge MP, Oliver Cromwell, led the cavalry. Brereton finally took Chester, on his third attempt, in January 1646, expressing his gratitude to Bradshaw in doing so for 'the very great obligations you have placed with me'. The Midlands now lost, a disguised Charles I slipped past the sentries at Oxford's east gate at three o'clock in the morning on 27 April, and presented himself to the Scottish army leaders at Newark, confident, it seemed, that his presence and willingness to negotiate would convince them to abandon their English allies and restore him to his throne.[24]

❦ ❦ ❦

It would be two and a half years after Charles I's arrival at the Scots' camp in Newark before John Bradshaw opened the proceedings of the court of law that was to try him. During this time both sides refused to make the compromises that could have brought peace and the return of the King to his throne, the outcome which most still sought. Frustrated at his refusal to accept the draconian conditions put to him for a restoration, the Scots handed the King over to English parliamentary commissioners. In London the parliamentary government had by now created the bones of a new reformed church and put bishops' land and property up for sale, executing William Laud in the process. But still there was no settlement with the King. Through this time of stalemate the army emerged as a powerful force in its own right, not now just a military but also a political player, distinct from its parliamentary masters. Under the influence of London radicals who had infiltrated the army's ranks, a religious and ideological extremism was taking hold that most in senior positions did not share. In the summer of 1647, acting on its own initiative (and fearful it was about to be disbanded with salaries unpaid), the army took possession of the King. To him were put surprisingly generous terms for peace. When the King still refused it caused the army's leaders to resent him even more. A final ferocious season of fighting ended in disaster for Charles and come 1648 he was held at Carisbrooke Castle on the Isle of Wight under a close guard. Terms for his capitulation seemed at last to be within reach.

The act that turned a civil war into a revolution took place in December 1648. Without it there would have been no revolution; with it the revolution that occurred would be forever flawed. As parliamentary representatives discussed the finer points of the treaty with the King, and it appeared an agreement was about to be reached, the army, with Henry Ireton the driving force, suddenly intervened. Feeling betrayed by the prospect of compromise with this 'man of blood', and 'convinced that they [Parliament] had deserted the common cause and interest of the nation', Ireton and his coterie took matters into their own hands. Marching 7,000 troops into Westminster, a menacing and unwelcome presence, they took the King from Carisbrooke to Hurst Castle and announced they would not return him until their concerns were addressed. Parliament was appalled, declaring the army to have acted 'without the Knowledge or Consent of the house', and sitting through the night, voted at sunrise by a hefty majority that the King's answers to their proposals were 'sufficient grounds for settling the peace of the kingdom'. The following day, 6 December, it happened. As the members of the House of Commons arrived at Westminster they found the grounds of the palace strangely thick with soldiers – not now the city militia, but the New Model Army itself. Armed men thronged the stairs up into the building and lined the lobby before the Commons Chamber. Standing at the door was the parliamentary officer Colonel Thomas Pride and in his hand was a piece of paper. As each MP approached and was identified by the doorkeeper, Pride checked his list and either allowed him to enter or turned him away – committing almost forty to prison in the process. In one shocking, audacious and utterly unlawful act 'Pride's Purge' removed all the moderate MPs from the House. The armed guard remained, and within a fortnight the remaining 'Rump Parliament' had repudiated the negotiations and declared instead that King Charles I was to be put on trial for high treason.[25]

Two

A New England

❦❦❦❦❦❦❦❦❦❦❦❦❦❦❦❦❦❦

W hen Sergeant Dendy arrived with the summons to Westminster
Hall, Charles I was waiting in the riverfront drawing room of Sir
Robert Cotton's house. This building, englobed within the Palace of
Westminster, was assigned the King for the duration of the trial. A
strange narrow room, just 6 feet wide, was all that separated Cotton's
drawing room from the Painted Chamber where the trial commissioners discussed the King's fate. Glazed bookshelves lined the space, from
the tops of which brass busts of Roman emperors gazed blankly into the
gloom. Beneath them were lodged hundreds of volumes bound in dark
red leather and stamped with a coat of arms and gold lettering.
Collected by Cotton over the decades before his death in 1631, these
were the founding texts of English history: the Lindisfarne Gospels, the
manuscript of 'Beowulf', Bede's 'Ecclesiastical History of England', the
diary of Edward VI, the will of Mary, Queen of Scots, and two of the four
original versions of Magna Carta. As Charles I rose to make his way to
Westminster Hall he was serene: all history was on his side.[1]

John Bradshaw and Charles I had never met until that day. But
Bradshaw knew what he felt about the small, whiskered man who took
his chair before him. In 1647 Bradshaw had become Chief Justice of
Chester, reflecting his rise to 'as it were Attorney General' for the
London government. The experience of practising law at this time

brought him into close contact with the extremes of life in Charles I's kingdoms. At the trial of the Irish lords he heard those who claimed to be privy to the intentions of the Irish rebels give gruesome details of the Catholics' plans to murder the entire Protestant populations of various towns, stab women and children to death and throw their butchered corpses into the rivers. This was the threat that English Protestants believed lay before them. Bradshaw's fellow lawyer at that trial was pamphleteer William Prynne. He cut a memorable figure. Judged to have impugned the Queen in his pamphlets, Prynne carried the marks of the sentence passed down by the now-abolished Star Chamber. His cheeks had been burned with branding irons to bear the letters 'SL' for 'seditious libeller' and his ears had been sliced off. Another of Bradshaw's cases in the mid-1640s was that of John Lilburne, who would become the most famous of the political radicals known as the Levellers. Bradshaw rehearsed for the court gory details of Lilburne's treatment by Star Chamber in the 1630s – his flogging through the streets of London, his violent gagging 'done with much Cruelty', his solitary confinement in hand and leg irons – calling the treatment 'unjust, illegal, and contrary to the Liberty of the Subject'. When he presided at a Nantwich court in 1648 Bradshaw had ended his speech with a passionate repudiation of Charles I as a King 'more cruel than Nero'.[2]

John Bradshaw regarded himself as a man of the law. He was prepared to uphold it, even when it disadvantaged his cause, as had happened in 1645 when he advised royalists against releasing parliamentary prisoners in return for money – to the bafflement of his fellow townsmen. And yet he came, like others, to believe that the trial of the King, though brought about by military force and with no precedent in law, was not merely justified but required. Somehow the manifest failings of Charles I, the death and destruction of the wars, the belief that profound change was God's will and a collective momentum carried matters through. The shift in attitude over those weeks of Bradshaw's fellow lawyer John Cook, one of the trial prosecutors, was witnessed by his friends. At first Cook had viewed the impending trial and the hysterical atmosphere that accompanied it with disbelief. 'They are all mad,' he remarked, reporting 'how a fellow cried out to the lord Fairfax, that if he did not consent to the proceedings, he would kill Christ and him'. But when his friends encountered him again a month later, they found him changed. As one recalled, seeing him in the streets late one night: '"Mr Cook" said I ... "I hear you are up to your ears in this business", "no" saith he "I am serving the people", "truly" said I "I believe there's a thousand to one will not give you thanks" ... "I hear you charge the king for the levying of warr against the parliament; how can you rationally do this when you have pulled out the parliament to make way to his trial". He answered me "you will see strange things, and you must wait on God".'[3]

Here was the rub. While those who did it claimed to be trying the King in the name of the people of England, the reality was that however much Charles I was resented, his trial for treason was not what the people of England wanted. Parliamentary procedure was utterly disregarded to achieve it: the House of Commons was ideologically cleansed and when the House of Lords tried to object they were simply ignored – the Commons breezily declaring that 'the Commons of England in Parliament assembled, being chosen by, and representing the People, have the Supreme Power in this Nation'. Even the 180 'Commissioners' chosen to sit in judgement at the trial were not convinced; over half did not serve and among those who did there were serious divisions on what the outcome should be. Despite all the talk of acting in the name of the people of England, those pushing the trial through were not actually concerned with notions of democracy or what 'the people' wanted. Ultimately, it was God's work they were doing, and their victory in the civil war had given them proof positive that he was on their side.[4]

Remarkably, the decision to undertake a military purge of Parliament involved neither of the two most senior officers of the army. Thomas, now Lord Fairfax, the head of the army, was strangely distant, and it was only after the decision was taken that he was informed of 'the necessity of this extraordinary way of proceeding'. His deputy, Oliver Cromwell, had not even been in London on 5 December, but was travelling south from Scotland. The person who took Fairfax the news, and the driving force behind the trial, was the army's Commissary-General Henry Ireton. Still in his thirties, Ireton had been raised a committed Puritan and, like John Bradshaw and Oliver Cromwell, was from a respectable gentry family. Early in the civil war he had become close to Cromwell, and in 1646 he had married Bridget, Cromwell's devout eldest daughter. Having orchestrated the New Model Army's occupation of London in November 1648, Ireton was one of the small group who drew up the list of MPs to be removed, which was then passed to Colonel Pride to implement. He was imaginative and energetic, 'full of invention and industry'. Like Cromwell, Ireton had initially hoped for an accommodation with the King, but frustration at Charles's refusal to compromise and experience of the growing appetite for change among the rank and file of the army had caused him to modify his view.[5]

But not all about him shared Ireton's clarity. John Bradshaw was one of many who wavered. Though named as a commissioner for the trial, he did not attend the first two meetings in the Painted Chamber and when on 10 January he was chosen as President of the court, it was again in his absence. Two days later when he finally appeared it was 'upon special summons' and he tried to decline the position, making 'an earnest apology for himself to be excused'. Many of the commissioners sought divine guidance during these fraught weeks. Colonel Hutchinson 'addressed himself to God by prayer, desiring the Lord that, if through any human frailty he were led into any error or false opinion in these great transactions he would open his eyes and not suffer him to proceed', but he found 'no check but a confirmation on his conscience that it was his duty to act as he did'. Whatever Bradshaw's own soul-searching involved, he came, eventually, to a decision. While more senior lawyers than he, men like Bulstrode Whitelocke and Sir Thomas Widdrington, had already declined to participate in the trial, he would not take this approach. His objections having been dismissed by his fellow commissioners, he would not concoct a flimsy excuse – an unnamed illness or invented incapacitation – to escape. He would have the courage to stand. God had delivered the King into their hands and his revenge on them would be ferocious – 'blood and desolation' – should they allow their prisoner to evade justice. As Bradshaw would put it to the King in Westminster Hall, the Bible was clear: to acquit the guilty was as much of a crime as to condemn the innocent.[6]

The overwhelming concern of those behind the trial was that it should appear as official and respectable as possible. Suggestions that the army should simply dispose of the King themselves if they were so keen to be rid of him were tartly rejected. As one contemporary put it, 'they were subtle enough to see and avoid that, and to make those whom they left sitting in parliament to be their stales, and to do their dirty work for them'. All the while London swarmed with soldiers. The legal infrastructure was quickly put in place; the Commons declared it treason for an English sovereign to wage war on Parliament and the kingdom. Officials of various degrees were appointed 'in order to the more regular and due proceedings of the said Court', proclamations were read drawing it to public attention and all who wished to were to be allowed to attend in person. When the issue of what seal to attach to the proclamation arose (the King clearly could not call himself to trial), a committee was asked to confer and a new seal was designed, which in place of the King's head depicted the assembled House of Commons. Henry Marten, one of only a tiny number of actual republicans, came up with a rousing alternative to the regnal year and the seal was dated 'In the first year of freedom by God's blessing restored'.[7]

❦ ❦ ❦

It took fifteen tense minutes for the King to reach Westminster Hall from Cotton's house. The south, high, end of the immense Westminster Hall was railed off and laid with matting to form an elevated court room, while the rest of the hall was available to the crowds of spectators who streamed through the north doors. This was the very spot where, for 500 years, kings of England had sat in state. Charles I was brought up a side stair straight into the court, and was conducted to a dock erected specially for the occasion; here he sat facing his judges with his back to the spectators (Colour plate 2). In the adjacent booth stood the three prosecution lawyers. Ranged opposite Charles, beneath the enormous Gothic window, the sixty-eight trial commissioners sat on their banked benches, the light from behind causing shadows to shroud their faces. Bradshaw sat at their helm, his papers on the sloping desk before him. Between prisoner and judges stood a table covered in a Turkish

The Great Seal of the Commonwealth, used 1649–53. One side depicted England and Ireland, while on the other the traditional image of the monarch was replaced by one of the House of Commons, now the sovereign body of the land.

rug, on which lay a sword and mace – emblems of the sovereignty which was itself on trial.

In the discussions in the Painted Chamber the commissioners had agreed that they would not seek to humiliate the King. He would not, like other prisoners, be required to remove his hat or to remain standing, and he was to be given time to speak in reply to the charge that was to be put to him. If he were 'insolent, outrageous or contemptuous', however, Bradshaw was to intervene and, if necessary, adjourn the court.[8]

Bradshaw rose and opened the proceedings. On the instruction of the House of Commons, he declared, they were assembled to try the King for the 'calamities that have been brought on this nation'; he then called on the parliamentary lawyers to read the charge. At this the King reached his gold-topped cane across the dock and prodded the leading prosecutor, John Cook, on the shoulder, instructing him to be silent. Bradshaw, eyeing his adversary coolly, ordered Cook to continue. The King sank back into his chair and gazed about him as the charge was read. When Cook came to the crucial words in his solemn speech, declaring 'Charles Stuart to be a Tyrant and Traitor', the accused simply let out a laugh.[9]

For much of the trial Charles affected an air of untroubled bemuse-
ment. 'I do wonder for what cause you do convene me here before you,'
he remarked after the charge had been read. Casting a quizzical look
around the hall, he continued: 'I see no Lords here, where are the Lords?'
Bradshaw ignored his questions and asked for an answer to the charge:
would the prisoner plead guilty or not guilty? Here the King changed

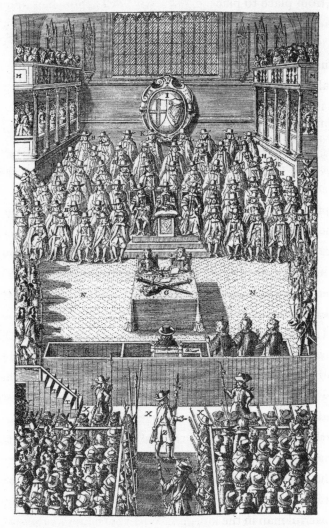

The trial of Charles I. John Bradshaw sat at the head of his fellow
commissioners under the great south window of Westminster Hall. The King
faced them from a boarded dock, his back to the crowds. It was from one of the
adjacent raised balconies that Lady Fairfax cried out in protest during the trial.

tack: he had been in the midst of negotiations with both houses of Parliament on the Isle of Wight, where 'we were upon conclusion of the Treaty', when he was suddenly carried off. On what authority, he demanded, was he being put on trial? 'I mean lawful; there are many unlawful authorities in the world, thieves and robbers by the highways; but I would know by what authority I was brought from thence, and carried from place to place, and I know what; and when I know what lawful authority, I shall answer.'[10]

This was as far as the trial ever got. Not accepting the basis on which the House of Commons acted, the King never entered the plea that would allow the trial to progress to hearing evidence. There was, of course, no historical basis for the King and the House of Lords being removed from the trinity of authority in the kingdom, and no acceptable account for Bradshaw to give of how this had come to pass. He was presented with an almost impossible task: to avoid, dismiss and close down each one of the King's contentions and questions on this point, and to plough on regardless with the course he and his commissioners had determined upon. Suddenly now the tables were turned, the King was arguing that he was upholding the liberties of the nation and its people in the face of their being trampled by Parliament, rather than the other way round. This was rich, as Bradshaw remarked, 'How great a friend you have been to the Laws and Liberties of the people, let all England and the world judge', but it was also hard to counter. 'Shew me one precedent' challenged the King, confident of his history. The lawyers reeled off a list of medieval and Scottish sovereigns who had been deposed by force, swerving entirely the uncomfortable question the King had posed.[11]

A further assault on Bradshaw's position and the court's authority came that day from an entirely unexpected source. When the commissioners had taken their seats, a roll of names had been called. First on the list after Bradshaw himself was Fairfax, Lord General of the army, and the most powerful man in the kingdom. When his name was read there was silence. As everyone looked around it seemed that Fairfax was not even in the building. The court official called his name again, and again there was no answer, until a distant female voice from the gallery at the side of the court cried 'he had more wit than to be there'. Those who knew her recognized the voice as that of Fairfax's formidable wife, Anne.[12]

For some months the great general, fearless hero of so many battles, had been fading as a presence. A professional soldier, war had been his métier and his choice as head of the army had been guided in part by the fact that this Yorkshireman stood at a distance from Westminster politics. But now events had overtaken him. He had been desperate for the Isle of Wight negotiations to succeed, which would have seen reforms confirmed in church and state and Charles I taking a newly limited position as King. But his men were against him; the army he had created had become more radical than its commanding officer. Unable to condone the trial and execution of the King, he also felt he could not stop it – though he was one of the few in the kingdom who might actually have done so. Fairfax spent those crucial weeks in limbo, his inaction hourly sapping his authority. Anne, braver even than the herculean husband she had accompanied on campaign, was certain that matters had gone too far, and attended the trial to cry out her impassioned protests.

Over three days John Bradshaw continued his battle of wills with Charles. Again and again the King was asked to enter a plea, and still he would not. Bradshaw's patience at his repeated claims to be upholding his subjects' liberties wore thin: 'you have written your meaning in bloody characters throughout the whole kingdom,' he retorted in exasperation. And yet, occasional expostulations aside, he was calm and curtly courteous in his chairmanship. While the attendant soldiers, egged on by various of their officers, jeered at and jostled the King, one even spitting on him as he passed, this was not Bradshaw's way. He remained professional, always addressing the King as 'Sir' and conducting his court with solemnity and dignity.[13]

While Bradshaw and his fellow commissioners were frustrated at the King's refusal to plead, their case, even if the basis of their authority were accepted, was shaky. The witnesses that had been lined up could certainly attest to the King having been in arms – among them the Hereford shoemaker who had seen him with a sword in his hand, and the man who had painted the shaft of the royal standard raised at

Nottingham. But all this hardly addressed the question of whether the King had initiated the conflict or was simply responding to an uprising, and it did little to substantiate the accusation that he had subverted his subjects' liberties. In the end, however, it did not matter. Many felt the outcome of the trial was inevitable regardless of what was said, and with no plea from the King the witnesses could not speak in court. As was usual when the accused would not plead, a 'guilty' plea was entered on his behalf and a week after the trial started the day of sentencing dawned.[14]

On the morning of Saturday 27 January it seemed that all was decided. The momentousness of what was happening was lost on no one. Bradshaw, whose mental and emotional strength was crucial to the prosecution of this unprecedented form of justice, was to be recognized in the highest terms. The day before sentencing the commissioners agreed that one of the most august and magnificent residences in the capital, the Dean of Westminster's house at Westminster Abbey – empty since the Dean had fled London with Charles seven years before – was to be given to him, furnished at the state's expense. Bradshaw put on a scarlet gown, usually reserved by the judiciary for royal or ceremonial occasions, and took his chair with the commissioners ranged behind him.[15]

As Charles I was brought in once again, the court officials struggled to bring the noisy crowd to peace. Bradshaw stood to address himself to the room, when the King suddenly intervened, asking to say something before judgement was given. Bradshaw agreed to hear him after his summing up. As he rehearsed the contention that the trial was conducted 'in the name of the people of England', a woman's voice once again rang out from the raised balcony to Bradshaw's right. 'It is a lie,' she cried, 'not half, not a quarter of the people of England.' A wave of shock ran through the room and the soldiers levelled their guns at the gallery, but Lady Fairfax melted into the crowd before they could locate her.[16]

When Bradshaw finally invited him to speak Charles I asked to put a proposal to the two houses of Parliament which he claimed would please all sides: 'I have something to offer unto them that will be satisfactory to you all, and will be for the immediate settlement of the kingdom in peace,' he announced proudly. Bradshaw was about to refuse this request when there came a shuffling from behind as one of the commissioners, John Downes, sitting a row back from Oliver Cromwell, stood to indicate dissent. While for some the purpose of the trial was always simply to bring about Charles I's execution, others, who still hoped some sort of arrangement might be reached which avoided his death, could not let this opportunity pass. When the commissioners trooped into the adjacent court of wards to confer, Cromwell was boiling with rage. Downes expressed his concern at the trial having not heard any witnesses and his belief that the King should be allowed to put his proposal – which was thought to be an offer to abdicate in favour of his third son, Prince Henry. But there was no question of such a meeting being convened. To involve the House of Lords at this stage would certainly destabilize and probably destroy the rickety legal and political edifice they had lashed together over the preceding weeks. Cromwell thundered to Bradshaw 'with a great deal of storm' that they should not be distracted by the King's disingenuous proposals and remember they were dealing with 'the hardest hearted man that lives upon the earth'. The question was put to a vote. The commissioners were divided, but the majority rejected the weeping Downes's objections and the King's proposal, and the court reassembled.

With the refusal of his request Charles's studied insouciance evaporated. As ever, his political judgement had been poor. He had left his gambit too late; as Bradshaw told him, 'your time is now past'. The sentence was read, the accused found a 'Tyrant, Traytor, Murderer and a public Enemy', and condemned to be 'put to death by the severing of his Head from his Body'. All the commissioners stood to indicate their assent. Bradshaw ignored Charles's repeated pleas for delay and ordered his removal. As he was led out of the dock he still called 'By your Favour (Hold!), the Sentence, Sir! – I say, Sir, I do ...' But to the King who claimed to rule by God's own command, the pale-faced Cheshire lawyer made no answer.[17]

※ ※ ※

Whatever his reservations had been, John Bradshaw had convinced himself of the arguments he set out in his lengthy summing-up to the court. The people were the source of all sovereignty and the basis of the law, the monarch was but an 'officer in trust'. Parliament was the means for ensuring that kings acted in the interests of the people. Charles I had set about subverting Parliament, 'uprooting' the 'great bulwarke of the Liberties of the People', and so had to be called to justice. As he had prepared to leave his lodgings on this last morning Bradshaw's wife had, it was reported, begged him on her knees not to go through with it, 'for fear of the dreadful Sentence of the King of Heaven'. He had reputedly responded that he was doing only 'what the Law commands'. For John Bradshaw, as for his colleague John Cook, initial uncertainty had been overcome by conviction. A few hours later Bradshaw passed the most extraordinary and momentous sentence in English legal history. If he had had doubts before, from that moment on he could have none.[18]

The execution took place two days later on the bleak, bitterly cold afternoon of Tuesday 30 January. The King was composed as he walked out onto the timber staging in front of the Banqueting House at Whitehall. In a speech which few could hear, he called his sentence unjust, but accepted it as divine judgement on him for having allowed the execution of the Earl of Strafford seven years earlier. He forgave 'the chief causers of my death, who they are God knows' and spoke of his hope that they would do their duty to the kings that would follow him. Finally finding the popular phraseology that had eluded him until now, he described himself as 'the Martyr of the people'. As the executioner landed the single blow that severed Charles I's head the crowd let out a deep collective moan.

❦ ❦ ❦

Though their sentence had been carried out, the commissioners of the High Court still had business to conclude, and they had several further meetings that week to mop up various administrative details. Bradshaw was characteristically concerned to ensure the court officers and guards were paid properly for their services – in his will he would leave individual legacies to dozens of employees and former employees, a fund for any recent recruits and a further £100 for his wife to distribute to them. The other more significant piece of business that remained was that of drawing up the official account of the trial. A group of seven commissioners, including Henry Ireton, was appointed to meet at Bradshaw's lodging at nine o'clock the following morning to 'peruse and consider the whole narrative of the proceedings of the Court', which was to be ready to present to the House of Commons three days later.[19]

As Bradshaw and his colleagues sorted through their bundles of notes and transcripts, a few hundred yards away the House of Commons was meeting. In recent years some 500 people had been entitled to sit in the House of Commons and the Chamber, the former Chapel of St Stephen, was famously noisy and overcrowded. Now fewer than eighty men sat on its opposing benches, the room's eerie emptiness an unavoidable reminder of what it had taken to bring their revolution to pass. On the morning of the King's execution the nation's future had remained unresolved – there was no statement of who or what was to take his place. A holding act had been swiftly passed ordering that no one should be declared king in his place without the Commons' consent. But this decided nothing.

In the days before the trial there had been discussion of the 'settlement of the kingdom' among the cabal of men at the heart of matters. A range of possibilities had been contemplated. Bulstrode Whitelocke and other senior lawyers had attended a meeting at the Speaker of the House of Commons' house, at which 'some were wholly against any king at all, others were against having the present king, or his eldest or second son to be king; others were for the third son, the duke of Gloucester (who was among them and might be educated as they should appoint)'. The parliamentarian preacher Hugh Peter and Henry Ireton had chewed the fat at Windsor in the days before the trial. Peter declared that not only was the King a tyrant and a fool, but the very office of king was dangerous, expensive and unnecessary. But such extreme views were not the norm even among their colleagues and the King's trial proceeded without a plan for the future. Eight days were to pass after the regicide before the matter was resolved.[20]

In order to determine the nature of the new regime the question of whose decision it was had first to be resolved. While the House of Lords had been excluded from discussion about the trial of Charles I, it was unclear if this was a permanent exclusion. On Tuesday 6 February the Commons debated whether the House of Lords should be allowed to re-enter the arena of government. This was not simply a debate about the upper chamber. It was obvious to all that if the Lords were allowed to return a less radical course would be taken thereafter. Seventy-three men voted on the question. Twenty-nine, including Oliver Cromwell, were for retaining the Lords but, with the republican Henry Marten using all his persuasive powers, forty-four voted against it. In a stroke, the upper house was abolished. With it, the chances of the monarchy surviving dramatically diminished. The following day, after discussion of Irish affairs and the question of who was to be the next Sheriff of Suffolk, the future of the monarchy itself was debated. The die already cast, it was resolved without a vote that 'it hath been found by Experience ... That the Office of a King in this Nation, and to have the Power thereof in any Single Person, is unnecessary, burdensome, and dangerous to the Liberty, Safety, and publick Interest of the People of this Nation.' The monarchy, the sovereign institution of England for as long as there had been an England, was no more. The country was instead to be a 'Commonwealth and Free-State', in which supreme authority resided in the representatives of the people in Parliament.[21]

❦ ❦ ❦

In those bewildering first weeks John Bradshaw may have felt his own part was almost complete. He was not an MP – despite his friends' attempts to find him a seat – so had no role to play in the deliberations in St Stephen's Chapel. He was occupied for a few weeks as the judge at the trial of four prominent royalists, and worked with colleagues on the official account of the trial of the King, which was taking longer than expected. Those involved in this project met in Bradshaw's expansive new lodgings, the Deanery in Westminster Abbey. Forming much of the western side of Henry III's great abbey cloister, this vast assemblage of rooms had been used mostly for meetings for the past few years.

Immediately after the King's trial John and Mary Bradshaw made arrangements to move in, and before February was out tapestries were being hung, furniture moved and repairs and improvements set in train. The Abbot's great chamber was redecorated and a new stair to it made, while as the shoots of spring began to appear the garden was attended to. Gravel paths were laid and rolled and colourful flowers – violets, pinks and gillyflowers – planted 'for the Lord President'. But if Bradshaw was hoping he would soon be spending his days tending his blooms, he would be disappointed. As he would explain to the Abbey authorities four years later, in the event he was able to make 'little use' of his splendid new house, as he was drawn instead to Whitehall where 'my whole tyme [was] spent in the publique service'.[22]

When the House of Commons decided to abolish the monarchy, and to declare itself the single sovereign body, it also announced that in place of joint Lords and Commons 'executive committees' which had been governing the country for the last few years, a new executive body, the Council of State, would be appointed to manage day-to-day government. The Council of State was constituted on 16 February 1649, a sub-group of MPs having been given the task of selecting its forty-one members, who were to serve for a year. The need to start broadening out the basis of the new regime was clear, and membership was to be mixed: the majority would be MPs, but there would be others, representatives of the army, five peers and a handful of senior lawyers, among them John Bradshaw. At first, in an egalitarian spirit, there was to be no single chairman, but after a month of meetings it became obvious that a 'Lord President' was in fact required. The only name discussed, and quickly agreed, was Bradshaw's, and so he found himself the closest thing there was to a head of state in the new English republic.[23]

In many ways Bradshaw was an unlikely choice as President of the Council of State. He had no parliamentary or government experience and (his stint as mayor of Congleton notwithstanding) he was a lawyer rather than an administrator. As his fellow council members would discover, his idea of chairing a meeting was not to solicit opinions and ensure business was dispatched, but to make the long, verbose speeches beloved of lawyers. However, his loyalty to the new regime and his political courage could not be doubted. As the man who had tried Charles I he had earned a special status that no one could better. Over the coming years he would attend almost every meeting of the Council of State, more than any other of his colleagues, and endeavour by force of sheer hard work to make the new regime a success.[24]

Bradshaw for his own part may well have hesitated in accepting the role. While no organized attempt had been made to prevent the King's execution, it was obvious popular feeling was against it. The fame of trying the King might have earned him this new office, but it brought with it great risks. One of his fellow trial lawyers, the Anglicized Dutchman Isaac Dorislaus, was stabbed to death by royalists in The Hague just a few weeks afterwards, and Bradshaw knew he, too, was a target. In early March he and fellow Council of State members were taking part in a funeral procession when someone identified him and an angry crowd swarmed forward with cries of 'There is Bradshawe, There is that Rogue, that Traitor, that condemned the King come lett us fall uppon him, lett us knocke him on the head, lett us teare him in pieces'. Bradshaw clutched Bulstrode Whitelocke, 'very much frighted ... & prayed me not to leave him', and together the two men narrowly avoided being lynched by escaping down an alleyway.[25] In interviewing informers Bradshaw was repeatedly confronted with the visceral fury that was felt towards him personally. A London grocer reported to the Council of State that he had heard a royalist vow that he 'would cutt in peices the said Lord President and boyle him and after give him to his Dogges to eate; And that if his Doggs would not eate himm hee would eate him himselfe.' The effect of this sort of testimony on one who had never seen battle or witnessed the bloody reality of war can only be imagined – despite his emotional fortitude, Bradshaw's physical cour-age was flimsy.[26] But these were the consequences of actions already taken. Bradshaw was now yoked to the regime for which he had done so much to clear the way. In the weeks after the trial those who wished to win favour or make connections in the new political world were already beating a path to his door. For better or for worse he was regarded as the 'parent of our State'. But just what sort of a world he had helped to sire remained to be seen.[27]

Three

Utopia

❦ ❦ ❦ ❦ ❦ ❦ ❦ ❦ ❦ ❦ ❦ ❦ ❦ ❦ ❦ ❦ ❦ ❦ ❦

O ne Sunday in early April 1649, some ten weeks into the life of the new Commonwealth, a small band of men set out purposefully from Church Cobham in Surrey. This large village 25 miles southwest of London nestled in a loop of the River Mole as it coiled its course east to converge with the Thames at Hampton Court. The river ran slowly through the Surrey commons and water meadows, its clear waters shaded by willows and specked with swans. The fertile fields on its banks were washed with nutrients in its occasional spates. Here in Cobham the larger houses were comfortable and desirable. When the Swedish Ambassador dined at Ham Court, in the heart of the village, in 1656 a contemporary marvelled at how it was 'seated like a ship, among ponds & water'. The smaller houses were framed of oak filled with soft red bricks, and furnished with benches, beds and painted hangings. The medieval church of St Andrew stood at the west end of the simple cross of streets, while to the east, past the Crown Inn, was the watermill to which the residents brought their wheat, barley and rye for grinding. As the band of men travelled north, they passed the capacious White Horse Inn in neighbouring Street Cobham, crossed over the bridge and walked out onto the uncultivated common land beyond. It was here, where the shallow, heathery slopes of St George's Hill rose ahead of them, that they would found their new Jerusalem.[1]

The leaders of the group were two men in their forties: a volatile former parliamentary soldier by the name of William Everard, and his thoughtful companion, Gerrard Winstanley, an erstwhile London cloth merchant who had moved to Surrey a few years before. With them were a handful of others, familiar local figures, and they carried on their backs the unlikely tools of their revolution. That afternoon they struck. They sank their spades into the sandy soil of the common, and began to turn and to sow this unpromising earth with beans, parsnips and carrots. As the light faded they returned the few miles to their respective homes. The following day they were back, bringing with them others who had heard of their enterprise. On the third day they lit fires to burn off the woody scrub, clearing some 10 acres to receive the plough. By Friday they were thirty-strong, and when some went to Kingston to buy more supplies they talked with urgent excitement of their cause. All were welcome to join them; they hoped to be thousands before many days were out. They were intent upon fulfilling the

Cobham, Surrey, home of the Diggers (from John Rocque's eighteenth-century map). The village was made up of two settlements: Cobham Mill and Cobham Street. The Diggers started their plantation on St George's Hill in the adjacent parish (top left), and then relocated to land in Cobham (bottom right).

promises of reformation which had been spoken of so often in the years of war: they were going to liberate England from the tyranny of ownership. As Winstanley recalled a few months later: 'I tooke my spade and went and broke the ground upon *George-hill* in Surrey, thereby declaring ... that the earth must be set free from intanglements of Lords and Landlords, and that it shall become a common Treasury to all.'[2]

For some months now the scheme had been forming in the remarkable mind of Gerrard Winstanley, a mind teeming with ideas and with anguish. In this he was not alone. When the country had dissolved into civil war seven years earlier and the national political and religious establishment had fallen, people who had never done so before began to query long-accepted certainties. If the King could be defied, the Archbishop of Canterbury executed and bishops and deans abolished, what else might not be open to question? New notions about society and religion began to germinate, put about and popularized by the printing presses which were now overrun with business. Among the noisiest agitators for change were the London radicals branded 'Levellers' for their egalitarian aspirations. With the distraction of war, and the divisions among the parliamentarians in the 1640s, censorship was patchy and popular debate and discussion reached levels never before seen in England.

Radical ideas were not simply the product of the loosening ties of government control in a period of civil war, or even of the fundamental questioning of hierarchy that the conflict represented; they were also a consequence of the economic conditions that the war itself created. From 1642 two armies had been kept in operation. In a kingdom with a population of under five million, it was a huge undertaking to support tens of thousands of men in arms, and therefore removed from the fields or the markets. Not only were they not being economically productive, but they needed to be fed, clothed and housed day and night. Food prices rocketed, with the cost of groceries almost doubling over the period of the war. Natural phenomena took a further heavy toll. In the summer of 1648 torrential summer rains spoiled crops across the kingdom; the following summer a severe drought had a similar effect. In an overwhelmingly rural society, hundreds of thousands depended for their livelihoods on the success of the harvest. Economic prosperity was fragile and even minor disruptions could cause financial ruin.

Come the republic's first year the cumulative consequence of all these factors was, in places, severe. England was already a country shattered. Something like 10,000 houses had been destroyed during the war, either in sieges or in anticipation of them. Towns in particular had been subject to wholesale demolition to create clear fields of fire outside their walls. As a consequence perhaps 55,000 people were already homeless. By 1649 a significant number of English families were destitute and facing famine. In Lancashire that spring lack of bread was causing widespread starvation. Not only did poor families have almost nothing to eat, but their homes were being used to house soldiers – one household was forced to look on as what remained of their precious seed corn was fed to the soldiers' horses. In Cumberland the number of families with neither bread nor seed corn was put at 30,000 in April 1649. Not without reason were there fears that the growing numbers of dispossessed would, with so little to lose, be attracted to radical new ideologies.[3]

❦ ❦ ❦

The economic extremes of the 1640s caused intense suffering, and amid the thousands of forgotten casualties was Gerrard Winstanley, the future leader of the group that would go on to call themselves the Diggers. In 1630, as John Bradshaw was qualifying as a lawyer, the young and hopeful Winstanley had arrived in London from Wigan. Bradshaw was county gentry entering the professions; by contrast Winstanley was 'bred as a tradesman' and beginning the long apprenticeship to become a clothier or merchant tailor. London was flooded with apprentices in their late teens and early twenties, but this young Lancastrian was cut from rather different cloth to his contemporaries. Bright, sensitive and empathetic, he was given to question, and to doubt, his own actions and the world around him. Apprentices all had a 'master' in whose house they lived and from whom they learned their trade. Winstanley had an unusual patron in the young widow Sarah

Gater. The death of her husband when she was just 18 had left Sarah to run his cloth business, and bring up their young son, alone. She did both ably, and for eight years Winstanley lodged with this remarkable young woman just four years his senior, learning at her side the names and qualities of cloth, the conventions and codes of trade, the arts of book-keeping and stock management. As well as organizing her personal and professional affairs, Sarah Gater read widely and developed a lively intellectual circle. Perhaps her closest friend was Izaak Walton, royalist writer and author of the bestselling fishing guide, *The Compleat Angler*. Dinner-table talk and the remarkable collection of books in this small mercantile household would all form part of the broad intellectual pastures available to her young apprentice. In time it would help feed in him dazzling ideological originality.[4]

In February 1638 Winstanley finally completed his apprenticeship. He was presented to the Master and Wardens of the Merchant Taylors' Company, probably by Sarah Gater herself, and at a ceremony at the Guildhall became a freeman of the City of London. He had now fledged, and was free to leave the security of the Gator household and forge out on his own. Wasting no time, Winstanley acquired a house and shop near the ancient London street of Old Jewry, site of the huge medieval synagogue until its desecration and the expulsion of the Jews 400 years before. The cloth trade underpinned the prosperity of the capital, indeed the country, and Winstanley chose premises deep in its affluent heartland. Old Jewry ran north from the main city thoroughfare of Poultry, and was synonymous with mercantile wealth. Among its tall, timber-framed houses were a series of great traders' mansions. The cloth merchant Kitely in Ben Jonson's play *Every Man in his Humour* had lived on Old Jewry, while at its south end was the magnificent Mercers' Hall, home of another of the city's great cloth guilds. From this prestigious address Winstanley started to trade textiles: acquiring linens and thick cottons such as fustian from wholesalers and the weekly cloth market at Blackwell Hall, just a stone's throw away, and selling them on to domestic and international buyers. Freed from the dependency of apprenticeship, he married Susan King, the daughter of a successful surgeon who would go on to be Master of the Barber Surgeons company

– her dowry presumably providing a valuable boost to his business. The newlyweds took on a domestic servant, Jane, and acquired a young apprentice of their own, Christopher Dicus.[5]

Setting up as a cloth dealer was a relatively inexpensive enterprise. Other than rented premises and funds to purchase stock, it required little more than a pair of scissors, shears and a yardstick. But as Winstanley would find, it was one thing to begin trading, another altogether to make a successful business in this highly competitive field. Despite his promising start, and Sarah Gator's tuition, he was not a natural businessman. Too trusting, too naive and too prone to operating on credit, and careless of paperwork, he did not prosper. The Winstanleys' income was among the lowest of the independent households in their parish; however, they were young and as yet childless. They took in a lodger and with time and connections there was no reason why their fortunes should not improve. But it was not to be. The outbreak of civil war brought a damaging interruption to trade – and opportunities for the unscrupulous – and Winstanley's nascent business quickly began to falter. In 1642 a deal with a slippery merchant named Matthew Backhouse, who was surreptitiously preparing to enter the West Indies slave trade, went disastrously wrong when Backhouse absconded to Barbados with several hundred pounds' worth of Winstanley's cloth. As the Irish uprising and its aftermath played out,

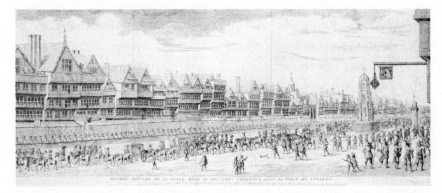

The timber-framed houses of Cheapside, the main thoroughfare of the City of London, shortly before the civil war. Gerrard Winstanley worked as a cloth merchant on Old Jewry, just off Cheapside, until bankruptcy and personal breakdown caused him to abandon the capital for Surrey.

seaborne trade was disrupted further and another of Winstanley's major customers, Dublin merchant Philip Peake, defaulted on a debt of over £100.

Now unable to pay his own suppliers, Winstanley's business was in free-fall. The pressure on him was immense and he was emotionally ill-equipped to withstand it. He would later write with feeling of the trader's lot: 'if he ask sometimes too little, or sometimes too much for his wares, then he is troubled, and do what he can, his heart is troubled, because he thinks he might have done better.' Finally, in the autumn of 1643, his business failed altogether. Bankrupt, he relinquished his paltry remaining stock to his creditors, vacated his house and shop and abandoned London. All he had worked for was dust.[6]

In fact, the Winstanleys were lucky. They had lost their business but they were not, and would never be, destitute. 'Friends' (probably Susan's father) provided the money for them to start afresh: the seriousness of Winstanley's breakdown necessitated a complete change, and they began a new 'countrey life'. They relocated to Surrey, where they lodged first in Street Cobham and then two years later settled a mile south in Church Cobham. Winstanley's new occupation was quite different from the teeming world of trade that was all he had known until now. He had become instead a grazier, a landholder who used his pastures to rear livestock for himself and others.[7] But while he had escaped the intense physical hardship that others were enduring, the experience of bankruptcy had had a profound effect on him. The desperate humiliation of personal financial failure, of disappointing those who had trusted him, was almost overwhelming – and was not diminished by the intervention of his successful father-in-law. He was mentally and emotionally traumatized. Shock gave way to self-pity and deep bitterness at those who had wronged him, and to the whole system which had so crushed him. 'Thou City of London, I am one of thy sons,' he cried, but by 'the theeving art of buying and selling', 'I was beaten out of both estate and trade.'[8]

While his new existence was more stable than what went before, life as a Cobham grazier offered little escape from injustice. The village was located on the road from London to Portsmouth, and was frequently required to house and feed soldiers. The colossal cost of the civil war, and of maintaining the armies, was funded largely through taxation of ordinary householders, who, county by county, had to provide most of the £45,000 needed every month to keep the army on the road. Charles I's infamous ship money was nothing compared to the tax burden that was now placed on the shoulders of ordinary English people by both sides in the war. While soldiers were meant to pay for their own food and lodgings from their wages, the practice of 'free quarter' was soon commonplace, whereby soldiers whose pay was in arrears (which was most) could require the local community to lodge and feed them for free. Added to this, soldiers tended simply to help themselves to whatever they liked in the name of the war effort. Winstanley and his Cobham neighbours had to look on as the village

A pillaging soldier making off with both the chicken and the cooking pot in a mid-seventeenth-century satirical print. The burden on ordinary people of billeting soldiers during the 1640s and 1650s was immense and often ruinous.

authorities distributed the soldiers among the poorer householders to save their own homes, compelling some to leave their lodgings altogether. His financial and personal struggle resumed, as 'by the burthen of Taxes and much free quarter, my weak back found the burthen heavier than I could bear'.[9]

While not obviously political in his London years, Winstanley was instinctively a parliamentarian rather than a royalist. The country's troubles had been visible in the City: Charles I had leaned heavily on the livery companies for funds during the 1630s when he had ruled without Parliament, and Winstanley's guild, the Merchant Taylors, had provided a substantial portion of that money. When the King dined at the Guildhall in November 1641, shortly before the outbreak of the civil war, many had taken to the streets in hostile demonstration, and when the five MPs whose arrest Charles had ordered fled to the City, they were probably hidden just around the corner from Winstanley's Old Jewry shop. Winstanley, like many others, had put his name to the agreement signed with the Scots to secure their military support in the civil war, the 'Solemn League and Covenant'. The document was designed to commit the English to a very particular form of Presbyterian church in return for the Scots' assistance, but it was its ambitious and uplifting language that lodged in Winstanley's mind. Talk of the quest for 'freedom', the 'many sins against God which had been committed in England', the 'common cause of religion, liberty, and peace' and the need for true 'reformation' stayed with him and in time he would begin to formulate his own response to these ambitious aspirations.[10]

Winstanley tried various things as he sought peace in his new life in Cobham – including briefly joining the Baptists – but without success. He began writing, soothing his mind by setting down the arguments that had begun to form: the importance of calm, the belief that no institution – not the monarchy, the church, universities or courts – held the answers, that they must be sought from God and within. Then one day in late 1648, while the negotiations with Charles I were grinding on miles away on the Isle of Wight, he had his epiphany. As he walked his pastures in autumn's rich colours, in a rural landscape which he had come to appreciate intensely, suddenly 'my heart was filled with sweet thoughts, and many things were revealed to me which I never read in books, nor heard from the mouth of any flesh'. He heard a voice say three times, 'Work together, eat together, declare this abroad'. When he awoke he knew what he must do. Spiritual salvation would come not from one sect or another, but from the blossoming of God within each man, and the promised 'reformation' would involve nothing less than the end of the very root of the 'thieving' practice of trade: private property itself. Freedom, complete freedom, beckoned.[11]

National events clearly influenced Winstanley, and the timing of his spiritual crescendo was significant. On 26 January 1649, as commissioners for the trial of the King sat around the table of the Painted Chamber in Westminster drafting the sentence, Winstanley completed his masterpiece, *The New Law of Righteousness*. Addressed to 'the despised ones of the world', it gave a luminous account of his powerful and optimistic vision of the future, the imminent rising of Christ in everyone – the true second coming – and the advent of a new spiritual and social Utopia. If the earth could be truly shared, and people could come together to work it, there would be an end to all hunger and want, all greed and envy. The way to realize this vision was to act: words were 'nothing at all, and must die, for action is the life of all'. As soon as God had guided them to the place, we 'that are called the common people' would begin his work.[12]

❦ ❦ ❦

In April 1649 such was the towering mountain of business before the new republic that the Council of State was meeting almost every day. The prevention of a royalist invasion, widespread discontent in the army, chaotic international relations, the search for funds in a near-bankrupt country and a situation in Ireland that was again spiralling rapidly out of control all required urgent attention. And this was not to mention the establishment of the new regime or implementation of any of its initiatives for reform. No one was more dedicated to its work than John Bradshaw. On Monday 16 April he was in the chair as usual when the Council first heard of the goings-on on St George's Hill. A local yeoman, Henry Sanders of Walton-on-Thames, gave a written account of the strange events there – the Cobham men planting and ploughing and their talk of the land being 'a common treasury'. The Council of State's overwhelming concern was simply to ensure the new republic's survival and on the face of it reports of the planting of vege-tables on common land in Surrey were hardly a national priority. However, other, unrelated, events of April 1649 caused them to take this report seriously.[13]

In the last years of the 1640s the London-based association of polit-ical radicals known as the Levellers had hugely increased their influence by managing to infiltrate the New Model Army. A number of charis-matic Levellers had enlisted and found in their fellow soldiers a sympathetic audience, men nervous of being disbanded without pay and concerned about the return to power of the King against whom they had taken up arms. In the autumn of 1647 the army high command had held a number of formal meetings at their headquarters at Putney to air the competing aspirations for the future governance of the nation within the ranks. Here, at the 'Putney Debates', a coherent and far-reach-ing proposal for constitutional reform was put forward which the Levellers had clearly orchestrated. This, 'An Agreement of the People', proposed a new written constitution based on the principle that all power emanated from the people. A new parliament would be elected on a dramatically extended franchise (because of a wealth requirement only a small percentage of the population was entitled to vote), parlia-mentary seats reduced and distributed more equitably, the legal system modernized, the national church abolished and freedom of worship introduced. What several centuries later would seem entirely reasona-ble looked dangerously anarchic to the governing classes in the seventeenth century, including many army leaders. Henry Ireton and even Oliver Cromwell might be content to put Charles I on trial, but to suggest that the poor should be allowed to vote was quite another matter. As the tempo in Putney had risen Fairfax and Cromwell, shocked by the scale of change their men were advocating, had closed the debate down. It was now returning in spades.[14]

When the army staged its coup in December 1648, a revised and expanded version of 'An Agreement of the People' was produced by a

group of army officers and leading Levellers, which amounted to nothing less than a manifesto for wholesale constitutional change, along the
lines of its 1647 precursor. But this clarion call for reform was to be
swiftly muffled. First its terms were moderated by the army high
command (Fairfax for one was no warrior for social justice) and then
when it was presented to the purged House of Commons, they – much
more interested in wreaking revenge on Charles I than reforming their
own institution – agreed only to look at it in due course. As one of the
trial commissioners put it, 'at that time every man almost was fancying
a form of government, and [was] angry when this came forth, that his
invention took not place'. The leading Levellers were indeed angry.
Feeling betrayed and fobbed off, and realizing that their window of
opportunity to direct events was about to pass, they started issuing
irate and inflammatory publications accusing the army leaders of
treachery and denouncing the new Council of State. Within weeks the
leading Levellers were in prison themselves accused of treason.[15]

It was in the midst of all this that Henry Sanders's report of activities
on St George's Hill was read to the Council. While there was actually no
direct connection between the Diggers and the Levellers, this was not
yet obvious (Winstanley added to the confusion by calling his manifesto 'The True Levellers Standard Advanced'). John Bradshaw wrote
immediately to Lord Fairfax asking him to send soldiers to disperse the
Diggers, adding by means of explanation that although the cause 'may
seeme very ridiculous, yett that conflux of people may bee a beginning
whence things of a greater and more dangerous consequence may grow'.
Captain John Gladman was dispatched to Surrey. But when his men
reached St George's Hill they found a scene that seemed almost laugh-
ably harmless: a handful of idealistic local men hoeing. Captain
Gladman wrote to Fairfax that he would try to persuade them to
disband, but that they posed no danger, indeed the whole thing was
'not worth the writing nor yet taking nottis of'. He was amazed the
Council should bother itself with something so insignificant. But this
would not be the end of it. With disarming self-confidence Everard and
Winstanley told Gladman that they would come to London to see Lord
Fairfax in person. And, sure enough, a few days later these two men

presented themselves at the palace of Whitehall for an audience with the Lord General of the army and his Council of War.[16]

Whitehall Palace had been the epicentre of the Tudor and Stuart monarchy ever since Henry VIII had acquired what had been the Archbishop of York's metropolitan palace from Cardinal Wolsey. A densely built-up complex of predominantly brick buildings on a narrow site along the Thames, it was a short walk north from Westminster. On the river side stood the king's and queen's apartments, a large privy garden, numerous courtiers' lodgings and Inigo Jones's great stone audience chamber, the Banqueting House. Across King Street on the edge of St James's Park was an assortment of brick tennis courts and cockpits where the royal family amused themselves. During the 1640s, with the King absent and the country at war, the palace's state apartments were little used. But as almost everybody was expecting Charles I's return sooner or later, there had been no colonization of his rooms. The palace was far from empty, however, as courtiers retained their lodgings and from 1648 a large garrison of soldiers was stationed there. During the winter of 1648–9, various army officers lodged at Whitehall, sharing quarters in inconsequential corners of the palace. However, as Bulstrode Whitelocke noted, by the time the trial began, the army's second-in-command, Oliver Cromwell, had taken as his berth one of Charles I's own 'fine' beds.[17]

With the execution of the King and declaration of the republic, things had changed. Crown lands and most royal buildings were to be surveyed for sale, while the royal collection of paintings and sculpture, tapestries and plate was also to be inventoried and auctioned to raise funds to pay state debts. In both cases a number of places and pieces were to be held back for the use of the new government. Whitehall itself was to be made ready for the Council of State: the supreme executive committee was to be served by the building just as the sovereign had been. The palace had become tatty and dirty through the years of disruption, and it was while repair works were underway, amid the coming and going of decorators and mat layers, inventory clerks and valuers, that the Diggers had their meeting on 20 April 1649. Everard and Winstanley stood before Lord Fairfax and gave an account of their

Imprinted at *London*, for *G. Laurinson, Aprill* 23. 1649.

William Everard, one of the leaders of the group of rural communists known as the 'Diggers', addressing Lord Fairfax at a meeting in Whitehall in April 1649. To Fairfax's amazement both Everard and his colleague Gerrard Winstanley kept their hats on throughout the meeting.

cause. Everard was not an appealing figure; he was prone to hectoring and eccentric behaviour that bordered on the lunatic, including claiming that his real name was 'Chamberlin' because he dwelled in the secret chambers of God's confidence. Gladman had predicted the General would be keen to be shot of he 'who is no other than a madd man'. Winstanley, however, was a different matter, and cut an altogether calmer and more reasonable figure.[18]

Fairfax listened to the strange claims of this unworldly pair. Since the Norman Conquest, they explained eagerly, England had been in a state of servitude. The moment was now coming when everyone would be freed, and the ancient order of things restored. Their work on St George's Hill was a beginning, and soon every man would willingly relinquish his property and join them, so that the bounty of the earth could, as God intended, be shared and used to 'feed the hungry and clothe the naked'. Alongside their apocalyptic vision, the pair were keen to stress their moderation. Despite what was being said, they had no intention of pulling down fences or attacking private property. They would work only on common land, and do so peacefully and without violence, trusting that their example, and God's intervention, would inspire all men to join them.

As the pair babbled enthusiastically, it was their appearance as much as their words that held the General's attention. Contrary to the usual practice when in the presence of a superior, Everard and Winstanley did not enter the room bareheaded, but came in with their hats on, and retained them throughout the meeting. As soon as they had stopped speaking Fairfax asked why they did so. They replied simply that 'he was but their fellow creature'. Did they then, he rejoindered, reject the biblical instruction to give honour to whom honour is due? At this they 'seemed to be offended', and vociferously denied they meant any dishonour to the General.[19]

It was a puzzling encounter. The two men were in themselves a contradictory combination; their activities were, too, being both shockingly radical and gently optimistic, and their tone was at once grossly insolent and placidly obedient. The General did not know what to make of them. While Henry Sanders had hoped his letter to London would see the Diggers swiftly stamped out, having met them the head of the army did not come to this conclusion. Indeed, the meeting had raised in him more curiosity than condemnation. Winstanley and Everard left Whitehall pleased; they had sensed a glimmer of sympathy in the Lord General's dark eyes.

Winstanley had other reasons to come to London that week. In the shadow of St Paul's Cathedral, on his old City of London stamping ground, was the shop of the radical bookseller Giles Calvert, identifiable by the large black spread eagle that swung on a painted sign over its door. That very week Calvert was publishing Winstanley's manifesto, 'The True Levellers Standard Advanced'. It set out, as its title page made clear, 'why the common People of England have begun ... to dig up, manure and sow Corn upon George-Hill in Surrey'. The timing was significant: the pamphlet was produced 'that the great Councell and Army of the land may take notice of it'. Calvert was famous for selling radical literature, or 'soul-poysons', and in 1649 he produced sixty-one new titles. Like many others, Winstanley had realized the importance of using the medium of print to articulate and disseminate his point of view. With its assistance the obscure doings of a handful of men could be broadcast and interpreted for the entire country. He returned to Cobham with a spring in his step, to tell his colleagues how the great General had treated them with 'mildness and moderation'. But if he now had hope that his prophecy would be realized, and all the common ground in England 'and in the whole world shall be taken in by the people in righteousness', events near and far were about to see it dashed.[20]

Four

The Ebbing Tide

❦❦❦❦❦❦❦❦❦❦❦❦❦❦❦❦❦❦❦❦❦

L ord Fairfax faced a series of threats in the spring of 1649 beside which the Cobham Diggers looked amusingly harmless. The four Leveller leaders were under lock and key in the Tower of London, but they and their colleagues had been so effective in their penetration of the army that their imprisonment only inflamed discontent among the republic's soldiers. In late April one troop about to be moved away from the capital and its fiery politics barricaded themselves into an inn on Bishopsgate. A stickler for military discipline, Fairfax had the leaders arrested on the spot and one, a young private soldier named Robert Lockyer, sentenced to death. He was felled by a firing squad on 27 April, making an eloquent case in his final minutes for the liberties of the nation. His funeral two days later became a mass popular demonstration; some 4,000 people participated, many wearing green ribbons to signify their Leveller sympathies.[1]

Political views aside, the rank and file of the New Model Army had other reasons for unhappiness. Their pay was in arrears and it looked certain they would soon be required to answer an unappealing call to arms. The extreme events in England over the winter of 1648–9 had been enough to spark a reconciliation between two of the warring parties in Ireland, and on 17 January the leaders of the Catholic majority had signed a treaty with the senior Irish royalist the Marquess of

Ormond. Now united against their common enemy – the new English Commonwealth – this Catholic–royalist alliance condemned the execution of Charles I and set out to consolidate its control of Ireland from its base in the medieval town of Kilkenny. The urgent need to reassert the authority of the English Parliament occupied the minds of the Commonwealth army high command. The soldiers who were likely to be sent there regarded the prospect with deep foreboding. After the failed uprising of 1641–2, tales of Catholic barbarism and bloodlust for Protestants abounded and long experience had shown that English military missions to Ireland seldom ended in glory. On the day Winstanley and Everard had visited Fairfax in Whitehall lots had been drawn to select the regiments to go to Ireland. Fourteen slips of paper had been shuffled in a hat, of which four bore the dreaded word 'Ireland'. The men selected were left gulping with fear. In early May this sparked outright mutiny. Some 900 soldiers rose against their officers, many demanding the implementation of the Leveller manifesto 'An Agreement of the People', and bills enumerating their complaints began to appear pasted on doors and walls. Fairfax at first tried to persuade the mutineers to back down, setting out how much reform had already been achieved and all that was still to come. They expressed their admiration for their Lord General, but would not capitulate, converging on the picturesque Cotswold town of Burford in Oxfordshire. Fairfax and his deputy Oliver Cromwell marched on the town, taking it and the mutineers in a swift and skilful nocturnal attack with few fatalities. Three days later the ringleaders were shot in Burford churchyard within sight of their captured colleagues. It was a stark reminder that while these army grandees had once been rebels themselves, they would tolerate no disobedience in their new regime.[2]

🎕 🎕 🎕

It was on the way back to London after suppressing the May mutiny that Lord Fairfax decided to pay a visit to the communists on St George's Hill. The General, head of the New Model Army, was now back at the centre of things. His crisis of conscience over the trial and execution of the King would never abate but, once the sentence had been carried out, he had agreed to participate in the new Commonwealth so long as he did not have to declare his support for the acts which had created it. His charisma, charm and tremendous reputation among the soldiers were valuable to the fragile new regime.

Winstanley and his colleagues had been at work for six weeks. The land they tilled was poor, but they chose to see this as an advantage – an opportunity for God to express his love. Rather than relying entirely on divine intervention, however, they had worked hard to improve its fertility. After burning off the heather, they had drawn the plough back and forth over the turned ground and forked in large quantities of manure. As the days grew longer and warmer and the gorse bushes on the heath were in full sweet-scented bloom, the pale soil became speckled with green shoots.[3]

The men who tended these crops were on the face of it an unremarkable bunch. Neither the poorest nor the most powerful of local society, they were from the middling families in between, an innkeeper, a bricklayer, a shoemaker, the younger son of a landowner. Unlike the Levellers, they were not part of the national political sphere, they knew and worried little about constituency boundaries, terms of Parliament or the voting franchise – this was not the world they inhabited. Rather, they cared about poverty and wealth, injustice and freedom on both an intensely local and an almost infinitely universal scale. They did not count among their number firebrands from London or organized agitators from elsewhere, but were almost all residents of Cobham inspired by Winstanley's radiant vision, the tempo of the times and the disappointments and hardships of their own lives.[4]

It was late May when Lord General Fairfax and his officers rode up the gentle slope to the Diggers' encampment. They found a dozen people at work on fields dotted with a series of simple timber 'houses' which they had built to allow them to stay overnight. The restless Everard had recently left their movement, and it was Winstanley who stood and spoke to their visitors. Fairfax's officers asked questions about the 'strangeness of their actions' to which he gave 'sober' answers, but his talk of an end to private property and the return to common and collective ownership made no sense to them. Fairfax made a short speech of reproof, but his attitude remained gentle. Winstanley spoke of the opposition they had faced from people of the parish, who had trampled their first lot of seedlings, but emphasized that they had not fought back, applying 'to all the golden rule, to do to others as we would be done unto'. The head of the army left the Diggers undisturbed and rode back to London. The Diggers returned to their work feeling they had secured the sympathy of the most powerful man in England.[5]

❦ ❦ ❦

The hopes of the minority who had pined for revolution were so high that the reality of life after the regicide was bound to be a disappointment. John Lilburne's expressively titled *England's New Chains Discovered*, published in March 1649, articulated his and the Levellers' anger at the new regime's reluctance to undertake the immediate wholesale constitutional reform for which they had argued. Meanwhile, Gerrard Winstanley's poetic optimism had to contend with the reality of the prosaic world around him. In the autumn of 1648 he had had an augury that the future might not amount to the social and spiritual nirvana he had hoped for. While 'Laudian' worship had been officially stamped out, there remained a requirement for religious conformity, just of a different stripe. Church attendance was still compulsory, as was adherence to a long list of beliefs, including the Trinity, the resurrection of Christ, the truth of the Bible and the resurrection of the dead, on pain of imprisonment. Winstanley had witnessed both his volatile colleague, William Everard, and another associate, John Fielder, being prosecuted for failing to adhere to these religious rules. This did not feel like the freedom that had been spoken of in the years before, and a frustration took root that would come slowly to the surface, brought on above all by the experience of the weeks that were to follow.[6]

The unedifying truth was that the real opposition to the Diggers would not originate from on high, the Council of State or the army – indeed, Fairfax clearly had a soft spot for these rural romantics – but from the ordinary people of their locality. A local yeoman had first contacted the Council of State and Winstanley conceded that despite their peaceful motives they had met resistance from their Surrey neighbours. Their first crop of barley had been destroyed by 'envious inhabitants thereabouts'. While Winstanley had reported hopefully that those who had opposed them were starting 'to be moderate and see righteousness in our work', even his billowing optimism could not long mask the bad feeling that lay about them.[7]

St George's Hill was only a mile or two from the Diggers' homes in Cobham, but it was outside the boundary of their parish, lying at the relatively unpopulated western end of the adjacent parish of Walton-on-Thames. The very fact of the Diggers being from the next-door parish fed local irritation and suspicion. Conservatism and the usual web of parochial grudges and rivalries combined to cause the people of Walton to regard the Cobham Diggers with distaste verging on disgust. While Winstanley and his colleagues were enjoying the tacit patronage of the head of the army, they hesitated to intervene. But when Fairfax's own soldiers acted, the floodgates of opposition were breached.

In early June a band of foot soldiers under the command of one Captain Stravie was stationed in Cobham, some even lodging in houses belonging to the Diggers. Thanks to the running commentary provided by Winstanley's publications and considerable press interest, the fame of the group was out of all proportion to their modest numbers, and 'our digging upon that common is the talk of the whole land'. One evening the soldiers set off for St George's Hill intent on stirring up trouble. They found two people quietly at work and, without preamble, launched an attack, bludgeoning the man in the head and beating the other, a boy, before stripping him naked. They then set one of the Diggers' buildings on fire and careered away. When Winstanley was told of the incident he was horrified. He wrote to Lord Fairfax and travelled to London to hand the letter to the General personally. 'Assured of your moderation and friendship', he asked the general to stand the soldiers down, certain they could not have acted on his orders. Surely there could be no reason for this unprovoked attack – unless, he added in a pointed aside, it was 'because we improve that victory which you have gotten in the name of the Commons over the King'.

Emboldened by the soldiers' attack, a pair of leading local landowners rode up the hill two days later followed by an armed mob. In a surreal gesture, presumably intended to humiliate, several came dressed in women's clothing. They pursued the Diggers with clubs, leaving the sandy hillside strewn with battered bodies. The uneasy peace of the spring was now gone, and within a fortnight the Diggers' occupation of St George's Hill was in the hands of the courts.[8]

A previous attempt to prosecute the Diggers had failed, but now Francis Drake, an MP and Walton landowner, brought a case for trespass against Winstanley and his fellow Diggers Henry Bickerstaff and Thomas Star at Kingston-upon-Thames court. In order to defend themselves, or even to learn the detail of the charge, the accused found they had to engage a lawyer. This Winstanley categorically refused to do, declaring it unjust that he should have to pay simply to maintain their innocence. One of the officers of the court gloated they were doomed anyway – a jury would be selected to find them guilty. As the system did not permit them to defend themselves in person, the three were forced to stand silent while the case was decided against them and a substantial fine issued. Further persecution was to follow. During Winstanley's imprisonment in Kingston, a group of Drake's associates stole onto his Cobham land and beat and then chased away the livestock they found grazing there. The men hit the helpless cows so hard with their clubs that the animals' heads and bodies swelled with injury. Their powerlessness and innocence, like that of the downtrodden poor, tore at Winstanley's tender heart: 'these cows never were upon George Hill, nor never digged upon that ground, and yet the poor beasts must suffer because they give milk to feed me.' It seemed now that the Diggers' enemies would stop at nothing to ensure their destruction.[9]

❦ ❦ ❦

When the Diggers were released from prison they found their plantation devastated. Determined not to capitulate they decided to relaunch their social crusade closer to home. Cobham also had a series of areas of common ground, including the wide, flat 'Tilt' across which the main road to Guildford ran. At the far east of the parish, at the end of long Fairmile Lane, was a smaller, less prominent uncultivated area known as the Little Heath. Here they would begin afresh.

Winstanley's financial failure seven years earlier had caused him a nervous breakdown, but he had now gained such clarity and conviction that even in the face of outright aggression he remained unshakable. While the new plantation was being established, he was at work on his latest publication. Throughout the year he had shuttled between manual labour on the hillside and his desk, where he scratched the pages full with his lucid, vivid prose. A combination of advocacy for the Diggers' movement, spiritual reflection and first-hand description of life on their plantation, this, A Watch-Word to the City of London and the Army, was another work bound for sale at Giles Calvert's shop. Until now Winstanley's tone had been positive, acknowledging setbacks but laced with uplifting confidence. The events of the summer had caused a darker note to enter his polemic. He now looked accusingly towards those in authority, brimming with bitterness that the new Commonwealth was so slight an improvement on what had come before. Livelihoods had been destroyed, people had died, families had starved, and all for what? This time he addressed himself to the city of London and the army, sibling authorities in this kingless new world. They had fought and fasted, prayed and toiled for liberty, and even executed the King, but 'now the common enemy is gone, you are all like men in a mist, seeking for freedom and know not where, nor what it is'. Particular bile was reserved for the legal system with which he had just had such an unhappy encounter. They had been prevented from representing themselves or even hearing the evidence against them. The jury had been packed with freeholders who were bound to oppose them and the case was decided against them in just a few days, when usually 'they keep a cause depending seven years to the utter undoing of the parties, so unrighteous is the law and lawyers'.[10]

Winstanley's critique was a powerful one. Hardly anyone took the Diggers' talk of communal ownership seriously, but his cry that the new authorities were falling short of the promises and sacrifices of the 1640s, and his condemnation of the inequities of society and the law, struck a chord with many. For decades, indeed centuries, the English legal system had been decried for its unfairness. The lists of its shortcomings varied, but most included the sheer time it took to resolve any case and the eye-watering cost in lawyers' fees of legal action. The indefinite imprisonment of debtors and the power of the central courts in London were also causes for repeated complaint, as was the fact that the law was a closed shop, conducted in Latin and French, to the absolute exclusion of non-professionals. The abolition of the central 'prerogative courts' in 1641 had been as far as many of the landed classes wished to go, but the Levellers and others pressed for more fundamental change. A petition in the summer of 1649 proposed that 'proceedings in law may be in English, cheap, certain &c and all suits and differences first be arbitrated by three neighbours, and if they cannot determine it, then to certify the court ...' Fairfax may have counselled patience to the Diggers, as he had done to the army muti-neers, but Winstanley's criticisms had real bite. In his writings he condemned the English legal system as an 'old whore' that 'picks men's pockets and undoes them'. Presented with such sharp reproofs, even the indulgent Fairfax began to look more coolly on the Cobham communists.[11]

❦ ❦ ❦

The army mutiny may have been suppressed, but in the summer of 1649 Fairfax, Bradshaw and the other members of the Council of State still had a monumental task on their hands to hold the new regime together. While the reformers cried for change, the truth was that the high-water mark of the English revolution had already passed and the tide was starting to ebb. The fact that only because of an outright military coup had so much change been achieved was inescapable – not least because of the daily reminders issued by the royalist presses. Moves were made to try to broaden the base of the regime. The House of Commons pledged to dissolve itself to allow new elections as soon as it was safe to do so and, once the incendiary business of the King's trial had passed, excluded members were encouraged to resume their seats, required to renounce the Isle of Wight deal with the King rather than to state their support for the regicide itself (though for a time Fairfax managed to avoid even doing this). As a result the revolutionary cohort of seventy MPs who had put the King on trial was gradually diluted by the reappearance of their more moderate colleagues, of whom well over a hundred would in time return.

In the first months of 1649, the Levellers had kept up the pressure for reform. While they were a live threat it was important to be able to point to evidence of change. In May a definitive statement of England's republican status was published; it was 'a Commonwealth ... without and King or house of Lords', and a committee to tackle reform of the legal system had been initiated. But with the defeat of the mutinous regiments the Leveller movement had been sapped, and the urgency of these initiatives receded. Moderates, on the other hand, were pleased at the absence of revolutionary social measures, and impressed at the enthusiasm with which Cromwell and Fairfax had crushed the radical uprising, and slowly more MPs trickled slowly back into the chamber.

There was a further fundamental tension in the regime that emerged in 1649. The violence and violation of Pride's Purge was something that many MPs could neither forgive nor forget. Perhaps as a deliberate act of retaliation, the committee of MPs nominating the forty-one members of the new Council of State had chosen just three soldiers, thereby largely disenfranchising the body which had brought the regime into being. While in the 1640s the army and Parliament had been held together by their opposition to the King, thereafter alienation gradually set in, and a growing sense of suspicion and distrust. In time these cracks would start to open up and threaten the revolution itself.[12]

✿ ✿ ✿

The Diggers began their new plantation on Cobham's Little Heath late in the summer of 1649. They felt that the Cobham villagers would be less opposed to them than their Walton counterparts – these were after all their neighbours and relatives. In this they were right, but the view of those in authority was hardening, and they had few of influence to whom they could turn. The lord of Cobham manor was a child whose widowed mother had recently married John Platt, the minister of West Horsley, six or seven miles away. For several years Cobham had been without a minister of its own, and as an outsider 'Parson' Platt had few of the local friendships and ties which might have tempered his approach. He became the ringleader of the opposition and the White Lion, the large coaching inn at the heart of Street Cobham, became his campaign headquarters. Here Platt and his colleagues gathered to drink wine, suck on their pipes and discuss how to crush the Diggers. If his encounter with the courts had caused Winstanley to experience the injustices of the English legal system, his dealings with Platt would see him condemn once and for all established religion and the conspiracy of oppression, as he saw it, between church and state. Platt for his part considered himself more than equal to the task of eradicating these local cranks, and recruited a rabble of young men to do his bidding.[13]

What followed was a campaign of intimidation and assault. Platt's mob, derided by Winstanley as 'knapsack boys' and 'ammunition sluts' after the hangers-on to the army, continued to target his own Cobham house, letting animals in to trample his corn and barley and, at such acts of sabotage, 'hollowing and shouting as if they were dancing at a Whitsun ale'. Meanwhile the plantation on the Little Common was under periodic attack. Platt went straight to the top. In early October the Council of State received a request for their assistance following a 'tumultuous meeting' in Cobham which the local authorities claimed to be unable to disperse. Outlandish claims about the Diggers' way of life were repeated, laced with slanderous rumours that they treated women as communal property and were secretly in league with royalists. After two weeks' petitioning by Platt, Fairfax was finally convinced to withdraw his tacit protection, though he stopped short of authorizing his men to use violence on the Diggers' persons.[14]

The harassment that followed was not unremitting, in fact there were even occasions when Winstanley engaged in thoughtful discussion with his adversaries. One soldier asked him how he could make claims for the common ownership of property, when such a state of affairs did not exist in any other country in the world. Winstanley's answer was simple: 'England hath lain under the power of that Beast, kingly property. But now England is the first of the nations that is upon the point of reforming.' Even Platt could engage in reasonable debate in person. But there was no disguising the malice of his intent.

A series of violent attacks were launched through the winter orchestrated by Platt and other figures of authority. A number of the Diggers'
families had joined them and were staying in the huts they had erected
on the heath. Here they guarded the winter crops of wheat and rye
that had been seeded over some 10 acres. The houses were a target for
attacks: in one assault a building was destroyed and the inhabitants,
an elderly couple, forced to flee and sleep in the fields. Determined not
to be undone by the destruction, the Diggers constructed small timber
'hutches' instead in which they lay among their crops.[15] As winter
advanced it was increasingly obvious that it would be only a matter of
time before the new plantation was eradicated. The Surrey Diggers
numbered fewer than fifty at their height, and both the landowners
and the army were now against them. So they changed tack, adopting
a martyr-like stoicism, and concentrating on addressing themselves to
the national audience that, through the printing presses, knew so
much of their work. Winstanley penned a new work calling to all
Englishmen, encouraging them to 'turn your swords into plough-
shares, and spears into pruning hooks, and take plough and spade and
break up the common land', urging them to act as 'a fruitful land is
made barren, because of the unrighteousnes of the people that ruled
therein, and would not suffer it to be planted, because they would
keep the poor under bondage to maintain their own lordly power'.
This publication spoke to those in Kent and Northamptonshire who,
inspired by the Diggers' example, had themselves 'begun to digge
upon the Commons'. In addition, Calvert reprinted a number of
Winstanley's early works, to meet a demand that was continuing even
as the Diggers themselves were faltering.[16]

Meanwhile, the noose about their necks tightened. New court
proceedings were instituted, and when Winstanley travelled to
Whitehall in mid-December to try to win back Fairfax's support, he
found that the bonds between them had slackened. He recounted as
further evidence of the Commonwealth's betrayal the sight of Fairfax's
self-satisfied officers batting away an impoverished elderly royalist
woman who had tried to present the General with her petition.[17] As
Easter neared, Platt was preparing for the final assault. One late March

day Minister Platt accompanied his men in riding over to the Common. He reportedly looked coolly on as they smashed down a house, and when the pregnant mother ran out protesting they kicked her so hard that she miscarried her child. Amid such violence Winstanley tried to maintain his pacifist's calm and to make his case to the imperious Platt. When he claimed all their doings were consistent with God's teaching, Platt replied that if Winstanley could prove it from scripture, he would not only leave them alone, but he would relinquish all his own possessions and join them. Ever a literalist, Winstanley called on Platt a few days later with his written 'proof'. Platt was placid and promised to read it and to give Winstanley an 'answer' shortly. But, as Winstanley later recalled, Platt's answer would not be in prose.

On Friday of Easter week Parson Platt rode to Cobham's Little Heath with fifty hired men and ordered them to torch the six remaining Diggers' houses, and with them the clothing and chattels within. While the vivid account of what followed is Winstanley's own, the court proceedings that ensued show that just such a large-scale attack did indeed take place. Winstanley described mothers and children running screaming from burning buildings as Platt declared: 'fire them to the ground, that these heathens, who know not God, may not build them again'. That night the Diggers were followed and threatened with murder if they returned to their plantation. Such was the delight among Platt's coterie that cries of 'the Diggers are routed' filled the air and the church bells were rung in jubilation. To this Winstanley made the soft reply: 'stay gentlemen, yourselves are routed, and you have lost your crown, and the poor Diggers have won the crown of glory.'[18]

In the summer of 1649 Winstanley had asked the House of Commons rhetorically whether, given their reluctance to undertake the reform that had been promised, it might not 'appear to the view of all men, that you cut off the King's head, [so] that you might establish yourselves in the chair of government'. Had they in fact executed 'the King for his power and government as a thief kills a true man for his money'? Now, as the Diggers' modest Utopia was consumed in vitriolic flames, his prediction to the leaders of the new Commonwealth was a chilling one: 'divisions shall tear and torture you,' he called, and 'the people shall all fall off from you, and you shall fall on a sudden like a great tree that is undermined at the root. And you powers of England, you cannot say another day but you had warning.'[19]

Five

Counter-Revolution

Charlotte Stanley, Countess of Derby, may not have been conscious as she turned 50. Her birthday in December 1649 came and went while she lay in thrall to an illness that was threatening to drain the formidable life from her veins. Her pale, ample body was ash-white against her nightdress and her fine linen sheets. Despite the constant attention of her ladies, the anxious concern of her husband and the ministrations of the doctor, she had barely slept or eaten for weeks. The light from her windows passed across her chamber in diminishing arcs as the days shortened, the sounds were the cries of seagulls following the fishing fleet into harbour and the rush of the waves on the shingle shore. Her chamber was furnished for the princess she was: the bed and black lacquered chairs upholstered in purple velvet, the stone walls hung with Flanders tapestries. The overall effect was claustrophobic rather than stately, however, as the room was too small for splendour on this scale. For Lady Derby lay not in the sprawling Stanley stronghold of Lathom House or the nearby hunting lodge at Knowsley, nor at their fine Westminster townhouse on Canon Row, nor in their suburban house in leafy Chelsea. Lathom was now a charred shell, burned by the victorious parliamentarians despite the Countess's celebrated attempt to save it. Derby House had been converted into committee rooms for the new republican administration. Even England itself was a ten-hour journey over turbulent seas. It was a measure of the fortunes of the royalist cause that the Derbys, premier noble family of the north of England, were holding court, and keeping the royal standard flying, from the Isle of Man, a windswept island that punctuated the rough seas between England and Ireland.[1]

The Countess of Derby, born Charlotte de la Trémoille, was a Frenchwoman of impeccable lineage (Colour plate 3). Her grandfather had been William the Silent, Prince of Orange and the founder of the Protestant Dutch Republic, and her father a distinguished French Huguenot nobleman, the Duc de Thouars, comrade of Henri IV of France. She had received the expansive education of a European princess, and as a child had been given rubies and diamonds as gifts by her doting uncles Frederick V, Elector Palatine and titular King of Bohemia, and Frederick Henry, Prince of Orange and ruler of the United Provinces. Charles I's sister, Elizabeth of Bohemia, had arranged her marriage to a young English nobleman in 1626, throwing a great nuptial entertainment for her at The Hague. Her dowry had been an almost unheard-of £24,000. The magnificent French and Dutch palaces of her childhood were a far cry from tiny Castle Rushen, the Stanley family's antiquated fortress on the Isle of Man, where she lay in 1649. But few women in Europe were more equal to the challenges and changes of such dangerous times as Charlotte de la Trémoille.[2]

When her thoughts were more coherent during those lost weeks, she felt sure that God was near and about to take her, as he had already three of her children. She faced that possibility without obvious fear, confident of her own salvation, knowing she had 'suffered for so good and holy a cause'. But it was not her time. As Christmas grew closer the fever slowly subsided and come the new year she was able to sit up and write once again. God had spared her and she would now return with renewed conviction to the cause of counter-revolution.[3]

By the end of 1649 the new 'Commonwealth' regime had seen off the Leveller uprisings and secured political and military control of mainland England. But England did not by a long chalk account for the totality of Charles I's territories. The Scots, though they had been the first to take up arms against the King, had played no part in bringing him to trial and were furious at the execution that had followed. They swiftly declared his exiled son their king, Charles II, though whether he would be prepared to accept the stiff terms they would be likely to offer to make this a reality remained to be seen. In Ireland Catholics and royalists had banded together into a 'Confederation' that was endeavouring to take full control of the country, while an English parliamentary army laboured to prevent it. Meanwhile, a series of smaller offshore territories remained in royalist hands. The Earl and Countess of Derby held the Isle of Man; the Isles of Scilly were still royalist thanks to the efforts of Sir John Grenville, while just off the northern coast of France, the Channel Island of Jersey remained loyal. Much further afield, Barbados, Charles I's most significant territory in the West Indies, was governed by Lord Willoughby, a prominent royalist. There was a great deal still to play for.

As 1650 dawned, and the Countess of Derby gradually recovered her strength, a ship was sighted from the telescope mounted on the ramparts of Castle Rushen. It carried an emissary from the young Charles Stuart, then on Jersey, who presented the Earl with formal letters and insignia bestowing on him the honour that many felt

Rushen Castle on the Isle of Man. The Earl and Countess of Derby held the island for the royalists long after their defeat on the mainland and hosted scores of exiled royalists here. They lodged in Derby House within the castle, its three dormer windows visible above the curtain wall.

Charles I should have given him years before: the Order of the Garter. There was no doubting its significance, the Earl and Countess of Derby would be needed again.[4]

Charlotte Stanley and her husband had, by 1650, been residents of the Isle of Man for almost six years. When she had landed there in July 1644 it was as a figure of national renown. She had arrived fresh from her famous defence of the family's Lancashire fortress, Lathom House, the only significant remaining royalist stronghold in the North-west, where she had withstood a violent three-month siege. In the absence of her husband, and immured with their young children, the Countess had stood resolute even as the attacking artillery had propelled iron cannonballs through the walls of her own chamber. The first part of the siege had been conducted by Thomas Fairfax himself, who – despite his clemency to defeated royalists and care to deal courteously with Lady Derby – had been unable to coax her into surrender. When he gave up, his successor Colonel Rigby had taken a less gentle line. On sending terms of submission with the blunt instruction to sign, he had had to stand by as the Countess shredded the document in his sight, declaring to rapturous cheers from her own men that 'my goods and house shall burn in his sight; myselfe, children and souldiers, rather then fall into his hands, will seale our religion and loyalty in the same flame'. By acting with all the guile and grit of a military commander, the Countess of Derby had polarized opinions. Puritan ministers thundered from their pulpits of this new 'whore of Babylon', while Charles I had spoken with grudging admiration of her bravery. She became a cult figure, emblematic among royalists of the strength and determination of the old noble families in the face of treachery and insurrection, and to parliamentarians of the devilish intransigence of their opponents.[5]

The Earl of Derby and Prince Rupert had finally arrived with troops to end the siege of Lathom House in the royalists' favour. But though the Countess had held the house, the North was slipping from the King's hands. Only a few months later, with the royalist defeat at the battle of Marston Moor, the Earl had been ordered to fall back to the Isle of Man, an ancient Stanley property in the Irish Sea. When

Charlotte had sailed to the island in the summer of 1644 the guns of Lathom must still have rung in her ears. As would often be the case, the couple smarted at their sovereign's instructions – to abandon the Lancashire lands she had just defended with such verve – but had submitted nonetheless.[6]

There was no inevitability to the Earl and Countess of Derby being staunch royalists, not least as they had little personal affection for Charles I or Henrietta Maria. The civil war did not divide along class lines. Senior noble families were to be found on both sides, particularly at the beginning of the war, and the founding commanders of the parliamentarian army were not disenfranchised revolutionaries, but the earls of Essex and Manchester. The Derbys did not love the Stuart court and had made for Lancashire soon after their marriage. This had suited Charlotte. She had not enjoyed the barbed questions the English court ladies revelled in asking about when her famous dowry would materialize. As her husband would note from the seclusion of Castle Rushen, 'court friendship is a cable that in storms is ever cut'. With their shared sense of the grandeur of nobility, husband and wife had preferred life in the North where their castle, Lathom House, had been considered 'both for magnificence and hospitality the onely court of the north part of this kingdom'.[7] Though Charlotte was a Frenchwoman, she shared little of Henrietta Maria's outlook and as a devout Protestant disapproved profoundly of the Queen's Roman Catholicism. But all this notwithstanding, the call from the King when it came was one to which both, with their strong sense of the inviolable loyalty of subject to sovereign, had felt compelled to respond.[8]

🐞 🐞 🐞

As the carpet of thrift on the Isle of Man's treeless slopes burst into pink bloom in the spring of 1650, and the puffins returned from the Atlantic to nest in their cliff-edge burrows, the Earl and Countess of Derby waited for news. For five years they had been able to do agonizingly little to further the royalist cause beyond holding the island in the face of parliamentary attempts to take it. The trial and execution of Charles I – called by Derby 'that fatal stroke which I cannot name without horror'

– had come and gone. They raised funds by intercepting trading vessels passing to and from Ireland and commandeering their goods 'for the king's use'. Ships carrying cloth, in the Anglo-Irish trade that had once sustained Gerrard Winstanley, were among those seized, their contents requisitioned and immediately run up into garments and equipment for their marooned community. The Derbys seem to have regarded all and any as fair game in the struggle for the survival of their cause, and gave little thought to the victims of their persistent privateering. Given Charlotte's reputation, such mercilessness was easily set at her door. Reports circulated that she had reprimanded a Manx captain for taking prisoners rather than simply throwing captured men overboard. But in truth both Earl and Countess considered the times to justify the means.[9]

When Henry Ireton had written to the Earl of Derby in the summer of 1649, asking him to surrender the Isle of Man and make peace with the new republic, Derby had returned an excoriating reply: 'I scorn your proffers, disdain your favour and abhor your treason,' he wrote, pledging to deploy 'the utmost of my power to your destruction'. He followed with an open invitation to all royalists to come to the Isle of Man where they would find hospitality, and others who in time could bring about 'the utter ruin of these unmatchable and rebellious regicides'.[10] Many responded and Charlotte became the chatelaine of a strange doll's house court. Castle Rushen, a diminutive medieval castle as far removed from Inigo Jones's Whitehall Banqueting House as could be imagined, became the palace of this miniature kingdom. One royalist who spent a month on the island talked of the 'great civility' he received as a guest of Lord and Lady Derby, recalling his hostess admiringly as 'one of the wisest and generousest persons that I have known of her sex'. The Earl and Countess, who had danced in one of Charles I's masques, began holding their own on the island each Twelfth Night. One of the great rooms in the castle was hung with tapestry and here guests and the senior residents of the island were invited to 'a great maske' followed by a feast. The Manx people present marvelled at the ladies 'most gloriously decked with silver and gould, broidered workes and most costly ornaments'. On an island where fireside fiddle music was the usual entertainment, this silk-draped vision of the world of Van Dyck and Ben Jonson was exotic indeed.[11]

❦ ❦ ❦

The Earl and Countess of Derby were in some ways an unlikely couple. For an indulged young Frenchwoman raised among the chateaux of the Loire a life in the wilder and wetter parts of England might not have been an obvious recipe for contentment. She had wealth and connections, if not beauty, and at 26 was not young to marry. Her expectations of matrimony had been low, but in the months after their marriage she had declared delightedly that her husband 'shows me the utmost affection, and God gives us grace to live in much happiness and peace of mind', thanking her mother 'for having married me so happily'.[12]

Despite their closeness, husband and wife had contrasting temperaments. Darkly handsome and six years his wife's junior, James Stanley, Earl of Derby, deeply respected the thoroughbred bride who had brought 'so great an honour to my family'. Perhaps because of his wife's status, or maybe just because of his character, he was unthreatened by her strengths, periodically using her maiden name after their marriage and asking her to manage many of his financial affairs.[13] The Earl had the tastes of an old-fashioned nobleman, wedded to his country estates and his large, liveried household. He was bookish and contemplative, and his enforced exile on the Isle of Man when it came suited him far better than his time as a loyal but unimpressive army officer. In the chamber over the gatehouse at Castle Rushen he tended his library. Here amid his hundreds of beautifully bound books and atlases he sat up reading well into the night. He grazed these volumes for wisdom as 'we gather flowers in our gardens from severall borders before we make a posie'. His writing projects included a history of the island, a set of devotional meditations and a letter of guidance for his eldest son. He even dreamed of founding a university on the Isle of Man.[14] Calm by nature, and cool and ceremonious with his inferiors, he had a special devotion to the couple's 'many sweet and hopeful children'. Other than recording civil war victories, his diary consisted entirely of notes of their doings. But love brought loss, and he had a deep well of melan-

choly within him. Every year on 27 March he marked the anniversary of
the death in 1636 of his most beloved child, 'my dear Son James'. 'He
was like an Angell with us. He is now an Angell with Thee,' he confided
in God, asking that He 'comfort me now, and to the end of my life, with
a comfortable expectation of a blessed meeting with my [child] in the
last day'.[15]

For those to whom she was closest Charlotte, Countess of Derby, also
felt and expressed deep love. As a child she had repeatedly implored her
mother 'pray love me' and she kept up a lifelong close friendship with
her sister-in-law, the Duchesse de Thouars, despite their decades of
separation. She was fond of her children – she had given birth to nine
and buried three – but she was devoted above all to her husband. When
in the 1620s he had had to leave Lancashire to attend Charles I's fractious parliaments, she had dreaded his absence and pined for his return.
The love was mutual, and as he sat in private prayer the Earl thanked
God for giving him 'a wife soe much according to my heart' who had
'made me soe exceeding happy'.[16] But Charlotte could also feel and
foster great hatred. Hers was a sharp, passionate temper, and she did
not share her husband's capacity for compassion and forgiveness. She
had grown up with tales of the struggles and setbacks of religious
conflict. Her grandfather had led the Protestants of the Spanish
Netherlands in the 'Dutch revolt' against the Catholic Habsburg monarchy, becoming the 'father of the fatherland'. As barely an adult she was
already speaking of 'going to war in defence of religion', and developed
a defiant, combative character.[17]

Although it was small, only 30 miles from north to south, the Isle of
Man was not without qualities to recommend it as a base for the Earl
and Countess. It was a tactically powerful spot, located in seas that
lapped all four territories of the British Isles – England, Scotland,
Ireland and Wales. Geographically there was no better springboard for
reconquest. It was also a place of great significance for the Stanley
family. While the island had been controlled by the English crown since
the fourteenth century, it was not, nor had ever been, part of England.
The Stanley family had been lords of Man since 1405, and though they
acknowledged the sovereignty of the English crown, and the title 'King

of Man' had fallen from normal usage, there was still much that remained regal about their status on the island. All justice emanated from the lord, all rents and incomes, feudal dues and taxes were paid to him. One well-informed observer reported in the 1640s that he could not find 'any difference at all ... betwixt a King and a Lord of Man'. Silk canopies of state hung over thrones in the formal rooms of Rushen and Peel castles. The Earl of Derby called this little kingdom 'my darling' and when he and the Countess were painted by Sir Anthony van Dyck in the late 1630s, he was depicted gesturing towards this beloved piece of his patrimony (Colour plate 3).[18]

❦ ❦ ❦

The Earl and Countess of Derby had, like their fellow royalist landowners, suffered greatly from the confiscations meted out by the victorious parliamentary side in the civil war. The cost of mounting the war had been immense for both sides; the participation of the Scots alone brought Parliament a bill of tens of thousands of pounds a month. The Painted Chamber, where Bradshaw and his fellow commissioners had met before the trial of Charles I, was more normally the meeting place of the Sequestration Committee, which had, since 1643, been overseeing the seizure (or 'sequestration') of the lands of affluent 'delinquents': wealthy Catholics and those who fought for the King. If after an investigation the charge of delinquency was proved, four-fifths of the delinquent's property would be removed, and the income from it kept by Parliament, and one-fifth returned to support the delinquent's family. Similar confiscations, without the allowance for the subsistence of the rest of the family, had been made by the royalists in areas they controlled until the course of the war turned against them. The pressure for money was such, however, that by the mid-1640s a practice had begun which was to prove much more effective in raising hard cash than taking the rents from such estates: that of allowing the royalist landowners to regain their estates on payment of a fine, a process known as 'compounding'. So successful was this model that in 1650 the Sequestration Committee was merged into the Committee for Compounding with Delinquents.[19]

There were some, however, including the Derbys, whose resistance was such that even the prospect of money was not enough to convince Parliament to allow them to compound. The Earl of Derby's English estates had been sequestered during the civil war, and in 1647, following the now established arrangement, one-fifth of the annual income had been returned. Six months after the execution of Charles I, Derby had offered to pay the fine to regain his remaining estates. Thomas Fairfax had spoken in his favour, telling the committee that he had received personal assurances from the Earl that he would not cause trouble. But the Council of State had disagreed and having canvassed views in Lancashire, and in light of the Earl's furious public response to Ireton's suggestion of surrender, they refused. While the Earl longed for his ancestral lands, his wife was less sentimental, writing to her sister as she convalesced that January that she thought it was probably for the best: 'if we had paid the composition fine which they granted us and have since refused, we would not be any safer', 'if one has the least enemy ... they can without any form of trial, take away your goods and your life'.[20]

One of the consequences of these shifts was that since the family had been allowed their 'fifth', the Derbys' two younger daughters, Catherine and Amelia, had been separated from their parents, remaining at the family's house at Knowsley in Lancashire to receive this income. Various trusted family attendants were with them. Their older sister Mary, now 18, and their younger brothers, Edward and William – Ned and Billy – 11 and 9, were with their parents at Castle Rushen. Charles, Lord Strange, the Derbys' eldest son, with whom his mother, in particular, was furious for having just married without his parents' permission, came and went.

While Lord Fairfax was at the fore, Lady Derby felt confident her daughters would be left alone. Though she and the great parliamentary General had eyed one another across the ramparts at the Lathom House siege, they had developed a mutual respect. He, after all, was head of another noble northern family. 'There are various opinions about his intellect,' Lady Derby remarked, 'but no doubt about his courage, and that he is a man of his word.' Fairfax had assured the Countess that her daughters would have his protection and so far this had held. But now the sands were beginning to shift.[21]

Enraged by reports of the Derbys' capture of parliamentarian prisoners and unhappy at the royalist enclave that remained at Knowsley, in May 1650 the Council of State ordered the girls' detainment and incarceration. Charlotte wrote to her sister-in-law in dismay: 'We hear that they are bearing it bravely, and I have no doubt this is true of the eldest; but my daughter Amelie is delicate and timid and is undergoing medical treatment.' Fairfax's protection was fading. He wrote to Lord Derby offering to release the girls and return to him half of all his estates if only he would relinquish the Isle of Man. 'I am deeply afflicted for the suffering of my children,' Derby replied, but he remained stalwart. If Lord Fairfax would not have mercy on his innocent offspring, 'my children must submit to the mercy of God Almighty, but shall never be redeemed by my disloyalty'. He may have lacked his wife's incendiary rhetoric, but he shared her steely strength. More than this, thrilling news had just reached the island which quickened the couple's spirits and stiffened their resolve.[22]

The Prince of Wales, now titular King Charles II, had been kept safely out of the country since the royalists began losing the war, variously lodged with his mother, Henrietta Maria, at the French royal palace of Saint-Germain-en-Laye, or with his sister, Mary, who had married William II, Prince of Orange, in The Hague. Since his father's execution discussions had been underway about how best to retake England, using one of the territories that recognized the Stuart monarchy as a launch pad. The Scots' demand that they would only welcome the man they had declared their king if he signed up to their religious programme in the form of the Solemn League and Covenant was unappealing. Added to which they had just executed one of Charles I's most loyal supporters, the Marquess of Montrose. However, the obvious alternative, sailing to Ireland, was worse still, as the military mission led by Oliver Cromwell against the royalist–Catholic confederation was proving brutally effective. Charles II swallowed his misgivings and agreed to the Scots' terms. On 2 June 1650 he sailed from the Netherlands to claim his northern kingdom.

Since the end of the fighting most royalists had either retreated into exile or returned to what remained of their estates to try to pick up the pieces. Attempts at grassroots uprisings against the new regime had been unsuccessful, thwarted by betrayals and disorganisation. But now, with the young King himself coming to the British Isles, the tempo had changed and orders were dispatched for the levying of men and arms in each part of the country to be poised to join their King the moment the call came.

The news of the deal struck between Charles II and the Scots generated intense alarm when it reached the Commonwealth government in London. During the preceding month or two they had sought to guard against any uprisings, making the 'Engagement', the oath of loyalty to the new regime, mandatory for all adult men, expanding pro-government propaganda and setting up a special court of justice primed to try any who conspired against them. With danger mounting, John Bradshaw wrung his hands, bemoaning the fact that despite all that he and his colleagues had done, he doubted they had changed a single royalist's mind. The Council of State met on 4 June in the former Queen's apartments of Whitehall Palace, Bradshaw as usual in the chair, and heard the news of Charles II boarding the Scottish ships in the Low Countries. They immediately dispatched a flotilla to try and intercept him, capturing him if possible, if not ordered to 'sink, burn or any other way destroy' the vessel that carried him. But they were too late. The ships had sailed and a new military front was about to open up for the Commonwealth government.[23]

Oliver Cromwell returned to London from his campaign to reconquer Ireland at the beginning of June and a fortnight later Parliament ordered that he and Lord Fairfax should together gather a 'northern expedition' to attack Charles II and the Scots. That Fairfax was deeply uneasy about the Commonwealth with its flawed foundations was widely known from reports that he had refused to swear the Engagement oath. Now he was being instructed to lead a military assault against Charles II and a sovereign country without any aggression on their part. He responded that he could not possibly participate. None was more dismayed at his stance than Cromwell, who pleaded with his old comrade, declaring sincerely that he would prefer to serve under Fairfax than to command the greatest army in Europe. It was Cromwell's suggestion that a special committee be appointed specifically to try to win Fairfax round, and they spent days closeted at Whitehall, arguing for the 'justness & lawfulnes of this undertaking'. But Fairfax was obdurate; his conscience would not permit his participation. If the Scots had invaded, he explained, he would willingly lay down his life in England's defence, but he would play no part in an unlawful and unprovoked invasion of a sovereign state. He sent his secretary, John Rushworth, to the House of Commons. At the bar, before the speaker, Rushworth laid on the table the first and last of the General's commissions. Finally, Thomas Fairfax, architect of the New Model Army and the parliamentarians' most celebrated general, was bowing out. He withdrew from Whitehall and parted company for ever with the Commonwealth government he had done so much to make possible. That same day, 26 June 1650, his deputy, Oliver Cromwell, was chosen as supreme head of the English army and, with his boots still muddy from his Irish campaign, was put on the road for Scotland.[24]

❦ ❦ ❦

It would be a year before the Earl of Derby received the summons to join Charles II. Cromwell and an army of 16,000 marched over the border and won a spectacular victory at Dunbar near Edinburgh in September 1650, giving the English Commonwealth possession of much of southeast Scotland. After a bruising time buffeted between competing factions within the Scottish ruling group, Charles II was finally crowned King of Scots and, in the spring of 1651, spurred into action by the English invasion, a Scottish army gathered in Stirling.

On the Isle of Man the Earl of Derby could make preparations, but could not himself set foot on English soil until the uprising was in train; being wanted for high treason, he would face certain arrest. Not so Charlotte, who had long shuttled to and from the island on missions to seek funds or assistance. In August 1650 she sailed to the Scottish mainland, hoping to make her way to the Dutch Republic and there secure support for Charles II from her powerful relatives. Instead, she discovered the presence of the English army and realized she could not proceed. With Fairfax gone she no longer had a contact in the high command, and risks could not be taken. After a fortnight sheltering in a small house in Kirkcudbright – 'I never saw anything so dirty' – living on oatcakes, she retreated again to Man.[25]

Then, finally, the order came. With Cromwell approaching across central Scotland, Charles II and his largely Scottish army of around 12,000 decided that, rather than confront him, they would make a break for London, the reconquest of England in their sights. Yoking their heavy artillery to oxen, and piling their horses with baggage, they set off at pace down the western side of the country. The news was met with exhilaration on the Isle of Man. Keeping a group of several hundred excitable royalists fed and orderly on the island for the best part of a year had been no easy task. At the end of the first week of August, Derby and his ten ships prepared to sail. The weather was atrocious and the Earl and Countess travelled from Castletown at the southern tip of the island to Ramsey at the northern end from where the fleet was to depart. Husband and wife parted, with the full responsibility and risk of what was in hand entirely plain to them. Three days later, Derby reappeared, blown back to shore. The couple were briefly reunited at Castletown, before Charlotte accompanied him again as he rejoined his ships at Douglas on the island's eastern flank, and set sail once more. It was now 13 August 1651. As his vessels disappeared into the mass of clouds and grey, rolling seas, Charlotte de la Trémoille was on her own.[26]

❦ ❦ ❦

There was much about the King's campaign that made the Derbys uneasy. While they were prepared to risk everything to come to Charles II's aid, there were lines of conscience that could not easily be crossed. The alliance with the Scots, and the compromises it had involved, worried them deeply. The Earl had refused to join Charles in signing the Solemn League and Covenant, baulking at its rejection of the Church of England and its denunciation of bishops and deans as 'Popery'. Charlotte, like her husband, was a moderate Protestant. They shared deep personal piety, and felt comfortable with the Anglican church of his youth, a reformed religion that retained some traditional ceremonies and offices. As her husband put it of the various controversies about church ceremonies, 'it matters not if we kneel upon a cushion or bare boards, or bare knees. What helps us to Devotion is good, whatsoever hinders us is bad.' Both abhorred the near-anarchy they saw in the new religious practices they had witnessed over the previous decade. Charlotte's sister-in-law, the Huguenot Duchesse de Thouars, questioned whether, as a proud Protestant, she should not welcome the parliamentarians' thirst for religious reform. 'Dear Sister', Charlotte had replied, 'if you had the least notion of the truth, you would change your opinions. The sects of which you speak increase daily, and it makes one's hair stand on end to think of it. The Koran is printed with permission. It is common to deny both God and Jesus Christ, and to believe only in the spirit of the universe.' For a couple who cared profoundly about hierarchy the new world was chillingly unstructured: 'every one who thinks he is able to preach, even women, may do so without examination'. Charlotte's personal experience in Scotland was salutary, the squalor of the Kirkcudbright cottage was 'nothing to the religion'. But as with their unrewarded loyalty to Charles I, their misgivings could not weaken their determination to serve their sovereign.[27]

Her husband gone, Charlotte returned to Castletown, and to Castle Rushen. Before Derby left he had formally signed over to his wife responsibility for the island and all decisions to do with it, declaring the confidence he had in 'the knowne wisdom and courage of you Dame Charlotte de la Trémoille my dear and welbeloved wife'. She was now the overlord of the island, with their able and loyal kinsman John Greenhalgh at her side as Lieutenant Governor.[28]

Because the lord of Man had usually been an absentee, the islanders had historically been allowed to manage their own affairs under the auspices of a resident Governor. Various officers drawn from the local population advised him; these included two Deemsters, who dealt with legal matters, and a Receiver, who collected the island rents. The leading figures of the island, the twenty-four 'Keys', participated in a consultative assembly, the Tynwald, which met periodically to discuss island affairs. The novel experience of having a resident lord, combined with the pressures of housing and feeding scores of exiled royalists and numerous incarcerated prisoners, was not a happy one for the people of Man. There had been considerable grumbling about the demands put on them, which Lord Derby had had to make various gestures to amelio-rate. Now that the Earl had gone, and with intense uncertainty as to what was to become of him or the kingdom, the task of keeping the islanders loyal became instantly more challenging.[29]

The Countess of Derby returned to Castle Rushen and the agony of waiting. The clock in the castle's bell tower metered out the endless hours, and all eyes scanned the horizon for sight of a vessel that might bring news. Lady Derby kept a miniature of Charles II within the folds of her dress, a talisman of their family's loyalty and hopes of success. The three children she had with her, Mary, William and Edward, shared her anxiety. There was no question of keeping anything from them; Mary had acted as her father's secretary, drafting his letters in the weeks before his departure, and father and children had had an emotional leave-taking. With them at the castle was a whole restless community of dependants who looked to the Countess for their lead. Most men of fighting age had sailed to England with Lord Derby, but there remained a garrison, servants and seven ladies-in-waiting. There to offer spiritual support was the family chaplain, Samuel Rutter, lifelong friend and tutor to the young Stanley boys. Beyond the castle walls the entire island, more than 10,000 people, knew that their fate lay in her hands.[30]

Days passed. After about a week, unable to bear it, Lady Derby dispatched one of her soldiers, Captain Smith, to the mainland to seek news. Shortly after he disappeared from view an approaching vessel was sighted. It brought a letter from her husband's cousin Sir Philip Musgrave: Derby had landed, had seen the King and was recruiting soldiers in Lancashire while Charles had ridden south. Cities were fast declaring their support. Overjoyed, Charlotte ordered the guns on the castle walls to be fired in celebration.[31] As the cannon boomed, across the Irish Sea Captain Smith was reaching land. Here he would soon learn that Musgrave's upbeat account was premature. On 25 August a battle was fought at Wigan Lane in Lancashire between Lord Derby and

Colonel Robert Lilburne, brother of the Leveller leader. The royalists were utterly defeated, and the Derbys' great friend Sir Thomas Tyldesley slain. Hundreds had been captured and the Earl of Derby had last been seen being lacerated by an enemy weapon.[32]

❦ ❦ ❦

The royalists' expectation that once Charles II was in their midst, his standard aloft, the country would rush to join them was being bitterly disappointed. Pitifully few came out for the King as he travelled down England's western flank, and many responded instead to the Commonwealth's call for recruits to their militias. War, almost ten years of it, had exhausted appetites for political or military campaigning. People longed for peace and order, not new conflict. Those who had just paid a hefty fine to regain their estates were reluctant to put this investment at risk, and nervous of being treated as collaborators should the King succeed. But more than this, Charles II, still only 21, may have been the Stuart heir, but he rode into England at the head of an army of foreigners, his 12,000 men overwhelmingly Scots. The English and the Scots regarded one another with dislike. Despite having shared a sovereign since 1603, they had remained quite separate countries. The Highlanders in Charles II's army cut frightening, even barbarian, figures to the conservative English townsmen and women they encountered. The speech of these 'Jockies' was unintelligible ('not one of a hundred can tell what they say'), they were armed with two-handled swords, some even with bows and arrows, and were widely rumoured to be unbaptized. Just as Lord Fairfax considered it unthinkable to ride into Scotland at the head of an English army, so the English recoiled at a Scots army thundering through their midst. For many conservatives the King's alliance with the low-church Scots was deeply distasteful, while the visible tensions between the royalists and their Scots allies made other royalists shake their heads.[33]

The Earl of Derby stumbled, wounded, from the battlefield at Wigan Lane. His own army of new recruits had been lost before it had even fully formed, and he and three companions could now only try to rejoin the King. As they rode south, the Earl fast losing blood from his injuries, they sought shelter with one of his old supporters, who in turn took them to the house of his friend Charles Giffard, nestled in wooded obscurity on the Shropshire–Staffordshire border. Here, at the aptly named Boscobel, they spent two nights tended to by Giffard's Catholic retainer, William Penderel. When dusk descended on Sunday 31 August Penderel guided the fugitives on their way. A day or two later, weary and weak, but hopeful now of a revival in their fortunes, they rode into the ancient city of Worcester.[34]

Six

Virago

C harles II may have had the initiative in his 1651 invasion of England, but he lacked almost everything else: men, munitions, experience, luck. Nonetheless the Council of State went into a feverish panic as they learned of his crossing the border. One of their number remembered the 'raging and crying out' in their meetings that August, the shouting and recriminations that 'Charles Stuart' should have been allowed to steal a march on them. John Bradshaw, he who had had the mettle to sentence Charles I to death, 'privately could not conceal his fear' at the thought of the royalists reaching London.[1] They directed their anger towards Oliver Cromwell, who they felt had failed them. But out in the field their General held his nerve. He knew the odds lay in his favour, and his highly organized professional army, twice the size of his opponents', soon caught up with them. On 3 September on the flood-plains outside Worcester he made just a few hours' work of their annihilation.

The news of the royalists' comprehensive defeat at the battle of Worcester did not reach Charlotte, Countess of Derby, for some time. She had been buoyed by Sir Philip Musgrave's report of her husband's warm reception by the King; even sending a ship to bring him over to Man to enable her to hear it again, first-hand. Further reports, including one from her agent, Captain Smith, had been prevented from reaching

the island by the swarming of Commonwealth ships along the English
coast. She wrote brightly to her sister-in-law on 1 September, unaware
of what was unfolding beyond the eastern horizon. Some days later the
seas cleared and a series of communiqués reached her in quick succession which revealed the events of the past weeks at sickening speed.
Captain Smith told her of the battle of Wigan Lane, her husband's injuries and the death of their friend. Shortly after she learned of the
royalists' defeat at Worcester. It was a catastrophe. The Derbys had
risen, had answered their sovereign's call, but pathetically few had
joined them. Now, after little more than a month, all their hopes had
been crushed and their fears fulfilled. For Charlotte personally
everything now had changed; she knew how suddenly exposed she and
her children were on their little island, and how skilfully she would have
to play her hand if she were to save her family.[2]

The extremes of civil war had brought about a change to the life of
many Englishwomen. The absence from home of the men who took up
roles in the army, for one thing, had brought them further into the
sphere of public life than had traditionally been the case. This happened
across the social scale. Charlotte, Countess of Derby, might have taken
responsibility for aspects of her husband's lands and affairs without the
civil war, but not to the same degree. Through the mid- and late 1640s,
as Lord Derby was exiled from England by the charge of treason and
Charles I's orders, she had shuttled back and forth to London. The
general assumption that women played no part in politics, and did only
their husbands' bidding, provided a cloak of innocence that she used to
her advantage. The Countess had been the conduit in those years for
much of the information that flowed between London and the Isle of
Man, reporting from the capital in 1647 'that the face of things here is
completely changed', ever carrying with her a letter from her husband
that she could present if necessary that declared his authority to have
been delegated to her.[3]

Through these years she had learned how to use the conventions of
her class and place to the advantage of the cause. During the siege of
Lathom House she had strung out the negotiations in the hope that
each new day might bring a relieving force. When Fairfax had proposed

she meet him for a parley at a particular location, she had delayed the meeting by replying coquettishly that surely it would be 'more knightly that Sr Thomas Fairfax shold waite upon her, than shee upon him'. She had then claimed to be unable to negotiate without her husband's permission, before, the next morning, launching a savage attack that killed thirty men as they lay dozing in their trenches. Like many a resistance fighter she exploited her sex and her social situation and had few qualms about using deception and violence to advance her cause.[4]

❦ ❦ ❦

The Earl of Derby was with the King and half a dozen others as they fled the battlefield at Worcester. They knew it was perhaps only a matter of hours before they would be hunted down. Derby suggested they make for Boscobel, where he had sheltered only a few days before. They arrived at nearby Whiteladies Priory in the black darkness of the early hours of 4 September. Here the King discarded his courtly costume and changed into the rustic dress of a forester. As his long cavalier locks were being shorn, Derby called for William Penderel who had helped him before. Introducing Penderel to the King, the Earl impressed upon him that 'the care and preservation of his most sacred Majesty [was now] committed to his charge'. Knowing the King would be safer without them, his noble companions dispersed. The Earl of Derby took 'his heavy leave' having by this one introduction to a Shropshire woodsman done more for the royalist cause than in all his endeavours over a decade of civil war. Penderel was the man who would protect Charles Stuart over the crucial coming days, and who would lead him to the great oak in Boscobel wood where he lay hidden from the Commonwealth search parties. Six weeks later Charles would finally sail to France and safety.[5]

Just hours after leaving the King, Derby and his companion the Earl of Lauderdale were being pursued by parliamentary soldiers. Their horses were collapsing with exhaustion and they knew their chances of escape were negligible. Encountering a solitary parliamentary captain, one Oliver Edge, a fellow Lancastrian, they were weak with relief when he consented to accept their surrender and, by giving them 'quarter', spare their lives. 'I and all who love me are beholden to him,' the Earl gratefully recorded shortly afterwards. Derby was now a captive and just a few days later was imprisoned within the red sandstone walls of Chester Castle. From here he would finally be able to write to his wife. 'My dearest heart', 'what I now write is a mass of many sad things in one'. His instructions, part written, part to be given by the bearer of the letter, were designed to 'save the spilling of blood in that island, and it may be of some heare, dear to you'. The Earl of Derby's hope was that having surrendered to Captain Edge, and with the Isle of Man as a bargaining chip, all might not yet be lost.[6]

❦ ❦ ❦

As Derby paced his Chester cell, Oliver Cromwell rode back to London in triumph. The defeat of Charles Stuart and his Scottish army at Worcester had been comprehensive. But much more than another battle won, it provided a crucial boost to the republic's morale. The people of England had not risen in support of the young King, God had expressed his approval of their work by bringing them this victory, won on the very day they had triumphed at Dunbar a year before. Cromwell neared the capital where a great deputation came out to greet him. On Hounslow Heath John Bradshaw as Lord President of the Council of State, the Speaker of the House of Commons, the Lord Mayor and aldermen met him with 'great state and solemnity'. Passing through the streets cheers rang out, and guns were fired in triumphant volleys. The General was modest in victory, 'he would seldom mention any thing of himselfe, but the gallantry of the officers & soldiers & gave (as was due) all the glory of the action unto God'. The young King and the Scots had been defeated and finally the republican regime seemed to be finding the security that had so far eluded it.[7]

❦ ❦ ❦

A shaft of light penetrated the Earl of Derby's bleak incarceration in Chester Castle. He was reunited with the three of his six children who had not been with them on the Isle of Man: his teenage daughters Catherine and Amelia, also in captivity in Chester, and his eldest son Charles, Lord Strange. All their efforts were now concentrated on trying to keep their father alive. There was good reason to hope. The Earl had not been taken in arms, but had surrendered. He was now in the charge of Colonel Duckenfield, Governor of Chester, an enemy, of course, but one from an old Lancastrian gentry family who Derby felt would treat him honourably. Duckenfield had already arranged pardons for a number of other royalists and was clearly surprised to receive instructions from London that the Earl was to be tried by a military court. When he queried this, he received only a reiteration. Derby was to be 'made an example of justice', as a 'terror to others, and prevent the like attempts against the peace'.[8]

On 22 September the Council of State wrote to the Colonel yet again, frustrated that the trial had still not taken place: 'we have no other direction to give you in that business.' Duckenfield was to try the Earl and then take possession of the Isle of Man. But still he demurred. On 30 September both Oliver Cromwell and John Bradshaw were at Council when two further letters from him were read. Derby was willing to discuss relinquishing the Isle of Man, so surely this should be acted upon. But the response remained unchanged. 'As to what you mention of the Earl of Derby, order has been given by Parliament concerning him which is to be effectually pursued without expecting any interposition from Council.'[9]

While the Commonwealth men argued among themselves the Earl's family was busy. Separated from his wife and her hard-line views on the matter, Derby had been reconciled with their eldest son, Lord Strange, and his unpopular bride. The young man would shortly ride 'for London with exceeding concern and passion for my good'. Meanwhile, Catherine Stanley was dispatching urgent letters to her mother's European relations pleading with them to intervene. This loving family's anguish was palpable; as Catherine put it to the Duchesse de la Trémoille, 'the thought of this [danger facing her father] is killing us and will certainly be the death of my poor mother when she hears of it'.[10]

❦ ❦ ❦

On the Isle of Man, Charlotte, Countess of Derby, had other setbacks to contend with. At exactly the moment he was most needed, her lieutenant and family friend, the Governor of the Isle of Man, John Greenhalgh, had died. On 19 September, with rumours circulating of the Earl of Derby's capture, the senior figures of the island gathered at the picturesque, whitewashed church of Malew for the funeral. As the congregation milled about the graveyard, the heather turning the hills beyond purple and the nearby meadows alive with bees and butterflies, a hushed conversation began. The islanders had little love for the Stanleys, who had systematically and unsentimentally squeezed them for rents over generations. As in many parts of the country, people's desire for peace and prosperity was stronger than their loyalty to one regime or another. The quartering of the royalist soldiers had been a bitter ordeal, harvests for the past two summers had been poor and food and fodder were in painfully short supply. Was this not the time to take matters into their own hands? To declare for Parliament before being forced to take up arms for a side which had clearly lost. The notion was put to the most senior Manxman on the island, William Christian, the Receiver, or collector of rents. Christian was instantly hostile to such dangerous talk; he responded: 'Pishh Pishh, and looked frowningly about him & bad them be quiet.' But the seed had been sown.[11]

Lady Derby swiftly appointed Sir Philip Musgrave Governor of Man in the place of Greenhalgh. For several weeks since reports of her husband's capture had reached the island she had not flinched; her men remained on high alert, readying themselves for action at the sight of any unfamiliar vessel. One day a Commonwealth frigate commanded by a Captain Young was spied, carrying an instruction to the Countess to surrender and the threat that her husband was about to be tried for his life. Lady Derby was resolute; her husband's orders were for her to stand firm. When Young started firing his guns on Derby Fort, an artillery emplacement built to protect Castletown, the Countess mounted her horse and rode out in person to lead its defence. A few days later it was reported in the English papers that 'that Amazonian lady' had replied to Young's threat that the Earl might be put to death that, in that case, she would execute every parliamentary prisoner on the island.[12]

All fight and fury in public, in private Lady Derby was desperate to save her husband. Receiving further news and instructions from Chester, she wrote to Colonel Duckenfield, expressing her distress at the Earl's imprisonment and her willingness to do anything in her power to 'procure his Lib[er]tie and save his life', and asking for his help in so doing.[13] To carry the letter she chose one John Fox, a Lancastrian she had known slightly for almost twenty years, who had been idling on the Isle of Man for some time. Fox and another man were to sail to England and seek out Duckenfield. All her hopes lay in the success of this mission. But as they made for England and she waited, two terrible truths were unknown to her. The apparently innocuous Fox was in fact a parliamentary spy sent to the island 'a long tyme before'. Over the preceding week or two he had used the island's tradition of hospitality to inveigle his way into the houses of a number of senior Manxmen and to inflame their discontent at the 'slavery' of their condition. He had found it remarkably easy to recruit the Receiver, William Christian, to the Commonwealth cause. While Christian had batted away the loose talk at Greenhalgh's funeral it was more from discretion than disagreement. His was an old Manx family that had long enjoyed a love–hate relationship with the Stanley Lords of Man. After several confidential conversations, Fox left him with an incendiary document: a commission 'to raise the countrey in Armes against the Countesse Derby'.

The second thing Lady Derby did not know was infinitely worse. Just a day or two earlier, a hundred miles away across the wide, iron-grey sea, her beloved husband of twenty-five years and father of her nine children, had mounted a timber platform and had been executed for high treason.[14]

❦ ❦ ❦

The attempts to save Lord Derby from death had continued until the very last. There was no doubt that he had taken up arms against the Commonwealth, but this was true of many others, among them the Earl of Lauderdale with whom he had surrendered, who would be spared execution. The question was whether he should be shown mercy. At his

Chester trial on 1 October, Derby pleaded that having been granted 'quarter' by the field officer Captain Edge he should be spared a military trial. When Captain Edge heard what was happening he hastened to London, appalled. Standing in person before the Council of State he gave a detailed account of what had passed between him and Lord Derby, and the undertakings he had given. Edge was humoured, and asked to submit his account in writing, but outside the meeting a payoff of £100 was quietly arranged and he was heard of no more.[15]

A number of influential Commonwealth men sympathized with the Earl's plight. John Bradshaw's elder brother, Henry Bradshaw of Marple, was one of the commissioners for Derby's trial. He tried hard to save the Earl's life, pleading with the chairman of the court to show mercy and writing to his brother in London in Derby's defence. He was unsuccessful, but his efforts would not be forgotten and, come the restoration, would save his own life. Colonel Duckenfield was another who remained convinced that the sentence would not actually be carried out – even sending his chaplain to the Earl to reassure him on this point. Derby himself was not convinced. Though he claimed to be reconciled to the prospect of death, he longed for life. Shortly after his conviction he managed to get out of his chamber onto the leaded roof of Chester Castle. From here he swung by rope down the precipitous medieval walls and dropped onto the muddy bank of the River Dee. But his disappearance was discovered almost immediately and three soldiers ran him down on the wide foreshore before he could make his escape.[16]

On 14 October the Earl of Derby knelt in prayer with his two teenage daughters on the roadside a mile from Chester at their final parting. At that moment in London an application for a reprieve was being presented to the Speaker of the House of Commons. The Rump Parliament agreed by a significant majority that the petition should be heard. Oliver Cromwell himself was in favour of a pardon. But it was not to be. There were too many who wished him ill, and the 'Paper was laid aside'. The Earl for his part was certain that it was not so much his support for Charles II as the settling of local scores that brought him to his death. He had been the leader of the Lancashire royalists during the civil war and there was little to induce those he had fought, now in positions of authority, to be magnanimous in victory. The timber of the scaffold on which he died had reportedly been stripped from the ruins of Lathom House. The place of execution was Bolton, a pointed gesture of retribution for the storming of the town in 1644, led by Derby and Prince Rupert, at which hundreds had been killed. His speech to the gathered crowd was largely a refutation of the charge that he had behaved dishonourably on that occasion; he bitterly contended that he was being executed for something that had not even been mentioned at his trial. Years may now have passed but the scars of the civil war were raw and they marked everything in the life of the Commonwealth.

The Earl's last letters were in the hands of his servant, Humphrey, as he mounted the scaffold. 'My dear Mall, my Ned, my Billy', he had written to his absent children, 'I am called away'. 'The Lord my Lord bless you and Guard you. So prays your father that sorrows most at this time to part with Malekey, Neddy and Billy.' 'Oh my deare soule', he wrote to his wife, 'I have reason to believe that this may be the last time that ever I shall write unto you.' He was grateful for the happiness they had shared, and concerned that he had not appreciated it enough. 'I shall live [on] in you, who is truly the best part of myself.' His partings past, he was content at least to meet a death 'worthy of my blood'. He had, he claimed from the scaffold, done no more than to answer the summons of his sovereign. He lay down to receive the fatal blow with the words 'I believe this nation will never be so well contented, never thoroughly happy, without a King.'[17]

※ ※ ※

Five days after Derby's execution on 15 October, the duplicitous John Fox reached the mainland with Lady Derby's offer to trade the Isle of Man for her husband's life. News of his death had not yet reached Man. Fox found Colonel Duckenfield already in Beaumaris harbour on Anglesey, with a fleet, thousands of soldiers and instructions to conquer the Isle of Man before sailing on to Ireland. Duckenfield had left Chester on the day of Derby's execution but thanks to powerful winds had not yet got out to sea.

The execution of the Earl of Derby in Bolton, 1651. The scaffold was
reportedly built from the charred timbers of his family seat, Lathom
House, which the Countess had refused to surrender through a famous
siege.

The easterly gale that kept Duckenfield in port also buffeted the Isle
of Man as the island's officials prepared to attend their biannual judi-
cial assembly, the Head Court, on Monday 20 October. Since he had
accepted his covert commission for the Commonwealth, William
Christian had been laying plans. He had not been hard to turn, and now
the same would be true for his fellow Manxmen. The Countess's asser-
tive style, combative language and the famous stories of her ferocity at
Lathom House made her easy to dislike. A reputation for heroism and
strength, especially in a woman, could also be one for arrogance and
brutality. Stories began to circulate that she had goaded her husband,
declaring that if he would not join Charles II, 'he should pull off the
breeches and shee would putt them on & then lead them on' herself.
With repetition the tales gathered details, one who had never met her
soon reporting confidentially that the Countess had forced her timid
husband to join Charles II by 'threatening him very often that she wold
publish him to be a coward' if he did not go. Such a harridan surely
deserved to be deposed.[18]

The night before the Head Court was to meet, William Christian and some associates gathered. The following day was clearly the ideal opportunity to begin the uprising and Christian had just the spark with which to light the fuse. 'The Countess of Derby broke her promise,' he revealed to his rapt companions: she had sent a letter to England offering to surrender the island to the Commonwealth army, and doubtless its inhabitants, too, without their knowledge. Word travelled with speed; come the meeting the following day it was the talk of the whole island that the Countess had sold Man and its inhabitants to Parliament. Within hours hundreds had joined Christian and sworn an oath to bring the Countess of Derby down.[19]

Lady Derby now had a monumental task on her hands. She knew her husband had been captured and that their cause was in shreds. On his advice they had played a dangerous game, continuing to hold Man on the pretext that she was ignorant of events in England. She was responsible for an island which she hoped to trade for his life and their survival, but to do so she had to prevent the population from turning against her. Unlike her stand at Lathom House seven years earlier, she could have no hope of a relieving force or loyal reinforcements. England, Scotland and Ireland were now in the Commonwealth's hands. She was alone. From the dormer windows in her lodgings at Castle Rushen she looked out to east and west, not knowing from which side, land or sea, the first assault would come.

Her children were with her in the small manor house within the castle walls known as Derby House. Between them and the world were two concentric curtain walls. The family chambers were no longer crammed with furniture, a consequence of the preparations that had been put in hand. A parliamentary fleet would probably come from the east, so the island's second fortress, the magnificently sited Peel Castle on the western coast, had been made ready. Most things of value at Rushen – plate, silver, tapestries and textiles – had been packed up and moved there. In the Peel Castle storerooms substantial supplies had been laid down: thirty-five barrels of gunpowder, a dozen or so cannon, piles of muskets and scores of barrels of fish and cheese – enough to enable them to withstand a prolonged siege.[20]

Secrets on islands are ever short-lived, and as Christian was recruiting supporters, word was brought to Lady Derby of what was underway. Keeping a cool head, she sent Musgrave to see him and – relaying her gracious concern – invite him to a personal audience. The meeting went well. Lady Derby agreed to address any grievances the islanders might have, and Christian pledged his loyalty – giving a written undertaking to stand with her in any assault that might be approaching and offering to swear his loyalty on the Bible. But each suspected the other was not in earnest. William Christian had not yet left the building when it was whispered in her ear that the garrison at Peel Castle had mutinied.[21]

Darkness was falling as Lady Derby descended the stairs of Derby House. The bells were rung and her orders were relayed that every soul in Castle Rushen was to muster immediately. Before the castle gates, where Musgrave stood at the head of the garrison, this extraordinary 51-year-old noblewoman made her address, crying out the words against the relentless wind. The rebels must be prevented from taking the island. Everything depended upon it. With her 'encouraging expressions' ringing in their ears, they rode west. That night in the wild darkness Musgrave managed to recapture Peel Castle, riding across its causeway as the tide rose to engulf it. The garrison was strangely small and it soon became clear why. The rebels' efforts were being directed elsewhere: the parliamentary invasion fleet had at last been sighted.[22]

Musgrave had recaptured Peel, but to hold it he had to remain there, leaving the Countess to lead the defence of Rushen alone. While the island's two strongest fortified buildings were still in her hands, the rest of Man was in chaos, its people unsure whether they should support the Countess, William Christian or neither, and terrified of the enormous armed force about to descend upon them. The Commonwealth ships drew near to the southern end of the island on the afternoon of 25 October, and were able to see the islanders mustering, but could not be sure whose side they were on. Before Duckenfield could disembark a further storm pushed his fleet north along the length of the island. Here, as the winds weakened, they dropped anchor and at 1 a.m. a Manxman, Hugh More, was rowed out. Believing Christian's tale that the Countess of Derby had sold the island and islanders to the invaders,

More 'seemed much terrified' when brought before the Colonel. Christian himself was rowed out soon after and together they explained to Duckenfield that they were ready to surrender, in the hope that 'their poor Island might be preserved from spoil'.

For two further days the weather prevented Duckenfield's army from landing. So powerful were the gales that one of his ships was wrecked, the hull smashed against the rocks as the soldiers and crew scrambled for safety. Finally, on Tuesday 28 October, three days after they had first approached the island, they were able to disembark, the men and horses weak and shaky from cold and seasickness. Despite the state of his army, Duckenfield had Christian and many of the islanders on his side, and had no difficulty in taking possession of the various defensive positions on the northern two-thirds of Man. But Peel and Rushen remained, and to take these they would need to contend with the Countess of Derby.[23]

It was evening when Colonel Duckenfield and his men marched on Castle Rushen. Making his own headquarters in Castletown, he ranged his men in siege formation around the castle's stone ramparts. Rushen was nestled in the midst of the town, with the quay and harbour on its north side. The besiegers, who numbered thousands, encircled it several men deep. Meanwhile, on the other side of the island a further thousand of Duckenfield's troops drew up outside Peel Castle. Still there was no sign of surrender. The following morning William Christian presented himself at the entrance to Rushen and was admitted. He gave Lady Derby a letter from Duckenfield, as both maintained the fiction of his loyalty. The letter took the form of a reply to that which she had written offering to trade the Isle of Man for her husband's life. The Countess read it with her children beside her. In it Duckenfield stated, quite truthfully, that he had already petitioned the Council and General Cromwell to look mercifully on her family. But he had not succeeded. 'I really believe there is no way left for your family of avoiding utter ruine, but by a present surrendering the Castles of Rushin and Peel.' What no one present would thereafter forget was the Countess's reaction when she read the words 'the late Earl of Derby', 'by which shee apprehended that her husband was deade'. The scream of desolation and loss which followed – raw agony and abandon – was terrible to hear. Her 21-year-old daughter, Mary, a fellow 'Virago', joined in. Lady Derby, recovering herself, shakily replied she would not be able to give the Colonel the immediate answer he required and Christian hastily withdrew.[24]

In truth Lady Derby probably already knew of her husband's death. The performance she put on at Castle Rushen was not a difficult one to mount, for her desolation was entirely genuine. At some point during the preceding days, as the rain and wind had beaten down, she had been brought the news. The shock was profound. But there was no time now for mourning, only to try to save what remained.[25] Late that evening a messenger was released out of the wicket gate of the castle's gatehouse and presented Duckenfield with Lady Derby's reply. It was, he explained, in the form of 'propositions' rather than a letter, as the Countess's grief prevented her from writing at greater length. While she had not, this time, shredded her besieger's communiqué before her cheering supporters, her response to her enemy's terms was hardly less bold. She would agree to surrender only if a list of conditions were met – gambling that pity might persuade the Colonel to negotiate. She, her children, her entire household and all her possessions, including their arms and ammunition, were to be transported safely to England or the Continent. All should be allowed to retain their lands and possessions, continue to receive their rents, and be safe from prosecution. Agreement was to be formally confirmed by the Council of State. Duckenfield was incredulous: these were the sort of terms that he would only consider if 'we had been at her mercy as she was at ours'.[26]

The following morning, Thursday 30 October, Duckenfield walked a circuit around the outworks of Castle Rushen. The walls bristled with the Countess's soldiers, visibly heavily armed, on the wall walks and towers. He had come to Man with no desire to besiege a beleaguered noblewoman, but Lady Derby's intransigence and the gossip he now heard of her conduct was hardening his view. There was no sign that she could be reasoned with. When Christian had delivered Duckenfield's letter Lady Derby's quivering chaplain Rutter had suggested they surrender. Her daughter, Mary, had responded that she 'wished he and all such as he were out of the Castle ... since they were afraid, and leave them alone who were resolved to sell their lives and their bloud at a dearer rate then so, and follow her noble father'. Infuriated by such defiance Duckenfield resolved that morning to attack. Before long the rumble of approaching heavy vehicles was heard – the wooden carriages bearing the heavy artillery – and the regular tread of hundreds more of Duckenfield's soldiers.[27]

Inside Castle Rushen, Lady Derby was convinced they could hold. They numbered about 130. Of these some 60 were the soldiers of the garrison, and a further 30 or so castle officials, including the staff of the kitchens, the surgeon and the locksmith, could be expected to fight. The rest were women, children and clergymen. While Rushen was not as well supplied as Peel – they had hoped to have relocated before facing attack – they still had supplies. In the old castle keep was gunpowder, muskets for 100 men, cannon and hundreds of rounds of shot. The granary held enough food to last weeks: barrels of oatmeal and beer, peas and barley. Duckenfield himself knew that it was possible she was right. Just as the mighty Fairfax had been unable to take Lathom House from the Countess in 1644, so he feared she might 'have wearied us out with a full winter's siege'.[28] In the end, however, Lady Derby and her children's courage did not falter, but it could not be matched by those who had little reason to share their appetite for resistance. The Castle Rushen garrison looked visibly appalled as the Commonwealth cannons and mortars were heaved into position. A 'strange kind of terrour' began to grip them. Suddenly, one desperate figure on the ramparts dropped his weapon, clambered onto the wall top and threw himself across the castle ditch. Before long others began to follow. Then, with scraping and crashing, some others of the garrison wrenched open a small doorway in the southwest tower of the castle's outer wall. As Duckenfield's soldiers flooded in like seawater, the Countess of Derby knew that the castle had been breached.[29]

On Friday 31 October 1651 the Countess of Derby surrendered. She and Colonel Duckenfield never met, each imperiously refusing to see, or ask to see, the other. Duckenfield's determination to teach his adversary a lesson would be visible in his decision to make the Countess and her children lodge in a 'poor ale house', dependent on their betrayer William

Christian for food, before they were conveyed off the island. The ignominy was more painful to Charlotte de la Trémoille than any wound.
Her representatives, Thomas Armstrong, head of the garrison, and her
chaplain, Samuel Rutter, attended the parley with Duckenfield's men.
The terms they came back with gave Lady Derby, her family and supporters safe passage off the island and Duckenfield's protection from
prosecution. All her goods and possessions, everything other than their
own clothes, were to be seized. These were not particularly punitive
terms, but Lady Derby felt only disgust. When her emissaries brought
the document back, she staged a final act of passive defiance: signing
her name to the articles of surrender without reading a single word.[30]

A week later the news of the island's fall was brought to the House of
Commons. They were delighted and rewarded the messenger with £100.
Well might they rejoice. As 1651 ended Ireland was now the republic's
to command, and Scotland had as a consequence of Cromwell's invasion become a further, almost incidental, conquest. Thanks to the
efforts of the able Admiral Blake, the Scillies had capitulated in June
and the Channel Islands were all but won. Lady Derby had held the Isle
of Man alone for almost three months. But, finally, the last remaining
outposts of royalism in the British Isles were coming to heel.[31]

The news of the capture of Man interrupted the day's business in the
House of Commons on Thursday 6 November. After prayers that morning, the first item on their agenda was the new committee charged with
'setting a certain Time for the Sitting of this Parliament, and for Calling
of a new Parliament'. Since the execution of Charles I, the Rump House
of Commons had been publicly committed to dissolving itself to allow
fresh elections. The criticism that it was in no way a representative body
had not dimmed. Some had thought new elections should happen
straight after the regicide, but there was general acceptance that the
immediate threats to the new regime needed to be seen off first. With
the cascade of recent victories national security was no longer a tenable
argument for delay. The newspapers reported that they 'have made a
very faire progresse therein'; a date for dissolution had indeed now been
set, but as it was three years hence, November 1654, it hardly represented urgent action. The great unspoken risk, of course, was that new

elections would return a moderate House of Commons which would bring a swift end to the young republic. It was also uncertain what would happen now the regime could no longer count on threats from without to galvanize unity within.[32]

❦ ❦ ❦

December 1651 was icy. Lady Derby and her children were finally back in England and the leaden chill mirrored her state of mind (Colour plate 4). 'Dear sister,' she wrote, 'there is nothing left for me but to mourn and weep, since all my joy is in the grave.' She was sustained only by her certainty that her husband's sacrifice had been pure and complete, a model of true nobility. He was 'that glorious martyr who showed such constancy', whose only concern as he faced execution had been 'the thought of the wretched condition in which he foresaw I should be'. His final request, she remembered, was that she should take care of their children. That he had also asked her to forgive their eldest son for marrying without her permission, she chose not to remember. For Lady Derby her purpose was plain: she had to secure the means to ensure their children could live in a manner befitting their birth. It was far from clear how this would be achieved, but she knew it would not be through melancholy seclusion or Continental exile, however tempting that might be. She made, instead, for London.[33]

❦ ❦ ❦

The young Dutchman Lodewijck Huygens had just dressed when he received a visit from one of the Stanley family chaplains on New Year's Day 1652. The visitor bore an invitation from Lady Derby, an old friend of his father, the distinguished diplomat Constantijn Huygens, from her days in The Hague. A few hours later Huygens was picking his way across the frozen ruts on London's streets on his way to pay his respects. Lady Derby hoped through this young man to gain access to the Dutch diplomats in whose entourage he was travelling. They might then be persuaded to put pressure on the government to allow her to regain the Stanley estates. She still had a few cards to play. Her own status, as a granddaughter of William the Silent, counted for a lot with the Dutch.

Huygens greeted her deferentially as 'your Excellency', and she was careful to ask after the health of her various powerful relations, including 'her little nephew the Prince of Orange'. Unblinkingly she milked the pathos of her situation. Though she knew he was coming, she left the fire in the downstairs chamber where they met unlaid, enabling her to apologize that 'she had not been left enough [money] to have one lit on her own account'. The prospect of a future meeting with the Countess's three unmarried daughters was dangled before him as he left.[34]

Lady Derby realized that if she were to achieve her ends she would have to build alliances; there was no place now for haughty standoffishness or the self-indulgence of mourning. When Huygens returned to her house a few weeks later it was to an evening reception attended by a sparkling company of young people, including the heir of a Cheshire gentry family recently returned from his studies in the Low Countries. Lady Derby's hopes that the Dutch ambassadors would intervene for her were ambitious. Relations between the English Commonwealth and the Dutch Republic had turned decidedly sticky and the diplomats had strict instructions not to stray beyond their brief. But they agreed to help informally if they could.

Charlotte had a job on her hands when it came to the Stanley estates. Her husband had been executed for high treason and her family officially banned from compounding for their estates. Furthermore, the one-fifth stake they had been allowed to retain since 1647 had itself been depleted by a fifth, allocated to one Robert Massey, a Liverpool merchant whose cloth they had seized from the Isle of Man. Massey had an axe to grind with the Stanleys, claiming to have been imprisoned at Lathom House for some weeks during the civil war, and soon Lady Derby was having to defend herself against accusations concerning her conduct during the defence of Man. Added to all these complexities the Commonwealth, desperate for money to cover the costs of its recent military campaigns, had just authorized the Committee for Compounding to start selling off the remaining delinquents' lands.[35]

But all was not lost. The republic had now existed for some three years and with the royalists decimated after the battle of Worcester, and many having paid the fines to regain their lands, a new sense of resignation was in evidence. Many moderate MPs who had not supported the execution of Charles I had returned to the House of Commons and in February 1652 an act of 'Oblivion' was passed giving immunity for all actions during the civil war, 'with the view of healing the long discords of the nation'. Those who had joined Charles II in 1650–1 were excluded, so this was no direct help to Lady Derby, but the spirit of reconciliation was nonetheless in the air.

The downfall of the nobility, even that part of it that had fought for Charles I, had never been the goal of the republican regime. The Committee for Compounding's overwhelming concern was raising money, not meting out political or social retribution, and in spite of the seismic shifts of the decade there was much by 1652 that was stabilizing. The majority of major landowners had kept their heads down during the wars, prepared to root for the royalist cause, to send arms or plate, but not to risk their patrimony for it. Perhaps a quarter of aristocratic and gentry landowners – some 3,000 families – had had their lands sequestered, but most would pay the fines to regain their property. Their ability to do so was increased considerably by the new London mortgage market and the facility the Committee made available allowing the delinquents to sell their lands before regaining title, thereby raising the funds to pay the fines. More by chance than design the Commonwealth had in its urgent search for funds found a mechanism that was beginning to bind its most powerful opponents into its fabric.[36]

Lady Derby pulled every string she could find. Lord Fairfax, though living in affluent retirement, was among her connections, and those who had argued for clemency for her husband – including Oliver Cromwell himself – seem to have felt his family now deserved some of the leniency that he been denied. By March the Countess's confidence was growing. She had successfully argued that she should be allowed the lands which had been her own as part of her marriage contract. As for her husband's estates, 'the most influential people tell me to hope'.[37]

The beauty of the two younger Stanley girls proved a significant advantage and Lady Derby's decision to bring them to London, and to receive visitors, paid off when her second daughter, Catherine, who had just turned 21, received a marriage proposal. The suitor was the Marquess of Dorchester, an old friend of Lord Derby's, who had been among the first royalists to pay a composition fine to regain his lands. 'I was very far from thinking such a marriage in our power, or indeed any marriage,' the Countess wrote excitedly to her sister-in-law early that summer. The marriage would not be a happy one but, bringing a title and £14,000 a year, it was more than they could have hoped for. Two further advantageous unions would follow, the gentle Amelia to the Earl of Atholl and the courageous Mary to the 2nd Earl of Strafford, son of Charles I's infamous Lord Lieutenant of Ireland.[38]

A gruelling two years after her husband's death Lady Derby achieved her goal. She saw off the legal case against her being pursued by Robert Massey and, thanks not least to Oliver Cromwell's own intervention, was finally given permission to compound for her husband's property in October 1653. The fine was set at a hefty £8,200, payable in two tranches. To raise this involved running up large debts, but it was managed without selling land and the following year her family, as fervent royalists as could be found, were returned much of their estates. As well as the title to the lands which the regime had not sold, they were given back their goods, among them the cases of furniture, paintings and silver from Rushen and Peel castles. So Lady Derby was reunited with the embroidered silk canopies of state from their island kingdom, the silver-gilt fruit bowls from which they had eaten their desserts and the oil-painted maps and 900 volumes of the Earl's beloved library. Whatever satisfaction she felt in her achievement, they were no compensation for her suffering – 'it is my irreparable losses that over-whelm me'.[39]

❀ ❀ ❀

The wages of the Derbys' uncompromising royalism were death, but they were not destitution. The Commonwealth regime was proving to be remarkably unvindictive in its treatment of its adversaries; the need for unity and reconciliation, not least given the tiny numbers who had actively wished for a republic, was obvious to many in positions of power. The same could not be said of individuals, and personal grudges lingered the longest. While her mother laboured for the return of their estates, Lady Mary Stanley complained of people who for their own reasons 'shut the mouths of those who feel pity for her condition and ask for some kind of justice for her'. While the Stanley estates were burdened with debt, the family came through the 1650s with much intact. The long-term value of securing their lands and making strong marriage alliances easily outweighed the effects of a one-off fine, steep as it was. But the personal injuries endured. Lady Derby's agony at the death of her husband, and bitterness towards those she felt had betrayed her – chief among them William Christian, Receiver of the Isle of Man – would never abate.[40]

There would, however, be an unexpected epilogue to the Countess of Derby's doomed defence of the Isle of Man. When Lord Fairfax had resigned his command of the army in 1650, having refused to ride into battle against Charles II and the Scots, he had been granted a magnificent pension by the Commonwealth government. Among the thousands of acres he was assigned in reward for his service was the Isle of Man, soon to be wrested from the Stanleys. Fairfax's days of office and government were now over. He was living with his wife at Nun Appleton in Yorkshire, rebuilding his family home and planting his gardens. In the maelstrom of the decade behind him he had developed an enduring admiration for Charlotte, Countess of Derby. Her fate doubtless played on his guilt at what he had helped bring to pass. More than this, perhaps he, whose own opinionated and demonized wife had cried out from the balconies against the trial of Charles I, had seen in Charlotte de la Trémoille qualities that he recognized and respected. When his agent finally took possession of the Isle of Man, Lord Fairfax issued a surprise instruction. The profits from the island were not to be retained. Instead, they were to be carefully accounted for, and then sent on to Charlotte, Countess of Derby. His baffled secretary queried the instruction, causing the General to restate testily: 'I shall desire your care ... that my Lady Darby be not prejudiced in any thing.' The man who gathered these rents was William Christian. Lord Fairfax remarked coldly that 'Receiver Christian hath proved a deceiver Christian' and ordered him to be dismissed. Lady Derby gratefully accepted the funds, and would later reflect that no act of kindness of the whole era had come close to this, from the founding General of the New Model Army.[41]

Seven

The Infamous Castle
of Misery

N ewgate was a byword for despair. The city of London had long
since spilled beyond the battlemented stone walls that had been
built to protect it, but those walls remained, and the hordes who passed
in and out of the metropolis each day still funnelled through its medieval gatehouses. Rising from the western wall of the city was Newgate.
Novel in name only, it owed its stately stone appearance to London's
celebrated fifteenth-century mayor Richard 'Dick' Whittington, who
had left money in his will for its reconstruction. Visitors to the capital
passed under this fine Gothic gateway, bristling with the teeth of its
raised portcullis, into a wide marketplace, the western termination of
the city's main east–west street, Cheapside. Among the traffic that clattered daily through the gate passage were scores of millers' carts bearing
the sacks of corn and flour that were the mainstay of the dry foods sold
in Newgate market. Beyond the stalls, and the great timber stand where
the flour was weighed, Bladder Street continued the thoroughfare east,
and when the wind blew from that direction it filled the marketplace
with the stench from the slaughterhouses set back behind the butchers'
shops.[1]

As the merchants and maidservants, tavern keepers and tourists
went to and fro through Newgate, other sounds mixed with the chatter
of the street and the calls of the market traders. They were the painful

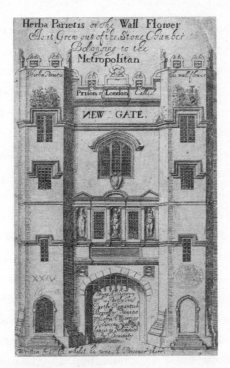

'Newgate', one of the medieval entrances to the City of London and an
infamous prison. Many political prisoners, among them the journalist
Marchamont Nedham, were incarcerated here. Prisoners lowered small purses
from its barred windows in the hope of donations from passers-by.

cries of the inmates of Newgate prison. Their calls and groans drew
attention to small canvas pouches dangling from the lattices of thick
iron that covered its high windows. These the impoverished inmates
lowered on strings to the street in the hope that passing strangers would
fill them with gifts of food or money that might prevent them from
starving.[2]

The 'stinking, lowsie, barbarous Gaol of Newgate' was the capital's
main holding place for those awaiting trial for serious crime. Among its
usual unsavoury assortment of swindlers and thieves, highwaymen and
murderers, Newgate in 1649 housed a number of other inmates. Men of
means, education and some status, they were the political prisoners
swooped down upon by the new regime as it attempted to secure its
position. Few individuals were more sought by John Bradshaw's Council
of State than the publisher of the excoriating weekly newspaper,

Mercurius Pragmaticus (for King Charles II), which tore unrelentingly into the weaknesses and shortcomings of the new republic. For over a year its editor, Marchamont Nedham, had been masterminding his covert publishing operation under intense pressure, producing his paper and getting it into the hands of the street hawkers without being captured. He moved houses, rearranged the letters of his name into his alias, Hamden, and darted from place to place, ever feeling the agents of the republic on his trail. Accounts of the cat and mouse pursuit added a further thrill to his journalism. His 1 May issue opened with the words: 'Now the Beagles must go a hunting again, and I must be the Hare; for so it pleaseth Master Bradshaw.'[3]

It was not surprising that capturing the editor of *Mercurius Pragmaticus* was a government priority in the summer of 1649. Not only was Nedham's paper a thorn in their side, made all the more dangerous as the Levellers were massing, but his attacks on its leaders were personal and unremitting. He taunted the Lord President of the Council himself as 'Bradshaw that dirty upstart, that half man and Beast ... that prodigious Monster, that walking hell', one who had to be 'guarded by Soldiers to prevent [the people] tearing in pieces'.[4] He repeatedly denounced the Rump Parliament, reminding his readers of its unorthodox beginnings and the soaring irony of its claim to be a representative body. As the excluded MPs slowly returned Nedham marvelled that they did not 'stumble at the door, though his Majesties blood lye at the threshold'. For all their talk of liberty, and taste for grandiose symbols of their new authority, these men of the House of Commons were 'supreme puppets', while 'poor Liberty lies fetter'd now like a flie in the Cob-web'. Reporting on a civic procession in which the Lord Mayor of London surrendered his ceremonial sword to the Speaker of the Commons in recognition of Parliament's sovereignty, Nedham told his readers that 'Oliver [Cromwell] laught in his sleeve' knowing that it was with his own steel blade, and the might of the army, that true authority now lay.[5]

Government agents prowled the city, searching the backstreets and warehouses for the hidden printing presses that were producing the literature they so loathed. During the trial of Charles I an almost complete news blackout had been achieved – not least because the army had been given a hand in press control – and even Nedham had struggled to put a paper to print in those febrile weeks. But, trial and execution over, the pressmen were soon back in business. Prominent among those trying to track down guerrilla editors in the summer of 1649 was the government agent Elizabeth Alkin, who would later become a newspaper publisher herself. Known by her prey as 'Parliament Joan', this portly middle-aged widow was a highly effective operator. Nedham's paper described her as an 'old bitch' who could 'smell out a Loyall-hearted man as soon as the best Blood-hound in the Army'. The sociable Nedham had had to change his gregarious habits, forgoing his epic drinking sessions, to evade capture; he confined himself instead 'to the narrow Circle of a Chamber where I converse with no other Creatures but paper worms, a Cat and a wife'. Whether it was Alkin or one of her colleagues who was responsible for his capture is unclear – it was certainly she who uncovered the four hidden printing presses of his acquaintance William Dugard, which saw Dugard's own passage to Newgate. Either way, in June 1649, aided by information from one of Nedham's associates, the Council of State issued a warrant for his immediate arrest.[6]

Newgate prison had expanded beyond the stone gatehouse itself into adjacent buildings centuries before. It now had a communal hall, where meals were taken by those who could pay for food, and the prisoners who were permitted to do so talked, smoked and took a glass of beer or wine. Separate 'common' chambers were designed for male and female prisoners while a chapel on the upper floor of the gatehouse was meant to provide spiritual succour, not least for those who left the prison for the gallows at Tyburn. Prisoners with no money to pay the keepers, or whose misdemeanour was felt to merit it, were incarcerated for large parts of each day in the room known as the 'pit' or 'dungeon', a miserable subterranean den beneath the main complex where they lay shackled in irons.

By contrast prisoners with means could improve their lot, prisons being businesses where opportunities to increase takings were seldom missed. An individual room rather than a crowded common chamber could be secured, a properly strung bed instead of bare stone or a heap of soggy straw, a fireplace, a window and access to books and writing materials. However, notwithstanding the petty perks which a full purse could purchase, imprisonment in Newgate was a grim experience. The corruption and negligence of the prison staff in 'that infamous castle of misery' was legendary, and its dim, fetid air hung with the stench of damp, despair and human excrement. Even in the relative comfort of his own chamber, Nedham was probably prevented from standing by chains holding his arms and legs together, though again a sufficient payment would have brought the keeper to smash these off with his hammer. It was perhaps a particular indignity for someone who, despite his less than heroic looks, was something of a dandy. But it was here he now found himself.[7]

Marchamont Nedham was a figure who could not have existed in any previous age. He was singular for many reasons. But most obviously, and least personally, because his was the first generation in British history for whom a career in printed news was a possibility. Newspapers, regular publications reporting contemporary events, simply had not existed in the British Isles before now. A market for information about the Thirty Years War, the great religious struggle that played out across Europe from 1618, was an important element in their genesis, as was the uncontroversial nature of their content, as these first papers steered clear of domestic news altogether. As a fragile news market slowly developed, it encountered the powerful political controversies of the late 1630s and early 1640s and suddenly flourished. The long-established censorship regime, which required all printed publications to be vetted and approved by the Stationers Company, started to falter and with out-and-out civil war broke down altogether. By the mid-1640s numerous newspapers had shot into being, dealing vividly and often virulently with contemporary politics and people. In London a variety of titles castigated the royalists, while from Oxford the official court paper led a vigorous defence of the King and cried out in horror at the parliamentary uprising.[8]

The rise of the newspapers was itself an aspect of the explosion in publishing which took place in the mid-seventeenth century. In the year

1500 just over fifty books were printed in England, in 1600 the number was 300, come 1648 more than 2,300 titles poured off the presses in a single year. Perhaps 30 per cent of all men and 10 per cent of all women could read, and over double those percentages in the capital, a reader-ship now offered an addictive weekly news fix that involved them as never before in the turbulent goings-on of their kingdom.[9]

When Marchamont Nedham was hauled into the porters' lodge at Newgate in June 1649 the gaolers found before them a curious figure. He was a small man of 28, with dark hair that had already dwindled to baldness and an ungainly figure. But to his unpromising parts he brought a flamboyant personal style. On his head he wore the latest fashion, 'false long hair (now much in date)', the colour of his wig vary-ing with his fortunes and mood. From his ears hung jewelled earrings. He was no dry intellectual. His personality was as engaging, irreverent and as sparkling as his prose. He loved wine and company, the taverns of London and Westminster were his stamping grounds, and his friends a bewilderingly wide circle. When the gaoler clanked shut the great iron door behind him, his prospects were not good. Printing seditious works could bring the penalty of death. However, hopelessness was not in his nature. Gambling that the talent for survival that had got him out of tight spots before might save him again, he took up his pen. Onto crisp, creamy paper he etched out a plea for clemency. Folding it twice length-ways he passed it to a guard unsealed, knowing his fate now lay in the hands of the very man he had pilloried every week in his celebrated paper – 'bloody Jack Bradshaw President of Hell'.[10]

🌑 🌑 🌑

In June 1649 Marchamont Nedham was married with a young family and had packed a great deal into his decade of adulthood. His back-ground was respectable but neither political nor literary; his grandfather had been the proprietor of one of the successful inns of the prosperous market town of Burford in Oxfordshire. He received a remarkable educa-tion from his stepfather, the vicar and schoolmaster of the town, and was bound for a career as a teacher himself. But his experience of employment at his stepfather's alma mater, the Merchant Taylors'

School in London, was a sorry one. The life of a junior schoolmaster, or usher, was one he would later recall with a shudder: the pitiful pay, the endless beating of pupils and an encounter with a sexual sadist who visibly revelled in 'such nakedness (of which Instances are not wanting, but that they are odious) it being a kinde of uncovering', caused him to change course. He was made for more than 'whipping Boyes at a penny a week'. He became instead a clerk at Gray's Inn, writing writs for a slight salary, before making an unexpected leap into another world. In 1643 he had joined the meagre editorial staff of the newspaper *Mercurius Britanicus*, a weekly title with a pro-parliamentary political line.[11] How he came to change professions is unclear. Perhaps he was helped with an introduction from Oxfordshire friends – the Speaker of the House of Commons, William Lenthall, was a neighbour and business associate of his stepfather. Or perhaps he simply saw the appeal of better pay and a more colourful existence and, impulsive and fearless, he abandoned a poorly remunerated steady profession for a potentially lucrative peril-ous one. Within three years he was the editor of the most successful parliamentary paper in the country, and his employer Captain Audley now did little more than cast an eye over his protégé's copy. Here Nedham's talent for language and his witty, scurrilous mind found its ideal application. For three years *Mercurius Britanicus* lampooned and taunted the royalists, entering into one-to-one literary combat with the Oxford royalist paper *Mercurius Aulicus*. The circulation was massive and socially diverse and in September 1644 Nedham boasted in an editorial that 'there is not now so much as a young apprentice that keeps shop, or a labourer that holds the plough, not only from the city to the coun-try' who did not read his newspaper.[12]

Three years of pro-parliamentary news editing had come to an abrupt end in May 1646 when Nedham's outrageous journalism finally brought him down. He had scandalized many when, in 1645, he had opened an edition of *Mercurius Britanicus* with a missing-persons advertisement asking whether 'any man can bring any tale or tiding of a wilful King, which hath gone astray these four years from his Parliament, with a guilty Conscience, bloody Hands, a heart full of broken Vowes'. He went on to add that if Charles I was in disguise he could be identified by his stutter. With the court absent it was not his insults against the sovereign which landed him in trouble, but a swipe at the House of Lords who remained in the capital. He was clapped in the Fleet prison and was only released having pledged to 'frame the whole course of my life' in loyalty to the Lords and to abandon journalism altogether.[13]

It was typical of Nedham's fluid political loyalties that his promises had not held for long. For a few months he had tried to wean himself from the world of news, turning his attention instead to a career in medicine. But the lure of the profession at which he so excelled, where the profits could be considerable and the lifestyle so suited his character, was irresistible. By a royalist intermediary, perhaps his Burford neighbour Peter Heylyn who was a royal chaplain, Nedham was admitted to Hampton Court, where Charles I was being held under house arrest. Here, before the sovereign he had mercilessly maligned, he knelt, asked forgiveness and pledged his loyalty. It was a remarkable turn of events, not least as the King's own stock was hardly high. A volte-face in print soon followed. In September 1647 Nedham, 'this piebald chameleon', brought his new royalist weekly, *Mercurius Pragmaticus*, into being. He now lauded as heroes the very men he had demonized only a year before. His timing was terrible. As he swapped sides his former allies pressed home their victory and the royalist cause he had just espoused crumpled. And so it was that only two years on, his new paper was on the brink of collapse and he was condemned to his malodorous chamber in Newgate prison.[14]

※ ※ ※

It was abundantly clear to John Bradshaw and the Council of State that the publishing free-for-all that had existed during the years of the civil war had to be stopped if there was to be any hope of the new republic properly establishing its authority. In the summer of 1649 attacks came from all sides, bringing, the government acknowledged, 'a suspition and hatred upon the courses and intentions of the Faithful Members of the People's Representatives in Parliament'. On the one hand, the Levellers were using cheap print to further their campaign for a more profound programme of social and political change. On the other, traumatized royalists provided a rapt readership for lachrymose meditations on the death of the King and the horrors of the new regime. Among the thousands of volumes that appeared in 1649 one, *Eikon Basilike* (The Portrait of the King), purported to be Charles I's own memoirs and meditations of his final hours. It slipped through the licensors' net and quickly ran

Catholics attacks on Protestants during the Irish uprising of 1641–2 were vividly reported in the English press, fuelling the violent retribution that would follow. James Cranford's *The Teares of Ireland* (1642) depicts the rape and murder of a pregnant woman and the stripping of a group of Protestants with the chant 'now are ye wilde Irisch as well as wee'.

into dozens of editions. As a cult of Charles the Martyr started to flourish, and the army succumbed to the Leveller mutiny, Bradshaw felt action had to be taken. In March 1649 he took personal charge of the issue, securing authority to sign arrest warrants for those who 'compose or print scandalous pamphlets against the commonwealth'. Work was set in train to 'prevent and punish' transgressors more effectively and to further control and regulate the press.[15]

The truth was that seven years of rampant political reporting, consumed by an increasingly literate nation grown used to reading such material, could not easily be undone. The army had been radicalized by the Levellers' rhetoric, much of it committed to print, and the networks and correspondents were in place to transmit news and ideas at speed. Gerrard Winstanley understood this and Marchamont Nedham's paper had that spring helped to carry tales of the Diggers' doings to a national audience. It was the highly partisan reporting of the 1640s which had helped raise animosity between the opposing parties in the civil war to fever pitch. Nowhere was this more true than Ireland. The violent Catholic uprising of 1641–2 had involved a series of brutal attacks on Protestants, which in turned sparked counter-attacks, resulting in broadly comparable fatalities on each side. The London press reported the killing of Protestants in every grisly detail but remained almost silent on atrocities against Catholics. Stories of Catholic barbarism and cruelty were embellished in the retelling and illuminated by horrifying illustrations showing pregnant women being raped and mutilated and children roasted alive. The narrative played to English distrust of both the Irish and Catholicism and the images haunted the minds of the soldiers who sailed to Ireland to assert English control there. What was to follow would both determine the fate of the English press in the decade to come and cast a shadow of hatred over Ireland for centuries.[16]

※ ※ ※

On 13 August 1649, the Commonwealth's second most senior soldier, Oliver Cromwell, sailed for Ireland with a plentifully equipped invasion army of 12,000 borne on a hundred ships. While the war in

England had been won, Ireland was still in play: the 'Confederate' alliance of royalists and Catholics held most of the island and only the very north and the area around Dublin remained in the hands of the English Commonwealth. A comprehensive royalist defeat at Rathmines shortly before Cromwell's army landed had been a significant boost to the parliamentary cause, and he arrived to find his task suddenly easier than he expected. Having unloaded, he announced his intention to begin the work of reconquest and set out for the walled medieval town of Drogheda, which straddled the deep River Boyne near the coast just 30 miles north of the capital. The royalists were now on the back foot and, outnumbered and outgunned, they steeled themselves for a siege, establishing the town's castle, Mill Mount, as their innermost bastion. When Cromwell invited them to surrender on 10 September they refused, and the following day the storming of Drogheda began.

What followed would never be forgotten. Once they had breached the 20-foot-high walls, Cromwell and his men surged in and proceeded to annihilate their opponents even as they capitulated, killing almost the entire garrison of some 2,500 soldiers and an unknown number of civilians. Cromwell himself issued the unequivocal command that every person bearing arms should be slain. Although the conventions of contemporary warfare meant a garrison which had refused an offer of surrender could expect to be killed, the complete absence of mercy, the sheer numbers involved and the inclusion of numerous civilians among the dead was immensely shocking. Furthermore, there would be widespread reports that much of the killing took place long after the beleaguered garrison had surrendered. With the fall of Drogheda the military reconquest of Ireland had advanced, but Oliver Cromwell and the republic's reputation had, in some quarters at least, been cut into bloodied ribbons.[17]

❦ ❦ ❦

As Oliver Cromwell had watched the Pembrokeshire coast recede on his way to Ireland, Marchamont Nedham had also been on the move. His petition to the Council of State had secured him neither release nor bail, despite his offers to put his journalistic talents at their disposal. 'Having little else to do in prison', he filled his days penning for publication a fulsome further appeal for clemency, in which he airily advised the Council of State not to trouble itself about those with an 'itch of scribbling' and to concentrate instead on rooting out the 'Eaves droppers, Whisperers etc' who were the 'very pest of mankind'. But neither manuscript nor print entreaties had had any effect. As the weeks passed and his trial grew closer, Nedham decided to take matters into his own hands. The very day the Irish expedition set forth, he made his escape. While other escapees would attempt daring leaps from the gatehouse roof, Nedham seems to have taken a subtler approach. In his own words he simply 'slip'd aside'. A quiet bribe or a time-honoured combination of alcohol and ingenuity may have smoothed the way. The moment he was out he fled London and disappeared.[18]

※ ※ ※

News travelled fast. It was quite normal for events on Ireland's east coast to be reported in the London papers inside a week. The fate of the republic's mighty expedition was of the greatest interest to people in the capital, not least as a colossal contribution to funding it had come from the city's merchants. Yet a fortnight after the event barely a whisper of the assault on Drogheda had reached London. When Oliver Cromwell's official report to the Council of State finally came, it was coolly factual in enumerating the enemy dead: 2,500 soldiers and 'many inhabitants' or civilians. Any doubt in Cromwell's mind about the cost of the victory was assuaged by the certain knowledge that it was God's doing.[19]

Strikingly, it was during just this strange fortnight's lull in September 1649 that Bradshaw's press crackdown took effect. On 20 September, just over a week after the siege, what would be known as 'John Bradshaw's press act' passed into law. To prevent the 'malicious misrepresentations' of print, the republican government was now assuming direct control of licensing. A new regime of fines and penalties was imposed and, crucially, all existing newspaper licences were suspended with immediate effect.[20]

The impact was felt instantly. While Nedham was not then publishing, other royalist newsmen remained at large; among them was George Wharton, of *Mercurius Elenctius*, who explained that the new act 'hath beene put so diligently in exeqution by the States Blood-hounds, that the last week I had enough to doe in securing myself from their hungry Jawes'. Noting the mysterious delay in the news from Ireland, he asked rhetorically why over a week after the siege of Drogheda there had still been no certain report of it even in Dublin. The answer was to him clear: 'the strictnesse that is here used to prevent all Intelligence, but what comes immediately from the hand of Cromwell, not any man being suffered to write to his friend either in England or Ireland nor to ride or walke a mile out of Towne without speciall licence.' A sister paper concurred: 'the news from Ireland is now forbidden so much as to be peep'd into by the Junto: the Post that brought letters sworn into Secrecy, and the Letters burid in the grave of oblivion.'[21]

In the fortnight that followed several papers tried to defy the new regulations and continue to publish, a number including verbatim the horrific accounts of the siege of Drogheda that were now emerging. Wharton reported how Cromwell's army had systematically slaughtered the garrison 'in the most cruell manner they could invent, cutting off their Members [penises] and peeces of flesh which they wore in their Hats triumphantly'. Another paper reported that two-thirds of those killed were not just civilians but women and children. Within a month Wharton and numerous other newspaper people were in prison and, for a time, every single one of the nation's licensed weekly papers had been shut down.[22]

🦋 🦋 🦋

Marchamont Nedham watched all of this unfolding from afar. Since his August escape from Newgate he had gone to ground. The obvious place for him to go, his childhood home in Burford, was too busy and populous for him to escape notice, but only a few miles away lay the reassuringly obscure settlement of Minster Lovell. Here he spent some weeks secreted at the home of the royalist poet and pamphleteer Peter Heylyn. The few houses of Minster Lovell were strung along the wide, reedy banks of the River Windrush either side of a substantial mill; Little Minster Hall stood at the far western end in useful seclusion. Heylyn had been the original editor of the main royalist paper of the early 1640s, *Mercurius Aulicus*, as well as a royal chaplain, and was now providing sanctuary for a variety of dissidents from the republic. Here Nedham was provided with a 'high room' where he could write in peace and observe the comings and goings of the landscape around him. He was painfully cautious, not even daring to contact his closest friends for fear of recapture. After a short time he left, feeling the safest approach was to keep moving, like 'a pilgrim about the Country'.[23]

But come late October 1649 Nedham had decided on a new course. He had run out of money and he was miserable. The lonely life of the outlaw gave him no pleasure and, with little personal attachment to the cause for which he suffered, he could not even enjoy the martyrish self-satisfaction of his fellow fugitives. Added to which the public relations fiasco of the Irish campaign, and the government's clumsy news shutdown, convinced him there was an opportunity to be grasped. In deep fear of recapture – his arrest warrant still stood – he adopted an elaborate disguise and crept back into the capital. Making contact with a single trusted London friend, he secured a dingy room in the streets to the west of Newgate 'where I hope nobody will imagine to find me' and set about dispatching a series of letters.[24] A new missive to John Bradshaw in which he recast his offer of his services as a propagandist to the republic was sent, together with another addressed directly to the head of the Commonwealth's intelligence operation, Thomas Scot. To his friend Henry Oxinden he wrote begging the loan of five pounds, explaining: 'I dare not so much as to peep abroad to converse with any, but am constrained to associate with Rats, old bookes and Cobwebs.' Even in the mortal danger in which he was operating he saw the humour in his own situation, remarking to Oxinden, 'Nay did you but see my clothes', and describing the red wig that formed part of his disguise as looking like it had been dropped by a condemned man on his way to the gallows.[25]

Marchamont Nedham's letters arrived as John Bradshaw and the Council of State looked grimly at the situation in which they found themselves. The legislation had been passed, the arrests were being pursued and two new pro-government papers had been established. But, regardless, unlicensed papers were still managing to get to press and were drawing painful attention to both the news crackdown itself and to the siege of Drogheda. There was only so much that could be achieved through the forceful suppression of their opponents. One paper printed a doleful roll of the recently deceased titles: 'No *Perfect Diurnall*, no *Moderate*, no *Weekly Intelligencer*, no *Weekly Account*, no *Moderate Intelligencer*, no *Occurances*, no *Faithful Scout*, no *Modest Narrative*! All wafted away by the breath of Jack Bradshaw.'[26] It was a measure of how desperate they were that on receiving this new petition from the most successful of their journalistic adversaries – a man who had compared the Rump Parliament to a public lavatory, talked of Cromwell's 'maggoty nose' and referred to them collectively as 'that Monster called the Council of State' – they decided to set him free.[27]

The Keeper of Newgate must have been as surprised as anyone when on 14 November he received notification from the Council of State of his former prisoner's release. Where exactly the idea had come from to liberate Marchamont Nedham, a man the republic had reason and evidence to execute, is uncertain. It was suggested later that William Lenthall, the Speaker of the Commons, who knew Nedham's family well, was behind it. Nedham himself laid the decision firmly at the feet of John Bradshaw. His begging letter to his friend was followed a few days later by an ecstatic postscript: he didn't need the money after all, 'for my Lord President's favour hath once more turn'd the wheel of my fortune; who upon a single letter has been pleased to indulge me my liberty'.

Bradshaw had learned more of Nedham's work in recent months, for shortly after his arrest the Council of State had instructed the staunch defender of the revolution, John Milton, to examine back issues of Nedham's paper and report on its content. It may be that it was Milton who realized that the talents of this errant newspaperman were exactly what the republic needed.[28]

❦ ❦ ❦

The sensational success of *Eikon Basilike* had surprised everyone, going through thirty-five editions in 1649 alone. Written in a highly personal style in short, easily digestible chapters, it portrayed Charles I not as the petulant, prickly prince he was, but as reasonable and reflective, a generous and forgiving father of the nation. He had called the Long Parliament, *Eikon* explained, not because he had been forced to, but 'by my Owne choice and inclination: who have alwaies thought the right way of Parliaments most safe for My Crowne and best pleasing to my people'.

The Council of State saw the impact all around them; as one contemporary remarked, 'multitides biassed by attention to the late king ... readily and very credulously take for current anything stamped with his effigy'. It was clear a powerful rejoinder was going to be needed to refute this ubiquitous and highly damaging account of the nation's recent history. John Milton was the obvious candidate, and through the spring and summer he had laboured on producing a response. The result, *Eikonoklastes*, went to press just as the Irish debacle was unfolding. It was a systematic and detailed dissection of *Eikon Basilike*, dismantling in turn each chapter, including the claim that it had been written by Charles I. But at twice the length of *Eikon*, and without its celebrity author or snappy first-person narrative, Milton's reply had little of its popular appeal. Milton wrote of his desire to 'set free the minds of English men from longing to return ... under the captivity of kings', but the realization was dawning that if the republic was to achieve such a shift it would not be by learned disputation. As Milton toiled over his refutation of *Eikon Basilike*, he paused to undertake the other task he had been given, that of reviewing Nedham's paper, *Mercurius Pragmaticus*. However much he loathed its content, here in Marchamont Nedham's audacious, darting prose, appealing squarely to the innkeepers and apprentices, was another way.[29]

Marchamont Nedham's release was not granted without misgivings. His claim that he could, by putting his own skills at the disposal of the republic, achieve great things remained to be proved. His reputation for unreliability was considerable and it was hard to see how one who had so vociferously assaulted the republic could now achieve such a complete act of reversal. Nedham, however, set to it. Over the winter of 1649–50, as Cromwell pressed home his bloody victories across the rain-swept pastures of Ireland, Nedham applied himself to the task of proving he could become the public relations champion that the English republic so clearly needed.

The result, the pages of which were peeled off the printing blocks six months later, was a short book, less than 100 pages long, in which Nedham demonstrated to the Council of State that he had the talent and application to join them. It was a remarkable feat, in which Nedham managed to perform the complete reversal (once again) of his political position without losing his footing. He did not attempt to conceal the change in his stance, indeed he addressed it head-on in the book's opening words: 'To the Reader. Perhaps thou art of an opinion contrary to what is here written. I confess that for a time I myself was so too, till some causes made me reflect with an impartial eye upon the affairs of this new government.' The book then set about using precisely the arguments he had used against the new republic – that it was based entirely on the brute force of the army – to argue for its legitimacy. Almost every significant ruler in history had acquired his or her place by superior military force, he contested. Whether motivated by self-interest or conscience every English person should knuckle down and accept their new masters. Any pragmatist would be a fool not to do so, while anyone resisting on the basis of conscience would be acting against 'reason and custom of the whole world'. Unlike other apologists, he offered no complex spiritual or moral justification for the revolution and regicide. To his former argument that Pride's Purge had robbed Parliament of any claim to represent the people, he simply replied that 'most princes came into the seat of authority not only without a call but absolutely against the wills of the people'. His argument was disarmingly simple: the people of England should obey those in authority whoever they were, for the sake of peace and order.[30]

The Case of the Commonwealth was a remarkable piece of work and, despite its bald premise, the Council of State was convinced. On its publication in May 1650, Nedham was paid £50 'for services alreadie done to the Commonwealth' – a substantial sum for a man who a year before had been prepared to work for £10 a year. But what lay ahead was more enticing still. For a salary of £100 Nedham was to start upon a fresh project to serve the Commonwealth: a new weekly paper of his own crafting which would be 'the stork of the Commonwealth' and secure for the republic the glowing reputation that had so far eluded it.[31]

Eight

Mercurius Politicus

❦❦❦❦❦❦❦❦❦❦❦❦❦❦❦❦❦❦

When the first issue of *Mercurius Politicus* appeared in the street hawkers' baskets on 13 June 1650 the contrast it struck with the other titles the government had recently sanctioned could hardly have been starker. Its format was familiar enough, though at sixteen pages and with a two-pence cover price it was substantial. But compared to their stolid prose and dull adherence to the party line, *Politicus* was a dancing, playful sprite. Whereas *Affairs and Transactions* had stated blankly that it would cover what was 'necessary for their [the public's] notice, which shall passe under a certain and strict examination', *Politicus* was engaging, flirtatious and ambiguous. Nedham's paper may have been published 'In defence of the Common-wealth', but it opened with a disarming line: 'Why should not the Common-wealth have a Fool as well as the King had?' Having thus piqued his readers' interest, Nedham played them with his gleeful, teasing prose. Charles II was rumoured to have left the Dutch Republic for Scotland, he confided, perhaps hidden in a barrel of herring so he could 'be landed any where in a Kingly pickle upon the Coast of Scotland'.

Nedham radiated delight: he was back. His second issue, a week later, wallowed luxuriously in the stir he had caused: ''Tis the talk of the Town who, and what this *Politicus* is.' Like generations of journalists to follow, he was creating a story where one as yet barely existed. His mission was to make his paper so spoken of, so celebrated, that no one of any political persuasion could bear to be without it. 'Those things called the *Fine Gentlemen* say he [*Politicus*] is a *witty Fellow* because they do not understand him', 'yet they buy him, that he may be produced as a Complement to their Mistresses'. Royalists would buy it for the quality of its news though they would 'shake their heads' at its editorial line.[1]

With his employment still on a probationary footing, Nedham had been careful to clear his concept for his new paper with his new paymasters before launching into print. It was not to be a blunt instrument of instruction, but something subtler. Humour and satire were to be its

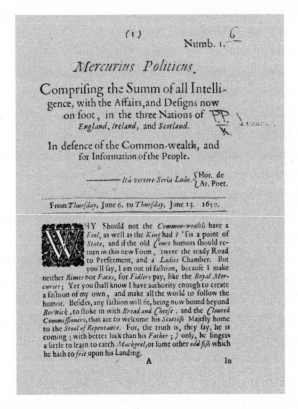

The first issue of *Mercurius Politicus*, the weekly newspaper published by Marchamont Nedham throughout the 1650s. The production and consumption of newspapers was a new phenomenon of the age and Nedham was a scurrilous, hard-drinking bon-viveur in the mould of many newspapermen to come.

methods. 'It must be written in a jocular way,' he explained; to sway the opinions of the 'multitude' required not dense disputation, but amusement and 'phantasie' that would delight and charm.[2] Satisfying his employers was not straightforward and Nedham's comic invective was not to everyone's taste. Like the court fools he referenced in his first issue, he found that mischievous humour laced with unpalatable truths could land a person in trouble. Only a few weeks into publication he referred to criticisms of his style, 'since my satyrs [satires] are offensive (though hitherto they have been moderate enough)'. These accumulated and after just three months Nedham's ebullient editorials, where the most untrammelled and elaborate of his satirical attacks on the Commonwealth's enemies were to be found, ceased. In their place came excerpts from his treatise *The Case of the Commonwealth* which served as a tutorial on acceptance of the new regime.[3]

The first issue of *Politicus* had a suitably spectacular lead story in the triumphant return of Oliver Cromwell from Ireland. The tone turned from one of amusement to one of awe when the General was mentioned. No longer the butt of Nedham's jokes, the 'town bull of Ely', he was now 'noble Cromwell', 'let them stoop with Reverence at the name of that victorious Commander,' he enjoined. Over the weeks and months that followed his paper became the indispensable house journal of the English Commonwealth.[4]

❦ ❦ ❦

Nedham was not content simply to produce a paper that would please his paymasters, or even to make people laugh; he wanted a title that would be read and admired. His editorial commentary might be impish, but he sought to set new standards in the range and accuracy of his reporting. He had been clear with John Bradshaw that to make a success of *Politicus* he would need access to 'the best Intelligence of State'.[5] This he got, and numerous official dispatches to Bradshaw were no sooner opened than they were passed on to Marchamont Nedham, giving him a significant advantage over his competitors. These reports he would supplement with his own network of foreign correspondents, whose letters came in from far and wide. More than half of each issue was made up of international news, which Nedham presented in short, lucid paragraphs 'From Venice' or 'From Madrid'. His net would soon stretch over oceans, as reports from Newfoundland and Barbados, Constantinople and China made their way into his sixteen weekly pages. In August 1651 he reported on the illness of Pope Innocent X, who had been supplying arms to the confederate army in Ireland, including details of the Pontiff's swollen legs. Nedham apologized that he could not say more: 'because his Attendants never stir out of his Chamber it is very difficult to know his condition' – adding for good measure that 'my opinion is he is dead'.[6]

It was a boost to the success of *Politicus* that its first fifteen months coincided with Charles Stuart's sojourn in Scotland. Nedham's playful style was a perfect match for the early days of this ill-fated escapade. His account of the 'famous adventures of yong Tarquin', the 'Baby-King', made for an addictively amusing read, and with every deft, derogatory metaphor the Stuart cause was diminished.[7] Royalists were lampooned for thirsting for rewards and court positions (dreaming of being 'mounted on horseback with golden Sausedges about their Necks'), and the Earl of Derby for lording it up on his 'petty principality', the Isle of Man, where rumour had it he had taken to parading in a lead crown. The Scots' motives for inviting Charles to join them were mercilessly impugned. *Politicus* accused them of having lured the young man with 'sugar plumes and sweet meats', weeping 'onion tears' for his plight, and begging him to join them with the sincerity of his beloved spaniels. Then, when they had him in their clutches, treating him as their errant pupil, 'down go his Breeches if hee refused to obey'.[8]

Come 1651, however, the situation had become altogether more dangerous. As Charles II started massing his Scots army, Nedham's reporting shifted, and the exiled King became a more serious and sinister figure. *Politicus*'s weekly reports of military manoeuvring, building up to the royalist–Scots march south towards Worcester in the late summer, had all the suspense of an episodic thriller.[9]

❦ ❦ ❦

Nedham's canvas was a large one. It was not just the people of the British Isles who thirsted for news of Charles II's fate in Scotland, but many of the political elite of Europe, which helped him to build an international readership at speed. This was an important part of his task, for the republic needed not simply to consolidate its mastery of England, but to establish itself as a credible force beyond its shores.

Europe's two most powerful countries, France and Spain, both governed by mighty monarchies, had looked on with rapt horror as the English had executed their King. But a combination of national self-interest and troubles of their own had prevented either from becoming much involved in English domestic politics thereafter – despite the fact that Charles I's widow, Henrietta Maria, was living as a pensioner of France. The Dutch, England's great trading rivals, were a different matter. This small but wealthy Calvinist country had won its independence from its Spanish Catholic overlords in a revolution led by Charlotte de la Trémoille's grandfather, William the Silent, in the 1580s. In the process they had rejected the absolute authority of monarchy and had become a republic, with a representative assembly, the States General, as their supreme body. As a Calvinist republic which had prospered for seventy years, the United Provinces provided a powerful exemplar to the young Commonwealth government. Its appeal had at first been dimmed by the fact that its Stadtholder, or senior executive, William II, was married to Charles I's daughter Mary, and The Hague had become home to a large group of expatriate English royalists. But when William II died unexpectedly in the spring of 1651, power shifted sharply away from the Orange family and the scene seemed set for an Anglo-Dutch alliance.

An elaborate embassy led by the lawyer Oliver St John was dispatched from London to The Hague and on 31 March 1651, St John attended a formal dinner with the States General where he set out their plan for 'a firm league and confederacy' between the two republics. The news of this notion had first been publicly aired by Nedham in *Politicus*, when he had reported two months earlier that a 'Union between this State and England is much desired by the Common people'. What was envisaged in London was something much more substantial than a trade deal or even a strategic alliance, nothing less than a 'union' of these two Protestant republics, one in which sovereignty would be combined and their shared ideological causes advanced. But the eager optimism of the English diplomats began to fade as the weeks passed and no firm commitments were forthcoming. The Dutch were a hugely successful nation, their prosperity generated in large part by acting as international carriers of goods. They had invested everything in establishing their own independence, and regarded the English proposal with scepticism. The ambassadors returned disappointed and snubbed, and the extensive coverage of the whole affair in *Politicus* helped ensure disgust with the Dutch was a national sentiment. A few months later, in November 1651, the Rump Parliament passed the Navigation Act, which banned imports to English ports from third-party ships, thereby dealing a nasty economic blow to the Dutch. It would have seismic long-term consequences.[10]

※ ※ ※

With the launch of *Politicus*, Marchamont Nedham quickly lost many of his erstwhile friends and colleagues. Rumours that the paper was from the same pen as the immaculately royalist *Mercurius Pragmaticus* seemed ridiculous at first. When confirmation came it elicited outright disgust. Peter Heylyn, who had sheltered Nedham from Commonwealth agents at Minster Lovell, was appalled that this 'zealous Loyalist' should have become an apologist for the republic – 'hired with the Wages of Unrighteousness, corrupted with mercenary gifts and bribes'. From that moment he refused to hear Nedham's name spoken. Another outraged former colleague declared he wanted to tear off Nedham's wig and brand his bald scalp with his own hypocritical words, hoping thereafter to see his head mounted on a spike.[11]

But a person as effervescent as Marchamont Nedham did not struggle to find new friends. Just as he equated himself with his newspaper in print – he and *Politicus* were one – he did not simply approach his new commission as a job that paid, but he became woven into the fabric of the republican regime he now championed. He had a talent for society which few could match. It was borne in part of his conviviality and

appetite for entertainment and amusement, and in part of his quick
and irresistible sense of humour, laced winningly with self-deprecation.
Nights on the town with Nedham were unforgettable, and his correspondence was peppered with references to drinking sessions in the
Mermaid, the Greyhound and the Rose, or the hilarious memory of
'those Turky-eggs at *The Trumpet*'. Even his enemies conceded he was
tremendous company, and those who became fond of him liked him
though they knew him to be unreliable and unpredictable. It was a
measure of his attractiveness as a person that he would go on to develop
affectionate relationships with several of the prominent Commonwealth
figures whom he had once mocked and insulted relentlessly. He was not
the first nor the last person to develop an enduring friendship with
those who ought to have despised him, in large part because he made
them laugh.[12]

In joining the government payroll, Nedham found himself rubbing
shoulders with the firebrand republicans who had created the
Commonwealth. He was temperamentally much happier with a fierce,
firm opinion than he was with middle-of-the-road moderates, and so
took to this company well. The job of vetting each issue of *Politicus* was
given at first to John Milton. As well as writing propaganda for the
Commonwealth, Milton worked at Whitehall as a diplomatic transla-
tor, acting as minder and guide to foreign ambassadors. On the face of
it this utterly committed republican, whose literary oeuvre was epic and
millennial in scope and seriousness, had little in common with a boozy,
popular journalist such as Nedham, who had already switched sides
twice. But Milton was warmer and more approachable than his literary
output implied, and Nedham more intellectually wide-ranging and
thoughtful than might be guessed from the pub crawls and his
two-penny publications. Nedham became, in the words of a contemporary, 'a great crony' of Milton's and the two men often spent the evening
together at Milton's home, entertaining visiting European intellectuals
who came to pay court to the famous poet and polemicist. Milton was
almost blind by now, and as his ability to do his day job gradually diminished, he suggested to John Bradshaw that a talented linguist of his
acquaintance, one Andrew Marvell (currently working as a tutor to Lord

Fairfax's daughter in Yorkshire), might be a suitable successor. But while his eyes may have dimmed, Milton's mind had not, and it was not long before he would begin composing and dictating the 10,000 lines of perhaps the greatest work of imagination in the English language, *Paradise Lost. A Poem written in Ten Books.*[13]

❧ ❧ ❧

The production of *Politicus* was an all-consuming business. Nedham had chosen Thursday for publication to ensure the paper could be distributed nationally before the weekend, but with over 5,000 words to compose every week, and ambitious aspirations for editorial sparkle and news quality, the task was a round-the-clock undertaking. The whole preceding week was devoted to preparation of the lettered blocks with which the pressmen, who operated the wooden printing machines, could begin their work. Nedham's own centre of operations was Westminster. He acquired a house next to St Margaret's church, a few strides from the Palace of Westminster. He seems also, like John Milton, to have had rooms in Whitehall Palace, where the Council of State and the other important committees met. On his desk scores of folded and sealed paper dispatches piled up through the week, bringing the news from his regular correspondents in Edinburgh, The Hague and Paris, further periodic reports from places such as Vienna and Cracow, Rome and Madrid, and occasional news from far more remote locations. Nedham's agents scouted inventively at home and abroad, jotting down in shorthand the first-person statements which made for such vivid reporting. They loitered in taverns, on market squares and harbour fronts where those with information – stock traders and ship's captains, soldiers and servants – might be encountered, bought a drink and persuaded to give it up. Only a dash down Whitehall's long corridors, from which much of Charles I's famous collection of works of art had now been stripped and sold, took Nedham to John Bradshaw's office or to the rooms of John Thurloe (Thomas Scot's successor as intelligence chief), where intelligence from government networks could be sought. All this he would read and digest, sift and sort before selecting, summarizing and synthesizing it into his bright, brisk copy.[14]

Thomas Newcomb's printing house, somewhere among the wharves and warehouses south of St Paul's Cathedral, received pages from Nedham daily, each marked up with notes of instruction. Here, on the cool north side of the printing house, Newcomb's 'compositors' would pore over the shallow wooden trays that contained the tiny metal letters. Their deft fingers darted across these cases, extracting ordinary 'minuscule' type from the 'lower case', and capital letters from the 'upper case', converting each line of Nedham's careful handwritten text into a row of tiny metal blocks ranged in reverse order along their iron composing sticks. The words would in turn be spaced to fit the line precisely, before being tipped into the galley case, ready for printing. By Monday much of Thursday's paper was set. If breaking stories came in that exceeded the small spaces left, the compositors could on Nedham's instruction use even smaller type to squeeze in extra lines. Such was the success of *Politicus* that soon booksellers and others were prepared to pay for notice of their wares to be included in its pages. On 29 January 1651, for instance, the publication of 'Cassandra, a Romance' was promoted in *Politicus* while a fortnight later it was a useful sounding book that promised 'a most compendious way for the speedie obtaining of the Latine tongue, So framed that the meanest Capacity may (in a short time) be enabled to turne any Sentence of English into pure Latine'. Like almost all printed material, including *Politicus* itself, both were available to buy from one of the scores of bookshops clustered against the cathedral and precinct walls in St Paul's Churchyard. Advertising soon expanded to missing persons' and classified notices of all sorts, and would grow into such a lucrative source of revenue that it far outstripped even Nedham's handsome salary.[15]

Nedham was required to submit the content of each issue of *Politicus* for approval, and only once he had done so could he send word to Thomas Newcomb that printing could start. In the age of the hand printing press the business of producing weekly over a thousand issues of a sixteen-page publication was a demanding physical operation. Each pair of pages of type, locked into place in an iron frame, was placed, face-up, on a block of stone set into a sliding carriage. The pressmen applied ink to the upturned letters by dabbing them with a soft leather inking ball. A wooden frame containing a large sheet of paper was then lowered onto the letters and this whole assemblage slid on wooden rails into the press itself. By means of a handle the pressmen lowered a block of perfectly flat wood or stone known as the 'platen' onto the paper from above, so pressing it down onto the inked letters. Raising the platen and drawing the carriage back, they opened the frame, and peeled the freshly printed paper off the metal type. This was handed over to their colleagues who draped each one over the latticework of wooden rails suspended from the printing house ceiling.

The pressmen worked into the night heaving down the platen, drawing the carriage back and forth, peeling off page after page, and replacing the paper and ink with each impression. The room rang with the creak and clatter of the press, governed by the rhythmic movements of the pressmen, who, like oarsmen, kept 'a constant and methodical posture and gesture in every action of pulling and beating which in a train of work becomes habitual'. By Thursday morning they had finished. Thousands of dry pages hung from the rails, and the air was thick with the caustic tang of the hot lye into which the ink-clogged letters were plunged for cleaning. By now the work of cutting, compiling and folding the sheets into individual issues was well underway. From Thames Street the completed copies of *Politicus* were carried forth. Many were sold to street sellers and 'mercury women', who hawked papers from baskets on London's pavements and taverns, crying out wherever they knew the trade was, from Westminster Hall to the Inns of Court. Large bundles went straight to the booksellers a few streets north in St Paul's Churchyard who piled them up on their counters alongside books and ballads, poems and pamphlets. Wholesalers bought quantities and carried them directly to market towns across England, supplying hundreds of copies of *Politicus* to booksellers and other intermediaries, including mercers and shoemakers, from Stamford to Chester, Ipswich to Gloucester. Nedham's paper 'flew every week into all parts of the nation', and was enjoyed by all manner of 'inconsiderable persons', so that farmers in Lincolnshire or merchants in Exeter might read weekly of the military exploits of the New Model

Buy a new Almanack.

An almanac seller touting books and newspapers from her basket, one of the seventeenth-century 'Cries of London'. The newspaper hawkers, who were often women, traded the day's papers across the capital while copies were transported to towns and villages across the country.

Army, the Turks' plans to besiege Crete, the effects of the earthquake on the Greek island of Santorini or the escaped tiger on the loose in the forest of Fontainebleau. And it did not stop there. Exiled royalists in Paris and The Hague waited for each issue, as did Continental diplomats and politicians who found the quality of its reporting outstripped domestic titles. Ships would carry copies to far-flung towns and trading posts, with *Politicus* even being enclosed in the post from London to Jamaica. When the English diplomat William Jephson wrote to London questioning the purpose of his posting, he pointed out simply that 'for the newes from the Hamburgh exchang[e], Mr. Needham hath it as perfectly every weeke'.[16]

❦ ❦ ❦

It was one thing reporting foreign affairs, and firing at easy targets such as the exiled Stuarts or the Scots, but Nedham's task became harder when it came to English domestic news. Cromwell's victories in Ireland and Scotland had brought the British Isles largely under the Commonwealth's control and with the battle of Worcester the royalists were spent as a political force. The General and his officers returned to London in the autumn of 1651 after an absence that had been almost continuous since the early days of the republic two years before. The months that followed would bring the fissures in the regime uncomfortably to the fore, providing turbulent political waters for *Politicus* to navigate. The fundamental problem remained that there was no consensus on how radical the Commonwealth should be. While the army was on campaign the Rump Parliament had become more moderate. Furthermore, as the various programmes of reform – of the law, religion and the voting franchise – were discussed, the complexities and drawbacks of radical change were encountered. Many MPs came to feel that what might have seemed like a good idea at the outset was, when the detail was contemplated, too difficult or dangerous to pursue. So it was that the soldiers of the New Model Army returned bloodied and bruised from the battlefield to find that a great deal of what they felt they had been fighting for – however ill-formed the notions might have been – had in the meantime been put on the back-burner by their parliamentary comrades.

When it came to delicate subjects, ones in which the republic's credibility or unity was most strained, Nedham generally adopted a policy of reticence. In June 1650, the first month of *Politicus's* existence, Lord Fairfax had resigned his commission as head of the army. Nedham reported briefly that the Commons had sat late debating the matter, before remarking 'it is best for *Politicus* to let ... [this] pass without a Commentary for fear of spoiling the Text and his own Reputation'. But Nedham was too restless and independent a man simply to trot out a party line every week, and his own sympathies began to show, some of which echoed the views of his paymasters and others of which did not. When the Earl of Derby was condemned to die in spite of having been granted quarter, Nedham's lengthy justification told of the widespread surprise at the sentence. He devoted much of the two following issues to Derby's execution, reporting on the last-minute attempts to secure a reprieve and printing verbatim his impassioned speech from the scaffold. On the other hand, the injustices suffered by Englishmen and women, which were the target of much of the reformers' ardour, also struck a chord with Nedham. Having had at least two spells in prison himself, he had more than a glancing experience of the torturous English legal system. In December 1651, when the pressure was on Parliament to demonstrate their reforming zeal to the newly returned army, Nedham printed a lengthy petition to Oliver Cromwell from the 'poor oppressed' people of the East Riding of Yorkshire. This dwelled at length on the injustices they suffered from heavy taxation, the slowness and cost of the legal system and the corruption of lawyers, and looked to Cromwell and his fellow officers, those 'who tender the welfare' of England, to bring remedy.[17]

The modernization of the English legal system had from the very outset been firmly in the reformers' sights. A significant moment, symbolically and in fact, came when on 22 November 1650 Parliament passed an act declaring that all legal proceedings, hitherto conducted almost exclusively in Latin or French, would be in English alone from the following Easter. Furthermore, the antiquated script, known as 'court hand', in which all legal paperwork was written, was to be abandoned and instead 'every of them shall be written in an ordinary usual and legible hand and character'. As a piece of legal modernization it may have lacked the complex cleverness beloved of lawyers but, in a single step, English people's ability to understand the legal processes to which they might find themselves subjected was transformed.[18]

The new dawn that early reforms promised did not quite come to pass. In early 1652 the 'Hale' Commission was appointed to consider the overhaul of the whole English legal system, looking at its slowness, cost and inequities. It met regularly for six months and drew up an ambitious range of proposals. None were ever passed into law by Parliament. The truth was that animosity between the Rump Parliament and the army remained the fatal fault line of the Commonwealth and it opened up dramatically after the battle of

Worcester. While the army leaders and their radical allies resented the Rump for its slow progress on reform and modernization, the Rump resented the army's assumption that it was in any way for them – Parliament's 'servant' – to decide the pace of change. When the work of the Hale Commission was being debated, Colonel Pride loitered ominously at the door of the Commons Chamber in just one of a litany of minor acts of provocation between the two institutions.[19]

Marchamont Nedham's lodgings near the entrance to St Margaret's church, Westminster, were barely a minute's walk from John Bradshaw's palatial apartments, formerly the Dean's House, in Westminster Abbey itself. Before long the two men who had been such bitter opponents became friends. No more was Nedham simply Bradshaw's employee and newsmonger, but they enjoyed one another's company though many Godly republicans were surprised that the Lord President could bear to have Nedham at his dinner table. John Milton joined this Westminster circle when in 1651 he moved from Whitehall to Petty France a few streets west of the Abbey. Milton would sing Bradshaw's praises as a host, remarking that though he was devoted to the business of state, 'at home his hospitality is as splendid as his fortune will permit'. In 1655 Bradshaw added a codicil to his will including Mr Marchamont Nedham and Mr John Milton among his beneficiaries.[20]

As the tensions between the Rump Parliament and the army mounted, John Bradshaw's own position as President of the Council of State came into question. The judge who had tried the King could hardly be faulted for republican credentials, and Hugh Peter described him as the bow of the ship of state. But, although he was not an MP, Bradshaw was a lawyer and as such, and someone so central to the Rump regime, a figure of increasing suspicion to the army high command. A strong spirit of anti-professionalism had come to the fore over the early years of the Commonwealth, not least as the lawyers of the new regime were blamed for the lack of progress on legal reform. Some, like the influential army officer Edmund Ludlow, felt sure they were deliberately dragging their feet for their own gain, 'it being in the interests of the lawyers to preserve the lives, liberties and estates of the whole nation in their own hands'. He accused them of holding up the proposals for change by spending three months debating a single word.[21]

Friction between John Bradshaw, as Lord President of the Council and head of the executive branch of the Commonwealth, and Oliver Cromwell, as head of the army, had also been growing. The two men were in a natural position of personal competition – vying for prestigious offices such as the Chancellorship of Oxford University. Rumours were rife in early 1651 that Bradshaw would not be renewed as President because Cromwell 'does not favour hime'. When, on the return of Cromwell and the army from Worcester in the autumn of 1651, elections to the chair of the Council of State came round again, they were moved from an annual to an unwieldy monthly cycle. The votes were cast and for the first time Bradshaw was not chosen. Cromwell's friends had warned him against wishing to be shot of one who had worked so hard, 'whoever succeeds hime, the commonwealth will finde a great misse of him'. Over the previous two years, the Council of State had met almost daily and Bradshaw had missed not a single meeting. But industriousness was not enough; his pre-eminence was waning, and the days of the Commonwealth itself were numbered.[22]

The other great subject of debate and disagreement was the question of when the Rump Parliament should itself make way for a newly elected House of Commons. The discomfort remained that, since so many of its members had been excluded, Parliament could not be claimed to be a representative body, and Cromwell and many others of a reforming outlook pushed hard for a date to be set for new elections. Marchamont Nedham added the voice of *Politicus* to the calls; when the Commons discussed the matter he commented approvingly that this was 'a worke much tending to their own honour and the satisfaction of the people'. But the distractions of the day-to-day intervened, all the more so when the escalating hostilities with the Dutch broke into outright war in the spring of 1652. For many in the army, the main attraction of new parliamentary elections was the opportunity to be shot of the Rump Parliament, who they now regarded as irredeemably complaisant and corrupt. Furthermore, as land threats to the new regime had diminished, it looked increasingly likely that Parliament

would start disbanding the army, thereby denying thousands a livelihood and lifestyle to which they had become accustomed. The question
increasingly became which of the army and Parliament would move
first to dispose of the other. Many key players were allied to one institution or the other; notable for being part of both camps was Oliver
Cromwell and the time was drawing near when he would have to decide
where his loyalties lay.[23]

Matters came to a dramatic head in the early months of 1653. With
the pressure on, Parliament finally agreed that it would bring forward
the date for its own dissolution to November. Details of how this would
work in practice were therefore discussed. There was general acceptance that there would need to be some sort of restriction or
'qualification' on those eligible for election to guard against royalists
and other conservatives being selected, but the question remained of
who should manage and enforce such a procedure. When it became
clear the outgoing MPs considered this vetting process to be theirs to
arrange, Cromwell and other army officers became increasingly alarmed
that any new parliament, far from bringing the reforming vigour they
longed for, would simply replicate the attitudes of the old.

The crucial bill setting out all this was due to be voted on by the
House of Commons on 20 April 1653. The night before, Cromwell called
an informal meeting of MPs and army officers in his lodgings at
Whitehall at which he made a surprise proposal. The task of 'managing
the affairs of the Commonwealth' until a new parliament met should be
put in the hands of a group of some forty men selected from Parliament
and the army. The length of the tenure of this appointed group was
unspecified; it was to sit 'for a time', long enough, it seems, to ensure
the process of reform was secured. The parliamentarians present were,
understandably, aghast at the notion, which signalled the abandonment of public election as the basis of sovereignty. Many army officers
were supportive. The meeting went on into the night and broke up without resolution. Among the last to leave were a group of MPs who
reassured Cromwell that they would ensure his idea was considered
further and that Parliament would make no decision until this had
happened.

The next morning a smaller smattering of men gathered again in Cromwell's rooms overlooking St James's Park. It was while they were continuing the conversation from the night before that news was brought that the Commons had already convened and was about to pass its bill. Cromwell was incandescent. Calling for a party of musketeers, he thundered down King Street and into the Commons Chamber. Here the atmosphere was electric. The thirty or so soldiers loitered in the lobby outside the chamber as Cromwell took his seat, a menacing, brooding figure among them. It was clear their bill was about to pass, by which, in Cromwell's own words, they 'would have thrown away the liberties of the nation into the hands of those who had never fought for it'. He rose to his feet, dressed in sober grey and black wool, and started to speak. He was controlled at first, but as the oratory and emotion rose within him, his voice filled with anger and outrage. This parliament, he intoned, had failed in its responsibilities, had acted with 'delays of justice, self-interest and other faults', and was comprised of 'Whoremasters', 'drunkards' and 'corrupt and unjust men'. Stalking up and down the central aisle of St Stephen's Chapel, his arm shot out to point pitilessly at individual MPs as he enumerated their misdemeanours, pawing the timber floor with his heavy boots as he did so. Never had Cromwell more fully embodied Nedham's 'town bull of Ely'. When MPs rose to respond to this diatribe they were roared back onto their benches. 'It was not fit they should sit as a Parliament any longer,' he bellowed, the feverishness and fury with which he spoke causing several to wonder whether he had lost his mind. He summoned his soldiers, pointed at the Speaker of the House of Commons, the figurehead of the chamber that for four years had been the sovereign body of the nation, and instructed them to 'Fetch him downe'. As the Speaker was hauled, shouting, from his chair, the Rump Parliament was dispatched with the same brute force that had attended its birth almost five years before.[24]

Later that day Cromwell, the wind in his sails, strode into the old Queen's Guard Chamber at Whitehall where the Council of State met. While John Bradshaw was no longer in the chair, this devoted officer of the Commonwealth had continued to attend as a member, and was among the faces that turned to the door as the General entered.

Oliver Cromwell expelling the Rump Parliament in April 1653. Cromwell
stands in bucket boots centre-left ordering the MPs from the chamber.
Although known as 'Parliamentarians', he and his army comrades got on no
better with elected parliaments than Charles I had.

Cromwell announced to them: 'Gentlemen, if you are met here as
private persons, you shall not be disturbed; but if as a Council of State,
there is no place for you.' Their reply, according to one contemporary,
came from John Bradshaw, he who had sentenced the King and devoted
his every waking hour since to the new regime and the principle of
parliamentary sovereignty that it rested upon. 'Sir,' he responded, 'we
have heard what you did at the House in the morning, and before many
hours all England will hear it: but Sir, you are mistaken to think that the
Parliament is dissolved; for no power under heaven can dissolve them
but themselves.' Fellow councillors weighed in, echoing his protest that
it was not for any individual, however armed, to dismiss this sovereign
body. But it was in vain. This group of lawyers and administrators, with
all their indignation, could offer no defence against soldiers whose
long-barrelled muskets hung primed at their sides.[25]

❦ ❦ ❦

The military coup that Cromwell staged in the House of Commons took place on Wednesday morning. All but the final two inches of page sixteen of *Mercurius Politicus* lay typeset and locked ready for printing in Thomas Newcomb's Thames Street premises. With such sensitive content to incorporate it was a mercy for Marchamont Nedham that Cromwell's coup came so late in the day. In the six lines that remained he chose his words with care, 'The Lord General deliver'd in Parliament divers Reasons' why Parliament should be dissolved, 'it was accordingly done, the Speaker and the Members all departing.' Lack of space enabled him to end simply, 'The grounds of which Proceedings will (it is probable) be shortly made publick'. A week later Nedham's loyalties, if they had ever seriously wavered from those who held the sword and paid his salary, had come to rest. Despite the closeness of his friendship with John Bradshaw (who would soon be asked to vacate his rooms at Whitehall), and though he would have missed nothing of the deafening hypocrisy of what had just happened, from the moment he had entered the government's pay two years earlier, he had accepted the logic of his own arguments in *The Case of the Commonwealth*. 'Those whose title is supposed unlawful and founded merely upon force, yet being possessed of authority, must lawfully be obeyed.' He might have friends who were prepared to be a 'fool's martyr' and resist, but he was not one of them.

Issue 150 of *Politicus* when it appeared a week later ploughed through news from Scotland and Paris, Stockholm and Hamburg before coming to Whitehall. Recent events, Nedham breezily reported, 'hath been already made publick' in declarations 'setting forth the grounds and reasons' for the dismissing of Parliament. While he could not 'let slip a matter of such concernment', neither was he willing to enter the fray by giving any sort of opinion. Instead, he simply reprinted Cromwell's 'Declaration', a lengthy essay in self-justification that described the shortcomings of the Rump Parliament and its misguided determination to 'recruit the House with persons of the same spirit and temper' as themselves in any new elections. The army, Cromwell explained, had acted on behalf of 'all considering persons' in deciding that this could not be allowed to happen. But more than this, he declared, 'we have bin led by necessity and Providence to act as we have done'. What happened next was in God's hands, and the task now was to 'wait for such issue as he shall bring forth'. In the meantime, all government officials were to continue to carry out their duties 'as fully as when the Parliament was sitting'. The Commonwealth and Parliament itself had passed. It was Divine Providence now, acting through its agent Oliver Cromwell, that was to direct the affairs of England.[26]

Nine

Tongues Like Angels

❦❦❦❦❦❦❦❦❦❦❦❦❦❦❦❦❦❦

A young woman stumbled unsteadily through the marshy fields beyond the village of Hackney one March evening in 1653, her clothes dripping with water. She was 32 years old and plainly but respectably dressed. There were rings on her fingers, her dress was almost certainly black with a white collar and her head covered by a tall, black felt hat. But the sobriety of her costume was in striking contrast to her demeanour. She moved feverishly, gesticulating and talking aloud as she did so to people who were not there. Her frame was sturdy but her cheeks were drawn from lack of food and her face waxy pale. Her manner was highly agitated and she seemed strange – mad even. She was desperate for solitude and for solace. Hastening on, she came upon a well. Here she stopped. Leaning forward over its low wall, she looked into its black depths and steeled herself to plunge downwards.[1]

For weeks now Anna Trapnel had been trying to kill herself. Her family had been on extended suicide watch; each night three of them took shifts sitting by her bed, feeling for the blades she concealed among the blankets. But now she had managed to slip their gaze and strike out into the fields. She had avoided the search party by lying in one of the watery ditches into which the pastures drained. With the chill night air rising, the waters had been sharply cold, but this physical pain was nothing to the torment in her soul.

Inside Anna Trapnel's mind a deadly battle was raging. This was no philosophical disputation, but an intensely immediate struggle between God and the Devil in which her ears filled with the voice of each, as vivid and real as any human. Satan urged her to do it, to let the still black water fill her lungs, whispering to her that it would bring no dishonour, as people would not know it was her doing, but would assume someone 'put thee inn'. He appeared not as a horned beast but as an angel of light, offering her soothing words and honeyed temptation. Then suddenly he became furious, imperious, filling her with paralysing terror.[2]

Anna Trapnel was tortured by the self-doubt and melancholy of her upbringing, by a fear that she was not one of God's chosen people. But this Hackney well was not to be her end. In despair she threw herself on

Anna Trapnel, daughter of a London shipwright, was attached to a congregation of Fifth Monarchists, the most political of the Puritan sects. Her powerful religious visions, some featuring Oliver Cromwell, made her famous across the country.

the hard ground and cried out: 'Lord there is no recovery, I shall surely go out like a snuff.' Then she felt a light shining around her, and a deep voice said, 'why lyest thou upon thy face?', 'pray and eat, this day is Salvation'. Somehow she was retrieved from the fields and awoke to find herself in bed at the house of her relation the merchant Mr Wythe and his wife. Several days had passed, as she toiled in the fever that had been brought on by her fasting and days of wandering. God was with her now and as she drifted back to consciousness she asked him earnestly what she was to do. He replied calmly that she was to 'go forth to the tempted, and whatever their temptations were, I should have to speak forth to them'.[3]

🦋 🦋 🦋

Anna Trapnel had from her earliest childhood been raised as a strict Puritan. Her father had been a shipwright, one of the hundreds of men who worked in the dockyards that fringed the Thames east of the Tower of London, hammering and sawing great ocean-riding vessels into being. While the fleet for which Charles I's infamous ship money had been raised was being built across the river at Deptford, Anna's father probably worked for the East India Company on the north bank of the Thames at Poplar, building ships for commercial trading to Asia. Memory of the exotic cargoes borne by such vessels stayed with her – the nutmegs that looked so 'barky and dull ... until grated', candied ginger, perfumes and other such 'costly things'. But her upbringing was one not of indulgence but of godly discipline.

William Trapnel's early death had left his wife and daughter alone, but Anna's mother remarried and her own religious education continued regardless. Working people of English towns and cities were particularly drawn to the purer form of reformed religious worship which many had sought in the past few decades. Charles I's campaign to make the English church less, rather than more, Protestant in its forms had only increased their determination, as had the refugees who fled to London from the bitter religious wars of the Continent.[4]

The leading figures of the Reformation, Martin Luther and John Calvin, had asserted that the Bible, rather than the accumulated traditions and ceremonies of the medieval church, was the source of all Christian truth. Anna, like many in modest Puritan families, had been brought up to read and write precisely in order that she might study scripture first-hand and understand its divine purpose. Close examination of the Bible, delving back beyond the relative clarity of the New Testament to the more obscure and incomprehensible books of the Old Testament, characterized Puritan education. Daily encounters with a stern and thundering Old Testament God, and with John Calvin's own grim analysis of humankind's sinfulness, made for a sobering diet. Calvin considered all people to be 'ignorant and bereft of God, perverse, corrupt and lacking every good ... inclining to all sorts of evil, stuffed with depraved desires addicted to them and obstinate towards God'. The belief that from birth God had already pre-selected those who were to be saved, and no amount of good works could change that, did little to encourage optimism in already anxious Puritans.

Anna's mother had been a stickler for Godly discipline, and had been quick to chastise her young daughter, seeing sin in everything she did, down to the tiniest actions 'that the world calls a trifle'. Anna grew up deeply fearful, 'persuaded I was for ever shut out from the presence of God'. In her teens she had fasted frequently, and attended church several times a day, taking it as yet another sign of her worthlessness if she failed to weep with Godly emotion at every sermon. Her mother reproved her for such fretfulness, saying curtly that it would only let in the Devil. It was while listening to the thundering Puritan John Simpson in the London church of St Bartholomew the Great that Anna's spiritual watershed had come. As he heaved forth on the words 'if any man have not the spirit of Christ he is none of his', 22-year-old Anna found herself crying out 'Lord I have the Spirit' and was suddenly washed with 'joy unspeakable'.[5]

Just as the civil war was starting, Anna's mother had died, calling out three times to Christ on her deathbed: 'Lord double thy spirit upon my child!' Anna was now alone. She had lived for a time on her own, the small legacy left to her by her mother making her independence as an unmarried woman possible. After a year or so, perhaps yearning for company, she had moved in with a series of friends and relations, living not as a servant but as a family member or companion. Ever ringing in her ears was her aunt's instruction on the death of her mother that she should now labour to be married to Christ.[6]

🏵 🏵 🏵

A few weeks after her recovery from the well incident in April 1653, Anna Trapnel travelled west to the village of Hillingdon which straddled the busy road between London and Oxford. Here she stayed with her friend Mr William Atcroft and mingled with the Puritans of the village. Among her acquaintances was the minister of the local church, St John the Baptist, the 35-year-old Oxford graduate Philip Taverner.

The past decade had brought great changes to the parish churches of England, the hub of social and spiritual life of almost all ordinary people. Charles I's innovations had seen some of the trappings of the Catholic church reappear, including more elaborate clerical vestments and the removal of the communion table from the body of the church to stand against the east wall, separated from the congregation by a wooden rail. The new rules of the early 1640s reversing his changes were vigorously enforced, and sometimes violently exceeded, by a fired-up parliamentary army as it marched back and forth across England during the war. At St John's Hillingdon, a marauding band of soldiers had burst in in 1642, having just burned the altar rail at neighbouring Uxbridge. The Hillingdon rail had already been disposed of, so they grabbed the parish priest's white surplice instead and tore it into strips which they rode off wearing wrapped around their necks.[7]

While the churches themselves had been stripped bare of all embellishments other than the pews, pulpit and communion table (now back in the body of the church once more), the ministry, too, was purged. Clergymen who were considered ideologically unsound – perhaps as many as a third of all ministers – were removed. Philip Taverner of St John's Hillingdon, altogether a kinder and gentler Puritan cleric than many, was among those who were appointed instead. By the time Anna Trapnel visited his Hillingdon congregation he and his wife had for three years been comfortably ensconced in the crumbling but capacious medieval vicarage.[8]

It was while among these friends in Hillingdon that Anna Trapnel saw the future. At William Atcroft's house she fell into a deep trance that would last a week, during which time she burst into involuntary hymns and was 'drawn into my visions'. As she lay barely conscious a series of scenes swam before her eyes: she saw the return to England of the Jews, exiled since the Middle Ages. In another apocalyptic apparition she saw the downfall of all nations. But it was the third that would attract attention. There appeared before her eyes the figure of Oliver Cromwell, in the guise of the Old Testament military leader Gideon, going into the Commons Chamber and demanding the resignation of the Speaker and the end of the assembly: 'I saw suddenly a departure of them, though they were very loath thereunto.' When, four days later, news reached the Hillingdon vicarage that exactly these events had just occurred in London, Anna's friends were thunderstruck. She was not mad. God himself was speaking through her.[9]

❦ ❦ ❦

Charles I's ceremonializing innovations in the church had been reversed to general applause in 1641, many keen to see things be 'as they were in Queen Elizabeth's time'. But this had not been an end of it. The terms on which the Scots had agreed to enter the civil war on Parliament's side had required the parliamentary regime to harmonize the English and Scottish churches. Any hopes that this would be simply a matter of revising the Book of Common Prayer were soon dashed. Wholesale reform was embarked upon. While the Elizabethan church had been doctrinally Protestant, indeed Calvinist, it had retained visible trappings of Roman Catholicism: the traditional hierarchy of bishops and archbishops, festivals and saints' days and various other ceremonies and institutions for which the Bible offered no precedent. In 1645 the English Prayer Book, in which these forms were set out, was abolished outright and in its place a spare new Directory of Worship was issued, omitting much of the familiar form and rhythm of the Anglican church calendar. Pictures, vestments, fonts and organs were banned in churches, as were festivities on saints' days, 'having no warrant in the word of God'. Even the Anglican approach to the feasts of Christ's own life, Christmas, Easter and Whitsun, were considered inappropriate. As public holidays these were as well known for boisterous and boozy celebrations as for pious churchgoing. It was announced that these were to be 'no longer observed as festivals or holy days' and every second Tuesday of the month was designated a public holiday instead, supplemented by occasional days of prayer and fasting.

When it came to church structure the unit of the parish church was to remain, but with a new administrative superstructure that omitted bishops altogether. The trouble was that this new system took some time to decide upon and when it eventually was agreed, the stable circumstances necessary for such drastic changes to take root simply did not exist. On the one hand most people were reluctant to relinquish the Book of Common Prayer and traditions that went back centuries, on the other there were noisy calls – amplified in mass-market printing – for further change including the end to any sort of nationally organized church.[10]

Since the early seventeenth century a small number of people, mostly in towns, had parted from the national church and taken matters of

A *Catalogue of the Severall Sects*, 1647, satirising the many religious groups that sprang up in the 1640s. They include the grandly robed Arminians (or Laudians), the Baptists or Anabaptists, shown performing adult baptism and the (probably fictional) nudist sect known as the Adamites.

religion into their own hands. Inspired by the Protestant emphasis on faith and an individual's personal relationship with God unmediated by a priesthood, they began to set up their own communities which conformed with their own notions of faith. The Baptists were among the first, believing in the importance of baptism only when a person's own spiritual awakening had occurred. The 'Pilgrim Fathers' who boarded the *Mayflower* in 1620 were themselves a small group of Puritan separatists who sought a new beginning. By the mid-1640s, with the traditional structures of church control removed and the new ones still shaky, many more grassroots groupings sprang up. The so-called 'Seekers' believed that no proper grouping or new church could be formed until clear divine guidance had been given. The 'Ranters', it was claimed, believed that the elect were free from sin and so absolved from earthly laws – and free to indulge in orgies of hedonistic abandon. While the radical sects only represented a tiny percentage of the population, their unorthodox practices excited huge interest and gave the young newspaper trade a field day. Many, among them the overwhelmingly socially conservative ruling classes, shuddered in response. Following the army coup of the autumn of 1648 it was unclear what was to happen. Was the new Presbyterian church structure to be upheld? Or was much even deeper religious reform now to follow?[11]

The religious grouping with which Anna Trapnel had become associated was known as the Fifth Monarchists. They weren't so much a doctrinally specific sect as a ramshackle association of religious radicals of various stripes who shared a common set of grievances. They had come into being as a direct result of the frustration and disappointment they felt at the Rump Parliament's reluctance to institute more far-reaching religious reforms. Many contemporaries – including Cromwell himself – believed that the conflicts of the times were part of the great battles that the Bible foretold would precede the second coming of Christ. This 'millenarian' outlook was taken literally by the Fifth Monarchists, among them a large number of soldiers, who dwelt obsessively on a series of strange prophecies in the Old Testament book of Daniel which told how four successive corrupt kingdoms would rise and fall before the advent of the fifth, the kingdom of God in heaven.[12]

In November 1652 the Welsh Puritan William Erbery slipped into one of the Fifth Monarchist services and marvelled at the 'confusion' he found. Their lack of ideological unity and their outbursts of anger brought its own disorder. At the front a wooden stand had been built with a lower and a higher platform for preachers of different persuasions, and from these successive and competing sermons were delivered. The congregation crammed in, sitting on the pews and perching on seat backs. Speakers leaped up onto chairs or stools to be heard, jostling and heckling one another during long, impassioned sermons, often lasting several hours. The gatherings were loud, emotional and highly political. The Fifth Monarchists had formed their manifesto at All Hallows the Great in the City of London immediately after an unsatisfactory meeting with Oliver Cromwell in 1651. First on their list was the uncompromising pledge that anything that was judged to stand in the way of the kingdom of Jesus should be 'utterly pulled down and brought to nothing'.[13]

Something of the atmosphere and energy of Puritan worship in the 1650s is captured in this contemporary print satirising Oliver Cromwell. The congregation is lively and engaged, the pews full, with several members, women among them, standing to speak.

Anna Trapnel's own enthusiasm for the movement had little to do with politics, however. She was first drawn to All Hallows, Thames Street, as its pastor was John Simpson, the charismatic preacher from the east London parish of her childhood, whose sermon had first caused her to feel the spirit of Christ. An unmarried woman in her thirties with neither parents nor siblings, she lacked the personal ties and bonds which most enjoyed. She had inherited enough from her mother in valuables and plate to enable her, with careful management, to live without working herself.[14] As a result she was not poor enough to be kept in one place by the need to earn her keep nor rich enough to employ her own household. With so little to anchor her, Anna's position was a lonely one, and the fellowship and community offered by the All Hallows congregation was its real appeal. More than this, it offered the fellowship of other women.

Women were strongly drawn to the hundreds of different independent congregations that sprang up in the 1640s and 1650s. The dislocation of the wars left many grieving, like Anna, for lost family and disorientated by the loss of social and religious certainties. Furthermore, reformed religious thinking made it possible for women, who were treated as inferior and subservient in almost all spheres of seventeenth-century life, to be taken seriously. If at the root of religion was each individual's relationship with God, then women, too, might find and deal with God directly – without having to defer to a clergyman or male member of her family as was required in almost all other matters. Women attended nonconformist congregations independently from their fathers and husbands, causing grumbling and rumours among their menfolk about the goings-on there. Women's individual access to God was acknowledged to a greater or lesser extent by most of the new sects, with some – as Lady Derby had heard – even allowing women to preach at their meetings.

The gatherings at All Hallows were attended by many women, indeed they probably made up the majority of the congregation. A sense of liberation from the restrictions and oppressions of their sex, and a feeling of sisterhood, seems to have been a common experience. For the solitary Anna Trapnel this was powerful indeed; she had always preferred the company of women, and for her the All Hallows congregation became the immediate family she had lost. Here she found the siblings she did not have, and even, in those she called 'Betty' and 'my Stripling', the children she would never bear.[15]

Anna Trapnel's vision of the expulsion of the Rump Parliament was not her first spell of clairvoyance. Five years earlier, when she was living with friends near the Tower of London, she had foreseen the New Model Army's occupation of London in the tense weeks before Charles I was tried. Two years after that she had experienced a further trance and this time saw an army on the battlefield, led by a figure of valour and courage, God indicating that 'Oliver Cromwell, then Lord General, was that Gideon'. Cromwell's defeat of the Scots at the battle of Dunbar soon afterwards offered Anna confirmation of the truth of her visions. While she was a person of no significant status, these strange turns by his young parishioner had begun to attract the attention of John Simpson.[16]

※ ※ ※

Having expelled the Rump in a burst of rage and self-righteousness in April 1653, Oliver Cromwell was faced with the problem of what was to take its place. Elections had not become any more appealing, and after some deliberation, and much seeking of divine guidance, Cromwell and his senior army colleagues announced that a new assembly would meet which would be formed of men whom he and senior army officers would choose from across England. Among the 138 who were selected at least a dozen were committed Fifth Monarchists, and more who shared their wide-eyed fanaticism. Their task was to guide the reform that the Rump Parliament had failed to institute. Cromwell set the assembly in motion burning with hope that this, finally, would bring about the stability and righteousness he sought. In his words, 'it was thought men of our own judgement, that had fought in the wars, and were all of a piece upon that account ... will do "it" to the purpose'. Others were less optimistic. John Bradshaw, as he vacated his Whitehall rooms, still reeled with disbelief that the Rump Parliament had been marched out of the chamber by the army. Others turned to satire, lampooning the new assembly for its flimsy constitutional standing and its ramshackle membership.

For some time Puritans had given their children distinctive godly or Hebrew names, born of their relentless biblical studies. Praisegod Barbon, a leather seller, whose brother was called Feargod, was one of the London delegates at the new nominated assembly, and in his honour the wags christened it 'Barebone's Parliament'.[17]

The dismissal of the Rump had been a momentous event for the Fifth Monarchists. Perhaps the Rump, rather than the Stuarts, was the fourth corrupt monarchy described in the book of Daniel, and its downfall therefore heralded the coming of Christ and their own elevation as the true believers or 'Saints'. After all, the end of the Rump had been revealed by God to a young woman of their own movement. But optimism on all sides started to evaporate with remarkable speed.

That summer the new assembly met and began its business. The more moderate members were soon shocked by the radicalism of their fellow delegates. Cromwell looked on nervously as 'the sober men of that Meeting did withdraw', while Anna Trapnel dreamed of the 'departures of those from the house, whom I called the Linsey-Wolsey party', those who, like linen mixed with wool, were neither one thing nor another, 'which the Lord said he would not have in his Tabernacle'. While a more robust attitude to legal and religious reform was precisely what Cromwell claimed to want, as soon as they began to tackle it he quailed. Ambitious proposals to achieve greater legal reform through abolishing altogether the Chancery, the strand of English justice administered by the Lord Chancellor, were defeated only by the Speaker's casting vote. A committee was appointed to consider the religious complexion of the nation, to which Cromwell was careful to have himself nominated. When it finally reported it proposed a broad and tolerant religious settlement, which was very much his goal but, to the ire of the Fifth Monarchists, not the end of a national church. Parish clergy were to remain as was the national system of taxation – tithes – which supported them, of which the English ruling class was fiercely protective.[18]

The changing tone of the speeches and incantations from the stacked lectern at All Hallows the Great could be read in Anna Trapnel's own darkening mood. In June 1653, before the new Nominated Assembly had even met, she was walking through Newgate market, in the shadow of Marchamont Nedham's erstwhile gaol, when she stopped to speak to one Mr Smith who sold linen at the sign of the golden anchor. He asked her what she made of the new assembly and her response was downbeat, replying 'that little good should be done to the Nation by their sitting'. This sense of growing dissatisfaction was something that Anna herself would soon reinforce.[19]

❦ ❦ ❦

In the autumn of 1653 Anna Trapnel was back in Hackney with her relations the Wythes. As the Nominated Assembly was having its torrid meetings, her feverishness returned. The fasting she undertook to try to get closer to God sapped her strength. She lay semi-conscious for ten consecutive days visited by further disturbing visions. The words inveighed from the pulpit at All Hallows echoed in her mind, mingling with dreams and memories. She saw strange things. A Christ-like figure surrounded by children bathed in light. A sinister white citadel being attacked by phalanxes of the wise. A great oak whose roots were so shallow it crashed to the ground. Then more immediate scenes, a herd of oxen, one with the 'perfect face of Oliver Cromwell', who appeared benign at first but then pinned her down with his great pointed horn pressed to her chest. The town bull of Ely had taken a new guise.[20]

News was now beginning to spread of this young woman and her 'visions'. With politics so febrile and the question of what God's own will was endlessly sought, people began to want to see for themselves whether Anna was indeed his intermediary. In early September as she lay entranced, Colonel John Bingham, a delegate to the Nominated Assembly, made the trip out to Hackney. He found a pale woman voicing her strange visions in sweet, tuneful songs. When he heard her sing of 'Gideon' having lost God's favour, and the 'breaking up' of the new assembly, he felt almost relieved, as it was clear to him the 'little parliament' was doomed. He travelled back to Westminster certain now that the utterances of this woman were nothing less than divine prophecies.[21]

❦ ❦ ❦

Cromwell looked back on the Nominated Assembly with bitter regret as 'a story of my own weakness and folly'. The membership was determined to make changes which he saw as the 'Subversion of the Laws and Liberties of this Nation, the destruction of the Ministry of this Nation; in a word the confusion of all things'. The appetite of the assembly as a whole for far-reaching reform went beyond what Cromwell and many of its moderate members were prepared to tolerate, particularly when it came to matters which impinged upon social hierarchy and property rights. It became clear to him that the Fifth Monarchists and their ilk would never make responsible governors of the nation; it was not in their nature. At All Hallows church, certain now that their former hero was not going to allow their programme to succeed, John Simpson and his fellow preachers sharpened their biting rhetoric. Reports reached Whitehall in early December 1653 that Simpson's colleague Christopher Feake had called the General 'the man of sin' and 'the old dragon'.[22] Cromwell's patience surprised those around him. He summoned Feake for a meeting, and tried to reason with him, but to no avail. As he would later tell a group of City of London dignitaries, the Fifth Monarchists 'had tongues like Angels but had cloven feet'. Taking matters into their own hands a group of senior army officers and members of the Nominated Assembly started to discuss how they could cauterize the danger they saw before them. As they whispered and conspired over the weekend of 10/11 December, Anna Trapnel had yet another vision. There was no doubting now who the malefactor in her imaginative firmament was. She saw once again a herd of oxen with human faces, one whose 'countenance was perfectly like unto Oliver Cromwels'. The rest of the herd bowed before him, recognizing him as their leader, their 'supreme'. He leaped up in vainglorious triumph and then turned to Anna and started to charge. Just as his horn was about to pierce her heart, she felt the strong arm of God encircle and protect her, and his voice saying 'I will be thy safety'.[23]

On the morning of 12 December 1653 some forty members of the Nominated Assembly put their plan into action. Knowing that most of the Fifth Monarchists would be distracted by the regular Monday meeting at All Hallows the Great, they gathered early and declared, sensationally, that 'the sitting of this Parliament any longer, as now constituted, will not be for the Good of the Commonwealth'. They had decided that the risks to social order if the volatile and uncompromising body were allowed to continue were too great. They were hereby resigning their powers, and delivering them up to the one person they felt had the authority to hold their fracturing regime together: 'the Lord Generall Cromwell'.[24]

Four days later, at one o'clock in the afternoon, a fine coach was drawn out of the court gate at Whitehall. It was the final and most important element of a procession in which all the greatest figures of the state participated. First to appear through the gate had been the judiciary dressed in their black robes. Then came a newly appointed Council of State followed by the Lord Mayor, aldermen and other officials of the City of London in coaches, their scarlet gowns bright splashes in the dull winter hues. The army came next, private soldiers respectfully bareheaded, and officers splendid in hats, swords and cloaks, all forming a sea of figures on foot lapping against the coach in which the new 'Protector' sat elevated. The procession passed south along King Street, under the two Tudor gatehouses that spanned the street. Reaching Westminster Hall, the riders dismounted and the procession passed through the north door. Inside the vast chamber the cavalcade formed a semicircle at the elevated southern end. At its centre was an empty chair. For the next hour the company stood while a secretary of the Council read aloud 'the rules for the new Government'. On its conclusion, having sworn an oath of fidelity to this new settlement, Oliver Cromwell took the seat. Here in exactly the spot where the King of England had been condemned to die, an erstwhile gentleman farmer from the Fens was declared His Highness, Lord Protector of England, Scotland and Ireland. The country had a sovereign, of sorts, once again.[25]

🦁 🦁 🦁

A month later, at the end of the first week of January 1654, Anna Trapnel was at Whitehall Palace. She and a group of fellow Fifth Monarchists crowded through the corridors and galleries towards the Council Chamber. On hearing of the abrupt end of the Nominated

Assembly, the Fifth Monarchists had taken to their pulpits to denounce Oliver Cromwell as 'the dissembleingst perjured villaine in the world'. A crackdown had begun: Simpson and Feake had been interrogated and their Welsh leader, Vavasor Powell, was now being interviewed by the new Protector's council. The day was cold and Anna and her friends clustered at a fire in an anteroom as they awaited the outcome of the examination. When Powell emerged, Anna found herself trembling with emotion. She had intended simply to return home, but the strength of feeling within her grew and started to overtake her. Consumed by 'troubled thoughts', she grew weak and had to rely on her friends to help her back down the stairs. Coming out into one of the courtyards near what had once been Henrietta Maria's Privy Kitchen she collapsed. A tavern and eatery had been established within the palace complex by one William Roberts and with his agreement she was carried inside and found a bed. Right at the heart of government and the nation, Anna Trapnel was once again falling into a trance. Suddenly, and entirely by chance, the bitterly disappointed radicals of the Nominated Assembly were presented with a golden opportunity to use this extraordinary young woman to try to save their fast-fading political cause.[26]

Ten

Cornhell in the West

❦❦❦❦❦❦❦❦❦❦❦❦❦❦❦❦❦❦❦❦

A nna Trapnel remained entranced at William Roberts's house at
Whitehall for almost a fortnight. She seemed, mostly, to be uncon-
scious, or at least in deep sleep. Her eyes were closed and her body limp.
A small group of her female friends tended to her, mopping her brow
and rearranging the blankets when she occasionally shifted. Then, each
day, usually in the afternoon, she came alive. For three or four hours at
a time words fell from her lips in a stream of murmurings and assertions and then in songs, sung in a sweet and tuneful voice, rhyming and
scanning with strange harmony. For the first five days she was not seen
to eat or drink at all. Thereafter she was able to sit up and take small
amounts of toast soaked in weak, watery beer. Sometimes she could not
even do this, and simply sucked liquid from the bread held to her lips.
Weeks later she tried to describe what it had felt like. She heard and saw
nothing, she explained, other than 'the voice of God sounding forth
unto me'. What she experienced was for the most part profoundly
joyful. At times she would cry out with happiness: 'Oh what brightness!
What glory! What sweetness!' God was with her, and he was not the
merciless, Old Testament figure of her upbringing, but an encouraging
and protective guide, brimming with strength, wisdom and reassurance
for his 'handmaiden'. Her dreams were full of invigorating imagery,
gusts of refreshing winds, glittering, glorious, sparkling encounters

with the holy spirit, trees, gardens and landscapes bright with light and optimism. But all this positivity was of little interest to the bitterly disappointed radicals of the now defunct Nominated Assembly. What they were searching for was something altogether more specific: proof positive that God had abandoned Oliver Cromwell.[1]

It took only a few hours before visitors started arriving, ushered past the royal kitchen and through William Roberts's door. These were not just passers-by or fellow radicals, but 'many eminent persons', who came to see the prophetess for themselves. They included Colonel Bingham who had visited her in Hackney, others of the Nominated Assembly, members of the new Council of State, noblemen and women. There was great excitement when she was revisited by the vision of Gideon-Cromwell as the malevolent ox. She went on to speak explicitly of how Oliver Cromwell had 'backslidden', asking whether 'he would be ashamed of his great pomp and revenue while the poor are ready to starve?' The public relations value of Anna's utterances had become abundantly clear and after three or four days a 'relator' had been engaged and stationed in the room, charged with getting all her words down on paper. His task was not an easy one: her speech was wandering and her songs sometimes indistinct, while at some points the sheer number of people in the room made it impossible to hear anything at all.[2]

The crowds flocking to Whitehall soon caught the newsmen's interest. While she was still installed, the *Grand Politique Post* and *Severall Proceedings of State Affairs* both covered the story. Each had to handle the matter of Anna's denunciation of Oliver Cromwell delicately given how closely the press was now monitored. The *Post* skated over it altogether, mentioning only her predictions of the rise of the glorious fifth monarchy of Christ. *Severall Proceedings* blended fact with fiction. It described her appearance and praised her 'excellent words and well placed'. But when it came to what she actually said, it changed the meaning entirely, claiming she had seen that God wished to keep the Protector close to him, as he had always done. *Mercurius Politicus*, on the other hand, with Marchamont Nedham at the tiller, for the time being made no mention of the Whitehall prophetess at all.[3]

❦ ❦ ❦

Marchamont Nedham had broadened his range during the torrid year of the Nominated Assembly. He remained the undisputed master of journalism and continued to act as an apologist for the regime through its changing forms, managing to turn out a detailed justification for the new Protectorate just weeks into its existence. He now turned his hand to espionage. He had no fondness for religious zealots and his talent for gathering information, and desire to please his masters, had caused him to offer his services. On 7 February 1654, a fortnight after Anna Trapnel recovered from her Whitehall trance, Nedham left the printing house at the west end of Thames Street and set off eastwards. All Hallows the Great stood at the long street's eastern end and here he joined the congregation, 'wishing to know how the pulse beats'. He reported back directly to the new Lord Protector on what he saw. A week earlier John Simpson and Christopher Feake had been imprisoned, their provocative sermons having finally caused the regime to act. Nedham found All Hallows 'a dull assembly' without them. Nonetheless, he recommended it be disbanded, for though it was 'but a confluence of silly wretches' their continued meeting was damaging to Cromwell's reputation, particularly with diplomats. The subject he was really trying to gain intelligence on, however, was Anna Trapnel.

The news that he came away with was startling. That Anna's words had been recorded was well known, and Nedham caught a glimpse of the bundle of transcripts in the hands of one of the congregation. It was no surprise to him that they intended to have these published – he had already provided the Protector with a sheaf of discrediting documents about the Fifth Monarchists with a recommendation that these also be quickly printed. What was new was what more was planned. A scheme was in formation to send Anna Trapnel out into the country to proclaim her visions, 'which are desperate against your person, family, children, friends and the government', 'viva voce'.[4]

❦ ❦ ❦

The idea came, it seems, from two men, neither of whom had known about Anna until the Whitehall trance made her famous. Robert Bennett and Francis Langdon were both army officers and Cornish members of the Nominated Assembly.[5] Bennett was a respected county figure who would serve as an MP in all the main parliamentary bodies of the 1650s, a significant landowner and a committed Baptist and millenarian. Langdon was a slighter figure but clearly also bitterly disappointed by the end of the Nominated Assembly. Their notion was to ask Anna to come to Cornwall so that she could share with the unenlightened people the extraordinary experiences God had given her. Anna was horrified. To leave London and part from her comrades at All Hallows – 'so dear to me and ... written in my heart' – and to do so in the company of perfect strangers, was unthinkable. She refused point blank and went home. But the following night she was haunted by the thought that she was failing in her calling. In the dark she voiced her doubts, and there came back the words '... *don't fear to go to Cornwall, though it be a long journey*, said the Lord, *for I will go with thee*'. The next day she agreed.[6]

Whether Anna entirely grasped the political motives of those around her – who wished to use her to undermine Cromwell and the new Protectorate – is not clear. She may have been too naive to see them. More likely, perhaps, she was aware of them, but they were simply eclipsed by the strength of her belief that it was her mission to recount her experiences. Over the days that followed she struggled with her growing apprehension at the prospect of the journey. It was to take her more than 300 miles from London and its hinterland, which was all she had ever known, with people and to places which were completely foreign to her. She travelled to Hillingdon to see her friends and seek their counsel, and then rode out to Windsor Castle where she was able to speak to the imprisoned Fifth Monarchist leaders, John Simpson and Christopher Feake. Their fortitude in prison, 'their courage for King Jesus', gave her strength. The night before she was due to depart she spent in prayer and comradeship with six close women friends from the All Hallows congregation. The following morning, Monday 6 March, she travelled by river to Westminster, where as public a departure as possible had been arranged. From an inn on King Street itself, yards from Whitehall Palace, the coach set out, waved off by a large crowd. One onlooker remarked that, had he known about it, he would have alerted the new Council of State, for Anna Trapnel was about to corrupt the whole country.[7]

❦ ❦ ❦

Aware of Anna Trapnel's preference for the company of women, her hosts had made the travel arrangements with care. The first leg of the journey Robert Bennett took responsibility for himself. While he shared a good deal of Anna's religious outlook, he was socially very much her superior: a member of the county gentry, educated, like her friend the minister of St John's Hillingdon, at Exeter College, Oxford. To put his clearly anxious guest at her ease he brought with him in the coach his daughter and a number of servants. The experience of days of travel on England's dirt roads, muddy and bumpy as they would have been in early March, was not a comfortable one. Anna suffered much from the jolting and rattling of the coach as they trundled west, stopping at Salisbury on their second night and reaching Exeter on the fifth. But conversation was possible and Anna began to relax a little. She found Robert Bennett to be less imperious a host than she might have feared. As one of the architects of the Nominated Assembly – he had helped Cromwell choose its members – he was part of the national political elite. But he was also an honest man with obvious integrity who had been robbed of his young wife and unborn child by the violence of the civil war. He asked Anna gently and solicitously about her trances, and encouraged her to talk freely about them. She warmed to him, as 'he manifested much kindness to me as we journeyed in company together, and charged his daughter to be very tenderly careful of me'. At Exeter, where they stopped for several nights, the party changed. Anna bade a sorry farewell to the Bennetts, and passed into the company of Francis Langdon, his wife and servants, whose house was almost a hundred miles further west. This second leg of the voyage was harder than the first. The company was new and less sympathetic, the landscape wilder and more hostile and much of the travelling now on horseback. The 'dangerous rocky places' that glowered around them as they traversed the bleak moorland of Dartmoor seemed a foreboding metaphor of the journey that was now nearing its end.[8]

Things did not improve when they finally arrived. At Francis Langdon's home, a rural manor house a few miles north of Truro, a crowd of his county friends had been gathered to meet this famous London visionary. With little time to recover or compose herself after thirteen days' travelling, Anna was expected to appear before them. She shrank from the scrutiny and the scepticism she knew awaited her. Langdon, who lacked Bennett's talent for coaxing and reassuring, dispatched a manservant into the garden to retrieve her. When she demurred, the man responded threateningly that 'it may be they would not take it well if I did not come and sit in the room with him'. With great reluctance she was persuaded to come into the house. The results were predictably unsatisfactory. She was faced with a group of strangers from a class and locality quite different to her own who regarded her with 'sour countenances and girding expressions'. They in turn were presented with an ordinary looking and uncommunicative 34-year-old working-class woman from the east end of London. They started to make disparaging remarks well within her earshot and the evening ended badly.[9]

The days that followed were to be mixed ones for Anna. On the one hand she was utterly isolated, 300 miles from home and with almost no control over her own movements. Naturally shy and self-contained she had no appetite for being gawped at and asked prying questions. On the other, the 'very sour' reception she had received began slowly to sweeten. While those who were expecting a powerful and charismatic prophetess were, on first encounter, disappointed, her modesty, dignity and absolute sincerity had gradual force. As another observer would remark later in the year, it was easy to dismiss her as a fraud until you actually met her – when the possibility became much more real that she might indeed be God's handmaiden. In the market town of Truro, nestled on the Fal estuary, she attended a lecture and then, after dinner at one Mrs Hill's house, townspeople crowded in to see her. Some came in rapt awe, others to stare and some to try to catch her out. Langdon instructed her to speak to them, which, with great hesitation, she started to do, addressing herself at first only to him. But as she spoke she grew in confidence and began to recount the story of her life, including her various visionary episodes. In revisiting these the emotional energy mounted within her and she broke into spontaneous singing and prayer. Come the evening she was entranced, and had to be carried from the room, insensible, in the chair on which she sat. The company was deeply impressed and whispered in hushed respect as she was taken out. But among them were those who, having witnessed the effect she was having, had made up their minds that she must be stopped.[10]

❦ ❦ ❦

While Anna Trapnel was sharing her visions with the people of Truro, in London Oliver Cromwell and his colleagues were engaged upon their own endeavours also in the face of a mixed reception. When Cromwell had sworn his inauguration oath as Lord Protector in Westminster Hall, it followed the reading of a written constitution for the new regime known as the 'Instrument of Government'. The first article stated that 'the Supreme Legislative Authority of the Commonwealth of England, Scotland, and Ireland, and the Dominions thereunto belonging, shall be and reside in one Person, and the People assembled in Parliament'. The document had been drawn up with considerable care in the autumn of 1653 by a small cabal of army officers, led by the talented soldier Major General John Lambert, who were determined to put an end to the Nominated Assembly. Cromwell was head of state, and the republic was no more, but this was to be a mixed monarchy: he could do little without the consent of a powerful Council of State, on which they sat, and legislation required the agreement of Parliament. Care was taken that this, England's first written constitution, should guard against the mishaps of the last few years. Parliament was to be elected (there was no more talk of 'nomination') and a new voting franchise and distribution of MPs was set out, including representation for Scotland and Ireland, making this the first ever British Parliament. It was to meet at least every three years and not to be adjourned (unless on its own initiative) for the first five months of any sitting. However, there was a catch.

This new parliament was not to be elected until September. In the intervening nine months, the Lord Protector and his Council were to have the freedom to pass 'ordinances' for the public good. This was a provision they put to speedy and effective use.[11]

The thing that Oliver Cromwell cared about above all was the religious settlement of the kingdom. The wording of the Instrument of Government had been broad. While there was to continue to be a national church, religious toleration was to be extended to all Protestants with the exception of those who insisted on bishops and those who were judged 'licentious'. The explicit stipulation that those who 'profess Faith in God by Jesus Christ, (though differing in Judgment from the Doctrine, Worship or Discipline publickly held forth)' were to be allowed to worship in peace was remarkable, and represented religious toleration on a scale never before seen in England. Cromwell's own instinct was broader still and his desire for there to be peaceful co-existence between people of a variety of different religious persuasions was ever present. He had reportedly exclaimed to one of the committee considering religion the year before that 'I had rather that Mahometanism were permitted amongst us than that one of God's children should be persecuted'. But while this was Cromwell's own inclination, the reality of religion in England and Wales existed not in Westminster or Whitehall but in the 9,000 or so parishes throughout the country.

The mass expulsions of clergymen in the mid-1640s, which had seen perhaps up to a third of all parishes lose their ministers, had brought with it the significant problem of who was to take their place. There were those, like Anna Trapnel's friend, the minister of St John's Hillingdon, who had been willing and able to step in, both meeting the criteria of supporting the new national Presbyterian church and the republic, and demonstrating the pastoral qualities required of a parish priest. In Cornwall, where Puritanism was not especially well-developed before the war, and which was hardly in the thick of things geographically or politically, the task of filling the vacant parishes was particularly challenging. The county had some 200 parishes from which more than eighty clerics were removed, leaving many people with no one at all to oversee religion and conduct parish life in their locality. The minister of

Truro remarked despondently in 1655 that 'many parishes are destitute of ministers, five or six together, because there is not a competence for a Godly one'. The problem was made no less intractable by the fact that, amid all the recent changes, tithes, the taxes from which the clergy's wages were paid were proving hard to collect. As a result the new Presbyterian Church of England was struggling. It was all very well for the government in London, and the new Protector, to wish both to maintain a national church to ensure order and stability and to allow broad toleration, but this made the task of parish clergy all the more difficult. Such a threadbare ministry was a gift to the recruiting sergeants of the new sects, and as Anna Trapnel was soon to discover, the tolerationist attitude of many of the London government was a far cry from that of the parish clergy on the religious front line.[12]

※ ※ ※

What followed Anna Trapnel's Truro trance was a swiftly orchestrated legal lynching. The organizer of the campaign to crush Anna Trapnel was the parish minister of St Ives some 25 miles away. Leonard Welstead began lobbying the civil authorities to intervene as soon as he heard of her arrival, and word was put about among his friends and colleagues that she was a dangerous imposter inciting disorder among the citizens of Cornwall. Anna's patron Robert Bennett, though a committed Baptist, acted with generosity and compassion in protecting erstwhile Anglican clergymen from persecution, but the same could not be said of Leonard Welstead. Furthermore, he saw the very existence of the 'prophetess' as destructive, presumably believing, in Anna's words, that 'the people would be drawn away if the rulers did not take some course with me'. Anna learned of the warrant for her arrest while she was paying a second visit to Mrs Hill in Truro. It struck at her core. Having lived a socially respectable and personally virtuous life, the prospect of being taken to court accused of a crime in this strange place was terrifying. She was overcome, God made 'his rivers flow' and she fell into a new trance.[13]

The following day, as Anna lay still insensible, a constable arrived with the JPs' order for her arrest. He was rebuffed by her supporters and a delegation sent back to protest. Anna was no rabble-rousing vagrant, they were told, but the honoured guest of a local dignitary. But Leonard Welstead and his cronies were not to be dissuaded. It was a measure of the head of steam that had been built up against Anna that Justice Launce came in person, accompanied by the relentless Welstead, determined to raise her from her 'trance'. It was a nasty encounter. Launce and Welstead pushed Mrs Hill's servants aside and mounted the stairs with their henchmen shouting 'Witch!' Here in the room where Anna lay the group of men stood over her limp body, scoffed that she was clearly acting and ordered the constable to rouse her. The officer stepped forward, pulled out her pillow, pinched her nostrils and pushed open her eyelids to try to elicit a response. Anna was absolutely motionless. Welstead blustered that 'a whip will fetch her up' but, disconcerted by her strange stillness, retreated.[14]

That night Anna awoke and the following day, Friday 7 April, she appeared before the Truro Sessions of the Peace. The irony was that as news of the failed attempted arrest began to spread, so did public interest in her fate. When she walked down Boscawen Street, the town's broad central thoroughfare, with a constable at her side, a crowd of people started following her, some in solidarity, some taunting her as she walked. The biblical overtones of the captive Christian being mocked added to her growing lustre and gave Anna herself a new certainty. The Truro Sessions House was fuller than it had ever been known to be as she took her low seat before the looming group of Justices on their railed-off dais. Anna was composed, feeling Christ to be by her side. She was accused of three crimes: being a vagrant, orchestrating unlawful meetings of evil intent and speaking against the government. She pleaded 'not guilty' to all three, looking her accusers steadily in the face as she did so. The foreman of the jury, whose hostility to nonconformists would become famous, declared that she should be referred up to the next Quarter Sessions where crimes of greater seriousness were tried.

Matters should have stopped there, but the Justices did not wish to let this chance pass to crush this ungovernable woman. The book detailing her Whitehall prophecies, which had now been printed and distributed, was waved before her. She was asked what she had to say for herself and who had brought her to Cornwall. In what followed Anna Trapnel was remarkable. She surprised herself with her self-assurance and dexterity, as she parried deftly each thrust from this hostile trio. She was pressed repeatedly on why she was in Cornwall when she had no lands or interests there. Her reply was serious yet airy: she was a single person, she could visit her friends where she pleased. When asked again who had 'moved' her to come, she responded unblinkingly that it had been God. The Justices started to become irate and spoke over one another, allowing Anna to request calmly that they should speak one at a time. It was then asserted angrily that she had been pretending to be in a trance the previous night, and that two witnesses would now testify to that effect. But of the women who were then proudly called forth, one, it emerged, had failed to appear and the other, when she was reminded of the consequences of lying under oath, ran from the building. At this a soldier standing guard shot a sideways glance and let out an involuntary laugh. One of the Justices exploded, shouting, 'He laughed at court' and had him ejected. Anna, embold-ened, ventured, with an uncharacteristic tinge of humour: 'Scripture speaks of such who make a man an offender for a word, but you make a man an offender for a look.' The Justices now looked understandably 'very willing to be gone'. As they broke up she stated, with powerful gravitas, that a time was coming when real Judgement would be meted out and 'you will hardly be able to give an account for this day's work'.

Outside the Sessions House Anna was given a rapturous reception. Her commanding performance in the court room, and the sight of a respectable, articulate and collected single woman seeing off the domi-nant middle rank of county authority had decided many waverers. The rumours that she was a witch were obviously false: 'she speaks many good words, which the witches could not.' She was what she claimed to be.[15]

Anna's Truro victory would be short-lived. Leonard Welstead and his friends saw now that their actions had only made things worse. If Anna were to remain in Cornwall until her Quarter Sessions appearance in August there was no saying how her influence might grow. A message was dispatched to London stating unequivocally that she was 'aspersing the government'. An order for her to be apprehended by the deputy governor of Pendennis Castle, which commanded the mouth of the Fal estuary, was dispatched from the Council of State by return. Ten days after the Sessions of the Peace, soldiers arrived at Francis Langdon's house and Anna was taken. Once she had recovered from the initial shock, she remarked to her host that at least she would be going home to London, and when she got there she would tell them about the place she regarded as 'Cornhell in the West'.[16]

❦ ❦ ❦

The new Lord Protector Oliver Cromwell and his Council of State were well aware that the window of opportunity they had to do things before the meeting of a new parliament in September 1654 was short. In the preceding nine months an accelerated programme of initiatives was raced through. These were in part Cromwell's own projects and in part what could be agreed between the Protector and his Council of State in the time they had. They expressed a desire for stability and certainty, for compromise and for social reform that would right glaring injustices. The problem of parishes without ministers was to be addressed by a new commission overseeing the process of vetting people for these positions. The sub-committee for Cornwall would include both the Justices who had presided over Anna Trapnel's Truro hearing and her sponsor, Robert Bennett. The conquest of Scotland was to be regularized by a formal union between the two countries, and the expensive war with the Dutch was to be brought to an end. Greater integration between old opponents was to be brought about by the repeal of the 'Engagement', the act passed by the Rump Parliament that had required all men to swear an oath of fealty to the regime. From now on no such ideological purity was to be required. The past had passed. Society was to be improved. New arrangements were put in place to ensure the roads, bridges and pavements of the country were properly maintained, for the regulation of London hackney carriages, and steps were taken towards establishing a public postal service. Duelling and cockfighting were to be banned as being accompanied by 'Gaming, Drinking, Swearing, Quarreling, and other dissolute Practices, to the Dishonor of God, and do often produce the ruine of Persons and their Families', and new arrangements were to be put in place for the care of lunatics. Some of this had begun under the Nominated Assembly, but there was clear desire now to ensure that momentum for this sort of reform was not lost. All this progress notwithstanding, it was far from certain whether it would be enough to distract the newly elected parliament from the military coup that had dispatched their predecessor and the drastic change in the constitution that had been effected entirely without them.[17]

❦ ❦ ❦

The journey which brought Anna Trapnel back to London from Cornwall took far longer than that which had taken her there. She was transported from Truro to Pendennis Castle at the mouth of the Fal estuary and there put into the hands of Captain John Fox. Adverse winds and the shortage of men and vessels meant it would be five weeks before she was eventually put onto a ship bound for Portsmouth. The journey did nothing to improve her opinion of Cornwall. The sea was frighteningly rough, the Cornish girl who had been sent with her as a maid was violently sick and Anna was thrown so suddenly by the swell that she injured her leg. But unpleasant as it was, worse was to come. For despite the great discomfort, she had been assigned the master's cabin and was treated by the crew with courtesy and dignity. When she reached London, she was lodged in some rooms in Covent Garden, waiting daily for her summons to appear before the Council of State. But none arrived. Then late one night a dreadful order was brought, signed by the new President of the Council of State, Henry Lawrence: she was to be taken to Bridewell.[18]

For a respectable woman of modest but independent means such as Anna Trapnel, even the idea of being incarcerated in Bridewell prison was shocking. Like Newgate, Bridewell was a place of detention for those facing trial, and among the inmates in the women's section of the prison were vagrants, debtors, thieves and prostitutes. The deep shame of being sent here jostled in Anna's heart with the belief that to suffer in this way was to truly fulfil her role as one of God's chosen people. As she was signed in just before midnight in early May the hard-bitten Matron, learning she was a religious prisoner, remarked disgustedly that she already had 'a company of ranting sluts like you' in her charge. The trouble was that some of the more outrageous religious radicals had, by their scandalous behaviour, thoroughly discredited the more thoughtful and credible nonconformists like Anna. The Matron asked her if she knew Mrs Cook, one such fanatic who had just been arrested after streaking stark naked through Westminster Abbey claiming to be the queen of Heaven.

Anna spent eight weeks a prisoner in Bridewell. Everything about it appalled her: the filthy stench, the swarms of rats, the 'harlots and thieves' she had for company. She was tortured by the thought of what her mother would have said if she could have seen her, and by the vision of the rejection and disdain she would experience when released. The anticipation of being pointed at in the street with jeers – 'there goes a Bridewell bird' – was almost unbearable. But again she persevered, discovering a strength that she did not know she had. Her female friends rallied to her, visiting her daily, bringing herbs and flowers to mask the smell, securing a copy of the warrant for her detention to prove to the Matron that it did not state any crime, simply that she was to be imprisoned. Her gentle and decent character wore a way into the Matron's cold heart, and soon her friend Ursula was permitted to stay in the prison as her companion. As the weeks went by the Matron was won over and became 'very loving and respectful' towards this unusual inmate.[19]

Then, on 26 July, the order finally came. It contained neither a charge, nor a summons to the Council of State. It was instead an order for her release. When the Keeper of the Prison told her the news, Anna was indignant, 'I told him they should fetch me out that put me in; had they put me among thieves and whores and now did they send for me without acknowledging the reproach they had brought upon me?' He shrugged and she had little choice but to acquiesce. Whatever her persecutors in Cornwall accused her of, the London government had clearly in the end decided to disregard. She walked out of Bridewell in the warm summer sun and made her way back east to the streets and the friends that were her home.[20]

❦ ❦ ❦

For Anna Trapnel and her Fifth Monarchist friends, as for John Bradshaw and the revolutionary corps of 1649, the rise of the Protectorate was a bitter betrayal. They each now set themselves against that which they had once looked to with such hope. Anna for her part had, until the events of 1654, been a single woman who heard God's voice. She had not been a campaigner or an activist, but a troubled person searching for certainty. She left Bridewell and the trials, injustices and indignities of the previous year changed. She would not slip back into quiet obscurity. Though the Fifth Monarchists' brief brush with power and influence had come and gone with the Nominated Assembly, Anna would henceforth devote herself to telling the truths that she now felt so strongly. She finished her detailed account of her experiences in Cornwall for publication just as the First Protectorate Parliament was about to meet. In it she contrasted the godliness of her supporters with the wealth and spoils on which, she claimed, Oliver Cromwell and his cronies now feasted: 'you cry to the Lord, and not for earthly palaces, nor Whitehall garden walks, nor kitchen-belly-cheer, nor lardery-dainties, not banquet sweetmeats, nor Council-robes, nor Parliament tithes, nor Emperor advancement, nor great attendance, nor for Colonels' and Captains' silken buff, and garnished spangled coats and gilded cloaks and brave London and country houses ...' She and her fellow Fifth Monarchists were in no doubt that 'This power and the old monarchie are one and the same'. No longer 'a silly nothing creature' who had gazed in despair into the Hackney well, she was now an agitator. In her visions and songs in the years to come God was a father figure no more: he was a husband and she 'Christ's beloved wife'. She had finally fulfilled her aunt's call for her to seek to be married to Christ. She travelled freely, visiting Cornwall at length again in 1656, and sang out her prophecies with little doubt or qualification: 'The voice and spirit hath made a league / against Cromwell and his men / never to leave its witness till / it hath broken all of them.'[21]

❦ ❦ ❦

In early February 1655, exactly a year after Anna had set off for Cornwall, a group of Fifth Monarchists came to Whitehall to meet Oliver Cromwell and immediately afterwards published an account of their experience. There were many women in their party; Anna herself may have been among them. Cromwell remained personally tolerant of their movement – despite their vocal campaign against him. Indeed (according to them) he conceded that 'I do know you have truths of Christ in you'. When they complained that there was not the religious freedom he had promised, Cromwell replied with fierce frustration, 'I tell you there was never such liberty of conscience, no, never such liberty since the dayes of Antichrist as is now, for may not men preach and pray what they will?' But the Fifth Monarchists were not satisfied for theirs was a political as well as a religious fight. Why, their spokesman John Rogers asked, were their members imprisoned without charge and trial? They had resisted lawful authority, they were told in reply. At this the Fifth Monarchists bridled. One retorted: 'We desire to be satisfied by what Rule you resisted the King, and warred against him and his adherents and destroyed the Government before, seeing they too were accounted a lawful authority'. Cromwell gave his stock answer at weary length: he had fought a war of self-defence against a king who had assumed absolute power. But this rabble of religious radicals would not be fobbed off. One of their number posed the fundamental question: 'And is not this Arbitrary? And is not your Power, with the Armies, Absolute? To break up Parliaments, and do what you will?'

To this towering question, which cast its black shadow over the whole edifice of the new 'Protectorate', Oliver Cromwell could give no answer.[22]

Eleven

Plough and Go to Market

❦❦❦❦❦❦❦❦❦❦❦❦❦❦❦❦❦❦❦

F or the oystermen who heaved their baskets across the endless sands
of Hunstanton at low tide in the autumn of 1653, the lean, angular
figure of Sir Hamon L'Estrange was a familiar sight. The shock of grey
hair which sprang almost vertically from his brow and his elegant dress
made him unmistakable (Colour plate 5). The old knight had lived on
his ancestral lands on the very northwestern tip of Norfolk for all of his
seven decades and knew their every mill and marsh, common and creek.
He attended to each tick and tock of the seasons' change with a fascina-
tion that age had done nothing to diminish. The labours of the seals
hauling themselves ashore to calve, the spinning of the smallest spider
among the sedge and the faintest call of an unfamiliar bird enthralled
him still. As October turned to November the migratory songbirds
swooped over Hunstanton's cliff, before gliding down to feed on the tiny
orange berries of the dune-top thorn bushes. From the icy north clouds
of grey geese and waders flapped thickly in, arriving to winter on the
L'Estranges' saturated salt marshes.[1]

Alice L'Estrange, by contrast, was not given to trying to unravel the
mysteries of the world (Colour plate 6). While her husband gazed at
their surroundings, or contemplated the intellectual landscapes
contained within the thousands of books of his library, she was busy
with more immediate concerns. For her autumn was a time for equip-

ping the household for the winter and laying the ground for the growing season to come. She moved purposefully between the larders and dairy herd, the dovecot and the barns. Under her watchful eye the ploughmen steered their heavy instruments across Hunstanton's stubbled soil and the taskers beat the summer barley on the estate's threshing floors.[2]

The L'Estranges were as ancient a family as Norfolk knew, they had farmed here, and christened their sons Hamon, since soon after the Conquest. Their seat, Hunstanton Hall, was a crenellated brick mansion on a moated platform. Improvements made by Sir Hamon and Lady Alice before the war had created spacious new accommodation which they shared with their eldest son and his young family. Nicholas (Sir Nicholas thanks to the baronetcy his father had purchased) and his thoughtful wife Anne had eight sons and one daughter (See family tree, page 365). While Little Ham and Nick had already passed out of their teens, their youngest, Thomas, was just 2 years old. The gently undulating landscape that stretched south from the house was enclosed as a park, specked with stately oaks and grazed by deer. To the north lay the church and village of Hunstanton, a cluster of low brick and rust-

Hunstanton Hall, Norfolk. Home to the L'Estranges since the Middle Ages. The importance of land and property to the gentry was paramount, and over half of gentry families had kept out of the civil war altogether rather than put them at risk.

coloured carrstone houses, with the sails of the occasional windmill breaking the skyline. Beyond the houses, past the drying nets, were the marshes, the dunes and the vast pale-sand beaches of the Norfolk coast.[3]

The weeks before Christmas were always busy ones for Alice L'Estrange. She might now be in her late sixties but she remained the mainstay of the lives of the family she had borne. Ever since her marriage at 17, in the last year of Queen Elizabeth's reign, she had striven to bring order and prosperity to her husband's impoverished estate. Sir Hamon was head of the oldest gentry family in Norfolk but he had been orphaned at 8 and his had been an inheritance of negligence and mismanagement. Alice had been no heiress, but she had proved herself to be valuable 'above pearls'. She brought to her husband's unpromising patrimony remarkable ability as an estate manager, an accountant and a businesswoman. Over the decades she had transformed Hunstanton through careful investment and tremendous care of every detail of their operation. As their family grew so did the profits, and her ability to sustain their tastes for handsome and hospitable living. Her husband and sons all had talents, but none had the unremitting application to dairy yields and crop rotation, sheep prices and wool weight with which Alice slowly rebuilt the family's fortune.[4]

Every year as December approached Lady Alice would prepare for Christmas – notwithstanding the welter of Westminster prohibitions of the church feast. The Puritan regime in London might outlaw religious festivals and even public entertainments, but they could do nothing whatsoever about what went on in people's homes. Butter and cheese, mutton, beef and chicken Alice could draw from the L'Estranges' own lands. Other seasonal delicacies came from far further afield, among them the raisins and figs, nutmeg and cinnamon, cloves and mace which gave her Christmas pies and puddings their exotic taste. Imported wines could be had in King's Lynn where the town's principal street, Winegate, was fringed with brick-vaulted emporia that backed onto the docks. Here Hunstanton Hall was supplied with claret from Bordeaux and 'sack', white wine from the Canary Islands. As Lady Alice applied herself to her preparations in November 1653, there was an added sense of anticipation. This year, for the first time in a decade, she would have her whole family about her. For her wayward third son had finally returned.[5]

The civil war had bitten hard into the prosperity that Alice L'Estrange had so painstakingly accumulated. Before the war Sir Hamon had, like generations of his forebears, been a prominent figure in the government of the county, as an MP, a Justice of the Peace and captain of the local militia. He was no lover of Charles I's policies, and he disapproved of Archbishop Laud's ceremonialism, but when war came he was only ever going to side with his sovereign. In 1643 a faction of King's Lynn's citizens had seized the town in the name of the King and declared Sir Hamon their military governor. After three weeks' siege, in which Sir Hamon commanded within and the Cambridgeshire officer Oliver Cromwell attacked from without, the town had surrendered.[6]

The impact of this episode had been profound. While Sir Hamon was in Lynn, the parliamentary soldiers had helped themselves to the Hunstanton livestock and produce. Over 1,500 sheep, numerous horses and the estate's entire crop of grain were taken. Added to this, and the sequestration of the Hunstanton estates that followed, Lynn's two parliamentarian MPs had managed to secure agreement from London that Sir Hamon should personally reimburse the town's citizens for damages to their property during the siege. This brought forth a never-ending list of claims for compensation which seemed to far exceed actual losses. To make matters worse, as his father was trying to negotiate the return of the family's sequestered lands, their third son, Roger, mounted an ill-advised attempt to bribe some Lynn townspeople into letting the royalists back in. He was betrayed immediately to the town's parliamentary governor, Valentine Walton, and found himself condemned to death for spying. A lucky escape from Newgate had allowed Roger to flee to the Continent where, for five years, he had lived on the annual allowance that his mother had issued out of the Hunstanton coffers.[7]

The decade since the siege of Lynn had been hard. Alice L'Estrange had, field by field, rebuilt the family's fortunes. Friends and relations – her son-in-law Sir William Spring, her cousins the Calthorpes – had helped with loans which she gradually repaid, and her own careful management of the estate before the war had stood them in good stead. She bore the fines and taxes exacted by central government with impressive calm, but what provoked her fury were the claims for compensation from citizens of Lynn, which she saw as blatant opportunism. The charges claimed ranged from the burning of a single haystack to an immense bill for rebuilding the Magdalen alms-houses in Gaywood on the town's outskirts. For Lady Alice the double injustice was searing. She complained bitterly of 'the unjust and tirannical oppression of Mr Toll and other of his faction in Linne concerning the siege'. But she had no choice but to pay up.[8]

❦ ❦ ❦

Christmas 1653 at Hunstanton Hall was a hearty affair. From the wealthy wool town of Lavenham in Suffolk, Sir Hamon and Lady Alice's formidable daughter Elizabeth, wife of Sir William Spring, returned to her childhood home for a festive visit. Elizabeth's favourite brother, the L'Estranges' second son, another Hamon, lived with his family only a mile or so from Hunstanton on one of the estate farms at Ringstead. And now the black sheep, Roger, had returned, too. During the short days, when shafts of low sunlight shot almost horizontally across the marshes, the L'Estrange men went wildfowling. Taking down the guns from the parlour wall they set out in the thin wintry light to shoot woodcock and snipe, partridge and duck. On the clifftop they plied the Hall's new hawking nets in the hope of snaring a marsh harrier, peregrine falcon or some other bird of prey, which might then be trained as a hunter itself. While the men were wildfowling the Hunstanton women oversaw other tasks, including the distribution of beef to the poor of the parishes of Hunstanton and Sedgeford. As the daylight faded, the leaded windows of the hall blazed with light from the candles that Lady Alice had acquired in quantities from Lynn a fortnight before.

At Christmas the cheese and fish which the L'Estranges often dined on were set aside and instead roast beef and turkey, venison and goose were served in quantities, enriched with capers and olives, sugar and spices. New Year's gifts were given, haunches of venison and cuts of veal were dispatched in the hands of retainers to gentry neighbours and civic worthies. At home Sir Hamon presented seasonal tips to his servants, several pounds each to his older grandsons and a few shillings to the littlest boys. The old man might have been ageing, and his health had not been good, but he was still beautifully dressed. A new 'Spanish' suit had been made for his thin frame that winter, with drawers, waistcoast and trimmings all in scarlet 'of the best dye'. Music was an essential feature of most English Christmases. Anne L'Estrange's sister, Catherine Calthorpe, always brought the Thetford fiddlers to her house at East Barsham. The L'Estranges, too, sometimes hired in players, but this year they had no need. The L'Estrange men were all accomplished musi-

The Vindication of Christmas (1653). The abolition of the church festival of Christmas was confirmed by the English parliament as early as the mid-1640s. Traditional celebrations continued throughout the 1650s regardless; here Father Christmas is shunned by the urban elite but welcomed by ordinary country people.

cians: Sir Hamon, Roger and little John in particular excelled at the viol. With their instruments clasped between their knees, three generations of L'Estrange men drew their bows back and forth across the strings, filling the oak-panelled parlours of Hunstanton Hall with rich, melodious music.[9]

The L'Estranges of Hunstanton Hall were not alone in celebrating the Christmas of 1653. Families up and down the country gathered to mark the ancient feast. The reality was that the Puritan government's attempt to stamp out the festivities of the church year had been largely unsuccessful. Christmas, along with Easter and Whitsun, had been abolished as church festivals five years earlier, partly because the only holy day mentioned in the Bible was the Sabbath, and partly out of disapproval of the drinking and indulgence they involved. But removing the church services had done little to diminish the entertaining and eating, card playing and carol singing that characterized English Christmas celebrations. A pamphlet published in London in 1653 summed up the situation vividly: the bearded figure of Father Christmas arriving in England only to be turned away by the great men of London. But when he ventured out of the capital into the frosty villages of the countryside he was welcomed warmly. Country people, families of farmers and yeomen, beckoned him in to join them eating meat and roast apples, singing carols, dancing, drinking and playing festive games.[10]

🏵 🏵 🏵

Amid the bustle and noise of Christmas Sir Hamon L'Estrange slipped away from his relatives to the quiet of his study. Here he was involved in a fascinating correspondence with the distinguished writer and physician Thomas Browne of Norwich. He had originally contacted the medic about one of his many ailments – which had long kept him in near-daily correspondence with his Fakenham doctor – but had become involved in a much fuller exchange with Browne about natural history. Browne's recent book *Pseudodoxia Epidemica* (or *Vulgar Errors*) was a remarkable analysis of popular myths and superstitions which sought to separate fact from fiction. Sir Hamon had been preparing a detailed set of comments and addenda. Doing so caused him to cast his mind back over the incidents and experience of his long life. He described the seal that had been caught in a fisherman's net during his boyhood and how it had lived for some time in the moat of Hunstanton Hall, answering to the name 'Ruff' and causing the pike to throw themselves onto the banks in terror. He remembered the great whale cast up on Hunstanton beach in 1626, and the detailed measurements and observations he had made of it, and he relived the day he had been ushered into a London house to see an exotic 'great fowle' – nothing less than a live dodo, one of the very last to be seen in Europe.

The other memory that Sir Hamon recalled for Thomas Browne that January was the mystery of his cliffs. At Hunstanton as the coast turned sharply south into the great inlet of the Wash, the otherwise low-lying Norfolk terrain rose for about a mile into cliffs of a strange composite geology. Here, Sir Hamon explained, very hard frosts occasionally sent slices of the rock face plummeting down onto the beach below. When they did so they revealed something extraordinary: 'excrecencyes' buried deep within the cliff itself. When these were picked out from the body of the rock with a sharp iron tool they were clearly identifiable as shells. How seashells of unfamiliar size and shape could possibly have found their way into hard stone 40 feet above the shore baffled him, 'I know not how to quiet my thoughts otherwise then with an opinion that they are the exertful froliques and enigmas of nature whereof to pose and amuse man in the highest acme and insight of his understanding'.[11]

For the L'Estrange family, as for so many up and down the kingdom, London and its doings was far away, and life since the revolution had mostly been one of simply getting on. After the siege of Lynn, Sir Hamon had laboured hard to get the punitive terms against his family overturned, making repeated trips to the capital to lobby those in power and having a series of petitions presented at the House of Commons. For a while he and Lady Alice were readying themselves for further conflict: in the first year of the Commonwealth she had laid in arms – pistols and powder flasks – in case of more fighting. But time had passed. In April 1650 the L'Estrange men had sworn the 'Engagement', the oath of loyalty to the new regime, and once they finally regained possession of their lands they seem to have determined to live a quiet life. Sir Hamon had applied himself with characteristic vim to his writing. This took the form, mostly, of fulsome and learned commentaries on the work of others, adding copious additional evidence or detailed analytical refutation. Lady Alice concentrated on consolidating their financial position: juggling their debts, draining marshy ground for crops and continuing her programme of rethatching in turn each of the estate's great barns.[12]

While Sir Hamon retreated to his study in January 1654, Lady Alice was not one for foregoing company. Her meticulous bookkeeping and her advancing age might have implied a severe or joyless figure. The opposite was true. She had a wicked and downright dirty sense of humour, and enjoyed nothing more than sharing funny stories and bawdy jokes. She was practical and unpretentious and could often be found in the Hunstanton larder, sleeves rolled up, skinning rabbits or sewing and dressing the wounds of injured villagers. Her children adored her and she was a kind and generous grandmother, buying bows and arrows, shuttlecocks and tennis balls for their entertainment. Her very age was itself a subject of humour. She loved the story of Lady Peyton, on marrying in her late middle age, being convinced she was soon to have a brood of children, and of deaf old Mrs Thurlow whose jocular host offered a glass of sack on condition she sleep with him, replying spryly that 'your worshipp knows what's good (meaning only the sacke) for an old woman'. She had been raised the daughter of the L'Estrange family lawyer in Sedgeford just a few miles from Hunstanton and hers was a firmly country perspective. She had visited London on more than one occasion before the war, and delighted in the beautiful things that could be bought there, but she had no appetite for metropolitan living. The stories that she told were not of high culture or intellectual endeavours but affectionate tales of the ordinary working people of Norfolk. Hers was an outlook expressed perfectly in the comment by a family friend, retold with approval at Hunstanton Hall, that London would be 'a marvelous fine sweet place ... if it stood but in the country'.[13]

In some ways life at Hunstanton had changed remarkably little with the seismic political shifts of the last decade. Norfolk had escaped most of the extremes of the civil war. Instead of being involved in county government Sir Hamon was now living a life of enforced leisure. The relentless taxation required to maintain the army and fight the Scottish, Irish and Dutch campaigns emptied their coffers as it did all those whose wealth met the threshold – direct taxes were now some ten times higher than when the L'Estranges were first married. The L'Estranges had to endure Toby Peddar, who owed his original appointment as chief constable of the parish to Sir Hamon, now taking any opportunity to report his former patron to the new authorities. But otherwise they got on. They did not join Charles II at Worcester or engage in counter-revolutionary plotting and when some royalist soldiers landed at Heacham Sir Hamon recommended that, while the men might quietly be allowed to 'escape', their presence should be promptly reported to the county officials.[14]

In the seventeenth century the overwhelming burden of government lay in the localities with the Justices of the Peace, sheriffs and constables who kept order and resolved disputes. The revolution had done almost nothing to change this structure. Sir Hamon L'Estrange was one of the familiar names now missing from this roll of local leaders, but many others remained. In Norfolk where the majority of the gentry had either supported Parliament or kept their heads down during the war, there was as much continuity as change. The county commissions of the peace now included a smattering of parliamentarian officers and promoted middling men such as Toby Peddar, but these newcomers sat alongside the scions of old county families, the Hobarts of Blickling and Townsends of Raynham Hall.[15] Other changes, such as the remodelling of the church or the campaign for moral reform, were less dramatic in many counties, including Norfolk, than might be imagined. The Puritans in power in London were certainly keen on stamping out drunkenness, vagrancy and sinfulness in general. But while they did so with fervour, they were often enforcing legislation which had existed long before the revolution aimed at the same thing. When it came to the religious life of the county, there was, to set against the crackdown on church ales and the festivals of the old church year, a great deal that was familiar. The vicars of all four local parish churches, Hunstanton, Heacham, Ringstead and Sedgeford, each of whom was appointed in the 1630s, remained in post right through the Interregnum into the 1660s. While they may have changed the form of their services when the Book of Common Prayer was abolished, their continuing presence was probably a more significant constant in the lives of their congregations than the differences in the liturgy.[16]

The Nominated Assembly had, before its dissolution, passed a significant piece of legislation regarding marriages which would change the status of another ritual of national life. In seeking to free religious worship from the offices of the state, they had declared that marriage – not since the reformation treated as a sacrament – should be conducted by secular JPs and not by parish clergymen. But once again the extent of change on the ground was masked by continuity of personnel. In Hunstanton, Toby Peddar, who had just become a JP, was now charged with officiating at marriages, but the person appointed to the new position of marriage 'register' was the long-standing vicar of St Mary's Hunstanton and chaplain to the L'Estrange family, William Harris. Similarly in King's Lynn Thomas Leech, one of the ministers of St Margaret's church, was appointed register. Sometimes the lightning crack of political change in London might be felt more as a rumble of thunder in the provinces.[17]

※ ※ ※

Roger L'Estrange's return to England in the summer of 1653 was prompted by several things. The dismissal of the Rump that spring had removed the vestiges of the body he had been opposing in 1643. More important was the new spirit of reconciliation that had followed the defeat of Charles II and the royalist cause at the battle of Worcester. Before its dissolution the Rump had passed the Act of Oblivion, 'desirous that the Mindes, Persons and Estates of all the People of this Nation, might be Composed, Setled and Secured, and that all Rancour and Evil Will occasioned by the late Differences may be buried in perpetual Oblivion'. This had pardoned those on the losing side in the civil war and instituted a far-reaching amnesty. For a family such as the L'Estranges it bleached away much of the stain of past actions and seemed to mark a new beginning.[18]

Roger L'Estrange's conviction for treason required a further degree of absolution than the Act of Oblivion alone provided, and towards the end of October 1653 he was admitted to the presence of Oliver Cromwell for a personal interview. He later boasted of having offered neither a declaration of loyalty nor a statement of contrition, but given that he was released, this may have been more swagger than fact. His claim that his father was on his deathbed and that he must urgently go to him seems also to have helped expedite the matter. Again Roger did not quail at embroidering the truth.[19]

A contemporary later described Roger L'Estrange as 'the scandal of a worthy Family, who have long been asham'd of him', and while this may have been an overstatement he certainly felt little need to conform to his parents' expectation. Almost ten years, and a great deal else, separated Roger from his older brothers. Sir Nicholas and Hamon were both confirmed countrymen, while Roger had an unslakable thirst for London. His older brothers had married in their twenties, thereby bringing new land and wealth to the family, but despite being almost 40 Roger still showed no sign of making such a commitment. He lost no time on his return to Hunstanton that winter in presenting his mother with a pile of unpaid bills. Ten days before Christmas Lady Alice paid out £50 to 'my Sonne Roger Le Strange by his father's apoyntment towardes the payment of his debts'. The sum would be £100 before many weeks were out. While his parents acted with their characteristic generosity to their children, the experience did little to help make the reunion a success. Roger did not linger at Hunstanton and was back in London as soon as priopriety would allow. Not without reason did one of the company at Hunstanton Hall joke that an expensive cheese was 'like a younger Brother. The coate is worth all the Body.'[20]

One of the further diversions at Hunstanton Hall as the new year dawned was the arrival of books and newspapers from town, some direct from the capital others via booksellers in King's Lynn. Marchamont Nedham's newspaper *Mercurius Politicus* was well read among the L'Estrange family. Sir Nicholas's brother-in-law, Christopher Calthorpe, ordered it by name for his house in nearby East Barsham and it was almost certainly among the many almanacs and newsbooks which were bought for Hunstanton Hall. Sir Hamon was a prodigious acquirer of books, with wide-ranging intellectual tastes. As well as collecting works of history, social science, philosophy and geography, he also bought books by those with whom he violently disagreed. A title by the radical Leveller leader John Lilburne, which was catalogued as 'Lillborns Railing Booke', and the Puritan polemic *The Practice of Piety* joined Sir Hamon's four copies of the royalist bestseller *Eikon Basilike* on the Hunstanton library shelves. As the L'Estranges recovered from their Christmas feasting in January 1654, Anna Trapnel was falling into her famous Whitehall trance – of which the papers soon brought them news. Among the parcels from London that January was another which thrust the politics of the metropolis further into their midst. Only a week or two after its publication Sir Hamon unwrapped 'a Booke of the Government of the Commonwealth', better known as the 'Instrument of Government', the controversial new constitution which had just made Oliver Cromwell Lord Protector of England.[21]

❦ ❦ ❦

Winter turned gradually to spring at Hunstanton in 1654. The indulgence of Christmas was followed by the parsimony of Lent. Very little meat was put on the Hunstanton dining table through February and March, instead the family dined on cheese from the dairy herd and fish. Plaice and ling were staples, crabs and lobsters were eaten when the season allowed and copious quantities of herring were served when the great silvery shoals surged down the country's east coast. Outside, Lady Alice's improvements were well underway. Among the new year's jobs was the erection of a large area of park paling or fencing. Trees had first to be felled and sawn into planks, which were then erected and new gates framed and hung. Outside the park the clogged-up drainage channels in a number of the estate's meadows needed to be cleared and the dikes recut. Seeds were germinated for planting out, and the orchard that Lady Alice had begun cultivating the year of Charles I's execution began to bud and blossom.[22]

As the weather improved Sir Hamon's health deteriorated; his symptoms came and went, dizziness and a strange numbness in his hands and feet. Ever intellectually curious he was keen to try unorthodox remedies despite the objections of the family doctor. It fell to Lady Alice to source the obscure ingredients: gum arabic and Cyprian turpentine as well as fruit syrups, figs and liquorice. She was sceptical about much of it, calling one of her husband's new medical advisers 'Playford the mountebank'. But her love for her husband, and his kind, fair-minded character, doused her disapproval and she loyally tracked down each exotic prescription.[23]

Easter 1654 was early. Before the war the vicar, William Harris, had come to the Hall on all the major holy days to administer the sacrament to the L'Estrange family and servants. He was still on the L'Estrange payroll but he now came on Easter Day only. The previous week a Palm Sunday communion was held at neighbouring Holme-next-the-Sea, to which Toby Peddar seems to have turned a blind eye.[24] That some people made for meetings of nonconformist conventicles while others remained in the parish churches had by now become familiar. Passionate preachers had long since appeared, and Anna Trapnel's brethren, the Fifth Monarchists, had already established several groups in Norfolk. But, as outsiders, the radical Puritans, just like the Laudians before them, were regarded with suspicion. When the ultra-high church cleric Matthew Wren had been made Bishop of Norwich in the 1630s he had reportedly asked a churchwarden to recite the Nicene Creed, to which the baffled fellow had replied, 'what's that? If you tell me the Toppe or the Tayle I can answere you.' Tales of ill-educated itinerant preachers and the promiscuous antics of the 'Family of Love' sect also provoked peals of laughter at Hunstanton Hall just as those of the prim affectations of the Laudians had before them.[25]

❧ ❧ ❧

Peace seems to have been in the mind of the L'Estranges as the elderly couple contemplated the world around them. A few years later it would be remarked in the House of Commons that 'the people care not what Government they live under, so [long] as they may plough and go to market'.[26] For most people there were simply more immediate concerns and priorities than the stripe of the men in power at Westminster. Ten

miles down the coast from Hunstanton in King's Lynn, the main port
on the Wash, what mattered to most of the mercantile population was
trade. Civil war, as Gerrard Winstanley had found, was a dangerous
disruptor of business and the war with the Dutch further disturbed the
vessels bringing timber from the Baltic, wine from the Rhine and coal
from Newcastle. Furthermore, there were worrying signs that the
massive programme of drainage and land improvement going on upriver
in the Fens was affecting the crucial channel between the town's port
and the open sea. When the news of the new Protectorate reached the
corporation of King's Lynn they did not hesitate. The bells of St
Margaret's church were immediately rung in loyal celebration and a
letter of congratulation dispatched to Oliver Cromwell – in which their
urgent concerns regarding navigation were humbly raised. The Protector
responded warmly. Delighted by the prospect of having their problems
discussed at the Council of State, the Lord Mayor and aldermen
commissioned a detailed report on the channel and risks to its naviga-
bility. At the same time they placed an order with a London goldsmith
for fine new civic regalia for the town engraved with the arms of the
Lord Protector.[27]

Sir Hamon L'Estrange had fought for the King because honour and
tradition required it, but it was not his or his wife's nature to let pride
or political dogma prevent them from pursuing peace and prosperity.
For them what mattered most was their family and estate. Now much
of the old enmity was, if not forgotten, then laid aside. Their own family
had been divided by the politics of the 1640s: their son-in-law Sir
William Spring had sided with Parliament, and Sir Nicholas had
declined to join his father and brother in defending King's Lynn for the
royalists. It had not dimmed their closeness. In King's Lynn Sir Hamon
had been succeeded as military governor by Colonel Valentine Walton,
husband of Oliver Cromwell's sister, Margaret, and one of the commissioners who had sat behind John Bradshaw at the trial of Charles I.
Come the early 1650s Walton was being included with the family and
friends to whom Sir Hamon and Lady Alice sent gifts of venison from
the Hunstanton herd. On more than one occasion Walton received a
whole buck with the compliments of Sir Hamon L'Estrange. Another of

the governors of King's Lynn was Robert Thorowgood, wine merchant, who was not inclined to let politics rob him of one of his best clients. He continued to sell copious quantities of claret and Malaga sack to the L'Estranges right through the 1650s, taking care to throw in extra bottles with the orders as a personal gift. In both cases, of course, the players were acting out of self-interest – but there were few more powerful balms when it came to the wounds of civil war.[28]

Sir Hamon L'Estrange's illness worsened with the weeks, and the old knight died in the spring of 1654 with the returning songbirds calling an exuberant elegy from every hedge and bough of his ancient acres. Almost his final act, a week before his death, had been to sign the paperwork for a £2,000 mortgage on his Ringstead lands, enabling Lady Alice finally to settle the composition terms on the L'Estrange estates. In his will he said nothing of war or injustice or personal achievements, but spoke of gratitude, peace and acceptance. He gave thanks for his long life – the 'great measure of daies' with which God 'had filled my glass of time' – and for the love and companionship of 'that life of my life my dearest wife'. He gave thanks, too, for his children, the 'olive branches' which he, an orphan, had been granted. While each of his servants, grandchildren and godchildren was individually named, he pointedly made no reference whatsoever to his youngest son, Roger. Whatever had passed between them at their last meeting had not enamoured father to son. His will contained words of advice to his descendants. Unlike Charlotte, Countess of Derby – a fellow vanquished royalist commander – Sir Hamon L'Estrange was an advocate of humility and reconciliation. He counselled his progeny 'to be affable, meeke, courteous, peaceable, easy to be entreated in all honest and lawful things'. With the passing of the Act of Oblivion and his estates secure, he could die peacefully, reassured that the civil war was finally over.[29]

🐝 🐝 🐝

While Sir Hamon's son Sir Nicholas L'Estrange was taking charge of affairs at Hunstanton over the summer of 1654, things in the nation as a whole were also shifting. Nine months after the Protectorate had been declared, the new parliament, the first to be elected since 1640, was finally to assemble at Westminster. The Instrument of Government had set out the voting franchise, which excluded royalists, Catholics and those with assets worth less than £200, and Irish and Scottish MPs now also made their way to Westminster.

The first day of its sitting was, quite deliberately, 3 September, the auspicious date of the battles of Dunbar and Worcester at which God had shown his approval of Oliver Cromwell and the regime. As there was now no House of Lords in whose chamber heads of state had historically given speeches to Parliament, the Commons was summoned to attend the Protector in the Painted Chamber, the room where just five years earlier Charles I's fate had been determined. Cromwell sat in great splendour, in a chair of state upon a dais shaded by a regal canopy. When almost four hundred MPs had crammed into the room, he rose and removed his hat to address them. 'Gentlemen,' he began. 'You are met here on the greatest occasion that, I believe, England ever saw.'

The purpose of their meeting, its 'great end', he explained, was 'Healing and Settling'. This was urgently needed, for until recently 'every man's hand (almost) was against his brother', 'the nation was rent and torn in spirit and principle from one end to another', exacerbated by the destructive doings of first the Levellers and then the Fifth Monarchists: 'family against family, husband against wife, parents against children; and nothing in the hearts and minds of men but "overturn, overturn, overturn".' But now, he intoned, change had come. Those opponents had been defeated, the war with the Dutch had been ended, new godly clergy were being found, a fresh push was underway to 'consider how the laws might be made plain and short and less chargable to the people'. In short, he and his council had already set the country on a better course, and this new parliament was now to take to the oars to propel it on.[30]

Among the members who heard Cromwell's powerful speech that day was one of the two representatives for King's Lynn. Guybon Goddard, the corporation's lawyer, or 'Recorder', was 42 and entering Parliament for the first time. He was born and bred in Norfolk and given his unusual Christian name was probably a relation of Francis Guybon, Lady Alice L'Estrange's cousin and close friend.

While royalists had been barred from standing, those who had been the architects of the revolution could hardly be excluded. John Bradshaw, though he was no longer a member of the Council of State, was elected an MP for his home county of Cheshire. Rubbing shoulders with parliamentary first-timers like Goddard gave him and other disappointed 1649 revolutionaries an ideal opportunity. Bradshaw was, in the words of a contemporary, 'very instrumental in opening the eyes of many young members who had never before heard their interest so clearly stated and asserted'. Not just the title of Lord Protector, but the creation of the whole Protectoral constitution, and the removal of the Rump before it, had all been done without any parliamentary discussion, let alone consent. And this in a country which just five years earlier had declared itself a 'free state' in which the supreme authority lay unequivocally with 'the representatives of the people in Parliament'. As soon as the business of appointing a speaker was concluded, Guybon Goddard noted in his journal that 'occasion was taken by some members to tell us that, until that time, they had not so much as heard the name of my *Lord Protector* within those walls'.[31]

All Cromwell's commanding, confident oratory could not drown out the indignation of parliamentary members at what had taken place over the previous eighteen months. Galvanized by the furious old-handers, the new assembly, like the Long Parliament in 1641, felt that their task was not simply to do the bidding of the head of state. They wished to discuss their grievances and constitutional irregularities and would not be dissuaded from doing so. A week later, Members of Parliament were summoned to the Painted Chamber again and, with companies of soldiers stationed conspicuously around the palace, instructed to sign their names beneath the Instrument of Government to signal their acceptance. Many refused outright. As Goddard reflected only four days in, 'the differences seemed so wide, the contest so hot, and the struggling so violent on both sides, as there seemed hitherto no hope of any fair agreement'.[32]

Come December 1654 the First Protectorate Parliament, as it would later be known, had decided that such were the shortcomings of the new constitution that no other legislation should proceed until it had been properly debated and resolved. Cromwell simmered with frustration. He could hardly march them out of the chamber as he had done the Rump, and they were never going to abolish themselves like the Nominated Assembly. On 22 January 1655 the *Commons Journal* recorded baldly that 'His Highness the Lord Protector, being in the Painted Chamber and the Parliament, with their Speaker, by his command attending him there was pleased to dissolve this Parliament'. The new constitution had set a minimum duration of five months for all future parliaments. The First Protectorate Parliament had lasted just four months and nineteen days.[33]

Twelve

Decimation

Sir Nicholas L'Estrange was 50 when his father Sir Hamon died. While in many gentry families the senior generation jealously guarded the family assets and charges, this had not been the L'Estranges' way. Sir Nicholas had lived with his parents at Hunstanton Hall all his life and had long shared in the responsibilities of the estate – including directing the agricultural improvements which had gradually been turning the Hunstanton salt marshes into productive arable fields. His assumption of the position of head of the family was therefore not a difficult transition. That said, the inheritance he now received remained compromised. The mortgage raised by Sir Hamon on his deathbed had placed a hefty debt on the estate which had to be repaid within three years, and he and his wife, Anne, had nine children, eight of them boys, for whom to provide.

Over the summer and autumn of 1654, while the newly elected House of Commons was picking apart the Instrument of Government, the timeless sorting-out after a family death was underway at Hunstanton Hall. The widowed Lady Alice packed up and moved to a house on her family's ancestral lands at nearby Sedgeford. In the Hall Sir Nicholas distributed his father's effects. Sir Hamon had left detailed instructions: Lady Anne was to have his watch, Nick, Sir Nicholas's second son, was to have his great English Bible with gilt leaves, John, his musical third son, was to have his bass viol and his largest sporting gun. Books could have been a difficulty, as Sir Nicholas himself had an extensive library, but Sir Hamon had anticipated this and had stipulated that any duplicate titles should be distributed among the ministers of the local parish churches.[1]

The new master of Hunstanton Hall may have been a bibliophile but he was no intellectual. His hooked nose and pale, thin face, sour in repose, were misleading as he shared with his mother a broad and boundless sense of humour (Colour plate 7). The people and pastimes of his own part of England were his principal preoccupation. The Hunstanton drainage projects interested him as much for the opportunities they offered to enhance the shooting as for commercial advantage. He loved music and among his guests at Hunstanton Hall was the celebrated composer John Jenkins – whose fantasias Sir Nicholas committed to pages of sheet music that became a prized possession. Above all he delighted in funny stories of country life in Norfolk and many years earlier had started to record these in a lexicon of 'merry passages and jeasts'. Here, neatly numbered and attributed to named family and friends, were hundreds of anecdotes: tales of bluff Norfolk farmers baffled by religious change, of drunken evenings in provincial inns and oak-panelled parlours, of saucy Norwich prostitutes and dour Dutch drainage engineers, of Cuckold the Calthorpes' dog and Wiggett the Hunstanton Hall fool, and of the many misadventures of Mr Prick, the unfortunately named minister of Denham. Here in a single small volume was enclosed one family's capacity for laughter even in the most serious times.[2]

Above all Sir Nicholas took a different approach to national politics from the other men in his family. When the war had broken out over a decade ago, he alone of the L'Estrange men had resisted the calls to join the royalist army. On the flimsy pretext of a lack of horses, he went on to sit out the turbulent years that followed. He was not alone in this as the majority of the Norfolk gentry families had done something similar, preferring to tend their estates and their families – whatever their personal sympathies – than run the risks of participation.[3]

Sir Nicholas L'Estrange's determined and sustained neutrality now looked set to pay off. As he took the reins of the L'Estrange estates he had a new opportunity to pursue his family's interests distanced from his father's active royalism. In his sights were the Irish lands they had lost in obscure circumstances before the war. He took up the case enthusiastically and within weeks of his father's death had written to a senior London lawyer of his plan to reclaim those lands. He hoped, he explained, that 'my own peaceable Acquiescence (without ostentation I speake it) in all the high distempers of this Age' would count substantially in his favour.[4]

While Sir Nicholas had kept assiduously out of politics during the preceding decade, his younger brother Hamon, now 49, was an altogether more politically minded figure. As a student at Cambridge Hamon had admired the muscular self-assertion of the Long Parliament, and published a treatise dedicated with wide-eyed enthusiasm to them and their 'great work of Reformation'. But age and experience had dulled his ardour and he had joined his father in the siege of Lynn and, like him, had suffered the fines and deprivations that followed. Now Hamon farmed a portion of the L'Estrange estates from a house at Ringstead, and kept in close contact with his neighbour and brother at the big house. But it was his sister-in-law, Sir Nicholas's serious-minded wife Anne, to whom he was closest. Indeed, the clever and contemplative Hamon would, on the face of it, have made a much more suitable husband for Anne than the jocular Sir Nicholas. Anne was not given to telling bawdy stories, but thought deeply about the troubles and contradictions of the times. It was during one of her discussions with her brother-in-law that Anne posed the question that set Hamon on the intellectual undertaking that would be his life's work.[5] Was there any truth in the Puritans' claim, she asked, that traditional Anglicanism – including feasts such as Christmas – was simply Catholicism by another name? His next book, published in 1651, was his first to address this question, and to argue for the antiquity and righteousness of Anglicanism, and its fundamental differences to 'putrid and ulcerous' Roman Catholicism. He wrote, he explained in his dedication to Anne, hoping to 'prove an Answer to you', signing himself 'your ... sincerely Addicted servant'.[6]

🐝 🐝 🐝

The L'Estranges may have been content to live a quiet life, but not all who had fought for Charles I were reconciled to such inactivity. Shortly after midnight on Sunday 11 March 1655 John Penruddock, an erst-while royalist officer, and around two hundred other armed men rode into the city of Salisbury. The Assizes, the travelling county court, was meeting in the town that week and the hostelries were full. Penruddock's men moved quietly along the dark streets lined with medieval houses to take up positions at each inn. Taking care to bolt the horses into the various stables, they made their move. The lawyers, JPs and other worthies were seized in their beds; some were dragged to the town gaol and others taken hostage. Penruddock proclaimed Charles II King of England, and then rode out of the captive city in triumph.

This incident, shocking as it was, came as little surprise to the able and industrious John Thurloe, Secretary to the Council of State. Since the new year the government's sophisticated intelligence network had been picking up whispers of a royalist uprising. A letter from the English diplomat in Hamburg had relayed a rumour that several major ports 'with many other places' were in danger and that Charles Stuart himself was to sail for England. Fragments of a similar story had been reported by Thurloe's spies and informants. With his characteristic self-posses-sion, Thurloe had dashed off letters authorizing arrests and interrogations, and dispatched men and arms. Thanks in part to his intervention several elements of the 'combustion', including those in Morpeth, York and Nottingham, had failed to ignite and Charles Stuart had not appeared. But in Wiltshire the rebels had kept their powder dry.

The Council of State in London sat in emergency session until midnight that night and Thurloe swiftly dispatched the Protector's order for General Desbrow to set out at once with 500 foot soldiers to suppress the rebellion. A tense week passed before a communiqué from Desbrow brought news. The rebels had ridden west hoping to draw recruits, but very little popular support had materialized and their numbers and momentum had dwindled rather than grown. A swift mili-tary assault on their base in the Devon village of South Molton had brought them down, and by 15 March Penruddock was in custody and the crisis over. The reluctance, once again, of even dyed-in-the-wool royalists to respond to the call to rise was testament to the regime's achievements and the royalists' disorganization. But as one of Thurloe's Warwickshire informants remarked, it could easily have been otherwise: this 'was a damnable rebellious riseing and plott intended by many thousand disafected, malignant, and desperate wicked men, to putt all the nation into a flame, and to involve and imbroyle us into a sadd warr and division'. Two months later Penruddock was beheaded in Exeter. His insurrection may have been both small-scale and short-lived, but its consequences would be neither.[7]

Penruddock's attack on Salisbury in March 1655 added further to John Thurloe's already formidable workload. The range of responsibilities of this middle-aged lawyer would have daunted a less remarkable man: as Secretary to the Council of State he was the nearest thing the age had to the head of the civil service, added to which he had special responsibility for national intelligence, foreign affairs and the postal service. When John Bradshaw had cleared his belongings from Whitehall in 1653 he had dropped all the papers he had amassed as an assiduous President of the Council of State 'being very many', on Secretary Thurloe's desk.[8]

While Thurloe examined the confessions of Penruddock's associates, he was also busy on another important national project. Peace with the Dutch had been concluded in the early months of the Protectorate and the English naval fleet thereby released from action. With over 150 ships, many brand new, now without employment and with no desire to scale back the nation's novel naval capacity, Cromwell and his council considered how best to deploy them. The approach they decided upon was an audacious one: a major assault on Spanish-held territories in the Caribbean.

From the last decade of the sixteenth century a series of tiny English colonies had been established on the eastern seaboard of the Americas: a cluster in New England spearheaded by Puritans in search of a new beginning, and another in Virginia and Maryland. To these a smattering of Caribbean islands, most importantly Barbados, had been added for straightforwardly commercial reasons in the 1620s and 1630s. Those who saw the potential to make money from the Caribbean had long argued that the English government should get involved and acquire territory in the West Indies.[9] Now the opportunity presented itself. The 400-mile-long Spanish-held island of Hispaniola (now Haiti and the Dominican Republic) was decided upon as a first step towards the complete conquest of the Spanish Caribbean. The enterprise was born of a combination of territorial acquisitiveness and ideological fervour – Cromwell among others saw it as the beginning of the extermination of Catholicism and the expansion of the Protectorate government and its great work of Godly reformation across the globe.

In December, with their precise mission still cloaked in secrecy, a fleet had set sail from Portsmouth manned by almost 3,000 men offered up from existing regiments, with a further 6,000 to be taken on in Barbados. Haste to stage the assault before the hurricane season set in caused the fleet to leave without a number of its supplies, which Thurloe was now vetting. The 'provisions' included maps, arms and armour, pistols, saddles and helmets plus a mass of practical equipment for establishing a colony: wheelbarrows, axes, fish and turtle nets, hammocks, food and supplies. That these had still to leave England in March 1655 was a sign that, already, all was not well with the 'Western Design'.[10]

❦ ❦ ❦

The Caribbean was a world away from north Norfolk and the L'Estranges were not travellers, but there were threads that tied this obscure corner of England to the wide world where the English army was making its very first foray into international colonization. An 'aethiopian or blacke a more' had lived with Sir Hamon L'Estrange at Hunstanton Hall in his childhood and been baptized a Christian at St Andrew's church in Ringstead. Heacham Hall, three miles away, was the seat of the Rolfe family, the L'Estranges' closest gentry neighbours. John Rolfe was only two years Sir Hamon's junior and both had spent their boyhoods scrambling about on the Hunstanton dunes. While Sir Hamon had remained at Hunstanton and married a local girl, John Rolfe had travelled to the English colony in Virginia and in 1616 returned home with Pocahontas, the daughter of Chief Powhatan, as his bride. From the security of

Hunstanton, Sir Hamon had been an investor in several international trading ventures, one west in search of the Northwest Passage to China and another to the East Indies. But he was no advocate of territorial colonialism, and disapproved of the motives and methods involved. In his view Englishmen should have 'better thoughts than to invade or exterminate natives and by means (to[o] commonly coarse) to get and to keep dominion'.[11]

The newspapers that were carried weekly from London across England gradually revealed the true goal of the Caribbean fleet. In March *Mercurius Politicus* reported the sensational news that the expedition was 'to make some attempt upon the islands and territories belonging to the King of Spain'. Almost 5,000 miles away English ships now bearing an army of 9,000 men had just sighted Hispaniola. The attention of Nedham's readership had been caught but as the weeks passed there was frustratingly little to report. In May *Politicus* apologized that there was 'nothing farther from Barbadoes'. Come mid-July there were tantalizing rumours of triumph, but Nedham had too keen a nose for truth (and was too close to the government) to be convinced, commenting 'we have nothing from our Generals, nor any other way as yet to confirm the Relation concerning the taking of San Domingo in Hispaniola, but it stands uncertain and every day some account is expected'.

The awful reality was, in fact, just being revealed to Cromwell, Thurloe and a handful of others. Though the English vastly outnumbered their Spanish adversaries, and despite the immense sum of £30,000 invested in the enterprise, the assault had been a catastrophe. The poor quality of the soldiers (many of whom had been offered up by their regiments in order to be rid of them), inadequate planning and leadership, the lack of supplies and bad luck had seen the whole attacking force founder. 'Tormented with heat, hunger and thirst', they had been forced to retreat after barely a fortnight on Spanish soil. In an attempt to retrieve some success from this unmitigated disaster the leaders of the expedition had captured the far smaller island of Jamaica before making for home, but this was cold comfort to the government in London. Cromwell himself was left reeling. The defeat was a bitter humiliation for the country, the army and the Protector personally. But far worse than all of these, it was a rebuke from God almighty. Cromwell could now see that God's Divine Grace, which had governed and guided him through everything, was being withdrawn.[12]

The summer of 1655 was a sobering time for the L'Estranges of Hunstanton. The new generation had been the owners of Hunstanton Hall for barely a year when Sir Nicholas's health began to decline. Lady Anne had at least the benefit of having her family close by as she tended to her husband: her mother-in-law, Lady Alice, her devoted brother-in-law, Hamon, her older sons Little Ham and Nick and her sister, Catherine, at nearby East Barsham. But further trials were to come. While Penruddock's attack on Salisbury had been short-lived, much more worrying to Secretary Thurloe and the Council of State had been that it exposed the existence of some sort of royalist network, calling itself the 'Sealed Knot', which, though they had failed in March, might succeed on another occasion. There was even a rumour that Thomas Fairfax, still in quiet retirement in Yorkshire, had been poised to join them. For months interrogations had been taking place and by June several thousand men – some implicated, many not – had been rounded up. Groups of soldiers had been dispatched to the houses of known royalists to investigate and report on what they found. In Norfolk the arrests had come over the unusually hot and dry high summer, and among those hauled from their homes, some in the middle of the night, were both Sir Nicholas's brothers, Hamon L'Estrange and the errant Roger L'Estrange. On 24 July Sir Nicholas died at Hunstanton Hall aged just 52. Whatever pain he suffered he must have struggled for life. He was leaving his wife Anne with their nine children to provide for, estates that remained heavily mortgaged, both his brothers in prison and nothing whatsoever to show for a lifetime of political neutrality.[13]

❧ ❧ ❧

Penruddock's uprising and the failure of the Western Design between them prompted a fundamental change of tack for the Protectorate regime. The components of this coalesced over the spring and summer of 1655. In addition to the army proper – which in England stood at around 10,000 – over 6,000 additional soldiers were now quickly recruited to form a new county-based militia. As was revealed at the Council of State on 21 September 1655, these soldiers were to underpin a whole new approach to governing England which was to be military as much as civilian. The country was being carved into territorial regions, each the domain of a senior army officer or 'Major General'. The Major Generals' remit was to be wide-ranging, but at its core was an ominous combination of eradicating royalist resistance and enforcing moral reformation. The first was a direct response to the March rebellions, the second reflected Cromwell's determination to win back God's approval.

The Major Generals, assisted by a corps of 'commissioners', were to identify all royalists and Catholics, imprison those believed to be active, force all others to enter into hefty financial bonds as security for their loyalty, confiscate their arms and support a new national surveillance regime. Furthermore, they were to enforce a whole raft of measures relating to social and moral reform. The funding of this massive new undertaking was a challenge, not least as maintaining the existing military establishment was already beyond the regime's means – added to which were the additional sums just laid out on the ill-fated Western Design. But a solution had already been identified: the infrastructure would be entirely paid for by a punitive new levy on all royalists of any wealth. The tax – instantly known as 'decimation' – was set at the rate of 10 per cent on the income of all those of means who had ever had their property sequestered or taken up arms against Parliament. This announcement was made without any reference to the Act of Oblivion, which had explicitly pardoned almost all royalists for their actions before 1651, and without any form of parliamentary consent. The end – protecting England from 'the endless designs of restless unwearied enemies' – was believed to justify the means. Cromwell's impassioned plea for 'healing and settling' just a year before now seemed a distant memory.[14]

🐝 🐝 🐝

The man given responsibility for imposing this new regime in Norfolk was Hezekiah Haynes. As his Old Testament name indicated, Hezekiah came of strong Puritan stock. He was born into an affluent Essex family which, while he was still in his teens, had moved to New England in search of a new Godly beginning. His father, John Haynes, had gone on to great things, becoming Governor first of Massachusetts and then of Connecticut. Hezekiah, like John Bradshaw and Hamon L'Estrange, was a second son with no expectation of inheriting the family lands. Instead, he had returned to England and taken up arms for Parliament in the civil war, rising to the rank of major under Cromwell's close friend and son-in-law Charles Fleetwood.[15]

The position of Major General for East Anglia and the middle belt of England was initially assigned to Fleetwood, who had succeeded Henry Ireton as the senior government figure in Ireland. But Fleetwood had immediately delegated his responsibilities and Hezekiah Haynes was assigned Norfolk, Suffolk, Cambridgeshire, the Isle of Ely and his own home county of Essex. Like a number of his fellow Major Generals, Haynes was not yet 40 in 1655 and this prestigious new appointment gave a young man a golden opportunity to shine before both Secretary Thurloe and the Protector himself. As a senior East Anglian army officer, he had led a thorough review of the state of the Protectorate's security within those counties following Penruddock's rebellion. It was he who, between March and September, had orchestrated the groups of soldiers sent to call at royalists' houses, and on whose say-so Hamon and Roger L'Estrange had been arrested and held without charge. His zeal and his desire to please were visible. Nonetheless, a member of the gentry himself, he hesitated to treat his social superiors with outright dishonour and detained many of his suspects in inns rather than in grim county gaols.[16]

Less than a fortnight after his appointment Hezekiah Haynes learned of the death of his only child, and before leaving Essex he had had to break the terrible news to his pregnant wife. But despite this, and his intense anxiety for her health, he allowed no note of melancholy to enter his professional dealings. Of the five counties in his charge, he had decided to start with Norfolk. He travelled to Norwich to marshal and brief the group of commissioners, local right-minded men appointed to help him. Then began the process of identifying and calling up all those royalists and Catholics who qualified and arresting others who were felt to be dangerous. For a week from 8 November the commissioners met every day. So industrious were they that Haynes wrote brightly to Thurloe, coordinating matters between the Major Generals and the government, that 'I am confident none in England will appeare to be more forward'.

Haynes's task was made easier by the fact that Norfolk, by his own admission, was not a hotbed of royalism. With the exception of Norwich, where there were rumblings, the county had been largely quiet for the past three years. Furthermore, thanks to his diligence over the summer he had already rounded up many of the affluent royalists who now qualified for the decimation tax. Soon both Hamon and Roger L'Estrange were released on heavy bonds for good behaviour, and able to return home, albeit with the tax itself still to pay. This, too, was soon addressed. By 19 November Haynes's Norfolk commissioners had summoned all royalists who were liable and the calculations had been done on their income and property to determine the sums. That he was doing God's work was completely clear to Hezekiah Haynes and his zealous helpers, and to this self-evident truth he ascribed the royalists' acquiescence. He noted with satisfaction that the 'delinquents' he dealt with all submitted to the requirements now placed on them and had 'not one word to say why ought should be remitted him'.[17]

The L'Estrange brothers may, like the other Norfolk royalists, have signed their names to the bonds for loyalty and shouldered the heavy burden of taxation placed upon them, but it did not mean they were reconciled. The injustice seemed to them bitter indeed. They had been pardoned for their actions, had compounded for their property and had played no part in royalist plotting since long before the regicide, and this was their reward. Roger L'Estrange returned to his London lodgings and Hamon to Norfolk, but neither was happy.[18]

That Hamon L'Estrange was among those arrested in the summer of 1655 probably owed as much to his recent publishing activities as to his bit-part in the siege of Lynn twelve years earlier. For he had followed his work on Anglicanism with a remarkable undertaking, a biography of Charles I licensed for publication in June 1655. *The History of the Life and Raigne of King Charles* was one of the first attempts to explain with some impartiality the forces and factors which gave rise to the civil war, written by one who felt he could comment without agenda, having lived a quiet country life 'in the vale of rural recesse, far from the Court'. It was an undertaking he knew would win him few friends, for to say anything in the late King's favour, 'importing [him] lesse then a Nero or Domitian, many will not endure', while on the other hand his criticism of the churchmen and policies of the 1630s was bound to enrage royalists. When he was released from prison he found that the book had already caused a stir. In October Charles I's former chaplain, Peter Heylyn, who had sheltered Marchamont Nedham at Minster Lovell before the newsman abandoned the royalist cause, published a stinging riposte. This then set Hamon L'Estrange to work upon a riposte to the riposte which was ready for publication early in 1656.[19]

With Hamon occupied with his writing and Roger L'Estrange back in the swing of London social life, it was, as ever, the women of the L'Estrange family who were to the fore in managing family affairs. Two generations of widows, Lady Alice, now almost 70, and Lady Anne, had the nine L'Estrange children to think about, and new debts to pay. Elizabeth, Lady Alice's daughter, had herself been widowed a year before on the death of her husband Sir William Spring. It was this black-draped assortment of powerful L'Estrange ladies who had to take matters in hand. Little Ham at 24 had become master of Hunstanton Hall, but he was not strong. He managed one Christmas at the head of the table, but as the shoals of herring teemed through the Hunstanton shallows in 1656 his coffin was lowered beside his father's in the red earth beneath St Mary's church.[20]

The family's perilous financial position needed to be tackled and the ever-practical Lady Alice and her well-connected daughter were not ones to let grief distract them from such an important undertaking. Marriage was the answer. Little Ham's younger brother, Nick, had now inherited, and in their sights was the Coke family at Holkham. John Coke, whose father Sir Edward Coke had been James I's celebrated Lord

Chief Justice, had an unmarried daughter, Mary. John Coke had long been a figure of fun at Hunstanton, ridiculed for being fat and stupid, having a loud voice and belligerent manner. However, he had married the heiress to the Holkham estate just 15 miles from Hunstanton and, despite being his father's sixth son, had inherited the vast Coke family lands. His daughter Mary was quite a prize, but it was also not an inconsiderable achievement for an untitled son of a lawyer, however distinguished, to marry his daughter to a baronet and the county's oldest family. The bargain that the L'Estranges struck with John Coke, which Lady Alice doubtless calculated with her characteristic care for every shilling and penny, was a hard one. Coke was to provide a marriage settlement for his daughter of £5,300 (more than twice the annual income of the whole Hunstanton estate) and, crucially, was to agree that if she died without children, her inheritance would remain entirely within the L'Estrange family, passing in turn to each of her new husband's six surviving brothers and after them to the remaining heirs of Sir Hamon L'Estrange. Added to all this, John Coke was to provide a further £4,000 on loan. The revolutionary age had diminished neither the prestige of the old families, nor their knack for turning it to their advantage. Old Sir Hamon L'Estrange had been right when he had described his wife, and her commitment to furthering the interests of his ancient family, as valuable 'above pearls'.[21]

※ ※ ※

When Hezekiah Haynes had reported on progress to John Thurloe in November 1655, he had pressed him for news on the other crucial component of the new regime, 'as yet we heare nothing of the regester's office at London, to which soe much of our worke relates'. For as well as the bonds for good behaviour on royalists, which meant any act of disobedience would bring financial ruin, there was to be a new national surveillance operation. A central intelligence office was being established in London. It operated initially from a room in a stocking merchant's house at the back of the Royal Exchange before moving into its own more respectable premises. All royalists arriving in or leaving the capital were required to report here, enabling the clerks of the office

(1) John Bradshaw, the Cheshire lawyer who sentenced Charles I to death. He was only 46 and far from being the most senior judge in the land but his calm self-possession gave the unprecedented trial much of its air of legitimacy.

(2) Charles I at his trial by Edward Bower. The king adopted an air of nonchalance for much of the trial. He tried too late to bargain with Bradshaw and the commissioners and was condemned to death without ever entering a plea.

(3) Charlotte, Countess of Derby with her husband and eldest daughter by Anthony van Dyck, c.1636. This formidable Frenchwoman came from a princely European family steeped in wars of religion. Her husband points to the Isle of Man, which Charlotte defended for the royalists to the bitter end.

(4) The Dowager Countess of Derby, after Peter Lely, 1657. Charlotte Stanley lost none of her force in widowhood and despite personally directing two major sieges managed, like most royalist landowners, to reclaim her forfeited estates by the late 1650s.

(5, 6) Sir Hamon L'Estrange of Hunstanton (left) and his wife Lady Alice L'Estrange (right) by John Hoskins. Living 100 miles from London, the L'Estranges, like many, were more focused on local affairs than trying to bring about a change in government. As far as anyone knew the end of monarchy was a permanent change.

(7) Sir Nicholas L'Estrange had studiously avoided taking any role in the war, though his father and two brothers had fought for the King. His book of jokes and funny stories shows how much laughter and amusement continued through these years.

(8) Wisbech Castle, Cambridgeshire, built for John Thurloe, Secretary to the Council of State. Affluent men, both Roundheads and Cavaliers, built beautiful houses and gardens in the 1650s following the destructive effects of the civil war.

(9) Dr William Petty by Isaac Fuller, *c.*1651, shown as Oxford professor of anatomy, with a human skull and *On the Fabric of the Human Body* (1627). Petty was the convener of the scientists of the Oxford Experimental Philosophy Club, which would later rename itself the 'Royal' Society.

(10) The army general Charles Fleetwood by Robert Walker. Fleetwood was a close friend of Oliver Cromwell and married his oldest daughter Bridget after the death of her husband Henry Ireton. He was Godly but easily dominated.

(11) Henry Cromwell by Samuel Cooper. The younger of Oliver Cromwell's two sons, Henry was given responsibility for Ireland after the civil war. Had he, rather than his brother Richard, succeeded his father, British history might have been very different.

(12) College Green, Dublin, showing the brick buildings with Dutch gables that characterised the city in the seventeenth century. The process of rebuilding the war-torn capital began under the aegis of Henry Cromwell.

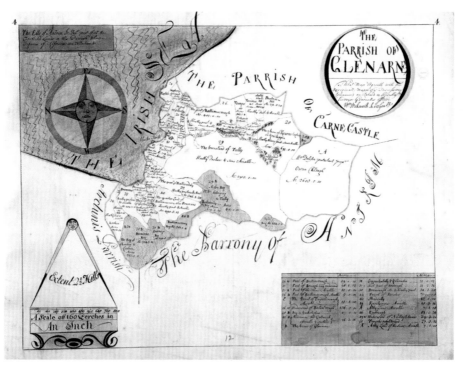

(13) The parish of Glenarm (sic) in Ulster, one of over a thousand from William Petty's survey. Here the Catholic Earl of Antrim was to have his estates confiscated and substituted for a far smaller parcel of property in Connacht.

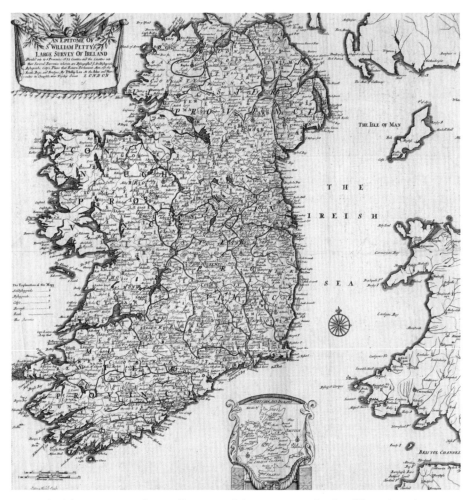

(14) 'An epitome of Sr. William Petty's large survey of Ireland' based on the
'Down Survey' of Ireland, 1654–8, one of the first detailed land surveys on
a national scale undertaken anywhere in the world. It would be
centuries before England would be as well mapped.

to document their movements and pass the information back to the relevant Major General. Further audits of how many royalists were living in London and at which addresses followed. So when the Lynn merchant John Morse travelled to the city on business in February 1656, he had to sign in at the Register Office, give details of the Vine Inn on Bishopsgate where he was staying and report again on departure in order that his whereabouts was always known to Hezekiah Haynes.[22]

Alongside this highly controlled but clear-cut area of work, which saw some 14,000 people designated as royalists and forced to follow the rigorous new reporting regime, the Major Generals were charged with a far-reaching but more nebulous range of responsibilities for moral reform. This involved closing down inns which did not offer accommodation for travellers, deporting those 'who live loosely and cannot give an account of themselves' and suppressing all social gatherings – such as horse races, cockfighting or plays – at which plotting might take place. In Norfolk the Quarter Sessions issued fresh regulations for alehouses, stipulating that only publicans 'well affected to the Government and of honest life', whose inns offered at least three rooms for travellers and had a proper sign outside, should be allowed to continue to operate. Ordinary people in the English provinces were feeling first-hand the effects of the new military regime.[23]

As Hezekiah Haynes totted up the decimation tax due in Norfolk, he had quickly realized that the funds being raised there would be insufficient to meet the direct costs of the new militia let alone the new national bureaucracy.[24] The scale of the mismatch between the costs of the Major Generals' regime as a whole and the takings from the decimation tax soon became horribly clear. Added to this the audacious provocation of the Western Design and the annexation of Jamaica had led England into outright war with Spain, which itself brought ballooning costs. The urgency of staving off a full-blown financial crisis was behind the suggestion, made in the spring of 1656, that the solution might be to call a new parliament to secure further funds from taxation. Given the debacle of the First Protectorate Parliament, this notion was met with deep caution in Westminster. But the Major Generals as a group took a different view. They were ideally placed, they argued, to manage affairs in their respective counties in a way that had never been possible before, and thereby to ensure the election of a pliable House of Commons. In the face of this enthusiasm, and with debts mounting by the month, Cromwell and the Council reluctantly agreed and at the end of June 1656 writs for new parliamentary elections were issued.[25]

The reality was that the Major Generals, as anyone who was not driven by fear or ideological fervour could have predicted, were destined to be despised. Hezekiah Haynes and his comrades were not on the whole dishonest or brutal, ignorant or illiterate, but their task was an impossible one. As both serving soldiers and a branch of central government imposed on the localities they were almost bound to be despised. For most people of any political persuasion the disturbance of the dignity and traditional order of country life was at best unwelcome. As the old lawyer William Prynne, he whose cheeks had been branded and ears amputated by Charles I, observed with disgust, these new men 'seise mens Horses, Arms, Swords, fouling, birding pieces (yea the very Armorets, Chandlers, Arms and Ammunition, though their stock, wares, trade, livelihood) at their pleasures, upon every pretended plot, fear, jealousie'. They were part of a regime that thought it nothing to 'break open, search, ransack mens Houses, Studies, Trunks, Chests, both by day and by night, and take away their Goods ...' These 'Major Generals and their Deputies [set about] suppressing of Innes, Taverns, Alehouses ... without any legal authority', thereby behaving 'like absolute Justices'.[26]

On 20 August 1656, as the elections to the Second Protectorate Parliament were underway, Hezekiah Haynes's friend, the Chelmsford clergyman Ralph Josselin, looked into the summer sky and saw clouds stretched across the firmament in the form of a cross. This boded well, he felt sure. But Haynes knew already that things were not set to go as planned. Some parts of the electorate had fallen into line. The corporation of King's Lynn, for instance, had been characteristically pragmatic. In the months before the election the town had voluntarily surrendered its charter to the Protector and received Haynes as guest of honour at a feast in their medieval town hall. Faced with new elections, they dutifully set aside local man Guybon Goddard and instead chose two of

Haynes's fellow Major Generals to represent them.[27] But things were
not so smooth elsewhere. Haynes was in the uncomfortable position of
trying to manage electoral affairs in Cromwell's home town, Ely, for
which the government candidate was his own superior, John Thurloe.
Furthermore, in Norwich, the nation's second city, which had been
dominated by Puritans since the revolution, things were looking shaky.
Here Haynes was 'doing my most to avoyde the election of John
Hubbert', but the signs were not good. In the days before the election he
wrote feverishly to Cromwell that resistance from those trying to influence the elections against them was mounting. The problem could be
overcome, he felt sure, if Cromwell would only send soldiers 'of a sufficient strength to secure the interest of these countyes'. It was a measure
of the mentality of the Major Generals that Haynes saw more soldiers as
the only way to persuade people to vote in the regime's favour.[28]

❦ ❦ ❦

The elections of 1656 were, to the horror of the government, even worse
than those two years before. Four hundred and sixty members were
returned (including Mr Hobart of Norwich), of whom over a hundred
were considered too dangerous to be allowed to take their seats.
Nonetheless, the government was determined to get what it needed. As
all royalists had been barred both from standing and from voting in the
elections, and with the most objectionable MPs already purged, there
was every reason to expect compliance. With steely determination John
Desbrow, Major General for the West Country and Oliver Cromwell's
brother-in-law, introduced a bill to continue the decimation tax. He did
so, pointedly, on 25 December, angry at people's dogged refusal to abandon the 'superstitious observances' of Christmas.

Desbrow put the case for the new bill with skill and some subtlety.
He knew where the objections would come – 'you will say the Act of
Oblivion is against it' – but the royalists had not kept to the terms of the
act, he contested, and so had forfeited its protection. It was only right
that they should bear the cost of the new security regime because their
actions had necessitated it – and they could easily afford it, for while
the Puritan government toiled at the responsibilities of state 'they grow

fat and live at home'. The attendance that Christmas Day was thin, but in the face of the brooding assertiveness of the army officers a small number of MPs, including some senior lawyers and, crucially, the Speaker, resisted. This bill involved the imposition of taxation and was arguably in conflict with existing legislation, so it should not be passed without proper scrutiny. The soldiers were furious. John Lambert, Major General for much of the North, pushed back, 'I have laboured to oblige that party,' he insisted, 'to win them as much as may be', but 'find it impossible till time wear out the memory'. Even as he spoke, he intoned, across the country, and in spite of all the prohibitions, 'they are, haply, now merry over their Christmas pies, drinking [Charles II] the King of Scots' health'. But it was in vain. Such was the disquiet about the police state which the military rule represented that within a month the bill, and the Major Generals' regime, was dead.[29]

❦ ❦ ❦

As John Lambert had spoken, a hundred miles north the L'Estrange family were indeed sitting down to their Christmas pies. Nick L'Estrange and Mary Coke, the new Sir Nicholas and Lady L'Estrange, were presiding over their first Christmas together at Hunstanton Hall following their marriage. Catherine Calthorpe, the L'Estrange boys' favourite aunt, was staying and the extended family enjoyed the traditional pleasures of the season. Hunstanton venison was eaten, Christmas presents given, card games played and gambled on, pipes smoked, wine drunk and jigs danced to the fiddlers' tunes. Nick L'Estrange's broad, ruddy-cheeked face beamed, being, like his father and grandfather, 'much addicted to the life that his ancestors led of keeping his chief mansion house by good hospitality'. Thanks to the wealth brought by his marriage, the futures of his six younger brothers had been resolved. John, still a keen musician, had been admitted to the Middle Temple and was now training as a lawyer, Edward had been apprenticed to a wealthy freeman of the Fishmongers' Company and annual allowances had been settled on the younger boys.[30]

Six weeks before Christmas old Alice L'Estrange had died, her work finally done. She left everything that remained at Hunstanton to her grandson Nick. Her 'beloved sonne' Hamon had moved to live with his widowed sister Elizabeth Spring in Suffolk following the imposition of the decimation tax. Alice left him the residue of her estate. To her third son Roger she bequeathed a paltry £40.

The L'Estranges of Hunstanton were a royalist family who, only a few years before, had more or less reconciled themselves to the new political order. Cromwell's policy of 'settling and healing' had accorded with their own resignation to the world as it was, and might well have succeeded in embedding peace where there had been war. But the past year had changed all that. The government had managed to alienate once again those who had lost the civil war without effectively emasculating them. As was pointed out that Christmas Day in the Chamber, the decimation tax had served an additional purpose, of positively identifying all those who had once been adherents of the Stuarts at a time when people had been beginning to forget – 'a character is set upon him that you may know a Cavalier from a Roundhead'. If the government had hoped that time might, in Lambert's words, 'wear out the memory' of old allegiances, the rule of the Major Generals had stopped this process in its tracks. Reconciliation and reintegration, once within reach, was now unthinkable.[31]

In Norfolk, Nick and Mary L'Estrange might be able to avoid national politics, perhaps feeling like Nick's father that so long as they could 'plough and go to market' it mattered little which government was in power. But Nick's uncle Roger L'Estrange could not take this view. He lived not in quiet Norfolk seclusion but in the political cauldron of London. With a talent for half-truths and a rhetorical agility that would one day come into its own, he had already rewritten his own story, ascribing his gentlemanly existence to 'the fortune my father left me' – when in fact it was only his mother's indulgence that had paid his bills. He was not made for rural retirement: he enjoyed 'fine conversation' and rubbing shoulders with important people – Oliver Cromwell once loitered at a Whitehall doorway to listen to him playing the viols. But a fury had been planted in his heart. 'By an order of Nov. 24 1655', he later recalled with bitter precision, 'no cavalier must be allowed so much as the least piece of defensive arms, no person suffered to keep in

his house as chaplain or schoolmaster any sequestered or ejected minister ... Nor any Persons of that Quality must be permitted to teach a
Schoole either Publique or Private nor Preach but in his own family, nor
administer the Sacraments, nor marry, nor use the Common Prayer
Book.' The insult to his family and class would fester, and the day was
drawing nearer where they, and he, would wreak their revenge.[32]

Thirteen

Ingenious Friends

W illiam Petty may well have been in the crowd that gathered to watch the execution of Anne Green in the yard of Oxford Castle. He lived just a short stroll away and he stood to benefit directly from her death. Anne was a 22-year-old domestic servant convicted of murdering her child. It was cold, 14 December 1650, as the stout young woman ascended the ladder to the projecting beam and the noose which was shortly to strangle her. Her time was short. She 'fixt her eyes on the Executioner' and said she hoped God would forgive her accusers, before singing a few lines of a Psalm. The noose was placed about her neck and seconds later she was pushed from the steps. She fell and the line snapped straight, arresting her drop with a sickening jolt. For almost half an hour she hung there, her not inconsiderable weight suspended from the rope around her throat. To ensure her neck was indeed broken, her limp body was lifted up and jerked down repeatedly and a soldier struck her chest hard with the butt of his musket. This done, she was cut down and dropped into the waiting coffin, where she was stamped on three times for good measure.[1]

Whether or not he witnessed her execution, William Petty was intensely interested in the demise of Anne Green. He had never met her and cared not a jot for her life or the justice or otherwise of her sentence. What interested him was her corpse – for dead bodies, especially fresh ones, were hard to come by. Soon after his arrival in Oxford he had arranged for a body to be brought upriver from Reading, but it had been necessary to pickle it first to prevent putrefaction. A cured cadaver was all very well, but its use was limited when it was the living body you toiled to understand.

The coffin containing the corpse of Anne Green was carried through Oxford to a medieval house on the south side of the High Street. Here, over an apothecary's shop, were Petty's own rooms. His colleague and fellow doctor, Thomas Willis, arrived promptly to join him in the dissection they were about to perform. With the blood still warm in her veins, Anne Green was a thrilling prospect to these two young men, their minds alive with the possibilities of Dr Harvey's radical contention that blood did not simply travel outwards from the heart, as had always been thought, but passed around the human body in a continuous circuit. It was only when they approached, their blades now just inches from her ashen flesh, that a faint rattling sound came to their ears and with it the realization that Anne Green was still alive.[2]

Anne Green, a servant girl hanged for the murder of her child, but revived some hours later thanks to the ministrations of William Petty. The 'miracle' of her recovery established Petty's reputation and his subsequent advancement.

✻ ✻ ✻

Oxford in the year 1650 was a new world. The city had been Charles I's headquarters during much of the civil war, the stalwart royalism of the town authorities and the ancient university having provided him a power base after the loss of London. The King had lived in splendour at Christ Church College and among those who had swarmed its cobbled streets had been Dr William Harvey himself, Physician to the King and the publisher of the greatest medical breakthrough since antiquity. Once the city had been forced to surrender, the parliamentarian authorities extracted an uncompromising revenge. By requiring its members to swear the Engagement, the victorious Puritans purged the university of over half its fellows. At William Petty's college, Brasenose, almost two-thirds were expelled. Petty, then only 26 and studying for his doctorate of medicine, was no politician; indeed, his political sympathies were largely invisible, but he, like many other young academics, found himself unexpectedly promoted thanks to this unprecedented clearout of the university hierarchy. Into the vacuum it created a whole new generation of scholars was being drawn and the consequences would be extraordinary.[3]

In the days that followed her 'execution' William Petty and Thomas Willis devoted their every hour to Anne Green. The remaining murmurs of life in the battered young woman had been feeble, but without hesitation the pair turned their efforts from dissection to resurrection. What came next would be the stuff of legend. They tended to her round the clock: taking her pulse, monitoring her colour, temperature and breathing and administering tonics and treatments. Her condition improved slowly at first and then at speed. Within a day she was uttering sounds, within a few she was speaking. It was not long before the whole city knew that Anne Green had been brought back from the dead. Curious callers flooded to Petty's door for sight of this lady Lazarus; at first they had been admitted but soon the crush became so great that Petty had to ask the Governor of Oxford Castle to station sentries at his door. Five days after her hanging Anne Green was sitting up in bed eating chicken legs. Her skin was black with bruising, her neck painfully sore and she could not yet walk, but given her ordeal she was remarkably well. Over those days she told Petty and Willis her story. Things were not as they seemed: she had been seduced by her employer's teenage grandson, and the murdered child was their miscarried baby.[4]

Anne Green quickly became a talisman to Oxford's young medical men. Money was collected for her from the visiting crowds, poems were printed in her name and William Petty himself drafted the petition seeking a reprieve from her sentence. This he argued for on the basis of its obvious injustice – something of which God himself had given proof in allowing her miraculous revival. A sympathetic account of Anne's plight was fed to Marchamont Nedham for publication in *Politicus*, and days later her recovery was the talk of the nation. Before the year was out Anne Green had gained her freedom and begun a career making celebrity appearances at fairs and markets, while Dr William Petty's reputation as worker of miracles was made.[5]

🜲 🜲 🜲

At the time of Anne Green's revival in December 1650 William Petty was 27 and on the brink of something great – though quite what it was remained to be seen (Colour plate 9). He had completed his doctorate and formally qualified as a medical doctor only two months before, but this underrepresented his achievements. While John Bradshaw and Thomas Fairfax, Hamon L'Estrange and Oliver Cromwell had all been born into landed families who gave their sons expensive educations, this had not been William Petty's lot. Like Gerrard Winstanley and Anna Trapnel, he came from a lowlier rung of the social hierarchy. Petty's father had been a small-time Hampshire cloth merchant, but while Petty shared this background, and an intellectual iridescence, with Gerrard Winstanley, it would be hard to conceive of men of more different temperaments. Winstanley worked by instinct and imagination and his fragile mind was haunted by feelings of failure. William Petty was a supreme logician who seems never to have experienced a moment of self-doubt in his life.

Petty's extraordinary intelligence had been obvious from the first. He had a phenomenal mind. He needed only to hear any sequence of fifty words or numbers once to be able to recite them perfectly, forwards or backwards, and to name the tenth or twenty-fifth or thirty-ninth at will. He knew his remarkable memory impressed people, but he thought it absurd for it was a 'thing of noe use'. Rather than being apprenticed in his father's trade, at the age of about 13 he had been sent to sea. He mastered the complex naval charts with a conspicuous cleverness that made his fellow sailors dislike him. A fall from the rigging left him with a broken leg and gave the crew the perfect excuse to be rid of their irritating young shipmate, putting him ashore in Normandy. This unexpected turn of events would have sensational consequences. Petty used almost the last of his meagre money to buy crutches and set about searching for opportunities. He lived on his wits and the proceeds from card tricks and buying and selling trinkets. The Latin and Greek he had already picked up caught the attention of those of learning he encountered and, through a mixture of obvious talent and sheer tenacity, he persuaded the Jesuits of the University of Caen to take him as their pupil. Here he would remain for three or four years, receiving almost by chance the advanced European education that would be his making. He emerged with perfect French, a respect for his Catholic schoolmasters alien to almost all Englishmen, and 'as much mathematicks as any of my age was known to have'.[6]

William Petty reached adulthood just as a scientific golden age was dawning that would give a man of his ability scope for personal advancement and intellectual invigoration such as had never before existed in England. Over the past two thousand years there had been remarkably little change in the understanding of the universe as articulated by Aristotle and others in ancient Greece. Christianity appeared in a world in which these truths were already long established. They included the belief that the earth was a static sphere around which various planets and stars travelled in circular arcs, and that everything on earth was composed of four basic elements: fire, water, air and earth. But a tiny number of intellectuals across Europe had started to perceive serious flaws in the received model of the physical world. The discovery of the Americas had thrown into obvious doubt the ancients' assertion that there were only three continents. Meanwhile, a Polish cleric, Nicolaus Copernicus, had challenged the whole basis of classical astronomy (and the teachings of the Catholic church) when he had posited that, far from being at the centre of the universe, the earth was one of a number of planets that instead orbited the sun. As soon as the edifice of the knowledge of the ancients had been shaken in the minds of the most inquisitive, questions upon questions arose which now demanded answers. The urgent need for tools to address them brought changes in technology, including – crucially – the invention of the telescope and the microscope, enabling a generation of scholars to see clearly things which had been absolutely invisible to their forefathers. It was a thrilling, and dangerous, time to be alive.[7]

Across a whole series of different disciplines – from astronomy to anatomy – new ideas were emerging that shared a common characteristic. The research from which they sprang was rooted not, now, in the studious contemplation of the writings of respected ancients, but in the methodical testing and examination of the physical phenomenon itself – be it the transit of stars or the functioning of the lungs. As yet many of the originators were treated as crackpots or heretics. While William Petty was studying in Caen the celebrated Italian astronomer Galileo Galilei was languishing in prison, having been condemned by the Catholic church for upholding Copernicus's views. Meanwhile, William Harvey's proposition that the blood was in perpetual circulation through the body's vessels, bearing an as yet unidentified substance to every organ, was regarded with profound scepticism, and in some cases downright ridicule, by his peers.[8]

The fracturing of the traditional structures of national life that accompanied the civil war made England particularly fertile ground for such new thinking. The lack of a single strong church or functioning national censorship regime in the 1640s gave rise to a disorderly but unusually free intellectual environment. Furthermore, the war caused many intellectuals, who were neither active participants nor the victors, to travel. Petty returned home in the early 1640s to find

England in turmoil, and so withdrew to Paris where he started to study anatomy, working in his spare time as an assistant to the philosopher Thomas Hobbes. In so doing he encountered men and methods which he would never have come across had he simply settled in a peaceful England.[9]

❦ ❦ ❦

Whether or not William Petty called the first meeting of the Oxford Experimental Philosophy Club, he was certainly one of its prime movers. This gathering of adherents of the new experimental approach came into being sometime in late 1649, and its Thursday afternoon meetings were held at William Petty's rooms on the High Street. Petty's downstairs neighbour, the chemist and apothecary John Clarke, provided the ingredients for many of their activities. They were not the first gathering of new scientists in England, but this was far more than a discussion group. It was a research society proper, with regular meetings and rules for election and the management of business. Individually and collectively this group would, through trial and error, observation and measurement, bring about fundamental changes in human understanding of the world.

Each week at their meeting this group of young men, almost all in their twenties and thirties, undertook practical experiments – the lifeblood of their association. Their research ranged across a dazzling array of subjects from the valves of the veins to the spots on the sun and its rotational axis, from the existence (or otherwise) of vacuums to the weight of air, from the hypotheses of Copernicus to the works of Galileo 'and divers other things of like nature'. Among their number was John Wilkins, the recently appointed Warden of Wadham College who, with his talented young protégé, Christopher Wren, was having an 80-foot telescope built for examining the moon. Another, Seth Ward, the first Oxford professor of astronomy to teach Copernicus, was setting up a chemical 'elaboratory'. To Wilkins it was clear that 'there are many secret truths, which the ancients have passed over, that are yet left to make some of our age famous for their discovery'.[10]

William Petty was as convinced a follower of the new philosophy as any of his contemporaries. He mocked those who still spent their time bent over books, for 'discoveries and improvements' would not be found in trawling the work of others. He had decided the previous year to stop reading altogether and instead to focus entirely on active experimentation, arguing that the club should have for their patron saint 'doubting' St Thomas the Apostle, who had refused to believe in the resurrection until he had seen Christ's wounds with his own eyes and touched them with his own hands.[11]

While Petty's subject was anatomy, his interests, like many of his contemporaries', were not confined to one discipline. They shared an appetite for encyclopaedic knowledge, for identifying all gaps in human understanding and seeking collectively to fill them – to which end many of the club were participating in the compilation of a great subject index to the books in Thomas Bodley's library. Above all, however, Petty was interested in things which might serve some practical purpose. As one who, growing up, had been entranced by the work of 'artificers' – watchmakers and blacksmiths, carpenters and joiners – he had limited appetite for advances in the abstract alone. Sons of the greatest families, he believed, should learn the practical skills of the artisan, while conversely 'many are now holding the plough which might have been fit to steer the state'. His deeply held belief in the marriage of the practical and the intellectual sometimes bemused his associates. At one meeting, after he and his comrades had spent a full afternoon inflating bladders with bellows and tobacco pipes, and suspending from them an assortment of weights, he recalled, 'I cried out for the aplication thereof to some usefull thing'.

More than this, Petty sought opportunities for the commercial exploitation of their work. He minded about money to a degree quite alien to the gentlemen scholars who had never known poverty, and the memory of the terrible week during his time in Paris when he had had nothing to live on but walnuts stayed with him for the rest of his life. For years he had contemplated how he would make his fortune, ranking and assessing the possibilities: practising as a physician, securing the patronage of wealthy men or coming up with a brilliant invention.

Throughout his time at Oxford he retained rooms in London and travelled back periodically to practise as a doctor, treating the families of wealthy City merchants for handsome fees.[12]

For some time now, Petty had believed he was on the brink of real riches. Having grown up in trade he was better placed than some of his cerebral colleagues to consider what an indispensable innovation might be. He had come up with just such a thing, he believed, a device for duplicating the written word, his 'instrument for double writing'. He guarded the details of his great invention closely, securing a patent and swearing the small number who knew its secret to 'absolute silence'. This, he felt sure, would be his making: an object 'of daily and almost hourly use to most men in most countries of the whole world'. But despite Petty's self-confidence, and almost paranoid protection of its design, the double-writing instrument would come to nothing. Instead, it was in another sphere, and on quite another scale, that Petty's remarkable abilities would find their release.[13]

On describing the Anne Green affair to his friend and mentor Samuel Hartlib, Petty had remarked mildly that 'my endeavours in this businesse have bettered my reputation'. And so it would prove to be. Just weeks after Anne's revival the Oxford professor of anatomy, Thomas Clayton, resigned. Indeed, it may have been Petty's famous success that precipitated Clayton's resignation: he had been in post for three years but had yet to give a single lecture and 'could not endure the sight of a bloody body'. Clayton nominated Petty himself and Convocation agreed without a murmur.[14] But his opportunities were not to end there, for just a year later he received a job offer that was so tempting it caused him to forsake Oxford altogether. In the autumn of 1651 Henry Ireton, Oliver Cromwell's son-in-law and the Lord Deputy of Ireland, died of disease camped outside the city of Limerick. His successor, understandably keen to ensure this would not be his fate, too, was casting around for a physician to take with him and offered the position, and the magnificent salary of £365 a year, to he who could bring back the dead.[15]

🐝 🐝 🐝

It was September 1652 when William Petty set sail for Ireland. He was still not quite 30 as the ship ploughed its way west across the ridge and furrow of the Irish Sea. He cut a striking figure. He was, in the words of one friend, 'a proper handsome man': 6 foot tall with a thick mop of dark brown hair and full eyebrows. His figure was slim and straight and his eyes a pale grey. To those who did not interest him he was sharp, unforgiving and supercilious, quick to dismiss or deride for stupidity. To those he cared about – his 'ingenious friends', his family and select others – he was altogether different: wry, funny and kind, if sometimes in a clumsy or ill-judged way. He was probably one of the last of the company to sight land on that voyage, for he suffered from acute short-sightedness, on the basis of which he would later dismiss an adversary's challenge to a duel by saying it would be a fair match only if it was fought with axes in the dark.

The journey to Ireland gave Petty his first opportunity to get to know his new patron. The freshly appointed 'Commander in Chief' of Ireland was Charles Fleetwood, friend of Oliver Cromwell and stalwart of the New Model Army (Colour plate 10). In the year since Ireton's death Fleetwood had not only been given Ireton's job (albeit with a lowlier title), but had married his widow, Oliver Cromwell's brisk and godly oldest daughter, Bridget. She was only 28 but already the mother of four young children. Fleetwood was a soldier but the task that lay before him as the regime's governor of Ireland was, at long last, not a military one.[16]

Ireland was of itself a country of great natural advantages. It was one of the things about it that attracted adherents of the new science. For here was an entire country which might be considered as a specimen of living geography on which, like the poor animals that the Oxford men injected with noxious substances, experimental approaches might be trialled. Petty himself may have been among those preparing for publication a remarkable two-volume *Natural History of Ireland*, based on the observations of a German doctor who had worked there in the 1640s. It described an island with great potential for economic development: a land of moderate climate, fertile soil, deep harbours, rich pastures and a healthy population. But as a consequence of the events of the last decade the Ireland of the *Natural History*, that visited by John Bradshaw's friend William Brereton in the 1630s, was barely recognizable as the place where William Petty and Charles Fleetwood were now each setting foot for the first time.[17]

❦ ❦ ❦

Come the summer of 1652 the relentless reconquest of Ireland which had been launched by Oliver Cromwell and Henry Ireton in the summer of 1649, had all but ended. The island was now under the steely thumb of the London government, but the human and monetary cost of the ugly war of attrition that it had prosecuted was epic in scale. The victims had overwhelmingly been on the losing side. Around half a million Irish people, by Petty's reckoning, had died, many from fighting but more from the disease and famine that accompanied it. This was of a total pre-war population perhaps approaching two million. It was, in the words of one contemporary Irish poet, 'the war that finished Ireland'. The numbers of English and Scots who perished were proportionately far fewer but still vast in quantity, perhaps something over 100,000.[18]

From Waterford where they landed Petty and Fleetwood made for Dublin, where both men set about acquainting themselves with the place and the tasks that lay before them. Dublin in 1652 was a shadow of a city. Before the war visitors had thought it fine and prosperous. Its handsome red-brick houses topped with ornamental Dutch gables regarded one another grandly across the broad streets, while the government of the country was conducted from within the ancient walls of Dublin Castle (Colour plate 12). Now, after years of war, Dublin was dirty, dilapidated and semi-deserted. As many as half the houses were completely empty, robbed of their inhabitants by fighting and famine, and even the government had periodically to evacuate the city to avoid disease. The Irish Parliament had been dispensed with and the chambers of the Commons and Lords stood gauntly empty, as obsolete as the antique armour mounted on their walls. The castle teemed with soldiers, eighty manning the gates day and night, and in place of a civilian government the country was ruled by the army that had just succeeded in bringing it brutally to heel.[19]

For William Petty, with a scientist's lack of squeamishness, Ireland was the opportunity he had been waiting for: a chance to have some position in the world from which to effect changes that would be both productive and profitable. His role was a dual one: personal physician to a powerful man and his family and the senior doctor to the army. He applied himself to the responsibilities with gusto, undertaking a comprehensive review of the costs and administration of the army medical establishment. Within a matter of months he had reduced waste and increased the efficiency of the supply of medicines and materials to the various garrisons and hospitals. His abrasive approach, particularly his attack on the Apothecary General and his staff, won him few friends, but he was not one to let other people's feelings get in the way when he knew he was right.[20]

Lieutenant General Fleetwood, by contrast, found the challenges of this battered and bruised colony altogether more daunting. He was a soldier taking control at a time when the soldiering was largely done. Instead, it was the task of rebuilding that needed to be taken in hand, and Charles Fleetwood had neither the personal authority nor the political agility to effect such a thing. The bloody business of war in Ireland had served only to steel the nerves and harden the hearts of those who had been left to lead it. Both among the common soldiers and in the high command the Englishmen who were now masters of Ireland had acquired a bitter intransigence, fixed by all that they had seen and suffered. For while the experience of ordinary Irish men and women had been appalling, the lot of the English private soldier had hardly been a happy one. Living in saturated field tents, engaged in a violent conflict in which norms of good conduct had long since been abandoned, ill clothed and fed, barely paid and beset by diseases that were felling whole companies, it was a horror of its own. Little wonder the soldiers who had been drawing lots for Ireland the day that Gerrard Winstanley had come to meet Thomas Fairfax at Whitehall had trembled at the thought of what was to come. When army commissioners had written to the Council of State in February 1652, they had had to report that of the new recruits sent over the previous year, two-thirds were dead already.[21]

The beginning of a new stage in the English exploitation of Ireland was sealed in the legislation that the Rump Parliament had passed just days before Petty and Fleetwood had set sail. Care had been taken to jog the memories of Rump MPs by having detailed testimony of the rape and murder of individual Protestants by Catholics in 1641 read aloud in the chamber in advance of the debate. The 'Act for the Settlement of Ireland' of August 1652 laid out the terms of the ruthless peace that was now to be enforced. The ramifications of this legislation were seismic. The very poorest Irishmen and women, the labourers and ploughmen with less than £10 to their names, were to be pardoned. But there the mercy ended. Everyone else who had not actively supported the Commonwealth army was to pay a towering price. A huge number of the prime movers and actual combatants were to be executed and all the rest were to suffer mass forfeiture of lands. Those who had surrendered and pledged complete loyalty to the new regime were to be allowed to retain a portion of their acreage, however this was not to be any part of their own property but a quite different allocation in the far west of Ireland. This was the infamous policy of 'transplantation'. It was harsher by far than anything experienced by the losers in the civil war anywhere else in the three kingdoms. More than this, it embodied the conviction of Ireton and his uncompromising comrades that such was the 'treachery, wickedness and malice' of the native population that the only possible future in Ireland involved absolute separation between English and Irish. The Protestant English soldiers were to be able to enjoy the lands they were about to receive in the north, south and east of the island 'without disturbance or danger of being corrupted by intermixing with the natives in marriages or otherwise'. Meanwhile, the Irish, overwhelmingly Catholic, were to be herded west, penned in beyond the far banks of the River Shannon, and banned from all ports and towns. Nothing short of complete ethnic separation was being legislated for, on a scale without any precedent in the British Isles before or since.[22]

The question of whether Charles Fleetwood was up to the task of seeing through this enormous undertaking did not take long to emerge in the mind of Oliver Cromwell, despite his personal affection for his new son-in-law. The following spring, in the final tense weeks of the Rump Parliament, the General was sufficiently concerned to dispatch an emissary to assess the situation. That emissary was his promising second son, Henry Cromwell (Colour plate 11). The young man, just 25, spent no more than a fortnight in Dublin in March 1653. His report was not encouraging. He set out the issues plainly: there were at the centre of the Dublin government a number of powerful and opinionated men, several committed Baptists, who were utterly merciless in their approach to Ireland and barely disguised their disgust at the management of affairs in London. Henry's brother-in-law, Fleetwood, 'does verry little' and was too much in thrall to his radical army brothers to moderate their measures. Fleetwood's chief subject of conversation was his desire to return home. Henry Cromwell made his assessment, but with no mandate to take any action, sailed home leaving the problems behind him. But it would not be the last time he would apply his shrewd eye to the troubles of this island.[23]

❦ ❦ ❦

The English reconquest of Ireland had been funded in two ways. First, a group of London investors or 'Adventurers' had, as long ago as the Catholic uprising of 1641, put up several hundred thousand pounds to be repaid in the lands that would be confiscated from the 'rebels'. Secondly, it was decided some time later that the soldiers themselves would also be part paid in forfeited lands. It was a funding structure that had made it impossible for any English soldier to contemplate any outcome short of total victory. Before Cromwell had even set sail, therefore, the need for total victory, and the bleak fate of Irish landholders, had been long since sealed.

In order for the two groups expecting payment in Irish lands to be satisfied now that the fighting was over, there was an administrative mountain to climb for there were no easy mechanisms to effect such transfers of land: maps barely existed and title deeds were nowhere to be found. A further Act of Parliament, passed by the short-lived Nominated Assembly in September 1653, addressed the question of how this was to be done. Connacht, the westernmost of Ireland's four large provinces, was to be allocated to the transplanted Irish and a highly ambitious programme of written and measured surveys was to be embarked upon, on the basis of which the reapportionment of a country could begin.[24]

As this mammoth task was being sketched out, William Petty looked on. The army was no longer campaigning, and scores of soldiers and hangers-on seeped back to Dublin, bringing with them the plague that had dogged them on campaign. Petty quickly developed a lucrative medical practice 'among the chief in the chief City of a Nation', and a new interest in demography. He began calculating the daily mortality rate, the numbers of English and Irish to have perished in the wars, the size of the population as a whole and other metrics for assessing the dimensions of a nation. He was also not without 'ingenious' company. Others of a scientific bent had also made their way to Ireland now that peace was descending. Among them was the person leading the national surveying project, an associate of a number of Petty's Oxford friends and fellow physician, Benjamin Worsley. Another was a man from an altogether loftier echelon of society, the youngest son of Ireland's wealthiest landowner, the Honourable Robert Boyle.[25]

William Petty had first encountered Robert Boyle in London some five years earlier, when, before his move to Oxford, he had been seeking sponsors for the double-writing instrument. Boyle was as rich as Petty was poor, and a few years his junior. The investment did not materialize but the two men had become acquainted. When Petty arrived in Ireland in 1652 Boyle, who had returned to his family's expansive lands earlier that year, soon sought him out. Boyle shared Petty's immense intelligence and after prolonged educational travels on the Continent, had been applying his mind to philosophy and theology. But he had recently developed a new, amateur interest in science – and having the Oxford professor of anatomy in Dublin was too good an opportunity to miss. Boyle and Petty started to meet to conduct experiments. It was through the gruesome dissection of a live dog that, with Petty's help, Boyle first saw for himself proof of Dr Harvey's theory of the circulation of the blood. He wrote to a friend in London enraptured that such an examination of nature itself had revealed more truth 'than all the books I ever read in my life could give me convincing notions of'.[26]

While Petty was not given to melancholy, Robert Boyle was, and the days he spent experimenting with Petty were one of the few things that took his mind from the darkness that otherwise filled it. Petty regarded Ireland with the same cool detachment as Anne Green's execution or the whimpering victims of his vivisection. For Robert Boyle the country, and the sight of its devastated people and places, was an altogether different experience. Ireland was the land of his birth and of the Boyles' wealth and titles. The family had been divided by the wars, different siblings taking different sides. He himself had taken none, but he was overwhelmed with sadness and anger at what confronted him on his return. His father's great castle that stood on a rocky crag above the Blackwater River at Lismore lay in ruins, the island's buildings and bridges had been reduced to rubble, his countrymen had been dispossessed and the burden of taxation upon them was unbearable – thirteen shillings a month for a single cow, he had heard. Along the roads he travelled between his house in Youghal and Dublin gaunt beggars and orphans were to be seen 'swarming', forced to feed like wild animals on weeds and carrion. And all this in a country famous for the fertility of its soil. He regarded the men now governing Ireland with absolute disgust, and what they presided over as a disgrace. How could it be that the people starved while his own brother, Roger, one of the senior officials of the new regime, 'hath found leisure newly to print foure Tomes of an English Romannce'?[27]

It may have been William Petty's irrepressible ambition, his friend's despair at the island's mismanagement, or simply his inability to watch others do badly what he knew he could do well, that caused the doctor to act. Tending to the medical needs of army officers and counting the dead was not enough. He was no politician, lawyer or soldier, so such arenas were not open to him. But he was an academic, a scientist and one whose life's work had been to look for the application of original thinking 'to some usefull thing'. The enterprise he had been watching with mounting frustration was that being led by Benjamin Worsley to produce the comprehensive maps of Ireland upon which the reallocation of lands was to be based. He could see how inefficient the process was set to be: it would take years, cost a fortune, be full of errors and omissions and establish an utterly inadequate basis for all future land ownership in the country. The time had come for him to step forward.

❦ ❦ ❦

In September 1654, Henry Cromwell was at his father's side as the new Lord Protector rode to Westminster to open the First Protectorate Parliament. In the crowd of MPs was Guybon Goddard, the lawyer from King's Lynn and, for the first time, elected MPs from Ireland and Scotland. Among the 'great works' with which the new Protector charged the assembled members in his opening speech on 'healing and settling' was Ireland. 'It is a great business to settle the government of that nation upon fit terms,' he boomed; but his impatience was already showing, 'there is not much done towards the planting of it, though some things leading and preparing for it are'. Five days later William Petty unveiled his proposition to the Commander in Chief in Dublin. As usual he did not sugar his words. Under the leadership of Benjamin Worsley the mapping project was 'insufficiently and absurdly managed' and set to be a disaster. He proposed that he, William Petty, take it on instead. Where Worsley was intending to map only the outline of forfeited lands, he would document all internal boundaries and land-scape features; instead of paying hefty fees to surveyors for 'an absurd and insignificant way of surveying' he would completely reorganize the process to reduce costs and achieve far greater levels of accuracy; and, crucially, whereas Worsley was expecting to take seven years, he would complete the entire task in just one.[28]

This Oxford academic, who had no experience of surveying or map-making whatsoever, nor even of managing any significant human enterprise, was now proposing to undertake the most ambitious feat of cartography in the history of the British Isles. The notion seemed ridiculous. But Fleetwood and his councillors felt the weight of the Protector's expectations heavy on their shoulders. Not until the maps were finished could soldiers be paid off, the army disbanded and the process of rebuilding begin. All their misgivings notwithstanding, this audacious proposition was too tempting to decline – and had Dr Petty not once before achieved the miraculous? Petty, for his own part, was driven by unshakable self-belief and a conviction that 'by attempting new difficulties' he would 'stretch my own capacity and intellect, the which (like leather on a last) is not only formed and fashioned, but much extended by such Employment'. But as the tall doctor leaned forward to sign his commission amid the crumbling grandeur of Dublin Castle on Christmas Day 1654, Charles Fleetwood and his fellow signatories must have wondered whether he could possibly be right.[29]

Fourteen

The End of Ireland

❦❦❦❦❦❦❦❦❦❦❦❦❦❦❦❦❦❦❦

The short, dark month of February was an inauspicious time to start
to map a nation. But having promised with such bombast to
complete his task within thirteen months, Petty could not afford to
wait. The start of the project had already been delayed six weeks by the
complications of agreeing terms, including – crucially – the remunera-
tion due on completion. Petty may have won the commission at the
expense of Benjamin Worsley, but Worsley was still Surveyor General
and all the details of how he was to proceed had to be agreed with his
vanquished rival. Not for the last time Petty's insensitivity to the feelings of those around him would have consequences.[1]

The thing which really outraged those who had been displaced from
the project, however, was how Petty proposed to complete it at such
speed. The answer lay in no ingenious mechanical innovation or new
scientific formula. Instead, he had looked at the small band of professional surveyors marshalled by Worsley, educated members of the
gentry whose 'practise [was] esteemed a mistery and intricate matter'
and had seen only cost and professional conceit. He envisaged a radical
alternative. He would not put the project into the hands of such men.
Instead he would break the whole process down into its constituent
parts and identify among the demobilizing soldiers of the English army
men with the right raw abilities to effect each element. Soldiers were

hardy, available in great numbers and had a vested interest in seeing the surveys done quickly and accurately. As they did not yet know which lands were to be allocated to which regiments, there was little risk of deliberate misrepresentation. There was also, Petty contended, no need to wait for all the equipment to be sent over by the specialist scientific instrument makers in London as, with the right guidance, many items could be made by tradesmen in Dublin. Irish watchmakers could assemble the large magnetic compasses, wood turners could make the staffs and stands for fieldwork and wire makers could manufacture the long measuring chains.

For the fieldwork itself, 'it being a matter of great drudgery (to wade through boggs and water [and] climb rocks', he intended to use English

Place this after the second Book to be laid open

A surveyor taking measurements assisted by putti with measuring chains. From William Leybourn, *The Complete Surveyor*, published in 1653. The mapping of Ireland under William Petty's direction in the 1650s was the most ambitious feat of cartography ever undertaken in the British archipelago.

foot soldiers familiar with the hardships of campaign. Here were men 'who could endure travaile, ill lodging and dyett, as alsoe heats and colds, beinge also men of activitie that could leape hedge and ditch'. They expected to sleep in tents and were trained to repel the hostility they were certain to meet. 'Steddy minded' soldiers who, like Petty, came from trading families and could read and write would be taught how to take the detailed measurements and assess land quality. Others whose backgrounds were in trades that involved painting or drawing could be shown how to use protractors and other instruments to create scale plans. Those who could draw would work up the fair copies and add decorative embellishments. Men with numerical skills could undertake calculations and the small number with the sharpest wits and eyes could carry out the exhaustive checks Petty required to ensure the accuracy of all that had been done. Here writ large was Petty's whole contention: that there were those in lowly positions across the land who with the right instruction might undertake the greatest work. And here, over a century before Adam Smith published *The Wealth of Nations*, William Petty was proposing dramatically increased productivity through the division and specialization of labour.[2]

🕸 🕸 🕸

To meet the expectations of his masters in London for the 'settlement' of Ireland – both metaphorically and literally – Charles Fleetwood had to achieve several daunting things. The vanquished Irish, the vast majority of the population, had first to be relieved of their lands, they then had to be shifted west and allocated new, far smaller landholdings in the rugged, boggy terrain of Connacht. At the same time the estates they released had to be precisely measured and assessed, and finally these acres had to be allocated on an equitable basis to new English owners.

The task that William Petty had undertaken to complete in just over a year was the mapping in fine detail of all the lands to be forfeited by Irish families in preparation for their apportionment to the disbanded English army. But such was the extent of confiscations, and so few the exceptions, that to do so entailed mapping the entire landscape of these areas. The counties on which Petty's survey was at first to focus formed a great diagonal stripe across most of the country, from Antrim in the north of the province of Ulster, to Cork in the south of Munster. The small area to the east was to be reserved for the commercial investors and for 'government use', while what lay to the west was principally the province of Connacht where thousands of dispossessed Irish families were to relocate.[3]

In theory the process of transplantation ought by 1655 to have been substantially advanced. But well over a year after the orders had been given, still only a few hundred had moved. While there had been some executions of the numerous people condemned, the regime hesitated to carry them out on the colossal scale entailed by the legislation, and many of those who were able to were opting for immediate exile over transplantation to Connacht. Most of those destined for transplantation hung back, some waiting for reassurance that there would, in fact, be lands for them in Connacht, some for the means to make the move and many simply in the desperate hope that something might yet save them.[4]

Over the winter of 1654–5, as Petty drilled his trainee surveyors, the Dublin government launched a further push to implement transplantation. Orders were issued that everyone was to be on the move by March 1655, on pain of death. When Edward Heatherington was executed in Dublin a placard was strung about his neck which bore the chilling words: 'for not transplanting'. Men were dispatched ahead to Connacht to establish what new lands the dispossessed Catholics were to be allotted instead. The immense numbers affected were made up of thousands of individual families and households, many already denuded by disease and famine. Some groups included the personnel of whole estates, such as that led by 31-year-old Matthew Hore from Waterford, whose party numbered 131, including his elderly father, 10-year-old son, servants and tenants, scores of cows and 300 sheep. In Limerick the red-haired Theobald, Baron of Brittas, registered as readying 'to remove' himself, his wife, two girls in their care – the young daughters of their friend Sir John Bourke – a handful of servants and a meagre three cows and six pigs. Another party was led by his elderly relation the Dowager Lady Castleconnell and included her servants, tenants, twenty cows, twenty sheep, ten horses and four pigs. No matter that in England, at precisely this moment, the Dowager Countess of Derby, who had personally directed two royalist sieges, was signing the papers to secure the return of the vast Stanley estates. Ireland, as ever, was to receive a different sort of justice. Tragedy hung over each sorry group – parents and children, employers and tenants, masters and servants – as almost every landowning Catholic family in Ireland faced dispossession.[5]

At just this moment a powerful voice of protest rang out from within the governing elite itself. Vincent Gookin was a Protestant and close ally of the Boyle family who had been impeccably loyal to the Commonwealth regime. But as an Irishman he looked aghast at the process of transplantation being conducted by this cabal of English army officers, none of whom knew Ireland other than as conquerors, appalled that such a policy could be thought in any way wise let alone workable. His pamphlet *The Great Case of Transplantation in Ireland Discussed*, published in January 1655, exposed the reality of what was in hand. This was not, he contested, about justice for individual actions in the late wars, as thousands who were now being dispossessed had taken no part in those wars and many others had been drawn in only by chance. It was instead a vindictive mission pursued by the Puritan officers of the English army to punish 'national blood-guilt', wreaking upon the Irish nation as a whole a merciless Old Testament vengeance such that 'noe eye must pittie them'. Not only was this unjust, contended Gookin, but it was also manifestly self-destructive, as if all those who made Ireland's economy work – the herdsmen and black-smiths, innkeepers and clothiers – were to be removed to the far west, how could any new settlers prosper? His publication was addressed to the MPs of the First Protectorate Parliament in the hope they would moderate the legislation that had been passed by their predecessors. But in London MPs were engaged in the bitter stand-off with Oliver Cromwell over the creation of the Protectorate and when they were abruptly dismissed a fortnight after Gookin's book appeared any hope of parliamentary clemency for Ireland was lost. But Gookin's pithy and persuasive case was too powerful to go unheeded.[6]

🏵 🏵 🏵

February and March 1655 were dismal. The rain was relentless even for a damp island, and the roads and tracks churned to mud. As Petty's recruits set out from Dublin, their instruments and tents, measuring chains and rolls of blank paper packed in carts, those whose entire patrimony was being taken from them were also taking to the roads. Petty's men travelled warily, keeping watch for renegade Irishmen ('tories') and the prowling wolves known to prey on the vulnerable. An enthusiastic group of sixty survey men had set out in early February in what was still deep winter. That first foray was a disaster, however, for they found the fields flooded, boundaries and landscape character impossible to divine, and were forced to wade 'up to the knees and middle in bog and water, the raine spoiling the instruments'. Petty lost hundreds of pounds in equipment and time that he could not spare.[7]

The task upon which Petty's surveyors were embarking was monumental. Scale mapping itself had only started to be widely used over the past century. In England the former royal and church lands had recently been assessed in preparation for their sale. But like many others, those surveys, while precise and comprehensive, were written documents and did not include any maps. With the exception of Connacht, which the Earl of Strafford had had measured in the 1630s and which was outside Petty's area, there were few suitable precedents from which to work.[8]

The maps were to take as their basic unit the sub-parish divisions known as 'townlands', of which there were some 60,000 in Ireland (Colour plate 13). The townlands of every parish might range from a few acres to several hundred acres each and were to be mapped at the scale of 1:50,000. These were then to be scaled up into barony and county maps (Colour plate 14). For each townland the surveyors were to record not just its extent and current ownership but its economic value: whether it was 'profitable', and if so arable or pasture, or 'unprofitable', in which case whether it was boggy, heathy, 'fursy', rocky, woody or mountainous. While the purpose of the survey was to catalogue the forfeit property, Petty had successfully argued that lands not subject to forfeit should also be delineated to create complete maps that would be useful in numerous other ways.

The maps themselves, on which the information was 'laid down' (which led to its name, the 'Down Survey'), were also to indicate natural boundaries and landmarks – castles, great houses, churches and earthworks – and the heights of hills. In addition to the maps and the raw data captured in the field books, Petty's teams were to compile exhaustive 'books of reference' listing the owners of each parcel of land, the names of towns and villages, the identification of land character and additional 'observations as castles, weares, mills, fords, passes, bridges, abbeys, churches, mines etc'. Furthermore, they were to set down markers to allow for the lands' subsequent division into portions for allocation to the soldiers, and they were to supply any recipient of over 1,000 acres with a specific map of his own estate. No mapping project of the extent or accuracy of the Down Survey had ever been attempted before in the British Isles and, with the exception of Sweden (ruled by the map-obsessed Gustavus II Adolphus), no country in Europe had yet been the subject of a comparable field survey.[9]

Before the survey parties set out, Petty had conducted a thorough search of what information of any sort already existed. Crucially, Benjamin Worsley had the previous year required the local officials of each parish to submit a written return detailing the condition of land in their locality which provided up-to-date guidance on what the surveyors should expect to find. The Ireland that this, the 'Civil Survey', described was as devastated as Robert Boyle had found his part of Waterford. Tipperary, for example, was a landscape of bleak ruination, in which most people inhabited tiny thatched 'cabins', one-room chimney-less dwellings, nestling amid the shattered wrecks of stone castles and surrounded by tumbledown mills, bridges and weirs. For good reason were Petty's surveyors being supplied with 'small French tents' for in many places there was clearly no chance of finding lodgings. It was not that nothing had escaped the destruction – there were intact Protestant lands, sturdy new English forts and properties already occupied by the new governing elite – but these stood starkly against a backdrop of post-war devastation that stretched far beyond the line of sight.[10]

So it was that as winter turned to spring the newly trained staff of the Down Survey made their way across the Irish landscape. There was no short cut to their laborious task. In each and every parish, having pressed a guide into service and viewed the terrain, they set up their instruments and began to take their measurements. The whole mapping process was done by means of trigonometry. The soldiers would run the measuring chains, each 66 feet long, along the hedges and ditches which formed the boundaries of each townland. Meanwhile, the surveyor would with his 'Circumferentor' – a magnetic compass with adjustable sights set on a stand – measure the angles between the various points. Each angle and length was systematically recorded in one of Petty's ruled-out field books, ready for drawing up. An array of measurements having been taken in this way, those doing the 'protracting' could by relatively simple geometry establish missing measurements and the acreage of any parcel of land. A similar approach, in which the instrument could be tipped up to

The South-East Prospect of Ballicar Castle, Co. Clare, 1681, showing a landscape of semi-ruinous tower houses with clusters of small cabins, entirely characteristic of the ravaged state of rural Ireland in the mid-seventeenth century.

assess angles of elevation, allowed the heights of landscape features to be divined.[11]

William Petty himself was not to be found leaning over the circumferentor on heathery hillsides or manning the measuring chains. He remained instead in Dublin, surrounded by a small group of trusted colleagues and collaborators, men who, as he put it, 'daily eat and drank with me', focused with relentless intensity on the task at hand. He dispatched replacement instruments and paper, money and clarifications of instructions to those who led the field parties, and stood ready to receive the books of measurements and the first drawn surveys. He was by his own description 'a sedentery schollar' not a leaper of hedges and anyhow his awful eyesight more or less disqualified him from any actual survey work. He was instead the conductor of a great orchestra, one that would soon have a thousand players, and the Down Survey would be his symphony.[12]

❦ ❦ ❦

Perhaps the last man in authority to accept that Henry Cromwell, and not Charles Fleetwood, was the person to take charge in Ireland was Henry's own father, Oliver Cromwell. Since 1654 John Thurloe and the Council of State in London had been putting Henry forward. On the day that William Petty signed the commission for the Down Survey, Henry Cromwell was at last appointed to the six-man Irish Council of State, in the capacity of Major General, or head of the army in Ireland. Oliver Cromwell's acute sensitivity to accusations of nepotism prevented him from formally naming his second son as Lord Deputy – indeed, Fleetwood himself had only finally been given the coveted title the year before. But as Fleetwood left for London just weeks after Henry arrived it was obvious who now was expected to wrestle with the intractable issues of Ireland.

Henry Cromwell was a different man from his brother-in-law. In place of Fleetwood's dogmatism, religious fervour and tendency to cede to those of stronger character, Henry Cromwell had real independence of thought and clarity of intent. He had seen during his short visit to Dublin how the radical army officers at the top of the Irish regime ran rings around his brother-in-law. Chief among them was Lieutenant General Edmund Ludlow, who, like John Bradshaw, had been enraged by the creation of the Protectorate and the abandonment, as they both saw it, of the founding principles of the revolution. Fleetwood lacked personal authority and even after a five-hour debate in his rooms at Dublin Castle he had been unable to persuade Ludlow and a number of other commissioners to proclaim the new Protectorate. It did not help Ludlow's case with Henry Cromwell that when he met the younger man he explained with sugary condescension that his objections were 'in no sort personal, but would be the same were my own father alive and in place of his'.[13]

As soon as Fleetwood left Ireland for England in September 1655, Henry Cromwell confronted Ludlow and ordered the arrest of various of his fellow agitators. He set the tone by explaining crisply that 'Liberty and countenance they might expect from me, but to rule me or to rule with me I should not approve of'. It was a clear enough message, but he, too, faced challenges in asserting his authority. Despite his authoritative tone he was painfully aware of his youth and inexperience – though he had served in the army in Ireland and had even been at Ireton's side at Limerick. He suffered periodic pulses of self-doubt, exacerbated by the fact that his father had given him responsibility for this nation without actually assigning him formal authority. As a consequence the disgruntled men Henry sought to bring into line retained a destructive back channel for complaints and counter-briefings to their titular master in England. Though Fleetwood had longed to return home, he nonetheless smarted at being supplanted and did not resist the temptation to encourage such communications and dish out unwelcome advice.[14]

❦ ❦ ❦

With Fleetwood gone, Henry Cromwell took stock of affairs in Ireland. It was an indication of the sort of man he was that he – like William Petty and St Thomas – wished to see and judge matters for himself. He set out from Dublin on 1 September 1655 and for the next month toured Leinster and Munster, the southern two of Ireland's four provinces. He returned in October with precious little to feel encouraged about. The country was in obvious physical disarray. Ireland remained largely under military rule, all the significant towns had lost their charters and were governed by English military commanders, almost all overseas trade was banned and taxation was ruinously high and set to increase every year. The English army in Ireland still numbered well over 20,000, double the size of that in England. The cost of maintaining it was over £300,000 per annum at a time when the funds available for all other government activities in Ireland came to less than £50,000. The process of transplantation had begun, it was true, but was disorganized and there was growing evidence that the substitute lands promised to displaced Catholics in Connacht would be insufficient for the numbers being sent there.

Rebuilding was urgently required, but it was not at all clear how this could be paid for. Any hope of securing financial aid from London was faint, particularly given the recent debacle of the Western Design. Charles Fleetwood unhelpfully pointed out to John Thurloe, as he travelled back to London, that it was hardly surprising that the Caribbean expedition had been such a disaster given that the soldiers sent to Hispaniola were those 'rejected and cast out from amongst us heere'. The Lord Protector wrote to his son promising 'more help' for Ireland, but this looked likely to be in the form of extra appointees to the Council rather than better terms or greater financial resources. Now that it had been 'pacified', Ireland had ceased to be a real priority for the Protector and the men at the centre of things in London. It was little wonder Henry Cromwell nursed 'melancholy thoughts' at all he had to shoulder.[15]

🐝 🐝 🐝

At 9 a.m. on Tuesday 11 March 1656, thirteen months exactly since William Petty's commission had been finalized, a special 'grand committee' of the Irish Council of State convened at Dublin Castle. Its sole business was to take receipt of the Down Survey. Petty was leaving nothing to chance. More than fifty of his surveyors and his eight 'examiners' hovered outside, poised on the doctor's summons to account for any measurement or address any discrepancy. On the table before Henry

Cromwell and his fellow councillors were placed a mountain of books and sheaf upon sheaf of plans in which some five million acres was rendered in ink on paper. The material was there, but its quality was unknown. Could the survey be as complete as it looked? Could the amateur personnel really have met the exacting standards set by Benjamin Worsley?[16]

A week later the three-man committee that had been charged with making a detailed examination of the survey reported back to the Council. Many of the surveyors, they found, were indeed 'persons who till that time had never been imployed in a worke of that nature'. However, their measurements and the maps created from them had, under Petty's system, been verified by the eight salaried examiners, who had redrawn every line and angle from a series of original measurements and compared their results with the maps created by the field teams. The committee inspected the 'foule draughts of the orignall mapps' rejected through this checking process and scrutinized Petty's payment arrangements to see whether they encouraged the acceptance of imperfect work. Having done all this still they could find no fault. Dr Petty had fulfilled the complex requirements of the survey and, in a masterful piece of reluctant praise, they concluded 'that noe other test cann be made of the survey' and 'whatsover fault may lurke in the said worke' could only be discovered 'by the care of the respective persons therein concerned'.[17]

The presentation of the Down Survey revealed to Henry Cromwell, if he was not already well aware, the remarkable talents of his doctor. Over the preceding months these two men, Cromwell just turned 27, Petty 31, got to know one another. As personal physician to the head of the army in Ireland Petty was responsible for the health of Major General Cromwell and his young wife. On 18 April 1655 Elizabeth Cromwell gave birth to the couple's second child at Cork House, the Boyle family's erstwhile Dublin townhouse where they now lodged. Petty must have been in close attendance throughout those dangerous days. In the end the birth was so straightforward, it was reported, that the mother's greatest hardship had been writing to tell everyone the happy news.

Henry Cromwell's priority was to uphold his father's Protectorate, and the birth of his first son provided a powerful portent. The child was named Oliver and a fortnight after he was born he was christened at Christ Church Cathedral, after which his parents hosted a lavish party at Dublin Castle. The baby was living proof of the strength of the Protector's line, and in giving him a traditional infant baptism, Henry Cromwell signalled that the Baptist army officers who had been so powerful during Charles Fleetwood's tenure held the reins no more.[18]

❦ ❦ ❦

Benjamin Worsley refused to accept that there were no flaws in William Petty's survey of Ireland and secured an additional three months in which to personally scrutinize the documents and maps. His doubts and those of the 'old surveyors' taken off the job had been many, including the imaginative objection that the soldier-surveyors' swords would distort the play of the magnetic compass needles.[19] But by the high summer of 1656 the deliberation was over. The faults he had found were all minor and explicable by the specific circumstances in which individual surveys had been done. This was not surveying under the peaceful conditions that had pertained when Lord Strafford's map of Connacht had been taken in the 1630s. In some areas it had been impossible to identify any boundaries at all as transplantation had denuded whole villages and there was simply no one left to ask. As well as the overgrown landscape and the reluctance of the locals to share information about boundaries, Petty's men were a sitting target for raiding gangs of 'tories', despite the armed guard that accompanied them. In one particularly gruesome case the notorious bandit Donnagh Doyle, 'Blind Donnagh', had ambushed a party of eight surveyors, dragged them into the woods and butchered them.

Now their extent and accuracy had been established, the scrutiny had to stop as Petty's surveys were urgently needed to allow the allocation of lands that was the prerequisite to disbanding the army. Some apportionments had been made the previous year, but the majority remained. It was clear that William Petty now knew more than any man alive about these lands and had showed his abilities as an administrator. Henry Cromwell had no doubt that here was the person to see through the process, both the distribution of the lands to the soldiers and the extension of his remarkable survey to cover the whole island of Ireland.[20]

* * *

William Petty would later look back on the summer of 1656 as a turning point. He had completed the survey on time and it had been accepted. He had bested Benjamin Worsley, he had proved that through his highly original approach to training and organizing his workforce he could perform the unthinkable, and he had had the satisfaction of seeing the professional surveyors 'unmasked'. His raw recruits, he later recalled with relish, had achieved far more than the 'ignorant immethodical, loytering, disunited, emulating and contentious Surveyors ... could ever do'. Thanks to the Down Survey he was rich: his own profits from the commission, simply by dint of its scale, amounted to an astonishing £9,000. He could now afford to resign his post and return to England. He could retire, or, with the backing of Charles Fleetwood or Henry Cromwell, walk into a position as a senior physician at the court of the Protector himself. He could have the satisfaction of being at the centre of power at a time when his Oxford friends were still inflating bladders and inspecting urine samples.[21]

That he did not was telling. It doubtless owed much to his desire not to let the perfection, as he saw it, of his survey be spoiled by a poorly executed process of land distribution, or completed with a substandard second survey. But it was also because of Henry Cromwell. Petty had developed a respect for his clear-sighted new master that he seldom felt for anyone. While Charles Fleetwood had thought highly enough of Petty to entrust him with the Down Survey, and had even tried to persuade him to return to England to continue as his personal doctor, Petty had never shown any particular regard for Fleetwood. He could see at once that Henry Cromwell, by contrast, had the instincts and judgement – and the balance and pragmatism – that his predecessor had wholly lacked.[22]

Petty was unsentimental to a fault about public affairs, but here was the opportunity to participate in the treatment of a place whose ills he had observed as closely as any patient, and to do it in the service of a man he genuinely admired. It was a decision that would prove definitive. He was choosing a path that led away from Oxford, from academia and from anatomy. Robert Boyle had returned to England and was just then moving to Oxford where he would take Petty's place in the Experimental Philosophy Club. Tales of Petty's new wealth, and his vanquishing of Worsley and the old surveyors, were also making their way there, where they would soon, in his words, begin to 'sew tares' into his old friendships.[23]

※ ※ ※

The next eighteen months passed in a blur. Having agreed to remain, William Petty was brought into the heart of the Dublin administration. Henry Cromwell saw in this prickly government functionary just what he needed, a brilliant man who would be loyal to him alone. On paper Charles Fleetwood was still Lord Deputy of Ireland, and even continued to draw his salary, while Henry Cromwell was just one of the six members of the Irish Council of State. Many around him retained the loyalties and priorities of the Fleetwood era – even when they pretended otherwise – favouring the relentless suppression of the Irish, both Catholics and the 'old' Protestants of the pre-war era, radical religious policies and the preference of the new settlers in all things.[24]

Henry Cromwell took Petty to 'his bosom', appointing him a secretary to the Irish Council of State and his own personal assistant and closest adviser. He wanted both Petty's remarkable brain and his undivided loyalty. Here Petty rose to the challenge entirely. It was no hardship for him to cut himself off from his master's adversaries. He closed his Dublin medical practice so he could not be seen as taking fees from people who might have competing interests, he declined invitations to dine or sup, turned away gifts and altogether refused to be 'mollified with warm entertainments, nor to be cajoled with Complements'. He was now entirely Henry Cromwell's man; 'alone with the alone' and acting for him on a whole host of affairs, from the appointment of government officials to the pardoning of crimes, from the export of goods to licences for the transplanted. He applied himself with absolute commitment, taking any instruction or matter for resolution away immediately, staying up through the night, sustained by bread and raisins, as he marshalled the arguments and organized the considerations. He would then appear as business began the next morning master of all the issues, ready, if any raised objections, to 'shoot them dead'. That he could be brusque and high-handed, and his manner 'obnoxious', did not concern him in his absolute concentration on his master's affairs. In all that Henry Cromwell did he was now assisted by the unstoppable machine of business that was William Petty.[25]

The arrival of Henry Cromwell in Dublin saw a clear shift in emphasis away from the settling of scores and exacting of revenge, towards the mending of bridges – literal and metaphorical – in this shattered country. William Petty's formidable analytical skills and lack of ideological *idées fixes* served Henry Cromwell well. While the horrific individual eyewitness accounts of the murder of Protestants in 1641–2 were still being compiled on the orders of the army, Petty's careful scrutiny quickly showed that the scale of the atrocities had been wildly exaggerated 'so as those who think 154,000 were so destroyed ought to review their Opinion'. Despite his parentage Henry Cromwell was no religious radical. He despised the Fifth Monarchist activist friends of Anna Trapnel indulged by his father, as the 'maggots, which ... are now again busily crawling out of the excrements of mr. Feak's corrupted church'. Rather than seeking to promote a strand of radical Protestantism, he was more concerned to try to revive some sort of national ministry that could tend to the spiritual needs of all Irish Protestants, wishing to 'hold forth a just liberty to all fearing God'.[26] William Petty shared his master's dislike of religious radicalism and was careful never to be drawn on the detail of his own religious loyalties, knowing privately that he would only feel completely confident when the time came for him to look at God with his own eyes. Henry Cromwell, who by William Petty's own admission knew him better at this time than any man living, may even have been treated to the doctor's comic impersonations

of the different preaching styles of everyone from raging nonconformists to mumbling Jesuits with which he would later reduce his friends to
hopeless laughter.[27]

Over the months that followed Petty helped effect policies which
began to shift affairs in Ireland. There was no reversal of the land settlement: indeed, its terms were fulfilled as soldiers were granted the
debentures for their estates and disbanding of the army at last began in
earnest. But the future rather than the past now became the dominant
concern. Henry Cromwell made no secret of his desire for demilitariza-
tion: he regarded the regime of the Major Generals in England as 'visibly
dangerous' and the decimation tax a 'calamity'. Just as military rule in
England was reaching its apogee, in Ireland, under Henry Cromwell's
steady hand, it was finally giving way to civilian authority. With
Fleetwood's departure, the Irish Courts of Justice were re-established,
and over the course of the autumn of 1655 and into 1656 numerous
Irish towns were granted new charters which enabled civilian local
government to resume. The ban on trade from Ireland covering pretty
much everything but fish was at last lifted and while the Irish were still
subject to import duties and strict measures to prevent their wool
competing with the English market, it was finally possible for Irish
produce to be sold overseas. As vessels carrying Irish beef and butter
began once again to sail east to Bristol and Chester, so ships from Wales
and the West Country arrived bearing the lambs and calves urgently
needed to restock Ireland's depleted pastures.[28]

The biggest issue that remained, however, was that of transplantation. This was a matter to which William Petty had, of course, given
detailed thought. It was quite within his intellectual range to hold two
arguably contradictory positions simultaneously. Indeed, his favoured
approach to any subject was to articulate in turn the positive case for
each viewpoint and to review them side by side. On the one hand he was
responsible for the Down Survey, 'such a service (being useful to all
mankind) for a victorious army, the first that ever totally subdued
Ireland, ... as great an honour as any other atchievement I could make
in so much time'. At the same time he had grave misgivings about the
mass transplantation with which it was inextricably connected.[29]

Vincent Gookin's lucid and reasoned analysis of the shortcomings of the policy was expressed in the same clearly marshalled practical terms in which Petty himself thought. Furthermore, as one who owed his own education to French Jesuits, Petty did not, like most of his countrymen, despise the Catholic Irish. On the contrary, he could see many merits in Roman Catholicism, among them its antiquity, the tremendous learning of its scholars and the practical benefits of the icons and ceremonies which characterized its worship as 'helps to devotion'. He also saw no evidence for traditional English tropes that the ordinary Irishman was lazy or treacherous. When it had been objected that his approach to the Down Survey would involve using Catholics as guides, he had shrugged his shoulders and retorted who else was he to ask, the Irish people were Catholic. Petty was deeply influenced by Vincent Gookin's publication and got to know the man himself well over those years. Among the numerous papers Petty wrote as he was forming the plan for the great survey in 1654 was his own 'Discourse against the Transplantation to Connaught'.[30]

Gookin and Petty saw the glaring flaws of the project to dispossess and relocate the vast majority of Irish people, but they were a long way short of having the power to prevent it. Both men were appointed to the committee charged with apportioning the confiscated lands to English soldiers and neither refused to serve. Petty was a rationalist and, just as Marchamont Nedham had maintained that the Rump Parliament had victor's right to the spoils, so he consoled himself that in Ireland the English had 'won' and had 'a Gamester's Right at least to their Estates'. Henry Cromwell may have taken a broader view of Ireland than his predecessors, but there was no question of this involving a reversal of the punitive approach to the Irish endorsed by every English Parliament since Charles I's day. However, it was one thing depriving the Catholic Irish of their lands, another altogether to physically shift hundreds of thousands of people west. The stories of those who did get to Connacht hardly encouraged others to move. The administrative efficiency of Petty's survey and land distribution was not mirrored by the commissioners doling out lands in Connacht. Corruption and disorganization saw many who were not entitled to them make off with thousands of acres, and many more realize that the dwindling portions of remaining land would never satisfy those transplanted from elsewhere.[31]

❦ ❦ ❦

By 1657 the project to effect an ethnic separation of Ireland had descended into a grim muddle. Most Irish people had lost some or all of their lands but still remained bitterly reluctant to move to the western enclave set aside for them. At the same time the flood of new settlement and investment anticipated by the various Acts of Parliament, and clearly needed if the fields were to sway with wheat once again, was not materializing. A thousand London investors and more than 30,000 soldiers had been expected to settle. In reality, the wealthy 'adventurers' treated their holdings as investments to be sold on and while perhaps half the soldiers did settle, as many decided against starting new lives as Irish yeomen farmers. Those who did take up confiscated lands quickly realized the truth of Gookin's argument that they could do little without an experienced workforce. William Petty was soon contending with a flood of requests from influential Protestants for specific groups of Catholics to be exempted from transplantation. Among them was a letter from Richard Cromwell asking that his footman's brother, Daniel Machona of Munster, be spared transplantation, 'for that it will be the utter ruen of him and his family'. Those in authority were capable of feeling a pity for the plight of individual Irishmen and women which never extended to the people as a whole. In many cases, including Daniel Machona's, Catholics lost the ownership of their lands but, rather than move west, stayed on to farm them as tenants of new Protestant masters. In the towns, from which Catholics had been formally excluded, many again remained despite the repeated instructions to leave, though under the terms of the new corporations they were barred from positions of authority.[32]

In the end the solution that was found was to draw a veil over the whole transplantation project by simply acting as if it had been accomplished. When Parliament considered Irish affairs in June 1657 the 'Act for the Attainder of the Rebels in Ireland' was passed. Despite its hawkish title, this piece of legislation effectively drew to a close the process of transplantation and reallocation of lands. Its opening line set the scene: 'The Rebellion begun in Ireland, the three and twentieth of October, 1641. is, and is hereby Declared to be Appeased and Ended.' Those who had received lands had their ownership confirmed, the pursuit of malefactors was effectively stopped and reference was made to various specific groups of Catholics who were to be allowed to remain. It was hardly a reversal of what had happened, but it drew a line of sorts under this ugly chapter of Ireland's history. The Down Survey was complete. All the books and maps were to be gathered together and within three months to be set among the records of the government of Ireland.[33]

          ❦ ❦ ❦

William Petty would later regard his time at Henry Cromwell's side with mixed feelings. He took pride in his own achievements. He had meas-ured a 'quantitie of line' by chain and compass which if strung out, he claimed, would wrap almost five times around the world. But it had come at a cost. His personal success, combined with his surfeit of self-confidence and shortage of charm, had multiplied his enemies and soon they began to mobilize against him. Baseless tales of corruption and financial embezzlement were told which reached his Oxford friends and before long they, too, regarded him with resentment rather than respect. But Petty had never worried too much what people thought of him and his admiration for Henry Cromwell was enduring. His master, he noted simply, was a person of 'Honour and Integrity'.[34]

Despite his personal loyalty to Henry Cromwell, Petty was never reconciled to English government policy towards Irish landowners. They had paid a devastating price for the violent barbarism of a small number of their countrymen during the uprising of over a decade before. As he put it in one of his own discussion papers, 'I cannt digest that Honest-Moderate-Wealthy Catholicks should lose their Estates for what a Company of Lewd, Ignorant, Barbarous and Beggerly Rascals did against the English in the Tumultary year 1642'.[35] William Petty reckoned that before the war the Irish had owned some two-thirds of the land. Now, he calculated, Protestants from mainland Britain owned three-quarters of the land, nine-tenths of the property in towns and two-thirds of all overseas trade.[36] Until the 1640s it was essentially religious allegiance which had separated the Irish from the English and Scots, the Irish were mostly Catholic, the incomers Protestant. Now Irish Catholics had been comprehensively disenfranchised and dispossessed: they had lost their lands, their ability to exercise political power at the local or national level and their pre-eminence as merchants and traders. The mass dispossession of the Catholic Irish was a policy on which the die had been cast long before the English revolution. Their bitter fate had in effect been determined when Henry Cromwell was a schoolboy, William Petty a pupil at the Jesuit seminary in Caen and Charles I still in charge of his dominions. It would have happened on some scale had there never been a revolution at all. But it was a punitive policy to which, nevertheless, history would always attach the name Cromwell.[37]

※ ※ ※

In mid-November 1657 Henry Cromwell finally received the formal commission from his father appointing him Lord Deputy of Ireland. While *Mercurius Politicus* as usual toed the official line, there was a ring of truth to its correspondent's comment that 'this news was very acceptable and revived the spirits of the people'. Henry Cromwell's abilities had been recognized on both sides of the Irish Sea, causing more than one person in London to observe, as the regime of the English Major Generals faltered, that he seemed to be making a better fist of governing Ireland than any of them had yet managed in England. Peace had held and Ireland's economic recovery had begun – and for the first time after years of war and famine grain was once again being exported from Irish ports. Standing proud on the Dublin waterfront was the new Council Chamber, a fine structure completed only months before, a beacon in a brick city that had begun to be rebuilt in stone. The paint was still fresh on the arms of the Protectorate on the wall behind him as Henry Cromwell was formally invested with the office of Lord Deputy. In the darkness of the late November afternoon he proceeded in a torch-lit procession up Cork Hill to the Castle gates with the church bells ringing, bonfires blazing and cannon sounding a reverberating salute. Gleaming gold in the fading light of the empty Council Chamber was the Protector's motto 'pax quaeritur bello': through war comes peace.[38]

This was the centuries-old ceremonial of English rule in Ireland. But on this occasion it meant something more. Henry Cromwell had secured the authority he had for two years toiled without. He could at last act upon the forward-looking projects he had discussed with William Petty – and of these there were many. The hopelessly debased Irish coinage urgently required attention, with the creation of a new national mint Henry Cromwell's long-held aspiration. The slowly growing export trade needed protection and a plan had been drawn up to encircle the whole of Ireland with a network of lighthouses. While the statute book required all Catholics to swear an oath comprehensively denying their faith – an 'extrame course' that Henry Cromwell had advised strongly against – it was now his choice whether this requirement would be enforced. Instead of retaining a substantial standing army he saw a system of civilian militias as a cheaper and less oppressive solution and, close to both Cromwell and Petty's hearts, was the aspiration to make a resurgent Ireland a great centre of learning. A second national college to sit alongside the Elizabethan foundation at Trinity, to be named after Oliver Cromwell, was envisaged. William Petty thrilled at the prospect of this 'great design' to promote knowledge and had pledged a handsome personal benefaction. Henry Cromwell was donating Cork House itself to be its home and had acquired the magnificent library of the pre-war Irish prelate Archbishop Ussher to form its founding collection. As the year ended and 1658 dawned everything at last seemed possible. All they needed was time.[39]

Fifteen

A Life in Fire

W hen Oliver Cromwell, Lord Protector of England, dressed in the
chilly January mornings of 1657 the body servants who attended
him in his riverside apartments at Whitehall Palace could see that
despite his 57 years their master remained muscular and 'well shaped'.
His 5 foot 10 inch frame was still strong and kept from corpulence by
restlessness, moderate eating and energetic weekend deer hunting. But
the Protector felt age creeping through him. As well as the periodic
bouts of illness to which he had always been susceptible he was troubled by a kidney stone, the joints in his feet were starting to swell and
bloom with gout and the dense brown hair that once covered the crown
of his head had dwindled into wispy tufts (Colour plate 15). While other
men had worked hardest in their prime and could in their fifties take
more leisure, his had been a life inverted. He had lived his first forty
years far from the national arena in rural East Anglia. Like the L'Estrange
men, whom he might easily have encountered at county weddings and
coaching inns during the 1620s and 1630s, he had enjoyed inherited
wealth and a university education, participated in local government,
kept hawks and horses and tended his family's affairs. His eldest children were already adults by the time war came to England and changed
everything. But the advancing years had deepened rather than diminished his difficulties. He had, he reflected in those weeks, 'lived the

latter part of my age in ... the fire, in the midst of troubles'. And in January 1657 these were about to become more intractable still.[1]

Marchamont Nedham's third issue of *Mercurius Politicus* of 1657 was one worth having. While he normally shied clear of anything but the blandest Westminster news, ever under the eye of Secretary Thurloe, this week he had covered two eye-catching national stories. The first was the denouement of a saga that had run for weeks: the effecting of the sentence against James Nayler. A member of the notorious new nonconformist sect known as the Quakers (after their habit of trembling with religious fervour), Nayler had been convicted of blasphemy for riding into Bristol in what was alleged to be a re-enactment of Christ's entry into Jerusalem. He had already been branded on his forehead with a 'B' for blasphemer and had his tongue bored through, and now he had been ritually humiliated. Nayler was stripped naked and paraded through Bristol sitting backwards on a horse before his public flogging. But the news did not stop here, for this report was followed by a second scoop: the uncovering of a plot to assassinate Oliver Cromwell.[2]

It was characteristic of Cromwell that he was more concerned about the first case than the second. While he belonged to no specific group among the kaleidoscope of Puritan sects, his deep and all-encompassing faith had much in common with theirs and he did not share the outrage of many MPs of the Second Protectorate Parliament, including committed Puritans, at their unorthodox beliefs and activities. The Quakers had caused a particular tide of revulsion for their rejection of all signs of social deference – in forms of address, doffing of hats and much else besides – which they, like Gerrard Winstanley, thought appropriate only for God himself. Through the 1650s Quakerism had spread at speed guided by their charismatic leader, George Fox. Parliament had set aside all other business in the last weeks of the old year to devote themselves to the Nayler case, and Cromwell had been unhappy at the harshness of the sentence that had been determined. He sent the Speaker a terse letter on Christmas Day 1656 acknowledging Nayler's guilt but reprimanding them for proceeding 'wholly without us' on this important matter.[3]

(15) Oliver Cromwell in the mid-1650s by Samuel Cooper. The later claim that
Cromwell had asked to be painted 'ruffness, pimples, warts & everything as you see
me' may have been made in response to this beautiful, candid portrait miniature.
His 'maggoty' nose was more referenced in contemporary satire than his warts.

(16) Hampton Court in the 1660s by Hendrick Danckerts. Oliver and Elizabeth Cromwell occupied the first-floor rooms in the two-storey range on the right of the palace. The grazing deer would have been part of the view in the 1650s, but not the canal which was dug for Charles II.

(17) Elizabeth Claypole (née Cromwell), Oliver Cromwell's sophisticated and politically active middle daughter, by Samuel Cooper. Grief at her death was widely judged to have caused the decline that ended Oliver's own life a few weeks later.

(18) Richard Cromwell was brought up to be a country squire and given neither the education nor the backing to make a success of the role of Lord Protector suddenly thrust upon him on his father's death.

(19) 'The Paston Treasure', *c.*1663, showing the collection of Sir Robert Paston of Oxnead, Norfolk who died that year. Shells, silks, exotic birds – and a young African man – all express the international reach of England in the 1650s. 'Indian' textiles, violins and globes were all to be found in Oliver Cromwell's apartments in the royal palaces.

(20) Oliver Cromwell depicted in the fashionable attire of the 1650s, 'bucket-top' boots and voluminous beribboned 'petticoat breeches'. As Sir Philip Warwick wryly remembered, by the 1650s Oliver had a 'better tailor' than when he first met him as a plainly dressed countryman in 1640.

(21) General George Monck by Samuel Cooper, c.1660. Cromwell's trusted General in charge of Scotland, Monck looked on as Parliament and the army turned on one another after Oliver's death. His sudden declaration for Parliament in October 1659 changed everything.

(22) Anne, née Clarges, who married Monck, probably bigamously, in 1653 and played a crucial role in the events that led to the Restoration. This portrait of Anne was a flattering image of one who was considered plain and later satirised as the 'Monkey Duchess'.

(23) A silk taffeta banner from the hearse in Oliver Cromwell's funeral procession, in which the arms of the Protectorate and those of his widow, Elizabeth, are combined.

(24) General Monck's army arrived in London to oppose military rule only to be ordered by the Rump Parliament to tear down the city's gates and detain prominent citizens. The orders horrified them and many Londoners and set the General on a path to readmitting the moderate MPs purged in 1648.

As the sentence against Nayler was being carried out, Parliament had returned to the debate on Colonel Desbrow's controversial motion to continue the decimation tax and thereby the Major Generals' regime as a whole. Oliver Cromwell's political troubles were made intensely personal by the fact that the differences of opinion on the widely disliked Major Generals' system, and on what form the government of England as a whole should take, did not simply exist in the nation or even in Parliament, but ran right through his own immediate family causing deep divisions between those whom he loved the best.

Within the Cromwell family there were two quite distinct groupings of opinion. Oliver Cromwell and his wife Elizabeth had six living children, four daughters and two sons (see family tree, page 366). His eldest child, Bridget, who had married first Henry Ireton and then Charles Fleetwood, was a deeply committed Puritan. Such was the strength of her 'affection for Christ' she needed no exhortations to religious devotion from her father, and as the widow of Ireton, mastermind of Pride's Purge, she was the one Cromwell child of whom the 1649 revolutionaries thoroughly approved. Fleetwood shared her religious fervour and was a Major General himself, responsible for the middle counties of England (though he had delegated his responsibilities to Hezekiah Haynes and others). John Desbrow, meanwhile, the military regime's chief champion, was one of Cromwell's longest-standing friends and for twenty years until her recent death had been married to his younger sister Jane.[4]

These older members of the Cromwell family had forged their allegiances, both to ideas and to one another, in the heat of the civil war. The younger members of the family were rather different. Oliver and Elizabeth Cromwell had brought up their sons with no expectation of being career soldiers or politicians. Despite Oliver's commitment to religious and political reform he was at heart a social conservative. He never lost his desire for change in some areas, among them the English legal system which 'would hang a man for six-pence'. But by the late 1650s he looked back on the experiment of putting the 'Godly' at the heart of politics, in the form of the Nominated Assembly, with a shudder, remembering how they had attempted to 'fly at liberty and property, insomuch as if one man had twelve cows, they held another that wanted cows ought to take share with his neighbour. Who could have said any thing was their own, if they had gone on?' The Cromwells' eldest living son, Richard, had, as his parents intended, taken up a life of rural leisure, living with his wife's family in Hampshire and spending his days hunting and horse racing. Oliver had wanted Henry, too, to live a 'private life in the country' and was only reluctantly persuaded other-wise. Come 1657, Henry was, with William Petty's assistance, well advanced in civilizing the government of Ireland and made no secret of his dislike of the Major Generals' regime. The Cromwells' cherished middle daughter, Elizabeth, and her husband, John Claypole, also shared much of the more traditional outlook of the country gentry from which they all sprang. The two younger girls were still in their teens and as yet unmarried but, like all the Cromwell children other than Bridget, it was to their capable brother Henry that they looked for example.[5]

As Oliver Cromwell surveyed his family and nation in January 1657 the fissures seemed more fundamental than ever. His brother-in-law Desbrow, who had served at his side in the army since the very begin-ning of the civil war, had risen in the chamber on Christmas Day to launch the legislation that would ensure the continuation of the Major Generals' regime. The first speech of opposition, on 7 January, had come from Cromwell's 32-year-old son-in-law John Claypole. Master of the Protector's Horse, Claypole was more interested in hunting than poli-tics, and his rising to say anything at all in the chamber was something of a surprise. But he spoke with sincerity – and from the vantage point of a younger generation – of the injustice of the decimation tax and of punishing sons for the actions of their fathers. Remarking nervously, 'I did only start this debate, and leave it to others who are better able to speak to it' he sat back down, but not before he called unequivocally for the bill's rejection.[6]

❦ ❦ ❦

Cromwell was troubled by the harsh punishment of James Nayler, but many around him, Secretary John Thurloe included, were much more worried about the assassination plot. The Sindercombe plot was uncovered when one of the conspirators confessed but had come uncomfortably close to success. Sindercombe was a disaffected army officer who considered the Protectorate a betrayal and dreamed of a return to the 'pure' early days of the republic. He had investigated a number of ways to kill Oliver Cromwell in order to bring this to pass, before this last in which the lock on Whitehall chapel was forced open and a basket of explosives planted, primed for detonation. While Sindercombe and his cronies were an incoherent bunch, there was no escaping the certainty that one day, whether by plot or providence, Oliver Cromwell would die, and what on earth would happen then remained shrouded in uncertainty.[7]

Royalist efforts to prise England back from Oliver Cromwell and his colleagues had made little headway over the past two years, thanks not least to the Protectorate's invasive surveillance regime. But things had grown far more uncomfortable for the London government when King Philip IV of Spain, furious at English exploits in the Caribbean, had invited the exiled Charles Stuart to take up residence in the Spanish Netherlands. Charles I's heir was now quartered only a short sailing away in Bruges. For the first time since his father's execution he had a sovereign backer who might at any moment decide to lend him the ships and men for an invasion. The obvious disharmony in England as Parliament voted down Desbrow's militia bill by a majority of almost forty on 29 January risked giving the royalists another advantage. MPs themselves were well aware of this and the need for unity. The formal thanksgiving for the Protector's deliverance from the Sindercombe plot, scheduled for just over a fortnight after the militia bill was defeated, was alighted upon as the ideal opportunity. As one MP put it, 'this will be a very good expedient to let the world see that there is a right understanding between his Highness and us and that we are cemented'.[8]

The day of thanksgiving on Friday 20 February began conventionally enough, with a service in St Margaret's church, Westminster. Afterwards, however, the solemn tone lightened. The Speaker of the House of Commons and all two hundred or so MPs were invited to return to Whitehall Palace to dine with the Lord Protector in one of the most magnificent banquets of the decade. The feast was served at long tables in the Banqueting House and enriched with music from the Protector's violins and trumpets. After dinner the whole assembly accompanied their host over the passage across King Street to the area of the old Tudor palace used for sport and recreation. Before the war Inigo Jones had converted Henry VIII's cockpit into an exquisite court theatre for Charles I and the room now served as Cromwell's private concert hall. Here, seated before Inigo Jones's Italianate staging, the parliamentarians were treated to a glorious performance of choral and instrumental music that went on late into the evening. The 'entertainment' was, according to one discerning contemporary, 'exquisite' and 'the rarest ever seen in England'.[9]

For one whose government's main policy of the past two years had just been comprehensively defeated in Parliament, Oliver Cromwell was in a surprisingly good mood in mid-February 1657. Another of his family who had spoken passionately against the Major Generals in the recent parliamentary debates was the Protector's cousin Harry Cromwell. Having been told how angry the Protector would be at his disloyalty, Harry went nervously to explain himself. Oliver's response to his earnest words was not a rebuke but laughter and 'rallary'. At the end of their meeting he swung the red cloak from his back and fixed it across the young man's shoulder, giving him the matching gloves for good measure, a clear signal of his continuing affection. The Lord Protector was, if another source is to be believed, in equally ebullient mood during the thanksgiving feast. As the candied apricots were brought round the diners in the Banqueting House, Colonel Pride spilled some liquid on the apron of a serving woman. Oliver, in mock reproach, pelted him with his napkin, causing a good-humoured fracas to break out on their table. The mood was heady. Many were doubtless just enjoying the plenty, relieved the last fractious weeks had passed. Others, however, knew what was coming. It was Friday afternoon and on Monday morning a bill was to be presented to Parliament for the restoration of both a House of Lords and the monarchy. Oliver Cromwell was about to become king.[10]

❦ ❦ ❦

The idea of reinstituting the office of king was not in itself new. Few even of those involved in the trial of Charles I, Cromwell included, had expected the monarchy itself to fall and after those radical first months the revival of the office of monarch had been periodically discussed. Only a small number were implacably opposed: republicans and men like John Bradshaw who had invested everything in the 1649 regime. Such scruples aside, kingship had much to recommend it to a regime that was struggling to embed its own legitimacy. Oliver himself, when strolling in St James's Park with Bulstrode Whitelocke in 1652, had, in the midst of a discussion of the shortcomings of the Rump Parliament, asked abruptly 'what if a man should take uppon him to be King?'[11] The idea had been raised again by John Lambert and his army colleagues in 1653 when, amid the increasing radicalism of the Nominated Assembly, they were drawing up plans for the Protectorate. The main stumbling block then and since had been Cromwell himself. The same aversion to being seen to seek personal advantage that had prevented him from making his second son Lord Deputy of Ireland caused him to resist. His greatest fear was that God would detect in him vainglory and mark him down as a man of ambition rather than of faith. He was at pains to impress on everyone around him – perhaps even God himself – that he had not wanted the high office he already occupied, 'I sought not this place. I speak it before God, angels and men, I did not'. But there were now signs that his attitude was changing.[12]

The defeat of the militia bill was a significant victory for those, like Henry Cromwell, who felt military rule and decimation had got out of hand and that a more moderate, civilian course was called for. Tied down in Dublin, Henry could take no part in the debates, but he could use his influence in other ways. He wrote to his father to entreat him to distance himself from the Major Generals and ally himself instead with 'men of interest and sober principles'. His friend Roger, Lord Broghill (Robert Boyle's older brother and sometime writer of romances) was among those who saw an opportunity to push home the advantage after the army's defeat in the House of Commons. Henry Cromwell referred in his letter to his father to a notion so sensitive that as soon as he had read it the Protector dropped the paper into the fire. But in doing so he remarked to Thurloe that 'he did very well accept what you [Henry] have sayd therein'. Vincent Gookin, author of the treatise against the transplantation of Catholics to Connacht, was in London as one of the Irish MPs and wrote home in cipher that 'kingship' was now on the cards, 'to which His Highness is not averse'.[13]

On Monday morning, their hangovers passed, those who had dined at Whitehall on Friday reassembled in St Stephen's Chapel. The moderates' nominee, Sir Christopher Packe, rose and asked that a proposal be put to the house for the 'settlement of the nation and of liberty and of property'. One of the military men protested nervously that they knew nothing of what was in this proposal. But plenty did and after a lengthy debate the motion to debate the bill passed. The next morning Henry Cromwell's agent wrote to his master of the news, 'we are now at the crisis which was expected'. Most people's loyalties were easy to identify: the army officers, John Lambert, Charles Fleetwood and John Desbrow were 'violently against it', while most prominent civilians, including Secretary Thurloe and the senior lawyers such as Bulstrode Whitelocke, were 'highly for it'. But the only opinion that really mattered now was one that no one could be certain of, that of Oliver Cromwell himself.[14]

🦡 🦡 🦡

Oliver Cromwell's emotions were seldom far from the surface. Faith, love of his family, comradeship, loyalty, pity all moved him to tears. It was remarkable that he who had presided over the brutal siege of Drogheda and 'could look with an uncomposed brow on thousands of men, and of his friends, lying dead on the Field after a battle', 'could not refrain from tears' on other occasions. Only days before the plan to change the constitution yet again was put to Parliament, Cromwell had been given an account of his son's successes in Ireland. As Henry was 'given the highest and well grounded aplauses imaginable', tears of joy seeped from his eyes and such was his pride in his son that he noted aloud that he himself 'might learn of him'. This was the mood in which he viewed the proceedings in Parliament and the proposal that in the place of the heavily militarized regime of the previous years, a new more civilian constitution should restore to England both a second parliamentary chamber and the office of king.[15]

The moment the debate had ended and the vote passed on 23 February, though it was now well into the evening, a group of enraged army officers strode to Whitehall and poured out their anger and indignation to the Protector. If they expected sympathy and comradeship they found neither. As was periodically the case, Oliver's calm and sometimes gentle personal demeanour was consumed by a blind flash of fury. 'What would you have me doe?' he demanded. It was they who had insisted on calling a new parliament, they who had chosen who could take up their seats and who not, 'and now doe you complaine to me?' And why were they so incensed at the proposal for reviving kingship when they had made exactly this proposal to him in 1653? Their extremism, he went on bitterly, absolving himself entirely from any blame, had caused every parliamentary mishap of the last four years and was precisely why a new House of Lords was needed. Balance had to be restored to national affairs or 'next time for ought I know you may exclude 400 [elected MPs]'. He had become their 'drudge' and he had had enough. And with this riposte, described delicately by one contemporary as 'a rownder answer then I believe they expected', he dismissed them. Oliver Cromwell had resolved to break company once and for all with his comrades in arms.[16]

❧ ❧ ❧

The Cromwell family of Huntingdon owed its ancestral wealth almost entirely to Henry VIII's notorious chief minister Thomas Cromwell. Through the Tudor statesman's nephew, Richard, a substantial share of his tremendous fortune, much of it from the dissolution of the monasteries, had poured down the generations. Oliver's branch of the family had been given extensive lands in Huntingdonshire. His grandfather, Sir Henry Cromwell, rebuilt what had been Hinchingbrooke Priory as a fine country house and was visited, and knighted, here by Queen Elizabeth herself in 1564. On the accession of the Stuarts the tradition of royal hospitality had continued, and Sir Oliver, Oliver Cromwell's uncle, had received King James and the heads of all the

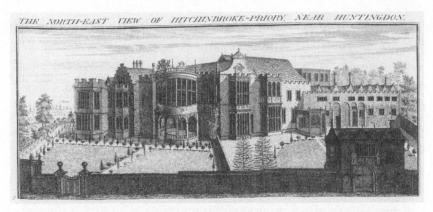

THE NORTH-EAST VIEW OF HITCHINBROKE-PRIORY, NEAR HUNTINGDON.

Hinchingbrooke House, the Cromwell family seat, just outside Huntingdon, where Oliver's uncle hosted James I and Charles I as Prince of Wales on numerous occasions.

Cambridge colleges when he had journeyed south in 1603. On that first visit the King was presented with gifts of horses, hunting dogs and first-rate hawks and it was not long before he returned to Hinchingbrooke to make use of them. Over the years that followed King James became a regular, almost annual, visitor at the Cromwells' house. He stayed at Hinchingbrooke on at least fifteen further occasions, sometimes for days, or even weeks at a time, and came to treat the house as his own, paying for improvements and sending ahead instructions to the gamekeepers. Young Oliver Cromwell was Sir Oliver's nephew, godson and namesake, and lived less than a mile away. As he passed through his teens and began his studies at Cambridge, he must have been at least an observer, and more likely a participant, in those lavish autumn hunting parties. Prince Charles, Oliver Cromwell's exact contemporary, accompanied his father on at least two of these visits and the two young men may well have met amid the thundering of hooves and reverberating calls of the hunting horn. Oliver grew up with a love of riding, hawking and deer hunting that would never leave him.[17]

As the son of a younger brother, Oliver's own portion of the Cromwell lands had not been great, and his father's death when Oliver was still at university had brought him considerable responsibilities – among them seven sisters, six still unmarried, to provide for. He had a formidable network of relations and probably thanks to his aunt Joan, Lady Barrington, married Elizabeth Bouchier, the daughter of a wealthy London merchant. The marriage was a happy one and the couple were blessed with a child almost every year through the 1620s. In 1628, like his father, uncle and grandfather before him, Oliver was elected a Member of Parliament for Huntingdon. A minor landowner and head of a growing family, he seemed set for a life in the mould of his forebears. But in the late 1620s the Cromwells experienced a series of setbacks which would change the course of their lives.

King James died in 1625 and following decades of extravagant entertaining the Cromwell family money had all but dried up. In 1627 Sir Oliver Cromwell was forced to sell Hinchingbrooke. The glory days were over. Meanwhile, Oliver, now in his later twenties, was beginning to have erratic episodes. He started to suffer from strange delusions, harbouring 'fancies' about Huntingdon's market cross and calling on the town doctor, Dr Symcotts, for assistance at all times of night and day – on one occasion convinced he was dying. He then became embroiled in a feud between the townsmen of Huntingdon about the use of a civic bequest. When the town decided to reform its governing body Oliver Cromwell was deliberately excluded from the new ruling group of aldermen. A fracas ensued in which an emotional Oliver, now just into his thirties, was accused of making 'disgraceful and unseemly speeches'. The dispute was referred to the privy council itself, and the person chosen to investigate was the Earl of Manchester, brother of the man who had just bought Hinchingbrooke. Oliver was subjected to a lengthy examination before the privy council at Whitehall Palace and remanded somewhere in London while Manchester deliberated. He was found in the wrong and made to apologize for words 'spoken in heat and passion'. After five days' incarceration he was released and slunk back to Huntingdon utterly humiliated.[18]

Within months Oliver and Elizabeth Cromwell were gone. The flat, marshy landscape and the slow, meandering waterways of the Great Ouse between Huntingdon and the Wash at King's Lynn were in the midst of being transformed by water engineers and their wealthy backers into fertile farmland and great, straight canals to the sea. Small farms specked the low-lying fields and pastures and it was to one of these, on the edge of the town of St Ives, that the Cromwells and their six small children moved. They were at the turning point of their lives. They had not simply moved house, but had taken the radical step of selling almost all their property, their only significant assets. Oliver was no longer a landowner, a collector of rent, a Member of Parliament and town dignitary, but had become a tenant farmer himself, resident of an 'old farmhouse' rented from the estate of Slepe Hall.

What exactly their plan was is unclear. The shame of imprisonment, even for a short time, was powerful, as Anna Trapnel had felt so keenly during her time in Bridewell. Perhaps, like Anna, Oliver found the prospect of his neighbours' sneers unbearable. Perhaps he had acted in the sort of sudden rage that would propel him to take rash decisions on other occasions in his life. Or perhaps he was implementing careful plans for a new start. Whatever it was the family left Huntingdon for a new beginning. The lands they sold raised £1,800 but this would not last long among so many. The days of employing their own falconer were already well behind them, but to begin with they at least retained a shepherd to tend the sheep on their St Ives fields. Money was soon in even shorter supply and before long the Cromwells were forced to sublet much of their farm to others.[19]

It was some time during these years, in the midst of all these troubles, that Oliver Cromwell underwent the spiritual awakening that would become the greatest force in his life. As for Gerrard Winstanley and Anna Trapnel, outright despair and a sense of personal failure might be the harbingers of spectacular religious rebirth. Oliver had not obviously been a man of exceptional religious conviction before now. But, as he told his cousin Elizabeth, in his moment of 'blackness' God came to him. 'You know what my manner of life hath been, Oh, I lived in and loved darkness and hated the light; I was a chief, the chief of sinners. This is true: I hated godliness.' Then, suddenly, God cast a dazzling beam into his abject darkness and he was reborn. He now had a certain purpose into which he could channel his abundant energy and emotion. He would henceforth be committed to honouring God, 'either by doing or by suffering', full of trust that he had been chosen and that God would one day 'bring me to his tabernacle, to His resting place'.[20]

The experiences of the 1630s sealed Oliver Cromwell's character and sense of personal calling. He had seen the darkness and he had seen the light. The faith he had emerged with was towering and unassailable. It was his salvation. While Anna Trapnel's mother saw the Devil and fault in her daughter's every action, the God to whom Oliver Cromwell now guided his children was a glorious vision of love. Instead of her bitter reproachfulness, tenderness, encouragement and a sense of the marvellous power of God suffused his counsels. He warned his pious daughter Bridget of the dangers of self-criticism and the overwhelming importance of love. She should remind herself 'What a Christ have I; what a Father in and through Him! What a name hath my Father: Merciful, gracious, long-suffering, abundant in goodness and truth; forgiving iniquity, transgression, and sin.'[21]

❦ ❦ ❦

After five years in St Ives the Cromwells had been delivered from their impoverishment by a substantial legacy of land and property from Oliver's maternal uncle Thomas Steward of Ely. They moved to a handsome house in the town and, wealth and status restored, Oliver became an active public figure once again. But there was no going back. He re-entered civic life brimming with his new Godly purpose, a powerful and emotionally charged Puritan religious fervour that he did not hesitate to express. All around him, including in the cathedral on his doorstep, Charles I's high church innovations were being promoted by the new Bishop of Ely, Matthew Wren – he whose punctilious interrogations of baffled Norfolk parishioners had caused hilarity at Hunstanton Hall. Fines and punishments were being meted out to those who failed to adopt them, including those of Oliver Cromwell's own religious circle. Anger grew within him. Years later, when he was Lord Protector of England, he would recall how men like Bishop Wren worked 'to eat out the core, and power, and heart, and life of all religion, by bringing on us a company of poisonous popish ceremonies, and imposing them upon those that were accounted the Puritans of the nation'. He was chosen as

MP for Cambridge in 1640 on the back of his opposition to government religious policy and entered the national political fray.[22]

When war had broken out in 1642 Cromwell had not hesitated to take up arms for Parliament. For him it was always about religion. His own conviction spurred him on and gave him the fearless bravery for which he would become famous. At the outset of the war he challenged his cousin John Hampden on their chances of success when the royalists had in their ranks the sons of the gentry who 'have honour, courage and resolution in them' while they had only 'old serving men and tapsters, and such kind of fellows'. What they needed was 'men of spirit that is like to go as far as a gentleman will go'. Men who, like him, believed theirs was a cause worth dying for. It was the recruiting and fostering of those 'as had the fear of God before them and some conscience of what they did' that Oliver believed would bring them victory. And it did. 'From that day forward', he later recalled with the nostalgia of the old-timer, 'they were never beaten'.[23]

After his first military successes, among them wresting King's Lynn from Sir Hamon L'Estrange, Cromwell had indeed chalked up an extraordinary record, each battle triumph reinforcing his confidence that they were doing God's work. Certainty deafened Oliver to the human cost, and any rumbles of doubt that the corpses on the battle-fields of Ireland might have elicited were drowned out by the booming report of God's favour. Cromwell's charisma, self-confidence and total belief in the righteousness of their undertaking made him a magnetic leader. He developed a rare talent for military strategy and for inspiring his men through heartfelt communal prayer and heart-stirring speeches. The unevenness of his own fortunes before the war had given him a flair for comradeship and he fraternized with the common soldiers and joined the jocular camaraderie of the camp with an ease few officers of his rank could match. Under his sure, paternal eye hundreds, and then thousands, marched, killed and were killed, on the road to victory.[24]

When Oliver Cromwell had had his religious awakening it had changed him but it had not expunged the man he had been before. The attitudes and affections of some thirty years remained within him. It was these that made him want for his children not lives of austere self-denial but comfortable affluent existences, with land and money, families and houses, love and plenty. His eldest son, Richard, had taken easily to the life of the country squire and soon got into debt. His father did not begrudge the boy his pleasurable pastimes and the costly attributes of status, and was happy to provide the money to fund them: 'truly I can find it in my heart to allow him not only a sufficiency but more.' He only warned him against making pleasure the 'business of his life'. For his daughters, as had been the case with his sisters, Oliver's material concern was that they should have decent dowries. But it was not the Godly Bridget, with her icy self-reproach, who was his favourite, rather his vivacious middle daughter, Elizabeth. 'Bettie', as he called her, had a less certain faith than her sister and was, he conceded, prone to 'worldly vanities and worldly company', but he loved her beyond words. So it was that there existed and endured within the Lord Protector a complex duality. He was both the country gentleman and the religious and political radical. He was of the world of Sir Oliver Cromwell and Sir Hamon L'Estrange, but also knew the religious ecstasy of Anna Trapnel and the Fifth Monarchists. For Oliver and for England, the search for a life that accommodated both was their monumental quest.[25]

War had been one thing for Cromwell. He had learned its ways, and God had favoured him. Peace he had found altogether more challenging terrain. It was now almost six years since he had commanded in the field. The flags and standards he had captured from Charles Stuart's defeated army at Worcester still festooned the walls of Westminster Hall but their colours were fading. Since then the signs from on high had been far more mixed. Gone were the relentless victories. In their restless pursuit of a parliament that made decisions of which they approved, Cromwell and the army had so far created and then swept away the Rump, the Nominated Assembly and the First Protectorate Parliament. Oliver remained uneasy about his own elevation to the position of Lord Protector which had been a further attempt at 'settlement', fearing it smacked too much of pride to meet God's purpose. The catastrophic defeat of the great army they had sent to capture

Hispaniola had shaken him profoundly. Never before had God issued him such a resounding rebuke, and now the Major Generals regime, which he had seen as the remedy, was collapsing, leaving the hostility between the army and the civilians of the governing class deeper than ever.[26]

❦ ❦ ❦

In the weeks after Sir Christopher Packe had presented his proposal for the settlement of the nation in February 1657 the new constitution was debated daily in Parliament. While it did not represent a complete rein-statement of the old constitutional order, it was a definitive move in that direction: monarchy and an upper house of Parliament were to be re-established, though neither quite as before – the monarch was to choose his own successor and the members of the upper house were to be his nominees rather than the peers of the realm. While it might seem to be an aggrandizement of Cromwell's powers it was arguably a curtail-ment. There were boundaries to the authority of kings, enshrined in the law and practice of centuries but, as recent events had repeatedly shown, Protectors working in tandem with an ideologically driven standing army could act almost at will. Parliament was to be called regularly, not to be 'broken or interrupted' or to have its legally elected members arbitrarily excluded, laws were not to be made, altered or over-ruled except by Act of Parliament. The leading army officers, the authors of the 'Instrument of Government' that had created the Protectorate, would see their power diminish: the succession was no longer to be decided by the Council on which they sat and the second house of Parliament was clearly designed to diminish their control. The irony was to many unmistakable: that precisely what the Long Parliament had accused Charles I of fifteen years before – raising unsanctioned taxes, dismissing Parliament summarily, forcing people to change how they worshipped, trampling on traditional freedoms, taking up arms against his own people – could all now be said of the English Protectorate. But with Cromwell distancing himself from the army, it looked as if now, at last, a decisive shift away from military rule was about to be achieved.[27]

In the last week of March, having worked their way through each clause, Parliament finally came to the controversial article stating that Oliver Cromwell should 'assume the Name, Style, Title, and Office of King of England, Scotland and Ireland' and should exercise them according to the laws of the nation. A 'pitch battell' with the Major Generals took the debate late into the night and tears rolled from Charles Fleetwood's eyes as he pleaded with his fellow MPs not to pass the bill. Finally, 185 MPs cast their votes. They divided and the tellers totted up the numbers. Those against the motion numbered 62, those in favour a resounding 123. There was no longer any doubt. The elected representatives of the nation were inviting Oliver Cromwell to adopt a new constitution and to assume the crown. Most of the big constitutional shifts of the last decade had happened without parliamentary consent. Here at last was a constitutional formulation that had originated in Parliament and had secured its unequivocal support. On the day that the 'Humble Petition and Advice', as the document was called, was presented to the Protector an elated John Thurloe put a clean copy in the post to Henry Cromwell in Dublin. It had happened, he reported breathlessly, the two apparently irreconcilable causes had at last been reconciled: 'the liberties of the nation and those of the people of God are met and doe embrace each other in this paper.'[28]

When Oliver Cromwell received the Humble Petition in the Banqueting House that day the Speaker of the House of Commons presented it with some flourish. It had been the work of forty long days, they had laboured to find a middle way that would meet the concerns and requirements of the majority, including of the Protector himself. But after the self-congratulation, the speech concluded with a pointed warning. The Protector must not imagine he could pick and choose from the clauses of this bill. 'They are all bound up in one link or chain; or like a building well knit and cemented, if one stone be taken out, it loosens the whole'. It was all or nothing.[29]

❦ ❦ ❦

As the parliamentarians had been working on the Humble Petition during March 1657, Oliver Cromwell had remained apart. His attendance at the Council of State, the executive body of the nation, was strikingly sporadic given the seriousness of the issues at stake. He attended only four of the fifteen Council meetings in February and March 1657, sometimes looking in just to sign documents and then going away again.[30] He seemed distant from state affairs, and when he met Marchamont Nedham in one of his chaplains' rooms at Whitehall it was Cromwell who asked Nedham for news, not the other way around. It was not that he lacked the energy or appetite for work. His stamina for the debates on the Scottish church then in train was unquenchable. The presenting clerics were left wilting and wishing they had eaten more breakfast while the Protector, invigorated, cleared his diary for a further four-hour session. He had time for pleasure, too, including inspecting the new Barbary horse, a prized breeding stock for racehorses, that had been imported from North Africa for his stables. It was choice not incapacity that kept him at a distance from the parliamentary debates. Like a diviner for minerals, anxious lest his own motion guide the hazel stick, he was waiting for Providence to show the way. Once the Humble Petition and its proposals for constitutional change had been presented, however, he could no longer remain aloof. Receiving it graciously, he asked the crowd of MPs to forgive his not responding there and then. Comparing himself to a groom on the brink of a betrothal, he asked for a brief pause before he signed so he might consult God and his own heart to ensure he had not misjudged 'the person he makes love to and ... it proves a curse to the man and to the family through mistake'.[31]

❦ ❦ ❦

The mood of expectation among the civilian party was palpable. This mixture of lawyers, moderates and county MPs who resented the power of the army thrilled at the prospect of a constitution of their own devising which would 'make penknyves of the soldyers swords'. It was a measure of the inclinations of the country that though royalists had been banned from voting, and though some one hundred of those

elected were then prevented from taking up their seats, two-thirds of
the chamber had still voted in favour of the new constitution and therefore against military rule. Its appeal was clear, a chance for a new
beginning. If the monarchy were restored then the issues at stake
between the erstwhile Roundheads and Cavaliers would be reduced to
merely a 'private quarrell between the House of Cromwell and Stuart'.
In such a dynastic dispute many, among them the affluent royalists who
had paid large sums to secure the return of their estates, would have
good reason to stick with the House of Cromwell. Above all, by adopting
the Humble Petition and Advice the indications that Oliver Cromwell
was done with the army and the social radicals would be built into a
firm constitutional edifice.[32]

Cromwell, however, had not yet formally consented. Under sustained
assault from two sources his resolve to accept the Petition began to
tremble. First were the army officers themselves, who had not let his
sharp words deter them and who redoubled their efforts to argue him
out of agreeing the new constitution. Second was Oliver's own
conscience. For the most part he was content with the clauses of the
Humble Petition, but it was the title that tortured him. Could it really
be that God intended him to be king, when he had sent them victory
after victory against Charles I and his son? The seriousness of his
doubts became sickeningly apparent to the moderates when, after
deliberating for three days, the Protector told an astonished committee
of Parliament that he could not go through with it.[33]

What followed was an agonizing tug of war as both interests sought
to pull Cromwell over the line in their favour. The moderates, Bulstrode
Whitelocke, Oliver St John (husband of Cromwell's first cousin
Elizabeth) and Lord Broghill, tried to talk him into accepting the title,
arguing again and again that if Parliament had voted for it, it was the
people's will, and therefore his duty to accept. In the Whitehall Council
Chamber – the very room in which Cromwell had stood in shame before
Charles I's privy council thirty years before – they laid out their case. In
the evenings, over games and pipes of tobacco in Cromwell's own rooms,
they pressed it more informally. As well as their own positive arguments, they felt the absence of alternatives in their favour, too. If

Cromwell declined the Humble Petition, what then? For the government to function it required the funds that only Parliament could grant, and without securing its support what possible course was open?[34]

But Oliver Cromwell was not William Petty; he did not approach personal or moral dilemmas with the scientist's rational eye. His responses were guided by emotion rather than logic and his communion with God was intense and private. His body servants would sometimes hear his muffled cries 'with great breakings of heart' from behind the closed doors of his inner chambers. After four weeks' prevarication John Thurloe was still 'not able to say' whether his master would accept the throne or not. As Oliver's old friend Francis Russell reminded Henry Cromwell, the mistake was to imagine that the Protector was himself certain, 'he often knows not his owne mind', for 'he is but a man'.[35]

Finally, seven weeks after Parliament had presented the Humble Petition and Advice, the House of Commons was invited to return to the Banqueting House to hear from Oliver Cromwell. Many moderates brimmed with hope: just two days earlier Cromwell had confirmed to two of their number his intention to accept the Petition, kingship and all.[36] But, unknown to them, 'in the very nicke of tyme' the 'three great men', Lambert, Desbrow and Fleetwood, had got to the Protector, talked of mutiny and told him that they, and many more army officers, would resign on the spot if he agreed. Their threats and pleas had an emotional force, and spoke to a personal experience, which all the urbane logic of the lawyers and administrators could not match.[37] Heart-rending entreaties were made. William Bradford, who had been a captain in the New Model Army, was among the numerous old army comrades who petitioned Cromwell during those weeks, beseeching him to decline the crown. Bradford pleaded with the Protector not to forget who his real friends were, those like him who had 'gone along with you from Edgehill to Dunbar'. They had been at his side in battle, and 'when we were in our lowest condition, your teares and prayers' had saved them. The Lord had been with them then, 'I am confident many of your teares was botled by God himselfe'.[38]

On Friday 8 May Oliver Cromwell made his reply. He commended the new constitution but stated unequivocally, 'I cannot undertake this government with the title of King', and so refused to give his assent. The moderates were stunned, 'all honest men here beeing at a stand and a losse,' wrote Henry Cromwell when he heard the news. They had strained every sinew to bring affairs to this point only to see their work dashed to pieces before their eyes. Oliver himself was elated. No matter that the government was in chaos and that, despite his fine words about liberty, he had yet again ignored the will of the people in Parliament. It was God's will that concerned him and now that he had made his decision he felt only delirious relief. The House of Commons had staked everything on their assertion that the new constitution was indivisible. But their bluff had been spectacularly called. While Oliver might be careless of the political consequences, they could not be. Ten days later, in a mood of gloom, they voted on whether to proceed with the new constitution with the title of Lord Protector rather than King. Some moderates felt that the substantial part had been achieved, important constitutional changes would now be effected and 'tis not names or words that governe the world, but things'.[39] But while the bill passed, and the new constitution was therefore agreed, others felt it was a Pyrrhic victory. The momentum and consensus of March had gone. Only half the number who had voted on the original bill were even present, scores having abandoned the whole enterprise, feeling 'that by refusing it', Cromwell had shown that he would always favour the army 'before a better and more solid interest'. And in place of the spectacular two-thirds majority that voted for the bill in its original form, the motion which brought in the new constitution passed by a single vote. This was the slender thread from which the nation's fate now hung.[40]

Sixteen

On the Watch Tower

❦❦❦❦❦❦❦❦❦❦❦❦❦❦❦❦❦❦❦

O n 26 June 1657 Oliver Cromwell was invested as Lord Protector of England for the second time in four years. The constitution had changed but, after six months' wrangling, the title had not, giving the ceremony a slightly surreal air. It was nonetheless a grand and closely choreographed affair. After attending Parliament, which was now dispersing until the new year, the Protector processed to Westminster Hall. Here, dressed in purple robes trimmed with ermine, he was enthroned on the ancient Gothic coronation chair, swore an oath to rule according to the law and was invested with a sword and sceptre of gold. The Venetian Ambassador commented that 'he lacked nothing but the crown to appear a veritable king'. But he was not a king. The symbols of power were handed to him by a representative of Parliament and while there were many regal trappings there was no crown. The ceremony represented the eclectic constitutional compromise which had eventually been agreed upon, and which would now be put to the test.[1]

Oliver was a man of the countryside and as soon as his reinvestiture had taken place, he escaped the fraught politics of Westminster for Hampton Court. The Tudor palace had been formally assigned to the Protector three years earlier and had become a place of sanctuary. The hunting parks, which had then been in the process of being sold, were hastily reacquired and stocked with game for his enjoyment. By 1657 a fine collection of horses filled the stables, hare and rabbits scampered over the rough grass of the warrens and two and a half thousand deer grazed the park (Colour plate 16). The huntsman, Thomas Lovell, and his seven staff managed a sporting landscape that was reminiscent of Hinchingbrooke in its prime, and which Oliver loved to traverse on horseback in pursuit of a stag. Meanwhile, the privy garden, between the palace and the River Thames, had been reordered for the Cromwells, probably following the new fashion for closely mown grass 'parterres', and ornamented with pieces of fine antique sculpture and a black marble fountain. The voluptuous bronze and stone figures of Venus and Cleopatra, Adonis and Apollo horrified hard-line Puritans – one, Mary Netheway, warned Oliver that the wrath of God would surely strike him down for allowing such 'monstres' in the palace gardens. But to her astonishment the Protector saw 'no evil' in such pagan pieces. In fact, images from classical mythology were found throughout their apartments at the palace, and the Cromwells' bedroom was hung with a celebrated set of tapestries from the royal collection depicting the goddess of love Venus in her adulterous affair with Mars, the god of war.[2]

When Parliament adjourned, the great men of government also left the capital. Oliver St John, Lord Chief Justice of the Common Pleas, who had been closeted with Cromwell during the many sessions in the spring of 1657, had built himself a magnificent new classical stone mansion, Thorpe Hall, on former church lands just outside Peterborough. John Thurloe, who had begun his career as St John's secretary, was using the same architect for his new house in nearby Wisbech – though the relentlessness of state business gave him little opportunity to enjoy it (Colour plate 8). John Lambert, architect of the 1654 constitution and one of the powerful army trio, had bought the former royal house of Wimbledon, celebrated for its magnificent terraced gardens, and filled its galleries and chambers with works of art purchased from the sale of Charles I's collection. Lambert had in the end been unable to stomach the new constitution, which represented a significant diminution of the army's power, even without the return of the office of king, and at Wimbledon that summer relinquished his commission.[3]

Lambert K° of ʒ Golden
Tulip.

Major General John Lambert, the most fearless and uncompromising of the army generals of the republic. His love of gardening and pursuit of rare horticultural specimens earned him the nickname the 'Knight of the Golden Tulip'.

The country houses of England were undergoing something of a renaissance after the destructive years of the civil war. Those in power were using their new wealth to build, while those excluded from public affairs, be they royalist aristocrats or retired parliamentarians like Thomas Fairfax or John Bradshaw, had the leisure to plan refurbishments, replant orchards and peg out parterres. The army officers just as much as the disenfranchised royalists took pleasure in tending their estates. Even before his resignation, John Lambert had been in extended correspondence with English exiles in the hunt for tulip bulbs and 'rare and unknown' anemones for his garden. Henry Cromwell had started work on Phoenix Park, the Lord Deputy's residence on the outskirts of Dublin, erecting an imposing new wing and stocking the mews with hawks and the kennels with beagles. In the fraught week when Oliver Cromwell had declined the title of king, the President of his Council of State and a number of its members had found time for a group outing to Deptford to visit the new garden being created there by the young royalist John Evelyn. Just as the disruptive and dispersing effect of war had brought William Petty and his ingenious friends into contact with new scientific ideas, so the adoption of fresh fashions in buildings and landscapes was being quickened by the turbulence of recent times.[4]

❦ ❦ ❦

When Oliver Cromwell had first been made Lord Protector in December 1654 he had been acutely uncomfortable with the paraphernalia of royalty that he had even then been expected to adopt. Seven former royal palaces had been assigned 'for the maintenance of his estate and dignity', into which his wife and mother had been reluctant to move. He had initially tried to avoid sitting on a throne and had actively prevented

The magnificent former royal palace of Wimbledon bought by John Lambert and filled with works of art, many pieces acquired at the sale of the royal collection.

foreign diplomats from kissing his hand. But international relations were managed through just such minute gestures of respect and hierarchy and to decline them was to cause confusion and offence. Diplomats began requesting in advance that the traditional procedures be followed and soon Oliver was forced to relent.[5] By 1657 he had made his peace with such expressions of status, and had found a way to feel pleasure rather than pain in the beauty and comfort that came with them. At Hampton Court and at Whitehall the Cromwells had declined to occupy Charles I's own rooms and moved instead into the erstwhile Queen's Apartments. Names associated with the ousted Stuarts were set aside. The Queen's Privy Chamber at Whitehall had become simply the Horse Chamber, after the equestrian tapestries that hung there. Charles I's Privy Chamber, one of the main audience halls of the palace, was now known as the 'Henry VIII chamber' after the large mural by Hans Holbein which still commanded the room. Both were used for much the same purpose by Protector Cromwell as they had been by King Charles, and were furnished with similar tapestries and suites of furniture but, as the recent constitutional debates had shown, names mattered.[6]

The tumults past, the summer days of 1657 were full of rest. Oliver was not completely well. His hands were shaking, among other things, and he had been given a 'course of phisick' by his doctor. While he may not have joined the younger men stag hunting that summer, he certainly played bowls on the smooth sward of the Hampton Court bowling green, which was fringed by shaded wooden seats and a brass dial on a pedestal for keeping score.[7] Remaining close to home had a special appeal as in early July his daughter Elizabeth, 'her father's darling', gave birth to a plump and healthy little boy, another grandson named Oliver. There was never any doubt among family or observers that the intelligent and ebullient Elizabeth was her father's favourite (Colour plate 17). She was neither biddable, especially godly nor given to the sugary terms of endearment her father sometimes favoured. Instead, she had a spry, sparky wit and her own views. When the philosopher James Harington remarked of her 3-year-old daughter, with whom he had been playing, that she was so lovable he wished he could have stolen her away, Elizabeth replied brightly, 'Stolen!', 'pray, what to do with her? For she is yet too young to become your mistress.' He had come, as many did, to ask Mrs Claypole to use her influence with her father in his favour. In his case it was to persuade the Protector to allow publication of his political treatise *Oceana*, which, after consideration, she agreed to do. She would often be a moderating voice with her father. Like her husband and brother, she resented the Major Generals' regime, and the power it gave men such as Hezekiah Haynes to override and invade traditional hierarchies and freedoms. In the month when her husband had launched the opposition to the militia bill in Parliament, she had attended the wedding of a government figure and on being asked where the Major Generals' wives were, had responded tartly, 'I'll warrant you, washing their dishes at home as they use[d] to.'[8]

Oliver Cromwell was delighted with his new grandson and made the baby's other grandfather, John Claypole senior, a baronet in celebration – his early reticence about granting hereditary titles having also passed. Elizabeth was now 28 and she and her husband John had extensive apartments at Hampton Court where they, too, spent the summer of 1657. Among them was a fine south-facing room which had been assigned to Archbishop Laud before the war but had become a nursery where their children could play and sleep in the long, warm afternoons. Andrew Marvell captured the happiness Oliver found here: 'With her [Elizabeth] each day the pleasing hour he shares / And at her aspects calms his growing cares; / or with a grandsire's joy her children sees / Hanging about her neck or at his knees'.[9]

Oliver Cromwell had always been fond of children. He had been a warm and demonstrative father when his own offspring were growing up, showing and telling them of his love at every opportunity. Of the nine children born to the Cromwells three had long since died. He must have mourned them all, but the sudden death of his first son Robert at the age of 18 had by his own admission very nearly killed him. It came in 1639, the period of Oliver's personal crisis. The loss, he remembered twenty years later, 'went as a dagger to my heart'. Like the Earl of Derby, who had been sustained as he prepared for the scaffold by the thought that he would soon be reunited with his beloved son James, so Oliver carried his grief for his own lost boy with him for a lifetime.[10]

As the only son in a family of seven daughters Oliver Cromwell had grown up with women and was naturally at ease in female company. His kindness and concern for the women of his family endured, extending beyond his own children to his daughters-in-law and other relations by marriage. The dominant role expected of a seventeenth-century father and husband came naturally to him, but he was seldom domineering and referred unashamedly to the need to confer with his wife before making significant family decisions. Elizabeth, to whom he was devoted, kept largely out of the limelight, but on occasion proffered frank advice to her husband on his professional conduct. Unlike Thomas and Anne Fairfax whose daughter received the elite education of a nobleman, the Cromwells did not regard educating their daughters as a priority. Oliver was no intellectual – he liked to say he studied men rather than books – and he saw his responsibility, beyond loving them, as encouraging his girls in their devotion to God and finding them rich and respectable husbands. As he had explained when negotiating the dowry that was to come with his son Richard's bride, he had to be careful of money for the simple reason that 'I shall need [it] for my two little wenches'.[11]

❦ ❦ ❦

The weather in August 1657 was mixed, summer sunshine interspersed with torrential downpours that sent palace life indoors. Morning and evening the Cromwell family attended prayers together in the palace chapel. The room had been stripped of stained glass and crucifixes nearly a decade before they had taken up residence, and its magnificent vaulted Tudor ceiling now sailed over a simple table pulpit and twelve rows of benches. Upstairs in the long gallery Andrea Mantegna's huge canvasses of The Triumphs of Caesar, the greatest Renaissance paintings in England, had been saved for the Protector's use. Wet afternoons could be pleasantly passed marvelling at their beauty or playing billiards on the tables erected below.[12]

For Oliver and Elizabeth Cromwell, however, the pastime that surpassed all others was music. Singing and organs had been banned from English churches over a decade earlier when the Puritans had forbidden everything that was felt to distract from the word of God. While Oliver would not have countenanced music in church, in a secular context he loved it. In April 1654, the month they first moved into the royal palaces, the Cromwells had hired a brilliant musician, John Hingeston, to be head of 'His Highness Musique'. Organist, chorister and virginal player, Hingeston had gone on to build up a group of talented musicians and singers to provide entertainment for the Protectoral court encompassing both traditional and up-to-the-moment instruments played together in 'consort'. It was on his instruction that an organ had been erected in the Cockpit theatre at Whitehall which was used for musical entertainments and celebrations – among them the concert staged after the great thanksgiving feast earlier in the year. It was when wandering past Hingeston's practice room near the Cockpit that Roger L'Estrange heard the chamber organ playing and was invited in to join the Protector's musicians on his bass viol. Cromwell himself, also passing, loitered at the doorway to listen. Hingeston had recently acquired the organ removed from the chapel at Magdalen College, Oxford, and had had it set up in the great hall at Hampton Court. This, the largest room in the palace, had ample space for accompanying strings, brass and singers as well as an audience. In mid-July an important Scottish visitor arrived at Hampton Court 'just whyl my Lord and his Lady was at their music'. Oliver leaped up and grasped the man's hand in warm welcome, before calling for a chair so that his guest could join them and the musicians could play on.[13]

❦ ❦ ❦

Under the terms of the old constitution, drafted by John Lambert and his army colleagues, the choice of Cromwell's successor as Lord Protector had belonged to the Council of State, on which they were well represented. The likelihood had therefore been that one of their number would fill the role when the time came, perhaps Charles Fleetwood or John Lambert himself. In a significant victory for the moderates, the new constitution of 1657 assigned the choice to Oliver Cromwell, instead, who was considered more measured and inclined to civilian government than his officers. Until recently Oliver had resisted any suggestion that his title might be hereditary. As with his attitude to taking the crown, he felt that God must surely disapprove of such an aggrandisement of his own kin. But now that the decision lay entirely with him, and his patience with his army friends had started to fray, he began to consider whether a reversion to the time-honoured hereditary principle might not, after all, be worth contemplating.

So far the Cromwells' eldest son, Richard, had taken little part in state or army affairs, unlike his brother Henry (Colour plate 18). Such was the disparity between the two brothers' positions that visitors to Whitehall frequently assumed that Henry was the older and Richard the younger.[14] Over that summer at Hampton Court Oliver began to draw Richard into the public arena, as if testing his suitability or otherwise for office. He was introduced to important visitors at Hampton Court and in July it was announced that Richard was to take over his father's position as Chancellor of Oxford University.[15]

The providential worldview in which John Bradshaw had been so thoroughly schooled in the 1630s was fundamental to Oliver Cromwell's whole existence – though the two men were now barely on speaking terms. It was Oliver's belief that everything was God's doing and nothing happened by chance that caused him such confidence in victory and such doubt in defeat. The signs of God's favour had been good that summer. Parliament had reached agreement and had willingly dispersed. Henry Cromwell was bringing new order to Ireland, Elizabeth had safely given birth to a healthy son and Oliver was just concluding the details of two advantageous marriages for his youngest daughters. But then, sometime in early August, things changed. A mysterious deadly 'sickness' broke out in London which claimed its victims at frightening speed, and was immediately interpreted as a sign of divine discontent. Then, shortly afterwards, while careering through the New Forest in pursuit of a stag, Richard Cromwell's horse fell, throwing its rider and then crushing him beneath its hefty flank. His knee was dislocated and his thigh bone shattered.[16] Surgeons and physicians hastily attended and after four days his leg had been 'set'. Richard's life had been saved, but the damage had been done. What did it mean? As John Thurloe observed, the Protector was in 'a very great affliction', for 'if a sparrow falls not to the ground without the providence of God' then Richard Cromwell's injury could hardly be chance. It was a sign.[17]

❦ ❦ ❦

September brought Oliver back to London, his medical treatment complete, and the resumption in earnest of government activity. Earlier in the year the English and French governments, each seeing the benefit of befriending their enemy's enemy, had signed a treaty committing them to join forces against Spain. The English were to concentrate on the Spanish Netherlands, with the promise of keeping the strategically important city of Dunkirk if it could be taken. In the third week of September the Anglo-French army launched a strike on the fort of Mardyck just outside Dunkirk. As ground troops bombarded the walls, the English navy attacked from the sea, under the command of Edward Montagu – son of the man who had bought Hinchingbrooke from the Cromwell family – who had been recently promoted as General at Sea. Mardyck fell and an English garrison of 1,300 was rapidly installed. Late one evening three weeks later the Spaniards staged a surprise counter-assault. Among the 5,000 assailants on the sandy ramparts that night were the 27-year-old Charles Stuart and his brother James, titular Duke of York. The night sky lit up as the garrison sent up flares to guide the fire from the English offshore gunships, and they in turn unleashed their artillery on the attackers. The fighting went on until dawn, when the Spanish at last conceded defeat. Retaining Mardyck was a modest enough victory in itself, but it provided a vital boost to English military morale. *Mercurius Politicus* reported triumphantly that the garrison had 'revived the ancient honor and renown of our Nation abroad'. Oliver for his part received a precious signal. Almost four hundred of those who fought alongside Charles Stuart that night were reported killed, while not a single one of Oliver Cromwell's men had fallen. God had not deserted him yet.[18]

❦ ❦ ❦

Despite its domestic preoccupations England under the Protectorate was a more cosmopolitan place than it had ever been before. Until war had drained the funds from city investors and interrupted shipping, English international trade had been steeply on the rise. The regicide was now almost a decade ago and trade had made a significant recovery. Since 1640 the volume of foreign imports to England had almost doubled, notwithstanding wars, high taxation and periodic poor harvests. Government anxiety about retaining control of an island nation with territorial outposts meant the navy was being maintained and manned to a degree that had not been seen before. The fractious and competitive relationship with the Dutch – and English government anger that their grand plan for a union had been rejected – had given rise to the highly protectionist Navigation Act which, when applied to this burgeoning international trade, would go on to bear extraordinary and unexpected fruit.

For fifty years English trade to the Far East had been almost exclusively the preserve of the East India Company. With the Dutch dominating the Far Eastern spice market, English interests had shifted northwest to India and to textiles. Cotton, with its fine fibres, softness and the ease with which it could be washed and dyed, was perfect for shirts and undergarments, napery and bedsheets. English merchants found a bountiful supply was to be had from Bengal, which came both as finished white fabric and as vividly printed calico (named after Calcutta) or chintz, prized for dress and upholstery fabric. India also offered a cheaper alternative source of silk, including the crisp weave known as taffeta (Colour plate 19). In October 1657, after a period of acute financial difficulty, the East India Company was granted a new charter signed by the Protector himself. On its favourable terms the Company would go on to dominate the oceans and markets of the world. While trade to the east was expanding, to the west the entrepreneurs of the English outposts in the Caribbean were shifting their agricultural exports from tobacco, the mainstay of the American plantations, to sugar. The production of this labour-intensive cash crop involved dangerous and back-breaking work in the sun-baked sugar cane fields, crushing mills and boiling houses. Its large-scale exploitation was made possible by the availability of forced labour, those who could not refuse, in the form of transported Catholic 'rebels' from Ireland and, increasingly, enslaved Africans purchased from the Guinea coast of West Africa.

The exploitation of these expanding international networks brought to the dim, oak-panelled, wool-hung parlours of England exotic colours, fabrics and finishes. By the late 1650s Mrs Cromwell's closet at Hampton Court was a gorgeous riot of green silk taffeta, on walls and furniture alike. Ebony stands and mirrors, red cotton curtains and Persian and Turkish carpets were found throughout the couple's apartments. Oliver Cromwell had, according to one wry observer, 'got a better tailor' since he had become Lord Protector, but he would never be a flamboyant dresser. His sons and daughters, however, were cut from different cloth. Elizabeth Claypole, who 'acted the part of princess very naturally', revelled in fine things and sent orders overseas for 'the richest gold and silver stuffs for her own wearing'. Even in the nursery, where her children played on their grandfather's knee, the armchairs and stools were upholstered in sky-blue silk taffeta embroidered 'after the Indian fashion'.[19]

The cheerless prohibitions of successive Puritan governments could not stop the people of England from enjoying and indulging themselves, and London continued to be the centre of commerce and consumption. Since the first coffee shop had opened in the early 1650s the 'Arabian bean' had taken the capital by storm and by 1659 the 'Turkish drink' was sold on 'almost evry street'. Sitting on wooden benches at long tables customers sipped coffee, drew on pipes stuffed with the leaves from Virginian tobacco plantations and thumbed and debated newspapers filled with dispatches from Europe and beyond. Even Oliver Cromwell himself occasionally took a pipe, puffing on it as he and friends sat in his closet at Whitehall, talking and playing riddle and rhyming games into the night. The ban on public theatres for 'too commonly expressing lascivious mirth and levity' had happened in 1642, and remained officially in place – not least because they were seen as dangerous breeding grounds for royalist plotting. But the appetites of audiences and the inventiveness of impresarios could not easily be suppressed. Other forms of entertainment flourished, among them

Southwark's bear gardens and the exhibition of 'animals' of varying degrees of authenticity – including a bull 'with wings ... newly sent out of Arabia' shown by Alexander Duncan in Islington. In September 1657, as Oliver Cromwell returned to Whitehall from his summer at Hampton Court, the celebrated acrobat known as 'the Turk' was in town. John Evelyn saw him in action, dancing blindfold on a high tightrope, a 12-year-old boy suspended 20 feet below from a cord around his ankle, 'as if [he] had ben but a feather'. Also that month Barbara von Becke, the celebrated marvel and musician whose entire face was covered in fine, dense hair, was in London giving harpsichord recitals. New amusements that evaded the ban were introduced, most notably the sung dramatic performances that Claudio Monteverdi had recently made popular in Venice known as 'Opera'. In promoting the benefits of an art form 'unpractis'd here; though of great reputation amongst other Nations', the enterprising William Davenant put it to Secretary Thurloe that, like the rulers of ancient Rome, the English government should encourage public entertainments to prevent the 'melancholy that breeds sedition'. Furthermore, he had in mind subject matter that could propagate patriotic, anti-Spanish feeling. His arguments found favour and in the summer of 1658 Covent Garden hosted its very first opera – complete with music, singing, perspective scenery and theatrical special effects. At three o'clock every afternoon a paying audience could watch Davenant's *The Cruelty of the Spaniard*. The curtain rose to reveal a scene of the West Indies as the musicians played 'a wyld Ayre sutable to the region'. Against a background of parched hills and shining sands the singers appeared dressed as 'Peruvians' wearing 'feather'd habbits and bonnets' and carrying lumps of gold and silver in baskets. Coconut palms swayed while 'on the boughs of other Trees are seen Munkies, Apes and Parrots' and in the distance valleys of sugar canes. Into this scene of idyllic plenty, with thrilling singing, acting and music, the villainous Spaniards would shortly make their entry.[20]

Hyde Park, now no longer a private royal hunting park, had become the fashionable place to see and be seen. Carriage rides and races were popular in which the Cromwell family were frequent participants. On one occasion in 1654 Oliver himself had ridden his team of carriage horses at such a lick that the vehicle overturned; the resulting panic was compounded when the pistol he always carried at his side accidentally discharged. New fashions were paraded, dresses and coats of the finest imported fabrics, and novel personal affections; the wearing of makeup and small decorative patches by women and of wigs by men took hold of high society in the late 1650s. After the Whitehall wedding of Oliver Cromwell's youngest daughter, Frances, in November 1657 the feasting and dancing went on until 5 a.m. Oliver himself led the high jinks, at one point snatching the fashionable peruke wig from his eldest son's head, threatening to throw it on the fire, and then sitting on it, to much hilarity.

Edmund Waller, poet and politician and builder of another fine new house, captured the growing affluence and international self-confidence of the capital in the mid-1650s in a poem of praise to the Lord Protector: 'The taste of hot Arabia's spice we know, / Free from the scorching sun that makes it grow; / Without the worm, in Persian silks we shine; / And, without planting, drink of every vine. / To dig for wealth we weary not our limbs; / Gold, though the heaviest metal, hither swims; / Ours is the harvest where the Indians mow; / We plough the deep, and reap what others sow'.[21]

🐝 🐝 🐝

When it came to the people he considered 'Godly' Oliver Cromwell was almost always compassionate, open-minded, accepting and untribal. He periodically displayed those same qualities to individuals who were not Puritans. Despite his antipathy towards the episcopacy, he had regarded Bishop Ussher of Ireland as 'pious and learned' and allowed him to be buried in Westminster Abbey. Even Catholics might experience his clemency and he repeatedly wrote to Dublin asking for specific Irish Catholic families to be excused the punitive terms of the post-war settlement. To the Dutch Rabbi Menasseh ben Israel who came to London to try to negotiate the readmission of the Jews, Oliver was warm and encouraging. While formal acceptance was not the result (probably because he knew he could not persuade the Council or Parliament), enough encouragement was given for the first synagogues in England since the Middle Ages to be established and Cromwell arranged for the Rabbi himself to receive a state pension of £100 a year. Largely to please Cromwell the new constitution allowed for freedom of worship for all adherents to 'the true Protestant religion' and stipulated 'that they may not be compelled thereto by Penalties, nor restrained from their Profession, but protected from all Injury and Molestation in the Profession of the Faith, and Exercise of their Religion'. This spirit of official freedom in relation to religion was a novelty of the 1650s, but it was not all it seemed. The 1657 constitution, like that which had preceded it, explicitly denied any such 'liberty' to adherents of 'Popery or Prelacy'. In a stroke all Catholics were excluded, as were millions, like the families of Alice L'Estrange or the Countess of Derby, who had been committed members of the Protestant church with bishops that had been the official state religion of the country for over a century. The Protector could not see how hollow his idealistic words rang to those who did not wish to worship his way. Many of the new sects benefited from his approach, but in all the Baptists, Fifth Monarchists and Quakers accounted for less than 2 per cent of the population (and the socially radical Quakers were also denied freedom of worship). Those parishes where the congregations shared Cromwell's desire for a strictly Puritan national church benefited, but they were unquestionably the minority. To the vast majority of the English population, who preferred the familiar form of religion codified in the Book of Common Prayer, was extended no such freedom. Instead, they were robbed of the social and religious rites of centuries past: church weddings and seasonal ales, Christmas and twelfth night services and celebrations, traditional baptisms and burials. Such was Cromwell's certainty in his course that he was untroubled by the loss that he and his fellow zealots had wrought upon Englishmen and women, or by the devastation being visited on the people of Ireland.[22]

The Protector's individual acts of kindness and toleration – and his sincere belief that he was doing the right thing – took place, therefore, before a national backdrop of the persecution of Catholics and the oppression of 'Prayer Book' Anglicans. According to legislation passed that summer, which Henry Cromwell had tried in vain to prevent, any

Catholic refusing to repudiate his or her faith was subject to both the forfeiture of the majority of his or her estate and a massive financial fine. Edward Montagu's young kinsman Samuel Pepys came to Whitehall on an errand from Hinchingbrooke in December 1657, and witnessed the Lord Protector's glee at the recent arrest of a coterie of Jesuits in Covent Garden. It was Oliver himself, Pepys reported, who encouraged his men to dress up in the holy vestments and caper about to peals of exultant laughter.[23] While Catholics were spared the religious executions of the sixteenth century, they experienced precious little freedom. On 25 December 1657 as, once again, people across England gathered to celebrate the feast of Christmas in spite of the prohibitions, Cromwell authorized soldiers to close such gatherings down. Bulstrode Whitelocke, for one, tried to talk him out of it on the obvious basis that it 'was contrary to the liberty of conscience so much owned and pleaded for by the Protector and his friends'. But Cromwell would not be dissuaded. The congregation of Exeter House chapel, a centre of covert Anglicanism, was in the act of receiving communion when the soldiers strode in to disperse them, levelling their muskets at the altar as they did so. Cromwell might proudly claim that 'there was never such liberty of Conscience ... as is now' but, not for the first time, his rhetoric did not marry with reality. Freedom there might be, but only for the Godly few.[24]

❦ ❦ ❦

London was white with snow when the new parliamentary session opened on 20 January 1658. The coach and superbly caparisoned horses which conveyed the Protector the short distance to Westminster passed through the palely luminous streets from which the dense fall had kept the usual crowds and muffled all sound. Cromwell was not feeling himself, and his usually leonine strength was less than rampant as he crunched over New Palace Yard. He remained anxious about the royalist invasion that might come at any moment, carrying a gun at his side and bolting his chamber door from the inside every night. But his spirit remained strong and he had reason for optimism. He had that autumn married his two younger daughters to wealthy and well-connected men,

Robert Rich, the heir of the Earl of Warwick, and leading moderate Thomas Belasyse, Viscount Fauconberg. The war with Spain had been going well, religious wrongdoers were being rounded up and the preaching ministry reformed, and now the new two-chambered Parliament which he had wanted was about to meet for the first time. He had taken immense trouble over naming the sixty-three members of the new upper chamber, striving for the balance and broad range of opinions that had been so absent in the early days of the republic. His two sons and his two sons-in-law were among those sent writs to attend, as were Fleetwood and Desbrow, the leaders of the army party. His friend Oliver St John and his army colleague George Monck were named, as was Lord Broghill, who had led the civilian group in the debate on the new constitution. Alongside them was Sir Arthur Haselrige, who had been one of the 'five members' Charles I had tried to arrest in 1642, and Thomas Pride himself, who had implemented the purge with which the whole enterprise of government without kingship had begun. For John Bradshaw, however, there was no place.[25]

In his opening speech in the old House of Lords, now in use once more, Oliver spoke movingly to the assembled members of the opportunity that lay before them. England was God's blessed nation, a people he had chosen to redeem from sin, and now they who gathered in these chambers would fulfil this destiny by bringing the peace and harmony for which they all yearned. Generations to come would thank them as the 'repairers of breaches and the restorers of paths to dwell in'. Theirs was nothing short of the greatest work that mortals could do on earth. He then called on Lord Fiennes to complete his opening remarks, murmuring, 'I have some infirmities on me'. But while he may have been a physically diminished figure, slumped in a throne beneath a canopy of state in the strange, snow-bleached light, his vision of paradise regained gleamed radiant before them.[26]

It took only a matter of days for the Protector's poetic prophecy of parliamentary peace and unity to be extinguished. Political miscalculations and personal grievances accumulated with horrible familiarity. The new constitution stipulated that the hundred or so MPs elected in 1656, but prevented from taking their seats, must now be admitted.

Among them was a small but potent crew of 'Commonwealthsmen' who, like John Bradshaw, regarded the whole Protectorate as an illegal edifice created by the army and wished to see the republic of 1649 revived. Several who had been nominated to the new second chamber chose to remain in the House of Commons. Meanwhile, the more powerful moderates appointed to the second chamber did move, thereby vacating their seats and interest in the Commons. As a consequence the House of Commons of January 1658 had a distinctly different membership and complexion from that which had voted through the 'Humble Petition and Advice' six months earlier. The picture was no better in the upper house. Of those summoned almost a third failed to appear. Many of the peers and more conservative country gentlemen named by Cromwell decided, in the end, that they could not go through with it – among them the Earl of Warwick whose grandson had just married Cromwell's daughter. To endorse the upper house was to give up on the House of Lords proper and the old royal constitution, to which by declining the title of king, Cromwell had shown himself irreconcilable. With the Protector's health visibly faltering the time might be approaching when a greater prize than this could be claimed. What followed was chaos. The House of Commons, fuelled by the Commonwealthsmen and missing the leading moderates, started picking a fight on various 'pettish' points, refusing to respond to any communication from a 'House of Lords' whose existence they questioned, and taking every opportunity to contest and challenge the new formulation. Cromwell's blood began to rise. Five days after he had opened Parliament he summoned both houses to the Banqueting House and gave a 'very long, plain and serious speech' expressing his concerns. Darkness fell and the clerks struggled to see the ink on their paper as he hectored on in a meandering extempore address. We must not return to folly, he intoned, the risks England faced from foreign armies and the Stuarts were very grave and yet still they squabbled. He had agreed to their new constitution but even then they would grant him no peace. What on earth was it that they wanted if not this? He had never sought status, but he was 'set on a watch-tower, to see what may be for the good of these nations, and what may be for preventing of evil'.[27]

Late at night the following week, matters came to a head. Oliver Cromwell had retired for the evening and Secretary Thurloe was laid up with a cold when the messenger came to Whitehall Palace. Thurloe read the letter and called at once for John Maidstone, one of the Protector's closest attendants, instructing him to take it to his master. Maidstone knew the fierceness of Oliver's temper and knocked gingerly on his door. When he received no reply he was forced to hammer with his fist. An irate voice eventually barked from beyond and Maidstone explained that he brought him a paper 'of great concernment'. Unlocking the door, Oliver took the letter and was appalled at its contents. One of his men had intercepted what appeared to be a summons to members of the army to join in some sort of an unauthorized action with the foreboding words 'I hope you will be at the House to-morrow to do service for the Army and the Nation'. Oliver immediately ordered the shifts of the soldiers on duty to be swapped, and called for John Desbrow to demand whether he knew anything of what was afoot. He then sat down to dispatch orders across the capital.

The following morning Cromwell burst into Thurloe's bedchamber, and announced to the invalid's bewilderment that he was going to Parliament. Striding through his apartments down the Turks Gallery onto the Privy landing stage to board his barge for Westminster, Oliver found that the river had frozen hard overnight and the barge could not be freed from the ice. He turned on his heel and walked out onto the street where he hailed the first passing carriage that crunched over the snow. His arrival at Westminster unannounced caused alarm among those milling about in the lobbies and courtyards. The Protector drank a glass of ale in a waiting room while the parliamentary officials gathered the members of both houses together. Charles Fleetwood, he who had made Henry Cromwell's life in Ireland so difficult, approached the Protector and asked what he was doing. Oliver replied archly that he was going to dissolve Parliament. Fleetwood protested that it would be a mistake, to which the Lord Protector and England's mightiest general responded in a flash of fury, 'you are a milksop', 'by the living God I will dissolve this house'. Shortly after noon Oliver Cromwell entered the old House of Lords and, yet again, ejected the institution in whose name and for whose rights he had fought the bloodiest wars in the history of the British Isles. They were further from peace now, he bitterly contended, than they had been at the height of the fighting. 'I think it is high time that an end be put unto your sitting, and I do dissolve this Parliament; and let God judge between me and you.'[28]

Parliament was sent packing just a fortnight after it had gathered. The threat of mutiny that Cromwell had felt that night spurred him into further action. Two days later he hosted a tremendous gathering at the Whitehall Cockpit for 200 officers of the English army. It was an event designed to calm nerves and galvanize loyalty – and to shore up the Protector's authority. Copious amounts of alcohol were served, and Oliver drank heavily himself. Amid the brotherhood and bonhomie he stood to address the gathering. 'Gentlemen,' he cried, 'we have gone along together, and why we should differ now I know not', 'if any of you cannot in conscience conform to the new government, let him speak'. An uneasy silence followed; no man raised his hand and the drinking resumed. A day or two later the ringleaders of the army who had indeed been agitating with the Commonwealthsmen for the end of the Protectorate and a return to the early days of the republic were called in. They remained defiant, even after he had given them a few days in which to consider their positions. Utterly unsatisfied with their answers, Cromwell sacked them on the spot.[29]

❦ ❦ ❦

The problem was that ever since Ireton and Pride had purged Parliament in 1649 to push through the trial and execution of the King, in which Oliver Cromwell had acquiesced, England had been ruled by men whose competing priorities made an unstable compound. The desire for more powerful and active parliaments, for social reform and for a quite different form of religion from the old Church of England could not easily be satisfied in a single government. The representatives of the people did not want the wholesale religious reform that the victors of the civil wars felt must happen and were unconvinced about many ingredients of the programmes for social and political reform. That the regime, or various versions of it, had endured so long owed a great deal to Oliver Cromwell himself. The variegated nature of his own character – country gentle-man, seasoned general and religious radical – enabled him to reassure enough people, be they committed Baptist officers in the army or conservative country people wearied by war, to prolong the enterprise. The steely, stabilizing force of the army had held the regime together and he was its commanding officer. Henry Cromwell put it with charac-teristic clarity: the whole regime 'depend[s] upon his highness life, and upon his peculiar skill, and faculty and personal interest in the army', 'beneath the immediate hand of God (if I know anything of the affairs in England) there is no other reason why wee are not in blood this day'.[30]

Oliver had seen off yet another crisis, he had dealt with both Parliament and the army and determined to keep both at arm's length. But he had found no peace. In the days that followed the events of February 1658 he was visibly shaken. He refused to join his wife and family for morning and evening meals, which until now he had always done, and insisted instead on dining alone. He suffered from insomnia and, it was widely reported, was taking strong doses of opium to help him sleep. His new son-in-law Robert Rich, heir to the fortune and title of the Earldom of Warwick, had fallen gravely ill. The disease he had contracted was scrofula, or 'the King's Evil', which, it was believed, only the healing touch of an anointed sovereign could cure. This striking diagnosis, which would have been a gift to Marchamont Nedham in the days of his rambunctious royalist newspapering, must have darkened Oliver's heart further. On 17 February the young man died and the Cromwells' youngest daughter became a widow at just 20.[31]

❧ ❧ ❧

Oliver Cromwell's qualities were such that even red-blooded royalists did not deny them. Richard Baxter considered him to be simultaneously a traitor and responsible for 'promot[ing] the Gospel and the Interests of Godliness more than any had done before him'. Edward Hyde, chief minister to Charles II, thought he would burn in hell but conceded he had remarkable virtues, and would be remembered 'as a brave bad man'. The Protector was a kind man who oversaw appalling atrocities; a consultative man who repeatedly dismissed elected parliaments in boiling rage; a passionate reformer who believed in the conservative ways of the country; a man of great personal humility who died in the bedchamber of a king with every power but the name. Taken on his own terms he had an intense integrity rare among rulers; he seldom acted for personal profit and almost always did what he believed to be best for others. His courage and conviction were crucial to winning the war that brought the English republic about, but he had not been its architect. It was a year and a half after Charles I's execution before he had even become head of the army, and five years before he was named head of state. His commitment and confidence and willingness to act prolonged a regime that might otherwise have crumbled within months, but a passionate providentialist did not make a natural politician. The sort of active political management, tactical compromises and careful forward planning that might have made a success of the 1657 parliamentary session were nowhere in evidence, and there appeared to be no plan whatsoever for what was to become of the nation on his death. Laying plans was not his way. God would decide what was to come and would reveal it when the time was right. His was an attitude born of deep personal conviction, but it also suited him to be perched high on his 'watch tower', removed from the detail, claiming ignorance of various endeavours and laying the political failures of the decade at others' doors. John Bradshaw had missed barely a single Council meeting during his years as its President, and committed his every hour to the regime he had done so much to create. By 1658 Oliver attended Council only occasionally, leaving his colleagues to manage the parlous shortage of money and paralysing ambiguity about the future. The Protector's eyes were now only periodically down on the detail and instead were drawn ever upwards to the heavenly sphere above.[32]

❈ ❈ ❈

John Thurloe's admiration for Henry Cromwell, now confirmed as Lord Deputy of Ireland, grew with every passing day and *Mercurius Politicus*, each issue approved by Thurloe before publication, was full of his admirable doings. Meanwhile, Richard Cromwell, now admitted as a member of the privy council, was seldom mentioned. It was obvious which son

the Secretary thought would make the better successor. As spring
turned to summer Oliver Cromwell's health steadied and he was to be
seen out hunting once again, but there was still no clarity on the succession. The civilian party rallied for another go at reviving kingship, and
were again given encouragement by the Lord Protector, who claimed he
had decided not to try to please his army comrades any longer but to act
instead by his 'own resolution'. Both Henry Cromwell and Elizabeth
Claypole were pleased to see their father parted from the army and
continued to press for moderation in the regime's dealings with royalists.[33] But the parliamentary session at which any further constitutional
change would need to be attempted was not due to take place until the
autumn and, given the changes in its composition, it must have seemed
to many that the moment for such a settlement had passed. That
summer Dunkirk finally fell to the English but the victory turned to ash
in the Protector's mouth. Days later his little grandson, Elizabeth
Claypole's son Oliver, born in such hope the summer before, died. His
mother, too, was gripped by illness. Oliver and his wife moved to
Hampton Court to tend to their beloved daughter. Her body became
convulsed by fits as a 'silent fire' consumed her from within. Her father
felt her every agony as his own. At last, on 4 August 1658, she fell still.[34]

The death of Elizabeth Claypole broke her father's heart. His devastation at the loss of his child, not yet 30, was universally recognized.
Andrew Marvell, who knew them both, described her end and the
personal tragedy it represented. Oliver had been by her side day and
night as she had strained for life, 'Like polished mirrors, so his steely
breast / Had every figure of her woes expressed; / And with the damp of
her last gasps obscured, / Had drawn such stains as were not to be
cured. / Fate could not either reach with single stroke, / But the dear
image fled, the mirror broke.'

Oliver's grief at his daughter's death overwhelmed him. In Elizabeth's
final days his family and friends saw 'his life suspended by her breath'.
Richard Cromwell wrote to his brother Henry that with their sister's
death the finest limb of their family tree had fallen, but now 'the axe is
layd to the roote'. Oliver himself felt death's proximity. When his wife
and children came to see him after they had dined on 23 August, 'he

broake out his more secreatt thoughts, assuring us of danger'. He pressed upon them the importance of their faith in Christ, and told them he had sent for his steward that he might put his financial affairs in order and 'setle his broken private fortune'. But of who was to succeed him as Lord Protector still he said nothing.[35]

Secretary Thurloe was beside himself with anxiety as Oliver's health deteriorated daily. He wrote to Henry Cromwell at 2 a.m. on 27 August of his fear of what would happen if the Protector died without determining the succession, 'which truly I beleeve he hath not yet done'. The year before Oliver had written a name on a piece of paper which he had folded and sealed, but when Thurloe had sent a servant to retrieve it from his desk, it could not be found.[36] His body was failing fast, consumed by 'ague' – perhaps malaria – but his spirit stiffened. On 2 September, with death palpably close, the Protector at last spoke. If Charles Fleetwood or John Desbrow had hoped he might choose them, they were disappointed. If John Thurloe had hoped Cromwell might name Henry Cromwell, he was also disappointed. Instead, this agent of revolution reverted to the time-honoured tradition of primogeniture. It was an act of almost blind faith – and of colossal political recklessness. He put everything in the hands of the son whom he had done almost nothing to prepare for the task, and in so doing passed over the son who might just have held the country and the Protectorate together. Less than twenty-four hours later Oliver Cromwell died in the royal apartments of Whitehall Palace and Richard, 32 and by his own admission 'more in the darke than others', found himself head of state.

Oliver showed little concern about the burden he was passing on. Instead he was filled with glorious certainty. Almost the last words he spoke before speech deserted him were 'God will not leave me'. His mind and heart were full – but not with concern for his country, for his family or for the unbearable responsibility which he was leaving others to shoulder. Rather, he was fixed entirely on the fulfilment of the spiritual epiphany he had experienced thirty years before. It was 3 September, the very day of his famous victories at both Dunbar and Worcester, and at long last God was bringing him home.[37]

Seventeen

This Lyon Rouzed

❧❧❧❧❧❧❧❧❧❧❧❧❧❧❧❧❧❧❧

A bove the broad banks of the River North Esk in the midst of Midlothian rose the noble castle of Dalkeith. Its position was winning. Past its western gates ran the road that led north the seven miles to Edinburgh and south the many more towards Kelso and the English border. To the east a tapering triangle of woodland terminated half a mile away at the 'meeting of the waters', the convergence of the Rivers North and South Esk, forming a magnificent enclosed hunting ground. Less than 3 miles beyond that lay the coast from which ships sailed daily to the ports of England, Scandinavia, the Baltic and beyond. Dalkeith Castle had been remodelled in Scottish Renaissance splendour by James Douglas, 4th Earl of Morton, Regent of Scotland during the infancy of James VI. It was, like Hinchingbrooke, an aristocratic mansion of such appeal that it was frequently requisitioned for royal use. The Scottish privy council met here often during James VI's reign, both before and after he became King James I of England. James's bride, Queen Anne, had lodged here, 'the nearest fair house to Edinburgh', on her arrival from Denmark, and on Christmas Eve 1592 she had given birth at Dalkeith to Charles I's short-lived older sister Princess Margaret.[1]

In January 1657 Dalkeith saw another birth. For the preceding three years the castle had been home and headquarters to General George Monck, Commander in Chief of the Army in Scotland (Colour plate 21).

Monck was a career soldier of a genteel but impoverished West Country family, who had fought in Charles I's ill-fated Continental campaigns during the 1630s. When the civil war erupted Monck continued in service, more from habit than conviction, until his capture at the battle of Nantwich in 1644. Thomas Fairfax, who had made his wintry odyssey across England to secure that parliamentary victory, had also been an officer in the pre-war English army and had singled Monck out from the captives as 'a man worth the making'.

For a year and a half thereafter Monck had been interned in the Tower of London where, with steady industry, he had written a manual of soldiery and warfare. It was while passing those slow hours of confinement that he had first encountered his future wife. Anne Clarges was a seamstress who called at the cells of the Tower to see to the prisoners' linen. Socially she was dramatically his inferior. Monck may have been a prisoner but he was nonetheless the son of a knight. Anne, by contrast, was the daughter of a London blacksmith. While Monck was handsome, in a thickset, dark-haired way, he was unused to female company and was reserved to the point of silence. Anne was already in her late twenties and despite her lowly social station and ordinary looks

The Castle of Dalkeith, just south of Edinburgh, rebuilt by the powerful Regent of Scotland, the Earl of Morton, in the 1570s and home to George and Anne Monck for five years from 1654.

brimmed with self-assurance and a fearless, irreverent wit that capti-
vated Monck (Colour plate 22). However unconventionally their
courtship unfolded within the unforgiving walls of the Tower of
London, the results were beyond doubt: they fell in love. From that day
on, according to his chaplain, George Monck 'never cast an amorous
glance upon any other Woman'. Monck was released from the Tower in
1646 on the proviso he join the ranks of his former enemies and sign
the Puritan Covenant, and Anne would soon follow him.[2]

Monck went on to impress Oliver Cromwell deeply both as a man and
soldier, and it was thanks to Cromwell's personal patronage that Monck
rose to the highest ranks within the army and navy. In 1653 when the
couple's first child was born in London, Monck was one of the three
Generals at Sea responsible for a significant naval victory in the war
against the Dutch. The birth of their second son in Dalkeith's imposing
grandeur came after Monck had returned to land service, and the infant
took his first breaths on one of those short January days. Like Anne of
Denmark's daughter, however, the Moncks' second son did not live long
enough to raise his head or form a smile. Anne was by this time 40 and
the risks of childbirth to both mother and son were considerable. The
baby lived only briefly during which time he suffered repeated convul-
sions. Grief descended on the household and the city governors and
councillors of state laid aside their business and travelled south from
Edinburgh to attend his funeral.[3]

While little George Monck's passing was marked with official obse-
quies, no such formality had attended the advent of his brother. In fact,
the circumstances of the birth of Christopher Monck, now 3 years old,
were oddly obscure. Suspiciously so. His parents had been unmarried at
the time of his conception in the autumn of 1652, though their relationship had by then already lasted eight years. Their marriage was
conducted in January 1653 at St George's church in Southwark, a parish
to which they had no particular connection and, highly unusually, only
their Christian names were entered in the register. Some time later their
full names were written out on a sheet of paper interleaved in the book.
There was a good, if extraordinary, reason for all this secrecy, for Anne
Clarges was already married.

Back in 1633, a decade before the start of the civil war, Anne, then only 17, had married a haberdasher from Derbyshire named Thomas Radford. Radford leased a shop on the side of London's great shopping emporium, the New Exchange. Here, under the sign of the Spanish Gypsy, he sold millinery – gloves and ribbons, pins and inkwells – to the well-to-do of the capital.[4] Then, sometime in the 1640s, apparently after she had met George Monck, Anne and her husband had parted. Thomas Radford simply disappeared, both from the New Exchange and from the capital's memory. It was later claimed that he had died, but when a careful search for evidence of his death was made in the London burial registers, none could be found – nor a single person to attest to it. Instead, Radford had, it seems, been persuaded to leave London, and would only re-emerge in the 1660s as a shopkeeper back in his native Derbyshire. George and Anne might have lived together quietly as man and mistress while they were childless, but the prospect of a child – and so the question of his status – changed matters. Monck's salary as a commander of the Commonwealth navy was more than enough to allow for a settlement to be reached, and a pay-off would have been an attractive proposition to a high-end haberdasher during the economically challenging war years. Radford's disappearance, and the discretion of a trusted few, paved the way for Anne and George's marriage. It was an astonishing business. The risks were colossal – not simply disgrace and disinheritance but death itself, as bigamy was a capital felony. But together, and for one another, Anne and George Monck ran them all.[5] The prize, it seems, made the risk worthwhile. As Monck would later remark of another gargantuan personal gamble, it was better to chance death in the jaws of a lion than to let yourself be slowly devoured by rats.[6]

🦁 🦁 🦁

George Monck arrived to take up his position as head of the army in Scotland in 1654 with some experience of the country to draw on. When Oliver Cromwell had invaded Scotland in 1650, Thomas Fairfax having refused on principle to lead the expedition, Monck had gone with him. At the famous battle of Dunbar, Monck had commanded the infantry, fighting alongside Charles Fleetwood and John Lambert, as between them they wrested a remarkable victory from a much larger Scottish opponent. Cromwell reported with exhilaration that they had killed 3,000 Scots that day and taken 10,000 prisoner while English deaths had been fewer than thirty. With the defeat at Dunbar, and the failure at Worcester of Charles II's Scottish-backed advance into England, Scotland was a nation conquered.[7]

The Scottish experience of subjugation to the English Commonwealth was, however, a different one from the Irish. The Scots were, on the whole, committed Protestants who had been the first to take a stand against Charles I's religious innovations in the late 1630s. There had been no equivalent in Scotland to the large-scale sectarian atrocities, so luridly and unevenly reported, that defined the English attitude to the Irish. Instead, the English parliamentarians had fought the first stages of the civil war in concert with Scottish comrades. As a consequence the Puritan government in London saw the Scots more as fellow travellers than ungovernable rebels. The conquest should, it was agreed, give way to a brotherly 'Union' between England and Scotland, in which free trade – never allowed to the Irish even under Henry Cromwell's persuasive captaincy – and an equitable allocation of taxes was to be part of the deal.

The task of imposing peace on Scotland was one to which George Monck was well suited. He carried little of the ideological or religious baggage of his fellow officers and as an experienced soldier knew how to master his terrain and read his adversaries. While the terms of the union were being hammered out there were still significant areas of royalist resistance to be quashed, mostly in the wild and inaccessible north. On 4 May 1654, a fortnight after his arrival in Scotland, Monck issued a proclamation from Dalkeith offering a full pardon to anyone who laid down arms. This added further scope for clemency to the wide-ranging Ordinance of Grace and Pardon issued at the same time. Not for the Scots the merciless collective revenge wreaked on the Irish. Monck then set out. Through the mid-summer months of 1654 he stalked the royalist leader John Middleton and his few thousand men across the majestic rain-buffeted hills and glens of Argyll and Inverness,

Perthshire and Ross with discipline and determination. Always one for careful planning, he used the Highland topography to his advantage, deploying glens and lochs as giant barriers with which to trap his prey. He burned hundreds of houses and acres of crops in royalist areas, seeing starvation as a useful weapon, sank all the vessels on Loch Lomond to close a crucial escape route to the south and spread the word that forced labour in the Caribbean awaited those caught in arms. Middleton's men steadily peeled away, weakened by 'cold and distress through mountains and hills' and 'hunted like partridge by the English'.[8]

Monck returned to Dalkeith having dispersed the rebellion and for the next few years lived there with Anne in an intense and busy peace. The Anglo-Scottish Union was passed by Oliver Cromwell, now Lord Protector, and a Scottish Council of State was established to manage the country. Henry Cromwell's friend Lord Broghill was appointed chairman and Monck one of its members. The two men worked well together not least because Monck, a career soldier rather than a Godly warrior, did not expect the army to be calling the political shots. Through concerted action they talked the London government out of more punitive policies – such as deporting all vagrants to the West Indies – which might have 'put the whole country in a flame'. As in Ireland, monarchy and the national parliament were abolished, and thirty Scottish MPs were to sit instead in the new 'British' Parliament in Westminster. When Broghill returned to London in 1656 to take his seat Monck, not naturally a political creature, was content to remain.

As de facto governor of Scotland in Broghill's absence Monck applied himself with characteristic determination to the management of the country. He was at work at the Dalkeith dining room table by seven o'clock each morning, reading news and correspondence, dictating replies to his secretaries, and seeing a stream of petitioners and agents ushered in and out by his Highland footboy. His formidable network of spies and informers allowed him to monitor any new royalist activity orchestrated from overseas along the thousands of miles of Scottish coast, so that he was able to reassure his London masters that no letters between Charles Stuart and Scottish royalists would be exchanged 'butt I shall know them'. Meanwhile, he directed the construction of hefty new forts at strategic locations: citadels were built at Ayr, Perth and Leith, and at either end of the Great Glen at Inverlochy (Fort William) and Inverness. Such were the numbers of soldiers garrisoned that half a century later a visitor to Inverness would marvel at the English accents, modes of dress and cooking seeded there by settling Cromwellian soldiers. Military management, designed to 'keep this country in awe', was mixed with pragmatism. Rather than forcing the Highland chief-tains into humiliating submission, Monck and Broghill devolved to them, on strict terms, responsibility for keeping the peace in Sutherland and the far north. In Edinburgh trouble was taken to craft new institu-tions which incorporated Scots and, thanks to Monck's lobbying, a new system of local justice, staffed by local lairds along the lines of English Justices of the Peace, was introduced. In 1651, the archives of the Scottish nation had been shipped to England in an act of cultural conquest, but now the legal registers at least were to be returned. While the Scots hardly welcomed their subjugation, the relative peace and stability it brought after years of war had their advantages. If the royal-ists had once regarded Scotland as a nation, and Monck as a man, as potential bridgeheads for their cause, they were to find themselves increasingly frustrated.[9]

⚜ ⚜ ⚜

From the time he started to serve under him, George Monck's fidelity to Oliver Cromwell, 'my deare friend', never faltered. As John Thurloe put it in March 1658 there was none in all three kingdoms 'more loyal and dutiful' to the Protector. George Monck and Oliver Cromwell had much in common though they had started the civil war on opposing sides: both were serious soldiers who combined military skill with a talent for winning the affection of their men; both were faithful husbands devoted to their families. They shared a past, too, as both men were raised in declining gentry families with high expectations but meagre means. Monck, like Cromwell, had experienced personal and financial shame as a young man. When Charles I was expected in Plymouth in 1625 a 16-year-old Monck had been dispatched to bribe a Devon under-sheriff so that his financially embarrassed father might be allowed to appear in the welcoming party. Just how bitter an experience it was for the teen-ager became clear when the official reneged and Monck, with his brother, tracked him down to an Exeter tavern where, after brutally cudgelling him, George alone chased him through the streets and stabbed him to death. Throughout his life Monck retained both the frugal habits of a man who knew what it was to be without and a simmering inner depth of feeling that only very occasionally burst forth.[10]

It was in matters of religion that Monck most differed from Cromwell. Monck was no less personally pious than many of his army colleagues, but his faith was governed by an overwhelming respect for order and propriety. He did not share Cromwell's affection for Godly eccentrics or the questioning, trembling relationship with God that guided his uncer-tain course. Monck did his best to encourage reconciliation between the warring religious factions in Scotland, swallowing his disapproval to deal respectfully with the more extreme Presbyterians, but he was appalled by the proliferation of sects and their unorthodox ways. The Quakers were growing daily more numerous especially in northern England and southern Scotland. Monck was baffled and affronted by their rejection of church structure and hierarchy, and the conventions of social deference that went with them, on the basis that Christ was to be found not in institutions or intermediaries but within each person. The Diggers had been crushed almost a decade before, but Gerrard Winstanley's belief that Christ dwelled within and his rejection of aspects of social deference had lived on and found a far greater audi-ence through the new Quaker movement. The Quaker leader, George Fox, saw Scotland and its soldiers as fruitful recruiting ground and made several visits to drum up support. On one occasion, probably at Dalkeith, Monck and Anne encountered two garrulous Quaker spokes-men keen to share their beliefs. Anne deftly dodged a lecture on the inner light by 'very pleasantly' drawing forward their chaplain John Price to listen in her place. The Moncks may have received such visitors politely enough, but George wasted no time in rooting proselytizing Quakers out of his army.[11]

❦ ❦ ❦

The news of Oliver Cromwell's death and Richard Cromwell's nomination as his successor reached Edinburgh in a matter of days. The messenger was Anne's brother, Thomas Clarges, an apothecary by training who, thanks to Monck's influence, had secured a lucrative job as London agent for both Monck in Edinburgh and Henry Cromwell in Dublin. There was no doubting the crossroads at which the British nations now stood. Monck had long been uneasy about Oliver's attitude to religion and his troubled relations with his Parliaments, and confided to his friends his belief that, even had he lived, he could not have held on to power long. Now that Richard was to fill his place there was a chance, slim though it might appear, for stability to be found. The soldier drafted in candid but courteous words a letter of advice to the new Protector. This was characteristically to the point. First came religion. Toleration had been allowed to get out of hand, so that religion had 'crumbled into dust by seperations and devisions'. The various parties should be gathered together and some sort of national religious structure established to put an end to blasphemy and disorder. Second was Parliament. This needed to be carefully managed, but if Richard assembled some of the moderate county gentry, men like Sir George Booth in Cheshire and Sir John Hobart in Norfolk, and convinced them of his good intentions he could bring about the harmony that had eluded his father and secure their support for a new religious regime. The final significant matter was the army. While Monck was one of its most senior officers, he disapproved of the 'insolent spirits' that had been allowed to operate within its ranks. These men needed to be systematically weeded out and replaced with officers loyal to the Protector. In these matters, he advised, Richard should work closely with the moderates and include Oliver St John, Secretary Thurloe and Lord Broghill – all supporters of the attempt to make Oliver Cromwell king – in his Council. Having dispatched his letter, he could do little more than watch and wait.[12]

※ ※ ※

Oliver Cromwell's funeral took place on 23 November 1658. His three sons-in-law, Charles Fleetwood, Lord Fauconberg and John Claypole, represented his family in the great cavalcade, walking immediately beside the hearse (Colour plate 23). Among the hundreds of people in the long procession that stretched out ahead of them walked John Milton and Andrew Marvell, as members of the diplomatic corps, Marchamont Nedham as state newsman and even John Bradshaw who despite being dropped from government at the fall of the Rump still held on to office as Chief Justice of Chester. But the appearance of unity among the chief mourners was as artificial as the robed and crowned effigy of Oliver that lay stiff on the hearse.[13] Richard Cromwell's nomination was supported by many of those who had hovered around his father's deathbed precisely because he lacked the experience, self-confidence and political instinct a proper tutelage might have given him. The factions with which his father had struggled remained at loggerheads: the civilian moderates who had advocated the almost-royal constitution of the Humble Petition and Advice (with or without the title of king), the army leaders who sought either their own elevation as Lord Protector or the primacy of the army in the regime more generally, and the Commonwealthsmen, still smarting from the expulsion of the Rump Parliament, seeing this as their moment for redress. It suited more than one group, as one observer put it, to 'have got a protector of wax, whom they can mould as they please'.[14] Also absent from the funeral cortège was Henry Cromwell. Shortly after his brother's accession Henry was elevated to the august position of Lord Lieutenant of Ireland. But what he really wanted was permission to return to London so that he could influence events and decisions. His wife was heavily pregnant and his mother pressing for his return to support his brother, but the permission did not come. Either Richard did not wish to be overshadowed by his more capable brother, or those around him saw that it would be to their advantage to keep him at bay.[15]

The first weeks of Richard Cromwell's 'reign' were unexpectedly peaceful and many commented on the calm with a note of surprise. But it could not last. Richard was a civilian with no following in the army and the fissures in the political establishment ran to its core. Within weeks of his accession the Protector's right to direct the army was being called into question. War and a standing army – and his father's failure to work with his Parliaments to agree new taxes – had left the treasury some £2 million in debt and army pay in colossal arrears. A new parliament was called. Those men who clattered into the chamber in January 1659 were a mixed bunch, a combination of men who had played a significant part in the events of the decade – John Bradshaw, sitting for his native Cheshire, Thomas Fairfax for Yorkshire and William Petty for an area of Cornwall where he had never set foot – and new men come to Westminster for the first time. Taken as a body they were more moderate and civilian in their outlook than either the army or the Commonwealthsmen. The atmosphere in the capital crackled with tension, each group hypersensitive to slights or affronts from its rivals. Tact and political sophistication, crucial if Richard were to win support in Parliament and manage the army, were in short supply. When Richard tried to disband the army's powerful Council of Officers, on the basis that their concerns were being addressed, and Parliament raised replacing the army with locally managed militia, the fragile peace shattered. Fleetwood and Desbrow told Richard that he must dissolve Parliament. When he refused they withdrew ominously to St James's Palace and Richard looked on with dismay as much of the army crossed the park to join them.

The denouement came on 21 April 1659. Late in the evening John Desbrow, lieutenant general of the army and Richard Cromwell's uncle, strode across to Whitehall and restated the demand that Richard dissolve Parliament. In the courtyards below his soldiers loitered menacingly, some breaking open the barrels in the palace's wine cellars. Richard offered brave words of resistance, but, shorn as he now was of the military support that had sustained every regime for a decade, they were words alone. Desbrow batted away his nephew's trembling assertion that he would suffer 'any violence' rather than concede, pointing out coldly 'that he was not in a position even to defer for an hour'. The outcome was inevitable. By daybreak Richard's signature was on the commission dissolving Parliament and soldiers yet again barred the doors to the House of Commons.[16]

❦ ❦ ❦

What exactly was happening was not immediately clear. The following week's issue of *Mercurius Politicus* brought little clarity, simply stating that the Lord Protector had dissolved Parliament 'for diverse weighty reasons'. But no amount of news management could disguise the fact that the new Parliament had been expelled on the army's initiative – not least because of the vocal anger of its dispersing members. It had existed for barely three months and during that time had not managed to pass a single piece of legislation. Meanwhile, the urgency of the need for funds had only grown. Under the pressure of necessity an unlikely alliance emerged over the succeeding days. Spotting their chance, the Commonwealthsmen proposed a solution: the Rump Parliament, dismissed in fury by Oliver Cromwell six years before, could simply be recalled. There was no need for new elections, with their unpredictable outcome. Instead the Rump could meet almost immediately – indeed, many of its members were in the capital at that moment – and agree the taxes necessary to stave off bankruptcy and pay the soldiers. After all, they cooed, was it not the army and the Rump Parliament working together which had brought about the revolution in the first place? Had it not been their bold brotherhood that had brought Charles I to the scaffold? With liberal references to bygone days when they had laboured together for the 'good old cause', directed largely at the younger soldiers who had not witnessed the fractious reality of those times, the Rumpers won over the army by whose force they had been marched from the chamber in the first place. Within a fortnight something much more substantial than the passing of one parliament had taken place. Richard Cromwell, now politically emasculated and personally broken, was being dispensed with and the Rump Parliament, and the republican constitution that went with it, brought back from the dead.[17]

It was an astonishing change. The men who had been the titans of the Protectorate were now facing the wilderness. Lord Fauconberg, husband of Mary Cromwell, was dismissed and command of his regiment was given instead to John Lambert, army leader *par excellence*, returned from his horticultural retirement at Wimbledon. John Thurloe, the Protectorate's most diligent servant, who confessed to being 'in such confusion I can scarce write', was sacked as Secretary of State. And John Bradshaw, who had tried Charles I a decade before, found himself once again with a seat on the Council of State. He received the unexpected news in Wiltshire where he was convalescing, and replied full of amazed delight at the re-establishment of 'this latelie languyshing and now revived Commonwealth upon sure and lasting foundacions'. His letter was dated, with a flourish, 'in the first year of the republic reborn'.[18]

Just how sure and lasting the foundations of this born-again republic actually were remained to be seen. The immediate question on everyone's lips during that extraordinary fortnight was whether the end of the Protectorate and the toppling of Richard Cromwell would pass without resistance. The two men on whose reaction everything depended were the heads of the other branches of the army, Henry Cromwell in Ireland and George Monck in Scotland. That Henry Cromwell would oppose the abolition of his father's regime and removal of his brother was a certainty; the issue was whether he could do anything about it. The peace he had established in Ireland was so fragile that he could bring no more than a fraction of his army with him or consign English rule in the country to chaos. If any act of resistance were to succeed he needed a brother-in-arms.[19]

※ ※ ※

The go-between Henry Cromwell sent post-haste to George Monck at Dalkeith in late April 1659 was no anonymous messenger. Cornet Henry Monck owed his position in the Irish army – and the escape it brought him from poverty and misfortune – to a favour Henry Cromwell had done for his kinsman George Monck two years earlier. The man was living proof of the debt that George Monck owed Henry Cromwell. In one of a number of warm letters between the two men at the time, George Monck had thanked Henry Cromwell for employing his luckless relation and pledged his service. On the death of Oliver Cromwell the previous September he had reiterated his pledge that no one would be more willing to serve Henry Cromwell than he, 'wherein you shall not find me to fayle upon any occasion'. That occasion had now come.

Monck's loyalty to the Cromwell family was well known, as was his lukewarm attitude to the religious and political priorities of the men who had just seized power. But he was a soldier rather than a politician and one who had been against Oliver Cromwell accepting the crown, though many of his circle had been for it. He was also a man of great self-containment, used to receiving and enacting orders, and not known for haste or emotion in word or deed.[20]

Cornet Monck arrived footsore at his cousin's Dalkeith headquarters on 7 May, a fortnight after Richard Cromwell had been compelled to scratch his name on the commission dissolving Parliament. He was not alone in making the journey: other agents, and many letters, had also made their way to Dalkeith, including a recent communication from Richard himself. But he and they did not find the encouragement they had hoped for. Instead, they met with a blank and total refusal. Only days later Henry Monck set out on his return journey to Dublin, carrying with him Monck's bald and crushing reply. It comprised no explanation or courteous words, only a copy of the letter of support that Monck had just sent to London, congratulating his army brethren on 'the greatest and happiest prognostick of our future peace and establishment that ever our eyes yet beheld'.[21]

❦ ❦ ❦

Richard Cromwell was broken by the fall of the Protectorate. While his failure was more or less guaranteed by circumstances entirely beyond his control he could not but feel it personally. Shame as much as anything had probably delayed the clear and immediate appeals for support to Ireland and Scotland that might have had different conse-quences. It was not until 12 May, three weeks after the coup, that he could bring himself to write to his brother, who was otherwise relying on patchy information from agents. He had tried to do what was right, Richard explained, in his dealings with Parliament and the army, and had not acted unreasonably – indeed 'I can assure you I stood not as highe as my father did'. Only George Monck could save them now, he

wrote, little knowing that at that moment Monck's letter of compliance
was already on its way to London. When this news reached Richard he
sank into despair. 'All the world is false,' he wrote bitterly, 'my friends,
my councel and my relations having all foresaken me.' His father's closest friends and his own kin – his uncle Desbrow and brother-in-law
Fleetwood – had betrayed him and with him the whole Cromwell family.
He was now to have no role or status but to be pensioned off. Little
wonder he wanted to 'throw myself in the dust and crye before the Lord'.
For Henry Cromwell, too, the end had come. He had never had much
appetite for conflict or personal aggrandisement and now his position
had become untenable. As the new government was preparing to
dismiss him, Henry Cromwell sent for William Petty and gave him a
letter of resignation to take to London. Its words were of sad acceptance. 'I acquiesse in the present way of government,' he wrote, 'although
I cannot promise soe much affection to the late changes, as others very
honestly may.' His hope was that the new regime would 'quietly search
out the ways of our peace', which, in his view, resided less in any one
constitution and more in the character of those in charge. He sailed
from Ireland leaving behind him, uncertain, all that he had toiled to
achieve. As the coast receded on the western horizon he could only
thank God that his father had not lived to see this day.[22]

❦ ❦ ❦

The abolition of the Protectorate and the 1659 Parliament was met
with disbelief in Scotland. The thirty Scottish MPs had been ejected in
April along with everyone else. But the restored Rump Parliament that
replaced them dated from a time before the conquest of Scotland and
comprised only English MPs. Furthermore, the repudiation of the
Protectorate overturned the Act of Union, leaving Scotland in limbo. An
Edinburgh resident wrote in dismay at the chaos 'in such a short space,
raising some and calling down others; and in raising parliaments and
dissolving of the same by a tyrannical power'. The usually tightly
managed Scottish political sphere, where publications had been closely
contained and the Kirk, the national church, maintained a firm hold on
national religion, was barely recognizable. With the English army had

come a whole range of religious groups and an expectation of some degree of religious freedom. Meanwhile, on the streets of Edinburgh pamphlets and newspapers were now bought and sold containing a plethora of different views. Some cheered on the coup and declared Oliver Cromwell to have been a worse tyrant than Charles I, others called the restored Rump the 'whorish good old cause', and more than one, among them a large publication by William Prynne, argued that the only viable solution was now the re-establishment of royal government in the person of King Charles II.[23]

❦ ❦ ❦

In a rented house in Brussels, somewhere in the streets below the Coudenberg Palace, another audience waited anxiously for news of the coup and what was to follow. Ever since the death of Oliver Cromwell, Charles Stuart and his advisers had been on tenterhooks, scouring daily intelligence reports and *Mercurius Politicus* for their opportunity and consuming any signs of political instability with greedy expectation. Charles, now 29, retained the tacit support of the King of Spain, but the bounty and military support he might have hoped for had not come. He was allowed to live in the Spanish Netherlands but only if his official base was sleepy Bruges rather than the capital. With no invasion army to command, any attempt to claim his father's kingdoms would need substantial support from within, support on a scale to defeat the New Model Army. It was a daunting challenge. When the Marquess of Ormond had travelled to England the previous year to meet the most powerful royalists and assess their readiness to rise up, he had returned dejected, having realized that despite the republic's problems, the royalists were for the most part cautious, uncoordinated and beset by squabbling.[24]

In the weeks after the end of the Protectorate and revival of the Rump Parliament two royalist initiatives unfurled. The first was an armed uprising, supposed to be nationwide but in fact only getting anywhere in John Bradshaw's native Cheshire. Sir George Booth, a staunch parliamentarian during the civil war and one of the moderate men Monck advised Richard Cromwell to listen to, gathered 4,000

CAROLUS II DEI GRATIA MAGNÆ BRITANNIÆ,
FRANCIÆ et HIBERNIÆ, REX, etc.

Charles Stuart, 'Kings of Scots', by Wallerant Vaillant, 1656. Charles was a complete stranger to almost everyone in England in 1660 and his return, and that of the monarchy, the consequence of the failure of every viable alternative.

supporters and took the city of Chester. Though many suspected their real goal was the reinstatement of the monarchy, the rebels' manifesto was for a full and free Parliament and attracted support both from royalists and from those who had supported the Protectorate. Chester Castle, from which James Stanley, 7th Earl of Derby, had almost escaped in 1651 was secured as their base, and prominent among those who rose with Booth was Derby and Charlotte de la Trémoille's eldest son, Charles, now himself 8th Earl of Derby.[25]

While the Cheshire gentry were taking up arms a more clandestine initiative was also afoot: a royalist approach to George Monck. Sir John Grenville was one of Charles Stuart's most loyal supporters and had held the Isles of Scilly for the royalists, as the Derbys had held the Isle of Man, until the collapse of the cause in 1651. Grenville was a cousin of the Moncks, and it was his idea that the General be approached through his younger brother, Nicholas. Nicholas Monck's daughter had for some time been living with George and Anne at Dalkeith, providing a convenient pretext for Nicholas, a clergyman, to make the voyage north. In early August 1659 he disembarked on the wide sands at Leith and journeyed the few miles to Dalkeith. Late in the evening he met his brother alone. No witnesses were present to testify to the conversation, but it was not the success that had been hoped for in Brussels. Charles Stuart's letter went unopened and no commitment to join forces was given. Edward Hyde, Charles Stuart's chief minister, recorded that Nicholas Monck was 'infinite reproached' by his brother 'for his daring to endeavour to corrupt him'. Just days later news arrived that John Lambert had crushed the Cheshire uprising, and both Booth and the young Earl of Derby were on the run. In only a matter of weeks Charles Stuart's high hopes had once again been dashed.[26]

🦁 🦁 🦁

George Monck was a man of secrets. His orders both on and off the battlefield rang with unambiguous clarity, but when it came to commenting on politics or sharing his personal views, he gave almost nothing away. It was for good reason that even those close to him considered him 'the most reserved man then living'. His taciturn manner was seen by his men as a strength, for their general was no honey-tongued mandarin but a tobacco-chewing man of arms like them. 'Old George' they called him, while Oliver Cromwell had seen in Monck's loyalty a guilelessness that caused him to term him 'plain hearted George'. But none of them truly knew the man of whom they spoke. The dark waters of George Monck ran as deep as a ravine, as his bigamous marriage would have revealed had any of them known it. He had meant it when he had pledged his loyalty to Henry Cromwell, but he was too level-headed to act when he knew it could only end in failure. Desbrow may have been leaning over him, sword at his side, but Richard Cromwell had nonetheless put his name to the commission to dismiss Parliament, so Monck could not easily object. Furthermore, many of his officers had, like the soldiers who left Whitehall for St James's, cheered for joy at the fall of the Protectorate and the return of the Rump. Seeing he had no choice but to accept the coup, he was sufficiently dispassionate to see that it would be better to do so with enthusiasm.[27]

Over the summer of 1659 George Monck kept his own counsel. Fleetwood and his fellow officers had taken his pledge of loyalty at face value. There was no reason for them to doubt him. Monck was army through and through; he had voiced no concern at the Rump's original expulsion or Oliver's fractious dealings with his parliaments, and had positively welcomed the creation of the Major Generals' regime four years earlier. Though he had once fought in Charles I's army, he had shown no enthusiasm for royalists or royalism since and his pursuit of 'the enemy' in Scotland had spoken for itself. But all that said, the tiny number of people whom he genuinely trusted knew how uneasy he was. His belief in the importance of order and stability in both religion and society was paramount and the events of the spring had brought dishonour to the family of his patron and had risked both. The country was subject to 'sword government' and the army ranks swelled with fanatics, men such as the soldier court-martialled for contending, to Monck's profound shock and disbelief, 'that our blessed Lord and Saviour Jesus Christ (I tremble to write it) was a basterd'.[28]

While George erred on the side of silence and caution, Anne Monck did not. In the long mid-summer evenings of 1659, after she had changed into informal indoor dress, she would slip into the Dalkeith dining room where her husband worked. Not for nothing did Monck's chaplain John Price call her evening dress her 'treason gown', for at these times this forthright former seamstress would broach with her husband the subjects that others dared not mention. Would he really stand by while the army leaders, with their ranks full of religious radicals, were flouting the nation's laws and liberties and 'dashing in pieces' Parliament? Would God not mete out a terrible judgement on them for failing to prevent it? 'Her tongue was then her own,' Price admitted, 'and she would not spare it', so much so that he would shoo out the servants and quietly withdraw, closing the doors behind him.[29]

When news reached Scotland that John Lambert had made light work of suppressing the Cheshire rising, the soldiers around Monck's table cheered with delight. As their spirits rose and the drink melted their caution, one overexcited officer cried in jubilation that it was only a matter of time before there would not be 'a steeple house [traditional church] or a parish priest left'. At this the usually placid Monck shot to his feet and snarled, 'Captain Poole if you and your Party come to pluck there, I will pluck with you', 'whereupon there was a sudden damp [and] they were but soldiers before their General and were silent'.

In late August 1659, like Thomas Fairfax before him, George Monck decided that his time had come. He could bear it no longer: he had to bow out. While Anne was a Londoner born and bred, Monck was a countryman who loved the land. At Dalkeith they had rented the gardens, park and orchard at considerable expense. Now the extensive property that he was to receive in Ireland as payment for his service there had, thanks to Dr Petty's surveyors, been mapped and apportioned and was ready to be 'planted'. He would leave the army pleading ill health, take his family west and start afresh in Ireland. As late summer rain whipped round Dalkeith's hefty walls, George drafted his resignation letter. It was sealed and dispatched on 3 September. Anne ordered trunks and portmanteaus and began to pack. And here, it seemed, the couple's part in the politics of the nation was about to end.[30]

🐝 🐝 🐝

The shotgun marriage between the army and the Commonwealthsmen was a mésalliance right from the start. They had shared a desire to dispense with Richard Cromwell and many wished also to see the end of the Protectorate but, as ever, agreeing on what to reject was the easy part. Once they had prevailed they were left with little in common and serious questions lay unanswered about the new constitutional settlement. As soon as the Rumpers received the keys to the House of Commons from the army, they abandoned their coaxing, solicitous tone and set about asserting what they considered to be the proper primacy of their civilian authority over the military. The defeat of Booth's uprising in August started a process of escalation which would change everything. Exhilarated by their victory, a group of soldiers produced a petition seeking to entrench the army's authority, and rumours began to fly that the officers were poised, once again, to 'violate the Parliament'. Thanks to Anne Monck's brother, Thomas Clarges, George Monck's letter of resignation had been intercepted and rather than being accepted had been set aside by the Speaker. A colossal stand-off was now looming between Parliament and army and, given the strength of the army, there could be little doubt who would come off the victor. When George Monck had accepted the spring coup he had warned Fleetwood that the revival of the Rump must be a new start; there could be 'noe more dashing in pieces or dissolving of them'. Now it seemed this was exactly what was about to happen. Just as Monck had risen in sudden fury to rebuke Captain Poole – and had long ago beaten a man to death in a dark alley – so something in him snapped. In a moment his plans of retirement were gone. He sprang into action for all the world – in the words of one at Dalkeith – like a 'Lyon rouzed'.[31]

Late at night on Wednesday 12 October, an exhausted Nicholas Monck arrived in London. He had journeyed for four days and nights from Dalkeith and made straight for the lodgings of Thomas Clarges. Early the following morning Clarges and Monck, brothers of Anne and George Monck respectively, had a meeting with the leading Rumpers. The message they conveyed to Sir Arthur Haselrige and Thomas Scot would change the course of British history. General Monck would stand back no longer, they confided. He was joining his cause to theirs and stood ready to march his army to London, and lay down his life, in mortal defence of the authority of the English Parliament.[32]

Eighteen

Mars and Minerva

O n 12 October 1659 the MPs of the Rump Parliament, now just sixty-five in number, voted to dismiss both John Lambert and John Desbrow, demote Charles Fleetwood and give command of the army to a seven-man commission. They seemed to be daring the army to eject them. The following day, sure enough, when William Lenthall, the elderly Speaker of the Commons, travelled by coach to Westminster he found the streets thick with soldiers. They massed into blockades as he approached New Palace Yard and he was forced to retreat. Discussions followed and the officers of the army agreed to pull back. But John Lambert, fiery and unrepentant, was not for compromise. He rode in, took possession of the chamber 'and lockt up the Doores, setting a strong guard upon the stayers'. It was more than six years since Oliver Cromwell and his soldiers had first marched the Rump MPs from the chamber, and eleven since the Rump itself had been born of the armed exclusion of their fellow MPs. Since that day in 1648, when Colonel Pride had stood on those same stairs and turned away the moderates of the Long Parliament, the English republic had been condemned to repeat itself.[1]

Four days later Anne Monck was one of the first at Dalkeith to learn of events in Westminster. She, more than anyone, had encouraged her husband to intervene but when the moment came she felt only dread.

She wished they had retired to Ireland when they had had the chance. She took her fears to their chaplain, John Price, who steadied her with his confident enthusiasm for the General's opportunity to shape events. Monck for his part did not underestimate the risk and responsibility he had taken upon his hefty shoulders. He took the eager Price aside and told him he could play no part in what was to follow. 'Be not discontented at it,' he explained, 'for you know not these people as well as I do, and cannot dissemble with them.' Monck knew he was embarking upon an enterprise that would require rather more than the honest soldiery for which he was renowned.[2]

The letters General Monck dispatched to the army leaders a few days later crashed into their schemes like a cannonball. They had had no inkling that their fellow officer and veteran of Dunbar would do anything other than fall in behind them. In that addressed to Fleetwood, dated 20 October, Monck was stark. 'I am ashamed of these Confusions and Changes that we have made', because of which 'we are now become a scorn and a reproach to our very Friends'. Parliament must be allowed to resume at once. If not, 'I am resolved, by the assistance of God, with the army under my command, to declare for them, and to prosecute this just cause to the last Drop of my Blood.' Fleetwood, Desbrow and Lambert, who had appointed themselves to a new executive 'Committee of Safety', were aghast. They, like almost everyone, 'looked upon George Monk to have no other Craft in him than that of a plain soldier'. They conferred at Whitehall late into the night in 'much confusion'. At midnight they called in Hezekiah Haynes, the officer who had managed East Anglia for Fleetwood during the Major Generals' regime, and asked him to find Thomas Clarges. Some hours later Clarges shuffled nervously into the chamber. Answering their questions warily, he was relieved, and rather surprised, when instead of detaining him they asked him to go to Edinburgh to treat with Monck on their behalf. Their sense of urgency was such that they gave him only three hours to prepare and by dawn he was on his way north.[3]

※ ※ ※

George Monck's purpose, as he made widely known by publishing his letters to Fleetwood and Lambert, was to 'reduce the Military power in obedience to the civil' and so end government by the sword. It was a remarkable goal for a soldier, especially given how much he stood to profit from his position in the army and how little he loved the Rump Parliament. He had no close friends among its MPs and resented their interference in appointments to the regiments he commanded. But he had served as a soldier for twenty years before the civil war, fighting for and with foreign powers, and he saw the relationship between the army and government with a clarity that few of his fellow soldiers shared. He also suspected the army trio, and Lambert in particular, of acting from personal ambition, eyeing for himself the lapsed office of Lord Protector. For Monck it was straightforward: the army was the servant of the civilian state and not the other way round. He had told Speaker Lenthall that summer that when he had learned his trade 'souldiours received and observed comands, but gave none'. Two decades of conflict heavy with righteous fervour had clouded this distinction in the minds of many – indeed it meant nothing at all to the men of faith whom Oliver Cromwell had recruited to their cause, who dealt directly with a higher power. While many officers paid lip service to the notion of parliamentary sovereignty, others barely bothered. Chief among them was Lambert himself who had remarked in the presence of a leading MP only weeks before, 'I know not why they [MPs] should not be at our mercy as well as we at theirs'.[4]

This aspect of his stand Monck was at pains to communicate clearly but in other respects ambiguity was every bit as important. To summon up enough support to challenge the might of the army Monck needed to achieve the seemingly impossible and unite its enemies. This would involve bringing together a whole host of entrenched opponents, royalists and republicans, Englishmen and Irishmen, Puritans and Laudians. Given the sheer incompatibility of their aspirations, only with immense skill and an iron nerve could he hope to prevail. Because he was not given to voicing opinions, sharing gossip or holding forth, and because he had a mixed record of allegiance, what he actually believed almost no one could say for certain. Crucially, he was tight-

lipped about his religious views, and Anne distracted attention by
asserting with playful aplomb that 'Mr Monk is a Presbyterian and my
[6-year-old] son Kit is for the Long Parliament and the Good Old
Cause'! Without evidence to the contrary and with the General's reputation for guilelessness, each could, with the right encouragement,
believe he was on their side.[5]

What General Monck was at pains to make clear was that he was not
striving for the restoration of monarchy. He envisaged the continuation
of the republic, but one in which Parliament rather than the army was
in charge. His reasons for this were not particularly dogmatic. He felt
sympathy for the executed Charles I, though he had clearly 'miscarried'
as a sovereign, and had served Oliver Cromwell with the loyalty of a son.
Like Henry Cromwell, George Monck was less concerned with the finer
points of any given constitution than he was with good governors and
governance more generally. For him a Commonwealth was the only
possibility for the future 'upon rational grounds'. Far too much had
happened for the clock to be turned back. Monarchy, and the church
hierarchy that went with it, would exclude all the new religious groups
from a national church, while the colossal changes in land ownership of
the past two decades – following the sale of crown and church lands, the
confiscation of Catholic estates in Ireland and royalists' estates everywhere – could not possibly be unpicked without plunging the country
back into war.[6]

While her husband marshalled men and munitions from his
Edinburgh lodgings Anne Monck was making preparations at Dalkeith.
Over the summer she had been planning for a civilian life in Ireland;
now she was preparing to take her son and household on campaign,
bound, it seemed, for London. Since her flash of fear on first hearing of
the breaking up of Parliament, she had regained her nerve. One of those
nights at Dalkeith she dreamed of a great dunghill, encircled by an
impenetrable ring of strong men. Atop the midden she glimpsed a
golden crown, and saw a dark figure come forward, break through the
ring and take it. What this meant, and who the figure was, she could
not say for sure. She had always been for action and now she felt more
certain of it than ever. She would not falter again. In all that was to

follow she became 'herself a Committee of Safety' to her husband, 'the Minerva and great Patroness of this grand design'.[7]

George Monck's rhetoric might have been powerful, but the reality of his position was much less so. The army in England alone comprised over 10,000 men with at least as many again in Ireland and Dunkirk. Its leaders had the keys to Parliament, control of London and of England's arsenals of weapons and ammunition, and could mobilize the navy. George Monck could marshal at most 8,000 men, of whom a significant number were Quakers or Baptists and supporters of the London generals. He was 400 miles from the centre of power and had land troops only.[8] But he had at least had some time to plan. For months now he had employed an agent to open and read the daily post between London and Edinburgh, establishing the allegiances of his men. He had the confidence and credibility to follow the advice he had offered Richard Cromwell, and root out unreliable soldiers. With remarkable speed he sacked well over a hundred officers, among them the outspoken Captain Poole, and promoted men he could rely on in their places. He knew only too well that money made such a process far easier, and he had recently secured a £20,000 advance from London. To loud cheers he pledged to settle the arrears of all those who stayed with him (those who wished to leave could petition the officers in London for their pay). He proceeded carefully, consulting repeatedly with his officers to keep them close, and securing the key citadels at Leith and Berwick. But all this notwithstanding, he remained at a disadvantage. The great fort at Ayr was against him, and by one reckoning he had only around 5,000 he could march south – not many more than had risen with George Booth. Meanwhile, John Lambert was advancing inexorably north at the head of a force that was expected to number 12,000 before it reached Newcastle. Were they to meet on the battle-field as things stood Monck knew he would almost certainly lose. He needed more men.[9]

🐝 🐝 🐝

The Rump's revival had given the ailing John Bradshaw a new lease of life. He had thrown himself into his unexpected new offices, as councillor and commissioner of the great seal, with gusto, attending almost every meeting in August and September and leading on the examination of Cheshire rebels, many of whom he knew personally. As one who, in his own words, had given his 'Hearts bloode' for the republic, no one wanted the restored Commonwealth to succeed more than he. The sight of the Rump Parliament being again despoiled by soldiers after just five months sickened him to his core. An army officer attended the now-redundant council to explain the righteousness of Lambert's intervention, and Bradshaw could bear it no longer. He rose shakily to his feet and, addressing himself solely to his fellow councillors, declared 'that being now going to his God, he had not patience to sit here and hear his great name so openly blasphemed'. He left the room in disgust and refused to have any further dealings with the army, or to relinquish the great seal. It would matter little, however, for a fortnight later, in the splendour of the Dean's House at Westminster Abbey, death finally claimed John Bradshaw. Marchamont Nedham wept for the loss of his friend, certain that it was the second expulsion of the Rump Parliament that had killed him. 'For the Commonwealth he always lived,' Nedham wrote, 'and for the sake of the Commonwealth he died so soon.' Bradshaw expired, his life and the cause to which he had given his soul entwined to the last.[10]

※ ※ ※

Given the fragility of his position George Monck had to play for time. He appointed agents to parley with the English army's representatives and supplied them with letters full of warm words about his desire to come to terms. The last thing he wanted was any sort of actual engagement, and he sent men ahead to Alnwick just across the English border to stave off an early assault by making 'them think him in greater readiness than he was'. He was now the petitioner dispatching a volley of letters to those who might be induced to join him, and he was now the recipient of the disappointment he had meted out to the Cromwell brothers in the spring. The navy, known to be shaky in the republican cause, did not offer its support and the hoped-for mutinies from English soldiers were nowhere in evidence. Instead, a troop of his own army deserted him to join Lambert, who as a Yorkshireman and erstwhile Major General for the North had networks aplenty in the northern counties. There would be no help from Ireland where, on Henry Cromwell's departure, the Baptists and militarists had swarmed back into Dublin Castle and consigned the Protectoral arms from the Council Chamber to the rubbish heap. Even the ejected former Council of State was slow to respond. With each rebuff Monck's prospect of success dimmed. It looked horribly likely that the name of Monck was about to join those of Derby, Penruddock and Booth as captains of uprisings that were crushed by the might of the English army.[11]

Hope, when it came, took an unlikely form. At the end of the first week of November two men arrived in Edinburgh: Monck's old friend the foul-mouthed, warm-hearted surgeon Doctor Troutbeck accompanied by Thomas Morgan, a short, bluff Welshman. Captain Morgan, whom Monck knew of old, was ostensibly travelling with Lambert's blessing to try to turn Monck's men, but in reality he was engaged on quite another mission. He carried with him a message from the single man who had the standing, the support and the sheer celebrity to turn the tide: the founding father of the New Model Army, Thomas Fairfax himself.[12]

For almost a decade following his refusal to participate in the invasion of Scotland, Fairfax had been living in rural retirement on his family estate, Nun Appleton, a few miles from York. He and Anne Fairfax had raised their daughter Mary, employing no less a man than Andrew Marvell as her tutor and, latterly, had married her to the 2nd Duke of Buckingham, son of Charles I's best friend. As Fairfax had been the beneficiary of the Buckingham family's sequestered estates, the match, like his decision to pay the profits from the Isle of Man to the Countess of Derby, had the effect of restoring something of the pre-war order. While his old deputy Oliver Cromwell was alive Fairfax had kept out of politics almost entirely. But lately things had begun to change. Fairfax had been elected to Richard Cromwell's Parliament and was incensed when it was closed down. He, like Bradshaw, was named to the

Council of State of the revived republic as a luminary of the Good Old Cause, but he would have nothing to do with it, and refused to attend a single meeting. Ten years earlier he had let the trial and execution of Charles I proceed when he alone might have prevented it. He was not going to allow such a moment to pass again. The message carried by Thomas Morgan to General Monck was that, with caveats, Fairfax would be willing to join him. The news was a godsend, and that 'little-man was of more worth at that time to us, than the seventeen score officers that had deserted the service'.[13]

※ ※ ※

John Bradshaw's funeral took place at Westminster Abbey on 22 November. The atmosphere was electric. John Lambert and the English army were just reaching Newcastle and George Monck and his officers rejecting the terms discussed by the two parties' negotiators. What the consequence would be, and what news might at any moment reach London, was anyone's guess. There was a terrific turnout for the old judge, he who had tried the King and had headed up the government during those first years of the republic. The legal profession was there in force as were the ejected MPs of the Rump, while many of the new Committee of Safety, not to be outdone, also appeared. The sermon was preached with unveiled anger on the death of the righteous, spared 'the evil to come'. John Milton and Marchamont Nedham, Bradshaw's great friends, were each named in his will in recognition of their enduring comradeship. While *Politicus* carried Bradshaw's glowing official obitu-ary, memorials of a different sort nestled alongside it in the street hawkers' baskets. Ten years of the republic had done little to diminish the abhorrence the name Bradshaw elicited among royalists and others as the man who had condemned the King to death, and the instability of the current regime only emboldened the satirists. Mock eulogies described the great welcome that Satan had ready for his creature, Bradshaw, and a spoof will was printed in which the lawyer bequeathed his possessions 'in the name of the Devil and his Dam[e], the Good Old Cause'. While disinformation was deliberately being spread about Monck's purpose and prospects, including a rumour that his officers had all deserted him, the London crowds were not so easily deceived. Feverishness filled the air and the great question hung heavy over Westminster of what would come to pass 'when Monk's to London got'.[14]

❦ ❦ ❦

The town of Coldstream in Berwickshire was barely a town at all. It was more a cluster of houses which had grown up around the remains of Coldstream Priory, a Cistercian monastery built on a bend of the great River Tweed as it flowed east to the sea. For centuries the river had formed the eastern stretch of the border between England and Scotland and at Coldstream a shallow section of water made for the first decent crossing point west of Berwick. It was one of the few places an army from Newcastle might pass into Scotland, and only a few miles south, at Flodden, an advancing Tudor army had slain the flower of the Scottish nobility over a century before. Come the first week of December 1659 Monck, accompanied by Anne and their son, had taken up quarters in Berwick, which as a heavily fortified town was well equipped for repelling attacks. Then, at 1 a.m. on 7 December, a messenger brought alarming news. General Lambert's men were advancing north, and were proceeding not along the coast road towards Berwick but along the Wooler road which led cross-country to the Coldstream ford. An hour later Monck was on horseback and in the freezing December darkness led his men along the banks of the river, the horses picking a treacherous course through the mud and ice. By eleven the next morning they had thoroughly scouted the 14 miles to Coldstream. While there was as yet no sign of Lambert's men, it was clear he was on the move. Here, at Coldstream, Monck declared, they would remain. With soldiers stationed to the east at Berwick, to the west at Kelso and to the rear at Duns, they were primed for the assault which might come at any hour.[15]

Coldstream had nothing like enough houses to lodge the men of Monck's regiment. The General set up his headquarters in a cottage, the best accommodation to be had, at the doors of which two great dung heaps stood sentry. Its main room was his office and barracks, though he barely slept. Instead, he stretched out, fully clothed, on a bench in front of the smoky fire, ready to rise and ride at a moment's notice. The sutlers made a mess tent of a barn and, the parish church being several miles away, a cow byre was requisitioned as a chapel, the manure shovelled out by the soldiers to make way for the benches. The weeks spent there would mellow with memory, but at the time they were bleak and relentless, the men of Monck's regiment chilled by both the bitter cold and the knowledge that if Lambert advanced with his full force they would surely be defeated.[16]

At his rustic table, a far cry from the splendour of the Dalkeith dining room, Monck wrote to Fairfax calling for his urgent assistance. He entrusted the letter to Thomas Clarges who rode at pace to Yorkshire. Lord Fairfax's hesitation was on the question of the ultimate goal. Monck had committed to restoring the Rump Parliament and maintaining a Commonwealth, but Fairfax wanted more – a full Parliament which should then be free to determine the future. Clarges explained how carefully his brother-in-law had to tread so as not to alienate those whose help was vital to unseating the army, and hinted that his 'real' goal was something other. It was enough. Fairfax resolved to act; he would both add his name to Monck's and, crucially, provide the armed distraction that would prevent Lambert from pressing north. He set the wheels in motion to rally Yorkshire and dispatched a messenger to Monck, pledging to be outside the gates of York at the head of an army on New Year's Day. All he asked was Monck's promise that he would, in turn, ride to Yorkshire's aid should Lambert attack in strength.[17]

A few days later, with plans well advanced, Lord Fairfax learned that his messenger had been captured. Thomas Clarges, meanwhile, had suffered a serious fall from his horse and was bedridden somewhere in the Midlands. Fairfax was distraught. Monck must receive his message or all would be lost. Casting about his household at Nun Appleton, 'troubled exceedingly', his eye fell on his young relation Brian Fairfax, making a family visit after the end of his term at Cambridge. 'Here is my cousin Brian,' Fairfax said, 'I will undertake he should do it.' Brian swallowed hard but accepted the commission on the basis that the mighty Fairfax had asked him and that two armies were facing each other 'and we were well-wishers to General Monck'. The direct route north from York to Coldstream was out of the question, for Lambert lay between the two at Newcastle and the roads were overrun by his spies. Instead, in the very deepest week of winter, Brian was to take an obscure route across the desolate fells and moors of Yorkshire's wide West Riding to reach the western side of the country. At Kendal he would turn north, skirting Penrith and Carlisle, before returning east to approach Coldstream from the rear. The young man made his arctic odyssey dressed in country clothes borrowed from the Nun Appleton park-keeper, passing over frozen streams and travelling long hours, as 'the moonshine and the snow made the nights as clear as day'. Terrifying moments came when an army agent stopped him near Penrith struck by his hands, too pale for a working man, and when he narrowly escaped murder by Anthony Elliot, the most notorious of the border bandits. Almost delirious with exhaustion, he finally stumbled into Coldstream on Christmas Day. He was taken to the General's 'poor little thatched cottage'. Here he delivered his message from Lord Fairfax to General Monck: 'that he would on the first day of January appear at the head of what force he could in Yorkshire and declare against Lambert's army'. He asked for reassurance that Monck would watch Lambert and intervene if he turned south. The strength of emotion Monck felt was evident in the great embrace in which the undemonstrative General clasped the young man. Thanking Brian for his efforts, Monck told him he planned to march into England the moment Lord Fairfax rose, and added, aglow, 'that he would watch Lambert *as a cat watches a mouse*'.[18]

When he had first left Edinburgh, Monck had not even been able to persuade locals to sell him horses; now, in the last weeks of December, his stock was rising rapidly. Earlier in the month Sir Arthur Haselrige, the leading Rumper, had reached Portsmouth and persuaded the town to declare for Parliament. This was little enough threat in itself, but things took on an entirely different complexion when on 20 December the soldiers sent by Fleetwood to recapture the city mutinied and joined the rebels. The English army could no longer be relied upon to follow orders from London. Meanwhile, in Ireland, Lord Broghill, erstwhile Lord President of Scotland, aided by Cornet Monck, had rallied the moderates and on 13 December Dublin Castle was stormed and seized in Parliament's name. The army leader with real steel, John Lambert, was in the field, and without him Charles Fleetwood, Commander in Chief in London, began to quail. The English army was months behind in its pay, deeply unhappy about the prospect of fighting their own comrades and shaken by rumours Lord Fairfax was to join General Monck. Meanwhile, Monck's agents had been agitating in the City of London and the discontent there, from the raucous apprentices to the sober men of money, was becoming ever more evident.[19]

Bulstrode Whitelocke, the senior lawyer who had been one of the decade's consummate survivors, visited Fleetwood in those days and told him that he must radically change tack before it was too late. It would not be enough now simply to concede to the readmission of the Rump. Only by taking much more drastic action, Whitelocke argued, could Fleetwood become the master rather than the victim of events. Either he had himself to declare for a free Parliament, or he had to contact Charles Stuart and set the terms for the return of the monarchy. But Fleetwood did not have it in him to make such a stand. Having at first agreed with Whitelocke, it took just fifteen minutes with Desbrow and his comrades to melt his resolve. He came back in a state of near-hysteria, telling Whitelocke, 'I cannot doe it, I cannot doe it'; he had promised Lambert he would take no significant step without his consent. Whitelocke protested that Lambert was hundreds of miles away; he had to act or he and his friends would all be ruined. 'I cannot help it' was all the defeated soldier, son-in-law of Oliver Cromwell, could mumble in reply. In this state of emotional collapse Fleetwood resigned his office, remarking in bitter self-pity that God had spat in their faces. On 26 December the triumphant Rumpers began sitting once more.[20]

On New Year's Day 1660 Lord Fairfax appeared at the gates of the nation's third city at the head of an army of almost two thousand. His recruits were not royalists but Yorkshire gentry fed up with years of military rule and political and religious instability. Although he was seriously unwell, and could travel only by coach with frequent stops to attempt the agony of passing a kidney stone, Fairfax's presence alone was enough to stir the spirits of those who had once served him and cause Lambert's men to lose confidence. He knew the strength of his reputation and he mustered his men on Marston Moor itself, scene of his own and the New Model Army's greatest victory, before leading them to York's western gate, Micklegate Bar. Once he had been sighted his agents within tolled the great bells of York Minster, the signal for the citizens to rise and overwhelm their military governor. As York fell Brian Fairfax watched the retired soldier, spellbound. 'He began to be another man,' he recalled, 'his motions so quick, his eyes so sparkling, giving words of command like a general.' When some republican soldiers proudly presented him with a declaration condemning government by a single person, Lord Fairfax, like Charlotte, Countess of Derby, all those years before, held it up and, to their horror, tore it into strips before their eyes. The gates to the great city were heaved open, 150 miles north General Monck and his army surged unopposed over the border into England and it was clearer than ever that the question of what exactly they were fighting for had not yet been answered.[21]

Once Fleetwood had conceded, the Rump MPs, in charge once more, recalled the English army, and John Lambert's position crumbled. His commission was withdrawn and his men melted away, enabling Monck to reach London without facing a single shot from the great army sent to defeat him. How Lambert must have cursed and wished that he, a man whose self-belief had never faltered, had been commander in chief instead of the faint-hearted Fleetwood.[22] Monck's journey south, meanwhile, became a progress of sorts, as he stopped at each substantial town to receive well-wishers and dignitaries. Soon the general messages of support and welcome from local worthies began to take on a familiar character. The gentry of Norfolk were among the first to set the tone. At a meeting in Norwich in January, they drew up a petition. Here they set out the grievances of a decade: they were tired of the 'miseries' of high taxes, constant 'interruptions of government' and economic hardship. It was not enough to recall the Rump, whose remaining members, less than a fifth of those originally elected, left whole swathes of the country – Norfolk included – entirely unrepresented. The 'secluded members', those whom Colonel Pride had turned away in 1648, must be readmitted, and until that time the county would not support the regime, or pay any further tax. Almost a thousand members of the county gentry signed their names, among them young Sir Nicholas L'Estrange, the master of Hunstanton Hall, and two of his brothers. From Monck's own home county of Devon a similar petition was presented signed by a number of his friends and relations. To this the General felt he must reply. In his public response Monck rearticulated his unequivocal commitment to republican government in general and to the Rump Parliament in particular – whose empty seats, he had been reassured, would be quickly filled. Now that Lord Fairfax's part was played, Monck's hints of a hidden purpose were revealed as nothing more than smoke and mirrors.[23]

❦ ❦ ❦

Anne Monck had been close at hand through all that had passed, lodging at Berwick while her husband was at Coldstream and riding over to visit him in his camp. On occasion she stayed the night in his famous cottage, undeterred by the mud and the stench, and she may have used those precious hours of intimacy – as she certainly had on other occasions – to quiz and cajole Monck on politics and public affairs. Her reputation as her husband's closest confidante had already spread and when, having sailed south, she arrived at Whitehall a few days ahead of him, she was inundated with requests for meetings. Those who wished to seek favour or size up the General's intentions came to her door, among them a number of Rump MPs and their wives. Anne welcomed these visitors with reassuring humility, serving them wine and cake and reiterating her husband's commitment to the republic. But Anne Monck, like her husband, was not a person to underestimate.[24]

❦ ❦ ❦

London in the winter of 1659–60 was a city in turmoil. At the centre of that turmoil were the apprentices, a vast and varied tribe of teenagers and young men, accounting for some 10 per cent of the capital's population. They ranged from those like Gerrard Winstanley and Anne

Monck's missing first husband, Thomas Radford, who sought the skills for front-line trade, to those, like Sir Nicholas L'Estrange's younger brothers, who would go on to be gentlemen-merchants of the leisured variety. What they shared, however, was youth. Few of them had any memory of England before the civil war, and many had not even been born when the first shots had been fired. Charles I and his shortcomings, the misdemeanours of Archbishop Laud or the injustice of ship money were as remote to them as the Spanish Armada and entirely overshadowed by the more immediate injustices, and far higher taxes, they had experienced first-hand.

Their natural antipathy to the army that had been stationed in the capital by Fleetwood was sharpened by General Monck's extensive use of printed material to make his case. From his very first stand he had been at pains to ensure the reason for his opposition to 'sword government' was set out in print – essential when he was hundreds of miles from those he needed to convince. A new paper edited by one of Monck's officers was launched from Edinburgh, which used the lively journalism Marchamont Nedham had pioneered to undermine the party line of Nedham's own government-sponsored title. Challenging the 'uncouth Catalogue of Lyes ... arrogantly intruded upon us by the late *Politicus*', the *Faithful Intelligencer* accused Nedham of being unable to 'carry a truth unmaimed from the Court of Aldermen to his own chamber'. The paper printed Monck's letter to the Lord Mayor appealing for the city's assistance in the face of an imminent threat to its own charter and the liberty of the entire nation.[25]

The last weeks of 1659 saw the usually rigid conventions of public life crumble and a state of near-anarchy break out in areas of the capital. In the city of London apprentices clambered onto roofs and bombarded the soldiers with bricks and tiles. Shopkeepers swung down their shutters and barred them for fear of looting, young men stalked the streets with cudgels and Godly vandals broke into Whitehall and smashed the classical statues in the privy garden. In Westminster intellectuals gathered at the oval coffee bar of the Turk's Head to discuss forms of government with a freedom unknown since the 1640s, voting after each debate by means of a wooden ballot box. William Petty was a regular, irritating his fellow debaters by seeking to calculate the benefits of each model of government in numerical terms. The printing presses, once again liberated by political breakdown, rattled night and day as books and pamphlets poured forth at a rate not seen since the war years.[26]

The difficulty for Monck and the Rump Parliament was that, having deliberately stoked the smouldering mass of public discontent aflame to bring down the army junta, they were faced with a blaze that they could not control. Roger L'Estrange, the errant younger son of old Sir Hamon L'Estrange of Hunstanton Hall, was one of those who had taken up his pen to denounce the army in the last weeks of 1659, stirred from his leisured life by the soldiers' behaviour, protesting 'we will not live to see our Wives and Daughters ravish'd: our houses Rifled and our Children Beggars'. When in January L'Estrange read Monck's statement of support for the Rump and a republic he was furious. He had become a naturalized Londoner but he shared the accumulated embitterment of the signatories of the county petitions, his nephews among them. It was not for a threadbare Parliament to determine the future, he cried, 'but the consent of the People that Must Settle the Nation'. Contesting Monck's case for a republic line by line, he protested that 'since the Death of the late King, we have been Govern'd by Tumult; Bandy'd from One Faction to the Other: This Party up to day, That to Morrow; but still the Nation under, and a Prey to the Strongest'.[27]

🌸 🌸 🌸

Matters came to a head in the second week of February 1660. On Monck's arrival in London the regiments stationed there were ordered to make way for him, and so it was his own men who now manned the streets. There were rumours that the city of London's governing body, the Common Council, would, like the various county petitioners, refuse to pay tax unless the empty seats in the House of Commons were filled. The Rump's reconvened Council of State was determined to see off such resistance, and positively sought opportunities to impose their will on the army. Though Monck had been their champion, some of their number doubted the depth of his loyalty. They met in his absence at Whitehall to discuss how to proceed. Anne was tipped off that something was afoot, rushed to the Council Chamber and hammered loudly on the door, on the pretext of seeking her husband, to try and break them up. But it was to no avail. When the meeting ended it issued its sobering instruction: Monck was to occupy the city of London, arrest eleven of its officials and emasculate its defences. The General's lofty assertions about the soldier's obligation to follow civilians' orders were being put to the test.[28]

Monck passed a sleepless night trying to decide what to do. Anne, always pushing him, argued that he must refuse or he would lose the support of his own men, let alone the capital. But Monck was both deeply uneasy about disobedience and knew that it would give the Rump a pretext to dismiss him. He rode out early the following morning and the citizens of London watched aghast as the men they had cheered as their liberators a week before dragged their civic representatives to the Tower and started to dismantle the city gates. The tension was tremendous. Monck's own men, who had risen to his cries against sword government, could hardly believe what was being asked of them. At Newgate, from whose squalid cells Marchamont Nedham had once made his escape, the soldiers protested to the ashen-faced onlookers that they had been ordered against their wishes 'to oppress their best friends' (Colour plate 24). One of Monck's officers distributed broken splinters of the shattered oak gate among his men, remarking grimly that here were the glorious medals with which a grateful Parliament was rewarding them.

All around General Monck the pressure was growing. From all sides – his own officers, the Lieutenant of the Tower, men he met in the street – he was beset with entreaties to change course. Late the following night he shut himself away in his rooms at Whitehall with the five or six people he trusted most, among them his wife and her brother Thomas. Through the night they conferred on the best way to proceed, Anne and the others urging him on, Monck cautious at every turn. Finally, a course of action was determined. Monck retired for a brief sleep while his friends drafted a 'brisk and smart letter' and gathered the General's most loyal officers. As dawn broke Monck moved east and by the time his letter reached Speaker Lenthall he had left Westminster altogether.

Lenthall opened it to read an ultimatum from the General: 'because they are not fully represented in parliament' the nation was in turmoil. Monck was giving the Rump until Friday to issue writs for elections to its empty seats; in the words of one of Monck's comrades, 'there was now a state of war between the Scottish Army and the Parliament'.[29]

Monck's ultimatum offered Haselrige and the Rumpers an easy way out – they could simply issue writs for elections to the vacant seats, which they had already promised to do. He had been clear that they could impose strict 'qualifications' on who could vote and stand and was unspecific about what would happen were they to refuse. But it did not matter. Monck was the Rump's servant no more and the subtleties

The 'roasting of the Rump': the downfall of the Rump Parliament, and the anticipated end of the republican regime as a whole, caused wild popular celebrations in London and across the country in February 1660.

were lost in the roar that followed. The 'sudden news rane like wild fier' through the capital, as it was reported that Monck 'should stand by them and they should have a free parliament'. The city of London erupted, by nightfall a bonfire blazed on every street and the bells of every city church rang in 'the greatest acclamations of joy that could posiably be expresed, and many drunk for joy'. Samuel Pepys stood on the river's edge and saw thirty-one bonfires from a single spot. The air was filled with the smell of burning wood and the rich aroma of singed meat as 'rumps' were carried aloft on poles and haunches roasted over the rampant bonfires. Pepys's ears rang with the bells and the shouts, and he strolled home marvelling at all he witnessed, 'passed imagination, both the greatness and the suddenness of it'.[30]

George Monck made his extraordinary stand, twice over, in defence of Parliament. But regardless the Commonwealthsmen of the Rump, barely more interested in a free Parliament than the army leaders they had seen off in December had been, declined to comply with his ultimatum. On the morning of Tuesday 21 February a group of middle-aged men gathered at General Monck's rooms and then proceeded to Westminster flanked by soldiers of the very army that had once removed them. The twenty or so MPs in the chamber looked to the door in astonishment as some seventy of their former colleagues, elected in 1640 and purged in 1649, flooded in to reclaim their seats, among them William Prynne who drew cheers as he walked through Westminster Hall. The terms Monck had agreed with the 'secluded' MPs was that they would return for a single purpose: to dissolve Parliament and call new national elections. After overturning the legislation which had excluded them, freeing a host of prisoners and ordering the gates of the city of London to be repaired, the Long Parliament did just that and voted for their own dissolution. Their last act on their final day of sitting was to confirm the 'ancient native right' of the House of Lords to be part of the English Parliament. It was little wonder that Anne and George Monck went to bed early that night 'in a very good humour', able, after the terrifying political high-wire act they had just performed, to sleep at last.[31]

※ ※ ※

Ever since his brother had approached him at Dalkeith with a letter from Charles Stuart, General Monck had refused to discuss the return of the King. His chaplain had alluded to it obliquely on one occasion the previous summer at which Monck had seized him 'in some anger' and he had promised not to speak of it again. Nicholas Monck had been sent away empty-handed and George Monck had repeatedly articulated his opposition to a restoration. Only Anne it seemed, in her 'treason gown', had been able actively to raise and discuss the possibility. Her fearlessness and closeness to her husband, physical and emotional, made her position unique. After dreaming of the tall black-haired man lifting a crown from a dung heap she had discreetly asked 'what manner of man the king was', and had been told by John Price, who as an Eton schoolboy had once seen the young Charles, that he 'was a very Lovely Black Boy' who had, it was said, grown very tall.

It was March 1660, following two great stand-offs, before the General would even have a conversation with anyone else on the subject, and by this time all other avenues had been exhausted. The Protectorate had failed, the Commonwealth had failed and the Rump had refused to fill its empty seats. George Monck had tried to make each 'settlement' in turn work, despite their many shortcomings, but without success. What now was left? Some suggested that Monck himself should become Lord Protector and one or two – including the widowed Elizabeth Cromwell – proposed the return of Richard Cromwell. The republicans clutched at such straws as the waters of public opposition engulfed them. But Richard's cause was lost and both Monck and Anne rejected any suggestion that the General should become head of state. The truth that Monck had long known, and had been the case since 1649, was that if a House of Commons was freely elected it was likely to dismantle the republic and recall the exiled monarch. Now that the Long Parliament had gone and nationwide voting was underway, Monck did what Bulstrode Whitelocke had advised a distraught Fleetwood to do two months before and, at last, opened his doors to the agents of Charles Stuart.[32]

For some days Sir John Grenville, George Monck's cousin and royalist agent, had been loitering among the throng in the outer chambers of

Monck's apartments in St James's Palace. Monck, ever cautious, avoided him until the Long Parliament had made good on its promise to dissolve. The next day a meeting between the two men took place in great secrecy in the rooms of William Morice, a Devonian neighbour and mutual friend of Grenville and Monck. It was nine o'clock in the evening in an obscure room in St James's Palace that the future of the monarchy was decided. Monck was at first curt and wary; he barely knew Grenville despite their family connection, but he opened the letter from Charles Stuart nevertheless. By the end of the meeting Monck's frosts had thawed and he was declaring that he was a wholehearted supporter of Charles Stuart, indeed no one 'desired his Restauration with more passion' than he. A year had not changed Monck's view that once you had decided on a course of action, even if with reluctance, it paid to espouse it with enthusiasm.[33]

The dangers that still lay ahead, both the practical problems with a restoration, and the risk that even now the army might change tack, were starkly clear to General Monck. Given the supreme sensitivity of the subject of the monarchy, it would not take much mismanagement for the officers of the army to desert him, not least as a charismatic opposition leader remained in John Lambert, albeit detained within the Tower of London. They must proceed without making a single false move, Monck told Grenville. Crucially, it was in conversation in William Morice's rooms that Monck set out his terms for a restoration. First, a free pardon must be given to everyone, with the new Parliament alone deciding on any exceptions; second, Charles must agree to whatever that Parliament decided regarding the lands sold and redistributed since 1649 and, third, the army should be paid in full. That there should be freedom of worship for peaceful Protestants with 'tender consciences' had already been accepted by the exiled King. Monck's terms addressed the issues of a national pardon, land ownership and army pay, but, knowing the controversy that would be involved in their resolution, he recommended referring them to Parliament – thereby both upholding the authority of Parliament and distancing Charles Stuart, and the return of the monarchy, from these difficult decisions. It was an ingenious piece of political manoeuvring. As Thomas Gumble would later remark, it was quite something to see a man 'bred in the midst of Drums and Trumpets from the Sixteenth year of his Age, to out-wit Politicians, and such as have been versed in the Arts and cunning of civil business all their Lives'.[34]

Still the General, ever watchful, refused to put anything in writing. Sir John Grenville memorized Monck's terms and set sail for the Low Countries. The gears of constitutional change had started to shift. Meanwhile, the mood in London roared ahead with expectation. At the Royal Exchange, a Latin inscription celebrating the 'Death of the Last Royal Tyrant' marked the place where Charles I's statue once stood. In the week the Long Parliament dissolved itself a London painter leaned his ladder against the wall and, pot in hand, clambered up and painted out the lettering. He then threw down his brush and announced to the crowd of shoppers who had clustered around him that he had 'put out rebells hand wrightinge out of the wall'. The crowd cheered, made a bonfire and cried 'God bless King Charles the Second' as it leaped aflame. Strength of feeling was widespread. In Boston in Lincolnshire the arms of the Commonwealth were torn down, dragged through the streets, and then urinated and defecated upon, 'such was there malice to the States armes in that towne'. Change was everywhere, springing like fungi from unseen sources. The royal arms started to reappear in public buildings and churches from Cork to King's Lynn. For many it was thrilling, for others it was ominous, even terrifying. At All Hallows the Great on London's Thames Street, the Fifth Monarchist headquarters and Anna Trapnel's own church, the congregation gathered for their meeting in April 1660 only to see that in the night the arms of Charles II had been once again mounted on the church's stone walls. Doom seemed to stand before them.[35]

It would take a month for the new Parliament to be elected and the complex choreography of which Monck spoke to be danced out. The tension did not abate. Monck mirrored his work in Scotland by purging radical officers from the English army. He acted not a moment too soon as in early April John Lambert escaped from the Tower of London, sliding down a rope into a waiting boat, and rode north to try to raise a rebellion. Marchamont Nedham, with his lifelong knack of backing the losers in a political crisis, attempted to stir up ill feeling towards the royalists through scurrilous publications but achieved little more than his sacking as editor of *Politicus*. Meanwhile, the royalist literature of Roger L'Estrange and others did a roaring trade, among them inventive accounts of the immaculate character and habits of Charles Stuart – his piety, sobriety and moral purity – that were lapped up by a credulous readership. The royalists gnawed their fingernails, hoping that there would not be a fatal slip. Still they could not be completely sure. As one of Charles Stuart's friends had remarked only weeks before, 'Monck is so dark a man, no perspective can looke through him, and it will be like the last sceane of some excellent play, which the most juditious cannot positively say how it will end.'[36]

On 25 April the new Parliament gathered and into the House of Commons trooped more country gentlemen and fewer soldiers and

Charles Stuart dining at the Mauritshouse in The Hague on the eve of the Restoration. After dinner Charles met the representatives of the English parliament, among them Lord Fairfax himself. The 'Ey[e]s of everyone' were reported to have been on the two men.

republicans than had been the case since 1640. Those hoping that the
terms of a restoration might yet limit the historic powers of the monarchy were disappointed, both by the conservatism of those elected and
by Monck's failure to enforce the 'qualifications' which had in theory
been imposed on its members. A week later Sir John Grenville attended
the Commons to present a letter to the Speaker from Charles Stuart.
As smooth and emollient as oil, it proposed the country's great wounds
be healed by the restoration of 'Kings, Peers and people to their just,
ancient and fundamental rights'. His proposed terms, the 'Declaration
of Breda', incorporated almost verbatim the points that George Monck
had dictated to Grenville at St James's, and offered no new restrictions
on royal authority. After the letter and the terms were read, William
Morice, Monck and Grenville's friend, was first on his feet to speak in
its support. There was no doubt what the response would be. A week
later heralds publicly proclaimed that at the moment of his father's
death eleven years earlier King Charles II had become 'the most potent,
mighty and undoubted King' and to him the people of the nation 'do
most humbly and faithfully submit, and oblige ourselves, our Heirs and
Posterities for ever'. A week later in the elegant grandeur of The Hague
the parliamentary delegation presented their agreement to the 29-year-
old man they now recognized as sovereign. At their head was Lord
Fairfax himself. The 'curiosity and eys of every one' was upon them as
the founding general of the New Model Army bowed before the son of
the king he had defeated, and the two men withdrew to confer in
private.[37]

❦ ❦ ❦

Charles II was rowed ashore in a barge from the ship that had borne
him across the English Channel at noon on 26 May 1660. Waiting on
the sandy shingle below Dover's chalky cliffs was a welcoming party
and a crowd of thousands. It was a glorious early summer day and the
silk canopy hastily rustled up by the town corporation flapped in the
breeze. Monck had been in Kent for several days organizing the 'incred-
ible' numbers who had come to witness this famous moment. He 'who
loved order and good government' disposed everyone into troops

under various noblemen and ensured that there were no fights over who had the best lodgings in the town's hostelries. To rapturous cheers and the thunder of cannon from sea and shore, the King disembarked onto the beach by a timber gangplank, followed by his brothers, the dukes of York and Gloucester, his footmen and his favourite spaniel. General Monck crunched forward to greet him. The square-set soldier, bare-headed, sank to his knees and kissed the hem of his sovereign's cloak. Monck had not set out to restore the monarchy, but now that it had been achieved, and with it a return to order and orthodoxy, his satisfaction was real. Charles Stuart for his part knew the debt he owed George Monck. He, too, dropped to his knees, and there on the sand the two men embraced one another, exchanging words that amid the clamour were lost to all but them. As they rose shouts of 'God Save the King' rang out, to which the young Duke of Gloucester replied, 'God bless General Monk', throwing his hat high in the salty air.[38]

Charles II landing at Dover on 26 May 1660, and being welcomed by a kneeling General Monck.

The royal party reached London, as was planned, in time for Charles II to make his triumphant entry on 29 May. In the evening John Price came to Monck in his rooms at Whitehall to congratulate him. On hearing his words, the General, who was at last relieved of the immense burden of the past months, broke down. 'No Mr Price,' he said, his great shoulders shaking with sobs, 'it was not I that did this; you know the jealousies that were had of me, and the opposition against me. It was God alone.'[39]

Anne Monck did not feature prominently in the pageantry of the restoration. She was given no seat in the royal coach to London and, a middle-aged woman of ordinary appearance, did not appear in Samuel Pepys's starry-eyed diary entries for those days. But those who had been close to events knew that her influence, above all, had brought them to this. At each step of the dangerous and uncertain journey they had made she had been with her husband, as confidante, coaxer and co-conspirator. Charles Stuart had already been told that 'Monks lady' had more interest with the General than anyone and that she was the person he must court. He had written to her almost the moment he had received the message containing Monck's terms for a restoration. Anne had replied conceding that 'her tears and prayers' had, indeed, played their part. A welter of further ingratiating letters addressed to Mrs Monck followed, among them one from the widowed Queen Henrietta Maria. Charles I's sister, the titular Queen of Bohemia, also wrote, describing herself warmly as 'your most affectionat frend Elizabeth'. The royal ladies' solicitousness of Mrs Monck, the outspoken daughter of a blacksmith, would be short-lived, but the Moncks' achievements would endure. 'In all places we will hang up Trophees and erect monuments,' one contemporary wrote that year, 'future Chronicles shall blazon your ladiship the best of Women and his Excellency the best of Men, [and] all Ages shall bless you.'[40]

General Monck acted as master of ceremonies for Charles II's entry into London and made sure the army had pride of place. The momentous day, the new King's thirtieth birthday, began with a military review on Blackheath, tens of thousands of soldiers and members of the local militias ranged in ranks, their hats tipped with feathers and their

harnesses gleaming. From here the procession set off, the soldiers themselves accounting for most of its great length, passing north over
London Bridge and turning west through the city towards Westminster.
John Evelyn watched them from the Strand and felt the wonder and joy
of most contemporaries. I 'beheld it, & blessed God,' he wrote, 'And all
this without one drop of bloud & by that very army, which rebell'd
against him.' Lucy Hutchinson, wife of one of the regicides, was also
among the observers. Well might the King ask, she noted bitterly,
'where were his enemies. For he saw nothing but prostrates, expressing
all the love that could make a prince happy.' She marvelled 'that day to
see the mutability of some, and the hypocracy of others, and the servile
flattery of all'. Chief among the 'prostrates' was General Monck himself,
riding immediately before Charles II, 'adored', she conceded, 'like one
that had brought all the glory and felicity of mankind home with this
prince'.[41]

EPILOGUE

The public gallows at Tyburn stood in open ground on the road west from London towards Oxford, the infamous vertical tripod of timber rising incongruously amid fields and farm buildings. Spectators walked or rode out to this pleasant spot to witness the capital's most notorious felons – murderers, highwaymen and swindlers – being strangled, dismembered and disembowelled. Here on 30 January 1661, the twelfth anniversary of the death of Charles I, an unconventional execution took place. Four days earlier the decomposing corpses of Oliver Cromwell, John Bradshaw and Henry Ireton had been carried up out of the vaults in Westminster Abbey, where they had been interred among kings and queens, with onlookers paying sixpence apiece to watch. On the morning of the 30th their coffins were strapped to timber sledges and pulled by riders through the streets. When they reached Tyburn the coffins were broken open, each long-dead body was heaved out, received a rope around the neck and was hauled up onto the infamous 'triple tree'.

It had been almost a decade since Henry Ireton, the moving force behind the trial and execution of Charles I, had died of disease outside the gates of Limerick, and his body looked 'like a dried rat' as he dangled from the rope that day, his groin 'corrupted'. Oliver Cromwell, who had been dead almost two and a half years, had been embalmed and his corpse was consequently 'very fresh'. Onlookers were struck as much as anything by his luxurious coffin, lined in purple velvet and embossed with gold studs and hinges. John Bradshaw had been in his grave just fourteen months. The winding sheet which had encased him was still wet from the seeping fluids of decay and his right hand and nose had disintegrated altogether. The three men hung there for just a single day, during which services of remembrance for 'Charles the Martyr' were held in churches across the kingdom. As the light faded they were cut down and decapitated. Their dismembered corpses were thrown in a pit dug below the gallows, while their heads were mounted on poles over the south front of Westminster Hall. John Bradshaw's had the place of precedence above the door of the room in which he had handed down his famous sentence.

Thousands travelled to Tyburn that day to see the corpses, among them Elizabeth Pepys who went with the wife of one of her husband's naval colleagues. A flock of apprentices escaped their masters to visit the macabre spectacle. A few enterprising young men even managed to reach up and pull off Bradshaw's toes, enabling a merchant named Sainthill to walk away clutching no fewer than five of the gruesome little trophies. Samuel Pepys had, like many, been a loyal servant of the Protectorate until recently and confessed that it 'doth trouble me, that a man of so great courage as he was should have that dishonour'. Charlotte de la Trémoille, Dowager Countess of Derby, on the other hand, felt not the faintest tremor of pity. She described the scene for her sister-in-law, satisfied for once: 'There is nothing which more fully convinces me of the vanity of this world, and that all but the fear of God is nothing.'[1]

🌸 🌸 🌸

The posthumous execution of Cromwell, Ireton and Bradshaw was a piece of revenge theatre that could be staged at next to no human cost. This was entirely deliberate, for Charles II was sincere about the clemency and compromise discussed with General Monck in the secret meeting at St James's Palace and enshrined in the Declaration of Breda. He had neither his father's proud implacability nor Cromwell's spiritual restlessness and was steady in his commitment to reconciliation. The 'Convention Parliament' elected in April 1660 drew up a wide-ranging 'Act of Free and General Pardon, Indemnity and Oblivion' which the King then signed into law. This remarkable document articulated the policy of the restored sovereign that no past crime against him or his father should henceforth be proceeded against or even talked of. He wished instead 'to bury all Seeds of future Discords' and all memory of discords past. Furthermore, the King had made clear his willingness to accept a broader national church, without the Laudian innovations so many had loathed and the strict liturgical rigidity his father had favoured and enforced.[2]

The Cromwellians who had helped secure the restoration were, as promised, rewarded for the near-miracle they had brought to pass. George Monck was the chief recipient, given his pick of court offices, a colossal pension and created Duke of Albemarle, Lord Lieutenant of Ireland and a Knight of the Garter. Sir John Grenville, his royalist cousin who had made the approach, became Earl of Bath, and Groom of the Stool to the King. Edward Montagu, lord of Hinchingbrooke, head of the navy, was made Earl of Sandwich and Lord Broghill, who helped secure Ireland, was given the Earldom of Orrery. Thomas Clarges and William Morice both received knighthoods and Brian Fairfax became a royal equerry. For Lord Fairfax, there were no honours, but then he probably sought none. He felt only too keenly the responsibility he bore for the events of the past, and had reportedly remarked that if anyone were to be condemned, 'he knew no man that deserved it more than himself, who being General of the army at that time, and having power sufficient to prevent the proceedings against the King, had not'.[3]

Of the small number excluded from the mass pardon of the Act of Indemnity, the most significant group were those who had signed Charles I's death warrant. These fifty-nine men had been a mixture of prominent Commonwealthsmen and relatively obscure figures whom Ireton and the cabal who brought the King to trial thought could be counted upon. Come 1660 many were dead, others had fled overseas and some were judged genuinely contrite, leaving just eleven to face immediate execution.

While this group of regicides was condemned to die, almost all the
senior men who had actually been in government during the republican
years, and from whom the restoration had been wrested, were allowed
to walk free. Many were saved from harsher fates by the intercession of
influential friends. Charles Fleetwood and John Desbrow, the army leaders and relations by marriage of Oliver Cromwell, suffered only a ban on
holding public office. The same mild censure was all that was meted out
to Cromwell's Lord Chief Justice, Oliver St John, and William Lenthall,
the Speaker of the Rump Parliament. Sir Arthur Haselrige, a die-hard
republican and one of the original 'five members' of Parliament whom
Charles I had tried to arrest, was slated for execution but was spared
death by the personal intervention of General Monck. John Thurloe was
too useful a figure to condemn: no one knew as much as he about the
administration of the past decade – and, anyhow, he was rumoured to
have kept a 'black book' containing information that could send half of
those who claimed to be royalists to the gallows in his place. John
Lambert, who had opposed Monck and the restoration to the bitter end,
was one of the few who was sentenced to death, but on Charles II's
personal intervention this was commuted to life imprisonment. The
soldier would spend the rest of his days watching the seasons change
from a series of prisons in the Channel Islands where his wife and
family were allowed to join him.[4]

The Cromwell family trembled at the thought of what awaited them
at the restoration given their 'obnoxious name', but they, too, were left
largely undisturbed. Henry and Richard Cromwell had left office with
the fall of the Protectorate in 1659. Richard was heavily in debt, causing
his brother-in-law Fleetwood to plead with Monck to help him – quite
something from the man who had hounded him from office as Lord
Protector only a year before. In the end it was angry creditors rather
than vengeful royalists who forced Richard to leave the country, and he
lived the next few decades of his long life in and about Paris. Henry
Cromwell, by contrast, remained in England and having professed
loyalty to Charles II was allowed to live in peace. Numerous senior
figures, Monck among them, testified to his character and achievements, one contemporary noting that in Ireland they had 'acknowlegd

that he deserved to have been the son of a better Father'. He was even allowed to retain over £7,000 worth of his Irish lands. He and his young family returned to the rich fields of the Fens, and here he would live out his days, a minor figure of the landed gentry like many Cromwells before him. Henry's closeness to William Petty endured and when he died in 1679, Petty called him simply 'my deare friend (who is now with God)'. In 1661 the bodies of the Cromwell family were removed from Westminster Abbey and reburied in St Margaret's churchyard nearby, among them Oliver's mother and his sister Jane. Only Elizabeth Claypole, Oliver's beloved daughter, remained, perhaps because of her support for a number of royalists. She lies there still, undisturbed among the sovereigns and statesmen.[5]

While the brokers of the restoration, including Hyde and Monck, nodded approvingly at all the peacemaking of 1660, others were not so pleased. Parliament might have established the principle that crown and church lands sold in the 1640s and 1650s should be returned to their institutional owners, but this did not help royalist families who had had their estates confiscated. They were left to pursue individual lawsuits for their return and received no reimbursement of the composition fines they had paid. While most were eventually successful in reclaiming their property, they looked on with indignation as their former oppressors escaped prosecution and in some cases profited from the change of regime. Prominent among the disillusioned was the Stanley family. Charlotte, Dowager Countess of Derby, attended the coronation of Charles II overjoyed at long last 'to behold the crown on the head of his Majesty'. But her anger was undimmed, both with those who had executed her husband and with her eldest son for having married without her permission. The Isle of Man was returned to the family along with other confiscated royalist estates that had been gifted to senior figures of the republic. A highly suspect trial followed at Castle Rushen which saw William Christian, he who had betrayed the Countess of Derby to the parliamentary invasion force, convicted of treason. He was executed by firing squad and buried in Malew churchyard, the very place where a decade before he had first been approached about the conspiracy. The privy council in London declared the sentence to have been contrary to the Act of Indemnity and ordered Christian's lands to be returned to his family. Charlotte de la Trémoille, Dowager Countess of Derby, was unmoved. She could hold a grudge like few others and she went to her grave in 1665 still furious with her son – leaving him just £5 in her will as a final rebuke – and incensed that the men who had beheaded her husband yet roamed free.[6]

The mounting sense of discontent among the royalists extended far beyond the aristocracy. Gentry families across the land would, like the L'Estranges of Hunstanton Hall, be slow to forget the insult and ignominy of being dragged from their beds by the Major Generals. Stoking the ire was Roger L'Estrange. Far from helping to crush the seeds of discontent, as the legislation of 1660 had stipulated, L'Estrange was propagator in chief. His new career as a pamphleteer had proved a runaway success. Determined to prevent bygones becoming bygones, over the first months and years of the restoration he churned out a series of publications railing at the injustice of including erstwhile Cromwellians in the new regime and the mortal peril posed by admitting 'the phanatique Fellowships' to the church in England.[7]

❦ ❦ ❦

Only a small number had been executed during the 1650s, the Earl of Derby among them, and so when the surviving men who had signed Charles I's death warrant were hanged, drawn and quartered in October 1660 the impact was significant. The executions were raucous, vitriolic affairs and the stench of burning bodies in Charing Cross where these sentences were carried out was unbearable, such that the residents wrote to the King begging that others might be dispatched elsewhere. When Charles II was pressed to take a more militant line against the surviving regicides he declined, declaring he was interested in his subjects' future actions not those of the past and was already 'weary of hanging'.

It was apparently the defiant and principled speeches of a number of the condemned regicides that inspired one of the more belligerent of the Fifth Monarchists to try one last stand. The movement, always political, had in the last year or so developed a terrorist wing. Anna

Trapnel, who had continued to travel and sing her prophecies, was among many who disapproved of this hardcore fringe. In mid-January 1661, undeterred by the disapproval of most of his brethren, Thomas Venner and fifty armed followers occupied St Paul's Cathedral. A shoot-out resulted in which several were killed and Venner captured. The incident never posed a serious threat to the new regime, but it was an absolute gift to those smarting at the clemency being shown to people they loathed. The newspapers, now under new management, covered the Fifth Monarchist skirmish in the same issue as the story of Bradshaw, Ireton and Cromwell's decapitations, spreading fear that it might be only the first of a new wave of insurrections from religious extremists. Those associated with the old regime quivered at the possibility that, having escaped retribution, they might now be condemned by association. Henry Cromwell wrote immediately to assert his absolute ignorance of any plan for an uprising, protesting 'I never so much as heard the least syllable' of it until he had read about it in the newspaper.[8]

Another group anxious to protect themselves against recriminations were the Quakers. So far Charles II had treated them as an amusing curiosity, much as Lord Fairfax had regarded the Diggers in 1649. But suddenly they risked being tarred with the brush of rebellion. It was in order to demonstrate their innocence and independence of the rambunctious Fifth Monarchists that George Fox published the Quaker 'peace testimony', A Declaration from the Harmles & Innocent People of God, called Quakers in February 1661. This definitive denunciation of war and conflict 'for any end or under any pretence whatsoever' marked the movement's abandonment of political agitation and began the explicit pacifism which endures to this day.[9]

Despite the protestations of innocence from various quarters, a bitter backlash against the spirit of togetherness of the Declaration of Breda followed Venner's uprising and reached its peak in the spring of 1661. It coincided exactly with elections to a new parliament, to devastating effect. Numerous men who had been elected the year before were rejected, their mixed credentials no longer welcome. This new assembly, which for good reason would be known as the 'Cavalier Parliament', would sit for almost twenty years. Among those who lost their seats was Lord Fairfax himself, he who, after Monck, had done as much as anyone to secure the restoration. Fairfax would return to Nun Appleton increasingly confined to his wheelchair by ill health, organizing his papers and writing poetry. Here he would remain, away from the heat of politics which had never been his forte, and here he buried his beloved wife, Anne, 'my best self'. He felt increasing melancholy, but took solace from the memory of his part in the restoration – and quiet satisfaction from the knowledge that the horse Charles II had ridden to his coronation was a gift from Fairfax's own stable.[10]

When it met in 1661 the Cavalier Parliament lost little time in grubbing up the tender seedlings of collaboration and inclusivity that had been planted by Monck, Charles II and others the year before. The spirit of compromise that had brought the restoration to pass was being borne away. The hopes of all those who wished for an Anglican church broad enough to embrace at least some of the numerous new groups and congregations were dashed as plans for a more flexible approach to worship were shelved. Instead in 1662 the pre-war Book of Common Prayer was reissued with few changes of substance and all clergymen were required by law to swear an oath to uphold it in every detail. All but the most traditional Anglicans – Presbyterians and Baptists, Quakers and Congregationalists of all stripes – were banned from meeting and worshipping, and excluded altogether from public life. At a stroke almost a thousand clergymen were ejected from the national church in England and Wales. They included hundreds of moderate Presbyterians like Anna Trapnel's friend Philip Taverner, the minister of St John's Hillingdon, who had himself been a vocal opponent of the radical sects. In barely two years Protestants with 'tender consciences' to whom the Declaration of Breda had categorically promised protection had been criminalized.[11]

❦ ❦ ❦

When the French physician and coin collector Charles Patin visited London in 1671 the fact that there had ever been a revolution or a republic might have escaped his notice altogether. Despite the recent great fire the capital was thriving, its population growing and an abundance of trade everywhere in evidence. The monarchy was back, as was the traditional church structure of bishops, deans and chapters; the church, crown and most landowners had regained their estates, and a narrow national Anglican church was again in operation. But just as Patin glimpsed, on looking up from the crowds, Bradshaw and Cromwell's monstrously shrivelled heads still impaled on their stakes, so the legacy of those years remained close at hand across the British Isles.[12]

In Ireland the impact was greatest. The systematic dispossession of Catholics would not be undone at the restoration, despite the fact that the Catholics had overwhelmingly supported the monarchy. Hundreds of Protestant Englishmen and Scots now held extensive Irish estates – among them Henry Cromwell, William Petty and George Monck – and British Protestant domination of the island, and the soaring sense of injustice that accompanied it, would be a defining feature of the next 300 years. The period had begun with the Scots setting the political pace in the British Isles, both in challenging Charles I and by requiring the radical remodelling of the English church as the price of their military support in the civil war. By the mid-1650s, however, the tables had been turned and Scotland was a conquered nation, forced to march to the English drum. This subordination would also endure, albeit in a less egregious fashion than in Ireland, and with the Act of Union of 1707 the Scottish Parliament voted for its own abandonment and Scottish MPs travelled south to Westminster once again.

The 'Interregnum' had been a period of destruction and disharmony, but it had also been a time of tremendous intellectual and imaginative creativity. The exotic intellectual terrain over which the minds of people like William Petty and Robert Boyle, Gerrard Winstanley and Anna Trapnel had roamed during those years would not be forgotten. The narrowness of the re-established Church of England fixed for ever the distinction between the national church and the 'nonconformists' who were now forced to worship illicitly, for a time at least. The Baptists and Quakers were among those well-established enough to survive the prohibitions, and many of the radicals of the 1650s found a home in their less formal, more egalitarian spiritual ways. Among them was

Gerrard Winstanley who, after the spectacular rise and fall of the Diggers, had remained in Cobham growing calmer and more conventional with age. After the restoration he returned to London where he re-entered the world of trade he had once denounced as theft, dealing in wheat and grain. He had two children and seems never to have published or planted again. He died a Quaker and member of the Westminster Society of Friends. Anna Trapnel had been harassed by Quakers as well as by the Cornish magistrates during her peregrinations in the late 1650s and whether she became reconciled after their declaration for peace is unknown. At the restoration she simply disappeared from view, perhaps dying or maybe simply settling, a chapter in the life of this remarkable woman caught only briefly by a passing beam of light.[13]

Political and institutional exile did not necessitate extinction; in some ways it had quite the opposite effect. The greatest works of creative imagination of the age were produced by those cast out by the fall of the republic and the cavalier backlash that followed. John Milton, ejected from the diplomatic service and narrowly avoiding prosecution, completed *Paradise Lost* in the years immediately after the restoration. Meanwhile, another of the Puritan preachers forced from English churches in 1662 was John Bunyan, an erstwhile soldier in the New Model Army, who would go on to publish in 1678 the most popular Christian allegory of all time, *The Pilgrim's Progress from this World to that which is to Come.*

The scientific endeavour of the decade would also take flight at the restoration. In November 1660 many of the Oxford Experimental Philosophy Club gathered once more in London, their proceedings marked with an inaugural lecture by Christopher Wren. Among them again was William Petty, whose employments in Ireland had ended with Henry Cromwell's resignation. The restoration brought an unexpected boost to their endeavours when it was discovered that the new King was a keen amateur scientist who would go on to establish a laboratory at Whitehall Palace. When Petty was introduced to the King he began with a faltering apology for his service to the republic. The King interrupted him and 'seeming little to mind apologies as needlesse replied,

But Dr, why have you left off your Enquiries into ye Mechanicks of Shipping?' Charles II granted them a royal charter as the 'Royal Society of London for Improving Natural Knowledge' and became their patron. Petty for his part lived the rest of his long life on the profits from the Down Survey. He became friends with the King, from whom he would receive a knighthood, but never again held a major public office or made another map. He remained intellectually irrepressible and his publications, *Political Arithmetick* and *The Political Anatomy of Ireland*, each drawing heavily on numerical analysis of people and places, established him as one of the founding fathers of modern economics, whose unique contribution would later be celebrated by Karl Marx among others.[14]

The economic reality of England had itself been changed by the republican era. Higher taxation and constant state debt which had been essential to maintain the Commonwealth army and fund its overseas activities, both in the Caribbean and on the Continent, had become routine during the 1650s. There was no reason for Charles II or his ministers to relinquish such useful funds, and after 1660 both phenomena continued, giving the English crown access to money on a new scale. As a consequence national overseas enterprises, both war and colonial expansion, could be undertaken to a degree previously unthinkable. In time this would help earn the inconsequential British archipelago an international standing out of all proportion to its size. The ability to raise funds through the burgeoning London banking trade that had enabled so many royalists, among them the L'Estranges of Hunstanton, to mortgage their lands and pay their composition fines was also transformational. This ready access to capital enabled scientists and entrepreneurs with more commercially viable innovations than William Petty's double-writing implement to raise the money to develop their inventions. Among such 'inventors' were those who at the turn of the century would demonstrate to the Royal Society machines for extracting water from copper mines. So was born the steam engine that would go on to power an industrial revolution.

Another change which had been brought about by the 1650s and could not be undone was public interest in news, current affairs and political debate. Marchamont Nedham went on the run at the restoration, certain that he would be singled out for prosecution for his role in promoting the republic and defaming the Stuart kings. In the end he secured a pardon, and would continue to haunt the backstreets of London both as a physician, his alternative career, and as a pen for hire. One of his rare acts of genuine principle was to publish a pamphlet arguing for fundamental reform of English schools where he had once had such an unhappy experience – pointing out that 'Were Parents obliged but for some time to the trouble of instructing their Children, (they think it trouble enough to have them in the same house;) they would quickly be convinced'. The national censorship regime was re-established at the restoration, and Roger L'Estrange put in charge, but with new levels of literacy, publishing and a nation that had for good reason lifted its sights from purely local concerns, even censorship could not ensure the government line was accepted. The political turmoil of the 1650s, including successive parliaments' struggles to be allowed to meet and arguments about the electorate's right to make a free choice of representatives, had given Parliament itself a new assertiveness. Taken together, these would help bring about 'the Glorious Revolution' of 1688–9, when Parliament backed the removal of Charles II's brother, the authoritarian Catholic James II, in favour of the Protestant William and Mary. The conditions of William and Mary's assumption of sovereignty, set out in almost contractual terms in the Bill of Rights, established just such limitations to sovereign power as had been discussed a generation earlier, among them the requirement for free elections and regular parliaments. After a generation of persecution and conflict, an Act of Toleration was passed in 1689 granting Protestant nonconformists the freedom to worship. The Licensing Act, which provided for a national regime of press censorship, was also allowed to lapse so that, come the end of the century, there was, in effect, a free press.[15]

🐝 🐝 🐝

George and Anne Monck gained immense wealth at the restoration: a pension of £7,000 a year, a palace, New Hall in Essex, lavish lodgings at Whitehall and numerous honours and offices of state. But the resentment that fuelled the election of the Cavalier Parliament also coloured their reputations. It was not long before they who had, more than anyone, brought the restoration to pass were also castigated. Monck himself, now Duke of Albemarle, had such standing, not least with the King, that he was spared much of the bitterness, but when it came to his wife, few held back. All those who had done less well than the couple – which was everyone – could look enviously at their wealth while Anne's flinty humour and outspoken style, the very qualities that had helped her guide her husband to the restoration, made her widely unpopular. Hyde, now Earl of Clarendon, and Pepys soon loathed her and even the Archbishop of Canterbury, Gilbert Sheldon, was reported to have called her 'the veriest slut and drudge, and the foulest word that can be spoken of a woman almost'. The Moncks were fish out of water at the self-indulgent restoration court, too serious, too salty and too spare in their tastes for its silk-slung blades and beauties. When the Grand Duke of Tuscany paid the couple a courtesy visit at New Hall he had already been told that the Duchess was 'a lady of low origin' who had once sold cloth in the New Exchange, and was primed to find fault in the hospitality, more 'a parsimonious collation than a handsome dinner'. Rumours of something disreputable in the Moncks' deep past drifted about unsubstantiated. Anne's clothes, her speech, her manners and her looks were denigrated and before the decade was out a vicious satire had appeared caricaturing her as 'the Monky Dutchess'. It was little wonder George Monck increasingly stayed away from court, sitting up drinking with Dr Troutbeck and bemoaning the 'rage of sin' at Charles II's court and the blasphemous 'Hectors and Roaring Boys that think they cannot speak with a good accent without Damme's, Bloods and Wounds'.[16]

In January 1670 George Monck died at Whitehall in the Cockpit rooms that had once belonged to his friend Oliver Cromwell. Anne Monck followed him just a fortnight later, accompanying him in death as she had done in life. The funeral that followed was a magnificent affair staged at public expense. Dr Troutbeck himself embalmed his old friend who then lay in state, and Christopher Wren, now Surveyor of the King's Works, arranged for the streets from Somerset House to Westminster to be gravelled for his funeral cortège. The oration in

Westminster Abbey was given by Wren's old Oxford colleague, Seth Ward, once Savilian Professor of Astronomy and regular of the Oxford Experimental Philosophy Club, and now Bishop of Salisbury. The General, he intoned, had been 'great of performance, little of speech'. During the dark years of the Interregnum, he continued – avoiding any reference to Monck's long service to the republic or closeness to Oliver Cromwell – 'The Sun was turned into Darkness, the Moon into bloud, the Stars thrown from their Orbs. Our Religion abolished, our Foundations overturned, our Laws abrogated. The Government of Church and State dissolved, the Governours Banished, imprisoned, murdered.' From this monstrous maelstrom Monck had delivered them. 'Such was his Courage, that though an Host of men were prepared against him, yet he did not fear. Audite posteri! if my voice would reach it, I would speak to the Generations which are to come.' But the generations to come would not be listening. The trophies and statues of the General and his wife that were foreseen were never to materialize. While the institutions they helped reinstate – the monarchy, the House of Lords, an Anglican episcopal church – still stand and are known the world over, George and Anne Monck are not, and within a generation their line and titles had died out entirely. The only monument ever erected to either remains their tomb, proposed and paid for by their one surviving son.

Three hundred years on, a royal commission considered which 'distinguished persons' should receive statues at the rebuilt Palace of Westminster, and was encouraged by Prince Albert to consider figures of the turbulent years of the seventeenth century. But when a public sculpture was eventually unveiled before Westminster Hall in 1899 it would not be of George Monck who had risked everything to uphold the power of Parliament. He had not even made the shortlist. Instead, the giant bronze figure immortalized the man who had consistently found the will of the people in Parliament incompatible with the will of God, and whose name would always eclipse all others of this utterly exceptional age: Oliver Cromwell.[17]

ACKNOWLEDGEMENTS

I would like to thank Dr Roland B. Harris and Dr Warwick Rodwell for their advice on the archaeology and topography of Westminster Abbey and Hall; Ros Westwood, Derbyshire Museums Manager, and Sir John Guinness, Thomas Hill QC and Ed Tollemache for advice on and access to portraits of John Bradshaw; Dr Paul Drury for generously sharing his work on Castle Rushen; Professor Jason Peacey for permission to consult his PhD on Henry Parker and parliamentary propaganda; Piers Townshend for his advice on seventeenth-century paper-making; Charles le Strange Meakin and Kiffy Stainer-Hutchins for access to the buildings and landscape of Hunstanton Hall, information on the L'Estrange family portraits and for permission to reproduce them; Dr Peter Barber, Visiting Professor at King's College London, formerly Head of the Map Library at the British Library, for his advice on British and European cartography; Stuart Orme, Curator of the Cromwell Museum in Huntingdon; the Duke of Buccleuch and Queensberry for permission to reproduce his wonderful miniatures of the Cromwell family and others; Dr Edward Impey, Master of the Armouries, for advice on military architecture and artillery; to the trustees of the Wisbech Society and the Diocese of Ely for permission to reproduce the painting of John Thurloe's Wisbech Castle; Kate Higgins, Assistant Archivist, The Mercers' Company, Tim Reid, Senior Archives and Local

Studies Officer, City of Westminster Archives Centre and, especially, Robin Harcourt Williams, Head of Collections and Archives at Hatfield House, for advice and assistance in tracking Anne Clarges/Monck and Thomas Radford through their respective archives. As well as benefiting from the assistance of the staff of many local and national libraries, and the programmes of digitisation of seventeenth-century printed material, this book could not have been completed without the staff of the London Library, whose efforts to supply books and resources to its members through the Covid-19 pandemic were outstanding.

I am immensely grateful to Professor Ronald Hutton of Bristol University and Dr Andrew Barclay, Senior Research Fellow of the History of Parliament Trust, for generously reading and commenting on this book in typescript. The errors that remain are, of course, mine alone.

Arabella Pike, publishing director of William Collins, took this book on, and has been a tremendous champion of it. Marigold Atkey, Richard Collins, Iain Hunt, Jo Thompson and colleagues at William Collins did a wonderful job of seeing it through to publication. Andrew Gordon my agent, of David Higham Associates, has been a wise guide throughout.

My father John Keay read this book chapter by chapter, from outline to epilogue, and gave incisive comments and unstinting encouragement. Simon Thurley discussed almost every aspect with me and has, as ever, been the best of colleagues and companions. This book is dedicated to our children with love and in gratitude to them for putting up with quite so much of the seventeenth century in their lives.

FAMILY TREES

The L'Estranges of Hunstanton

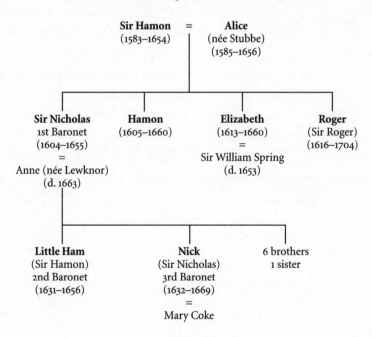

Sir Hamon = **Alice**
(1583–1654)   (née Stubbe)
                (1585–1656)

Sir Nicholas   **Hamon**   **Elizabeth**   **Roger**
1st Baronet   (1605–1660)   (1613–1660)   (Sir Roger)
(1604–1655)   =   (1616–1704)
=   Sir William Spring
Anne (née Lewknor)   (d. 1653)
(d. 1663)

Little Ham   **Nick**   6 brothers
(Sir Hamon)   (Sir Nicholas)   1 sister
2nd Baronet   3rd Baronet
(1631–1656)   (1632–1669)
                          =
                    Mary Coke

The Family of Oliver Cromwell

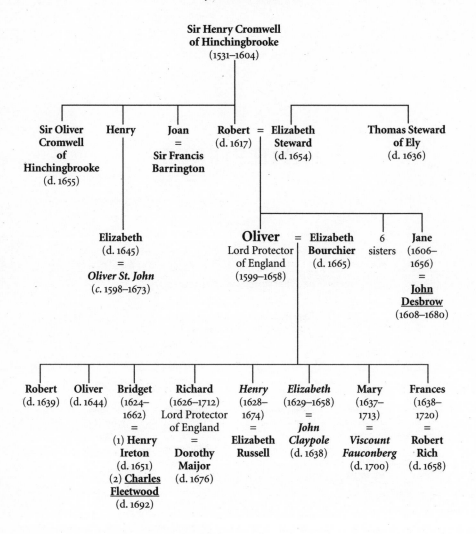

Sir Henry Cromwell
of Hinchingbrooke
(1531–1604)

Sir Oliver
Cromwell
of
Hinchingbrooke
(d. 1655)

Henry

Joan
=
Sir Francis
Barrington

Robert = **Elizabeth**
(d. 1617) **Steward**
(d. 1654)

Thomas Steward
of Ely
(d. 1636)

Elizabeth
(d. 1645)
=
Oliver St. John
(*c.* 1598–1673)

Oliver = **Elizabeth**
Lord Protector **Bourchier**
of England (d. 1665)
(1599–1658)

6
sisters

Jane
(1606–
1656)
=
John
Desbrow
(1608–1680)

Robert
(d. 1639)

Oliver
(d. 1644)

Bridget
(1624–
1662)
=
(1) **Henry**
Ireton
(d. 1651)
(2) **Charles**
Fleetwood
(d. 1692)

Richard
(1626–1712)
Lord Protector
of England
=
Dorothy
Maijor
(d. 1676)

Henry
(1628–
1674)
=
Elizabeth
Russell

Elizabeth
(1629–1658)
=
John
Claypole
(d. 1638)

Mary
(1637–
1713)
=
Viscount
Fauconberg
(d. 1700)

Frances
(1638–
1720)
=
Robert
Rich
(d. 1658)

underlined   Significant 'military' men, 1657–8
italic   Significant 'civilians', 1657–8

TIMELINE

		REGIME and EVENTS
1648		**MONARCHY: *King Charles I (1625–49)***
1649		***The COMMONWEALTH, Parliament sovereign, no head of state, council of state executive***
	Jan	Trial and execution of Charles I
	Feb	House of Lords abolished
	April	Diggers start work on St George's Hill; Levellers uprising quashed at Burford; Cromwell and Ireton sail for Ireland
	Sept	Siege of Drogheda
1650	June	*Mercurius Politicus* launched; Charles II lands in Scotland
	Sept	English army wins Battle of Dunbar
1651	Sept	Charles II and royalists defeated at Battle of Worcester
	Oct	Fall of the Isle of Man
1652	Feb	Act of Pardon and Oblivion; Act for the Settlement of Ireland
	Sept	Fleetwood and Petty arrive in Ireland
1653	April	Cromwell dismisses the Rump Parliament
	June–Dec	
	Dec	The Nominated Assembly dissolves itself
1653	Dec	***The PROTECTORATE Parliament and Lord Protector share sovereignty***
		Oliver Cromwell Lord Protector
		The *'Instrument of Government'* sets out constitution; Council of State to choose the Lord Protector's successor
1654	April	Act of Union passed between Scotland and England
1655	March	Penruddock's uprising
		The 'Down' Survey of Ireland begins; Failure of the Western Design expedition to the West Indies; Creation of the MAJOR GENERALS; Decimation tax levied; Henry Cromwell takes charge in Ireland
1656		
1657	Jan	Decimation tax defeated in parliament
	June	The *'Humble Petition and Advice'* sets out constitution; return of an Upper House of Parliament, Lord Protector to nominate his successor
1658	Sept	Oliver Cromwell dies
		Richard Cromwell Lord Protector
1659		
	April	Richard Cromwell ousted
1659		***The COMMONWEALTH restored***
	April	Army and Commonwealthsmen take control
	August	Booth's rebellion
	Oct	The army expels the Rump Parliament and seizes executive control
		General Monck declares his support for the expelled Rump
1660	Jan	Lord Fairfax takes York
	Feb	
		The RESTORATION OF THE MONARCHY: King Charles II (1660–85)
	April	
	May	Restoration of the monarchy voted through Parliament
1661	April	Thomas Venner's uprising

PARLIAMENT

The Long Parliament, 1642 until 'Pride's Purge' December 1642–8

The 'Rump' Parliament (Dec 1648–April 1653)

The Nominated Assembly ('Barebone's Parliament') (June–Dec 1653)

The First Protectorate Parliament (September 1654–Jan 1655)

The Second Protectorate Parliament (Sept 1656–Feb 1658)
First session: Sept 1656–June 1657

Second session: Jan–Feb 1658

The Third Protectorate (Richard Cromwell's) Parl. (Jan–April 1659)

The Rump Parliament recalled (1659–60)

The Long Parliament recalled (Feb 1660)

The Convention Parliament (1660)

The Cavalier Parliament (1661–79)

NOTES ON SOURCES

This book deals with a period in British history which has attracted a monumental amount of debate and discussion. I have not even attempted to reference the range and depth of scholarly work on the many areas the narrative touches upon. Instead, the notes are designed principally to identify the primary evidence for the lives and actions of the book's protagonists. Readers who wish to know more about politics and society in the period may want to explore this further reading list, and the sources cited therein.

FURTHER READING ON THE PERIOD

Barnard, Toby, *Cromwellian Ireland: English Government and Reform in Ireland 1649–1660* (Oxford, 1975, 2000 edn).

Braddick, Michael, ed., *The Oxford Handbook of the English Revolution* (Oxford, 2015).

Coward, Barry, *The Cromwellian Protectorate* (Manchester, 2002).

Dow, F. D., *Cromwellian Scotland 1651–1660* (Edinburgh, 1979).

Durston, Christopher, *Cromwell's Major-Generals: Godly Government during the English Revolution* (Manchester, 2001).

Holmes, Clive, *Why Was Charles I Executed?* (London, 2007).

Hutton, Ronald, *Restoration: A Political and Religious History of England and Wales, 1658–1667* (Oxford, 1986).

Kelsey, Sean, *Inventing a Republic: The Political Culture of the English Commonwealth, 1649–1653* (Stanford, 1997).

McElligott, Jason, and Smith, David L. (eds), *Royalists and Royalism During the Interregnum* (Manchester, 2010).

Woolych, Austin, *Britain in Revolution 1625–1660* (Oxford, 2002).

Worden, Blair, *The Rump Parliament* (Cambridge, 1974).

The *Oxford Dictionary of National Biography* has been extensively used throughout.

NOTES

ABBREVIATIONS

BL	British Library
Clarke Papers	*The Clarke Papers: Selections from the Papers of William Clarke*, C. H. Firth (ed.), 4 vols (London, 1901)
CRO	Cheshire Record Office
CSPD	*The Calendar of State Papers, Domestic: Interregnum*, Mary Anne Everett Green (ed.), 13 vols (London, 1875–86)
CSPV	*Calendar of State Papers and Manuscripts, Relating to English Affairs, in the Archives and Collections of Venice, and in other Libraries of Northern Italy*, Rawdon Brown (ed.), 38 vols (London, 1864–1947)
EHR	*English Historical Review*
HMC	*Historical Manuscripts Commission*
NRO	Norfolk Record Office
ODNB	*Oxford Dictionary of National Biography* (Oxford, 2004)
State Papers of John Thurloe	*A Collection of the State Papers of John Thurloe*, Thomas Birch (ed.), 7 vols (London, 1742)
TNA	National Archives
VCH	*Victoria County History*
Whitelocke, *Diary*	Bulstrode Whitelocke, *The Diary of Bulstrode Whitelocke*, Ruth Spalding (ed.) (Oxford, 1990)
Whitelock, *Memorials*	Bulstrode Whitelock, *Memorials of the English Affairs from the Beginning of the Reign of Charles the First to the Happy Restoration of Charles II*, 4 vols (Oxford, 1853)

1. THE FORCED REVOLUTION

1. Christopher Wilson, 'Henry III's Palace at Westminster', in Warwick Rodwell and Tim Tatton-Brown (eds), *Westminster. II. The Art, Architecture and Archaeology of the Royal Palace*, BAA Transactions, XXXIX, part II (Leeds, 2015), which argues that the January 1237 'parliament' met in the Painted Chamber; *A Short History of Parliament: England, Great Britain, the United Kingdom, Ireland and Scotland*, Clyve Jones (ed.) (Woodbridge, 2009),16; I am grateful to Dr Roland B. Harris for his advice on Westminster Palace.

2. *A Complete Collection of State Trials*, T. B. Howell (ed.), 21 vols (London, 1816–28), V, 1201; Bulstrode Whitelock, *Memorials of the English Affairs from the Beginning of the Reign of Charles the First to the Happy Restoration of Charles II*, 4 vols (Oxford, 1853), II, 499–501.

3. S. Kelsey, 'Bradshaw, John, Lord Bradshaw (b. 1602, d. 1659), lawyer, politician, and regicide', *Oxford Dictionary of National Biography*.

4. Cheshire Record Office (CRO), DX69, no. 11; *Ceremonies of Charles I: The Note Books of John Finet. Master of Ceremonies, 1628–1641* (New York, 1987), 296–7; Thomas Birch, *The Court and Times of Charles I*, 2 vols (London, 1848), 79; David Cressy, *Charles I and the People of England* (Oxford, 2015), 69.

5. Gilbert Mabbot, 'A Perfect Narrative', *State Trials*, IV, 994; *The Memoirs of Edmund Ludlow*, C. H. Firth (ed.), 2 vols (Oxford, 1894), I, 214; for the shortcomings of the *Memoirs* as a source, see Edmund Ludlow, *A Voyce from the Watch Tower*, A. B. Worden (ed.) (London, 1978); Blair Worden, 'Whig history and puritan politics: The *Memoirs* of Edmund Ludlow revisited', *Historical Research*, 75/188 (2002), 209–37; *Trial of King Charles I*, J. G. Muddiman (ed.) (Edinburgh and London, 1928), 'Bradshawe's Journal', 203–4, Bradshaw's entourage were to accompany him 'to and from this court and through Westminster'; J. Nalson, *A True Copy of the Journal of the High Court of Justice for the Trial of K. Charles I* (London, 1984); *The Moderate Intelligencer*, 200, January 1649.

6. *State Trials*, V, 1080.

7. For the life of the Bradshaw family, see the account book of Bradshaw's brother, Henry, CRO, DDX69/9, Henry Bradshaw of Marple's Account Book, 1638–1644. The only modern biography of Bradshaw is Richard Lee Bradshaw, *God's Battleaxe: The Life of Lord President John Bradshawe (1603–1659)* (Manhattan Beach, Ca., 2010)

8. Chester Archives and Local Studies, Diocese of Chester Parish Baptisms 1538–1911, St Mary's Stockport, John Bradshaw son of Henrye baptised 10 December 1602. Findmypast.co.uk; Samuel Yates, *A History of the Ancient Town and Borough of Congleton* (Congleton, 1820), 147.

9. CRO, DDX69/4, Mary Bradshaw to Mrs Newton, 29 January 1642.

10. 'A Letter from John Bradshawe of Gray's Inn to Sir Peter Legh of Lyme', *Chetham Miscellanies*, II, Chetham Society (Manchester, 1855). While the editor of the letter points out there was another JB at Gray's Inn at this time, the close links between JB of Marple and the Legh family, and the signature, make it highly likely this letter is from him; TNA, PROB/11/296, 457.

11. William Urwick, *Historical Sketches of Nonconformity in Cheshire* (London and Manchester, 1864), 151ff; R. Baldwin, Aldersey, Thomas (1521/2–1598), merchant. *Oxford Dictionary of National Biography*; *A History of the County of Chester*, Victoria County History, 5 vols (1979–2005), III, 249–50; 'Original correspondence of the Lord President Bradshaw', A. C. Gibson (ed.), *Transactions of the Historic Society of Lancashire and Cheshire*, new ser., 2 (1861–2), 41–74, 60, in which Bradshaw wrote to the parishioners of Feltham of 'prvyding you every Lords day and othr ffytting tymes an able & ffaythfull minister to dispense unto you ye mysteries of ye Gospell'. In Congleton, Bradshaw again had a distinguished Puritan clergyman: Dr Thomas Dod, nephew of a radical Calvinist John Dod, and himself famous for his eloquent oratory. Bradshaw may also have had a hand in the appointment of Dod's next but one successor, John Ley, who came to Congleton from Great Budworth, where Bradshaw had been involved in a legal case in the mid-1630s, CRO, DCN 1984/65/70.

12. Cheshire Historic Towns Survey. Bunbury. Archaeological Assessment. English Heritage. 2003; Peter Rutter, *The Haberdashers' Oldest School: A History of the Aldersey School, Bunbury 1594–1994* (Cambridge, 1993), 6–36; S. Guscott, 'Hinde, William (1568/9–1629)', *Oxford Dictionary of National Biography* (2004); *A History of the County of Chester*, 3, C. R. Elrington and B. E. Harris (eds) (London, 1980), 227, 249–50; Ronald Hutton, *The Rise and Fall of Merry England: The Ritual Year 1400–1700* (Oxford, 1994).

13. *Memorials of the Civil War in Cheshire and the Adjacent Counties … and Providence Improved by Edward Burghall*, James Hall (ed.), The Record Society for the Publication of Original Documents relating to Lancashire and Cheshire (1889), 1–2, 10–11.

14. *The Register of Admissions to Gray's Inn, 1521–1889, together with the Register of Marriages in Gray's Inn Chapel, 1695–1754*, Joseph Foster (ed.) (London, 1889), 162, 26 May 1620, 'John Bradshawe, son and heir of Henry B. of Marple, co. Chester, gent.'; E. K. Chambers, *The Elizabethan Stage*, 4 vols (London, 1923), III, 233–5. Peter Brereton was named as one of Bradshaw's three heirs in his will. Milton, 'The Second Defence of the People of England', *The Prose Works of John Milton*, Charles Symmons (ed.), 7 vols (London, 1806) VI, 413–14.

15. 'A Letter from John Bradshawe of Gray's Inn to Sir Peter Legh of Lyme';
    'Houses of students of the common law', in John Stow, *A Survey of London.
    Reprinted From the Text of 1603*, C. L. Kingsford (ed.), 2 vols (Oxford, 1908),
    I, 76–9.

16. *CSPD*, 1628–9, 27 March 1629, 504; *Memorials of the Civil War in Cheshire*, 2.

17. CRO, DDX69/4; CRO, DCN1984/65/70; Robert Head, *Congleton Past and
    Present* (Congleton, 1887), 87, 79; *Memorials of the Civil War in Cheshire*,
    1–18; Edward Hyde, Earl of Clarendon, *The History of the Rebellion and Civil
    Wars in England*, W. Dunn Macray (ed.), 6 vols (Oxford, 1888), IV, 474–5.
    See also John Milton's reference to JB's hospitality: Milton, 'The Second
    Defence of the People of England', 413–14; *CSPD*, 1639, 11 June 1639,
    264–322; J. Earwaker, *East Cheshire: past and present; or a history of the
    Hundred of Macclesfield ... From original records*, 2 vols (London, 1877), II,
    69; CRO, DDX69/10–11.

18. John Milton, *Milton: Poetical Works*, Douglas Bush (ed.) (London, 1966),
    48; Yates, *A History of the Ancient Borough and Town of Congleton*, 32–6; *Notes
    and Queries*, 6th series, IV, 1881, 199; Head, *Congleton Past and Present*,
    71–6; CRO, DDX/69, January 1640/1; see January 1638/9 and 'my shipp
    money' payments in Henry Bradshaw's account book; *Commons Journal*, 2,
    89. Henry Bradshaw owned a copy of Henry Elsyng's 'The Manner of
    Holding Parliaments', Parliamentary Archives, HC/LB/1/13.

19. Micheál Ó Siochrú, *God's Executioner: Oliver Cromwell and the Conquest of
    Ireland* (London, 2008), 22–32; *Commons Journal*, 3, 651, 674; Whitelock,
    Memorials of the English Affairs, I, 313; *State Trials*, IV, 653ff.

20. John Morrill, 'Sir William Brereton and England's Wars of Religion',
    Journal of British Studies, 24, 3 (Jul., 1985), 311–22; John Morrill, *Cheshire
    1630–1660: County Government and Society during the 'English Revolution'*
    (Oxford, 1974), ch. 2; *A Declaration and Ordinance of the Lords and Commons
    assembled in Parliament for the seizing and Sequestring of the estates ... of
    Notorious Delinquents* (London, 1643).

21. *Lords Journal*, V, 208.

22. *Memorials of the Civil War comprising the Correspondence of the Fairfax Family*,
    Robert Bell (ed.), 2 vols (London, 1849), I, 74–5; *The Journal of Thomas
    Juxon, 1644–1647*, Keith Lindley and David Scott (eds) (Cambridge,
    1999), 44; R. N. Dore, *The Civil Wars in Cheshire* (Chester, 1966), 33–9.

23. CRO, DDX69/9, Henry Bradshaw's account book, 23 May 1645; *Letter
    Books of Sir William Brereton*, R. N. Dore (ed.), 2 vols (1984, 1990), I, 100,
    158, 172, 422, 450–1.

24. *Letter Books of Sir William Brereton*, II, 470.

25. *Commons Journal*, VI, 93; Whitelock, *Memorials of the English Affairs*, II, 467;
    Memoirs of Edmund Ludlow, I, 208–9, 212; Ian Gentles, *The New Model Army*
    (Oxford, 1992), 276–83.

2. A NEW ENGLAND

1. Kevin Sharpe, *Sir Robert Cotton, 1586–1631: History and Politics in Early Modern England* (Oxford, 1979); C. G. C. Tite, *The Manuscript Library of Sir Robert Cotton*, Panizzi Lectures, 1993 (London, 1994); *Wren Society*, XI, Sir John Cotton's house; 'John Bradshawe's Journal', *Trial of King Charles I*, Muddiman (ed.), 203–4.

2. *Mercurius Elencticus*, 1647, 21–28 June 1648, 8; *State Trials*, IV, 653ff, 1128; *Lords Journal*, 8, 13 February 1646, 163–6; Kelsey, 'John Bradshaw', *ODNB*.

3. *Letter Books of Sir William Brereton*, II, 208; Morrill, *Cheshire*, 231; *State Trials*, V, 1089–90.

4. As Bradshaw put it to Charles I at the trial, 'God hath reserved better things for us and has pleased for to confound your designs, and to break your forces', *State Trials*, IV, 1011; *Commons Journal*, VI, 3 January 1649, 109–10.

5. *Memoirs of Edmund Ludlow*, I, 208–9; Whitelock, *Memorials of the English Affairs*, II, 474.

6. 'John Bradshaw's Journal', *Trial of King Charles I*, Muddiman (ed.), 198; J. Nalson, 'A Journal of the High-Court of Justice, for the Trial of King Charles', *State Trials*, IV, 1054–8; Mabbot, 'A perfect narrative of the whole proceedings of the High Court of Justice', *State Trials*, IV, 1017; *The Diary of Bulstrode Whitelocke*, Ruth Spalding (ed.) (Oxford, 1990), 227; Clarendon, *History of the Rebellion*, IV, 474–6; Hutchinson put it 'God would require at their hands all the blood and desolation which should ensue by their suffering him to escape, when God had brought him into their hands', Lucy Hutchinson, *Memoir of the Life of Colonel Hutchinson* (London, 1973) 189–90.

7. *Memoirs of Edmund Ludlow*, I, 214–16; Whitelock, *Memorials of the English Affairs*, II, 480. The literature on the trial of Charles I is considerable, and I have made no attempt to reference it fully here, concentrating instead on contemporary sources. For recent debates see Sean Kelsey, 'The death of Charles I', *Historical Journal*, 45, 4 (2002), 727–54; 'Staging the trial of Charles I', in Jason Peacey (ed.), *The Regicides and the Execution of Charles I* (Basingstoke, 2001), 71–93, 'Politics and procedure in the trial of Charles I', *Law and History Review*, Spring 2004, 22 (1), 1–25, and Clive Holmes, 'The Trial and Execution of Charles I', *Historical Journal*, 53, 2 (2010), 289–316.

8. Mabbot, 'A Perfect Narrative', *State Trials*, IV, 993–4; 'John Bradshaw's Journal', *Trial of King Charles I*, Muddiman (ed.), 208.

9. *State Trials*, V, 1079–82, 1086; Mabbot, 'A Perfect Narrative', *State Trials*, IV, 994–5; Hutchinson, *Memoir of the Life of Colonel Hutchinson*, 190–1; Whitelock, *Memorials of the English Affairs*, 499–500.

10. *State Trials*, V, 1078–84; Mabbot, 'A Perfect Narrative', *State Trials*, IV, 995–6; Whitelocke, *Memorials of the English Affairs*, II, 499–501.

11. Mabbot, 'A Perfect Narrative', *State Trials*, IV, 999.

12. Clarendon, *History of the Rebellion*, IV, 486–7; *State Trials*, V, 1148, 1151, 1153; *Trial of King Charles I*, Muddiman (ed.), 71–4.

13. Mabbot, 'A Perfect Narrative', *State Trials*, IV, 1004; Clarendon, *History of the Rebellion*, IV, 486–7; *State Trials*, V, 1215.

14. Nalson, 'Journal of the High Court of Justice', *State Trials*, IV, 1102–11. See the recent work of Sean Kelsey and Clive Holmes, referenced above, for the debate on whether or not the outcome of the trial was a foregone conclusion.

15. 'John Bradshaw's Journal', *Trial of Charles I*, Muddiman (ed.), 21; J. F. Merritt, 'Reinventing Westminster Abbey, 1642–1660: a house of Kings from Revolution to Restoration', *The Journal of Ecclesiastical History*, 67, 1, January 2016, 122–38; Mabbot, 'A Perfect Narrative', *State Trials*, IV, 1004.

16. *State Trials*, V, 1148, 1153.

17. *State Trials*, IV, 1125–30; *State Trials*, V, 1211–14; *The Memoirs of Edmund Ludlow*, I, 216–20; 'John Bradshaw's Journal', *Trial of King Charles I*, Muddiman (ed.), 225; Whitelock, *Memorials of the English Affairs*, II, 509–10; Clive Holmes, 'The Trial and Execution of Charles I', *Historical Journal*, 53, 2 (2010), 289–316, 304.

18. Roger Manley, *The History of the Rebellions in England, Scotland and Ireland* (London, 1691), 200.

19. *CSPD*, 1648–9, 350–3; *Trial of King Charles I*, Muddiman (ed.), ix–xi, 230; TNA, PROB11/296.

20. Whitelock, *Memorials of the English Affairs*, II, 481; *State Trials*, V, 1123.

21. *Commons Journal*, VI, 132–3; Whitelocke, *Diary*, 230; Whitelock, *Memorials of the English Affairs*, III, 22; *Memoirs of Edmund Ludlow*, II, 220–1; Blair Worden, *The Rump Parliament 1648–1653* (Cambridge, 1974), 172; *CSPD*, 1649–50, 6; 11 May 1649, 'An Act Declaring and Constituting the People of England to be a Commonwealth and Free-State', *Acts and Ordinances of the Interregnum, 1642–1660*, 122. The word 'Commonwealth' had a variety of meanings in early seventeenth-century England: general or common good, a state or body-politic and, specifically, a republic, OED.

22. Westminster Abbey Muniments, 42,756B-E, 42,755; I am grateful to Professor Warwick Rodwell for his advice on the Westminster Deanery.

23. Sean Kelsey, 'Constructing the Council of State', *Parliamentary History*, Vol. 22, pt 3 (2003), 217–41.

24. TNA, SP25/62, fol. 71; Whitelocke, *Diary*, 234; Whitelock, *Memorials of the English Affairs*, II, 552; for Bradshaw's assiduous attendance of the

Council of State for the whole Commonwealth/Rump period, 1649–53, see the lists in the preface to *CSPD*, 1649–50, 1650, 1651–2 and 1652–3.

25. Whitelocke, *Diary*, 255; BL, Add MS 37,345, fol. 54r-v.

26. BL, Add MS 78258, nos 52, 58, 63, 121; Hutchinson, *Memoir of the Life of Colonel Hutchinson*, 201–2. 'Bradshaw himself, as stout-hearted as he was, privately could not conceal his fear' at the prospect of a Scottish/royalist army marching towards London in 1651.

27. Payne Fisher, *Veni, Vidi, Vici: the Triumph of the most execellent and illustrious Oliver Cromwell* (London, 1652).

3. UTOPIA

1. Whitelocke, *Diary*, 446; John Gurney, *Brave Community: The Digger Movement in the English Revolution* (Manchester, 2007), 1–62; 'The New Law of Righteousness', *The Complete Works of Gerrard Winstanley*, Thomas N. Corns, Ann Hughes and David Loewenstein (eds), 2 vols (Oxford, 2009), I, 476; *A History of the County of Surrey*, Victoria County History, H. E. Malden (ed.) (London, 1911), III, 442–7; a house associated with one of the Diggers, Anthony Wrenn, still stands on the Ridings, *The Surrey Diggers Trail: Sites Associated with the Movement 1649–50*, printed pamphlet, the Elmbridge Diggers Heritage Group.

2. 'A Watch-Word to the City of London', *Complete Works of Gerrard Winstanley*, II, 80; *The Clarke Papers: Selections from the Papers of William Clarke*, C. H. Firth (ed.), 4 vols (London, 1901), II, 209–12; Whitelock, *Memorials of the English Affairs*, III, 17.

3. Steve Hindle, 'Dearth and the English Revolution: the harvest crisis of 1647–50', *Economic History Review*, New Series, 61, S1, 2008, 64–98; Whitelock, *Memorials of the English Affairs*, III, 24, 25, 40; Stephen Porter, *Destruction in the English Civil Wars* (Stroud, 1994), ch. 4.

4. Gurney, *Brave Community*, 62–9; James D. Alsop, 'Gerrard Winstanley: What do we know of his life', in Andrew Bradstock (ed.), *Winstanley and the Diggers*, Prose Studies, 22, 2, August 1999, 1936. For the nature of apprenticeships see Daniel Defoe, *The Complete English Tradesman* (London, 1726).

5. *Complete Works of Gerrard Winstanley*, I, 9; Alsop, 'Gerrard Winstanley: What do we know of his life', 23–4; Ann Saunders and John Schofield, *Tudor London: A Map and a Plan* (London, 2001); John Stow, *A Survey of London*, 2 vols (Oxford, 1908), I, 81, 276–82, 288–90; William Herbert, *The History of the Twelve Great Livery Companies*, 2 vols (London, 1834), I, 225–96; II, 383–525; Matthew Davies and Ann Saunders, *The History of the Merchant Taylors' Company* (Leeds, 2004), 127–41.

6. J. D. Alsop, 'Ethics in the Marketplace: Gerrard Winstanley's London Bankruptcy, 1643', *Journal of British Studies*, 28 (April 1989), 97–119; R. J. Dalton, 'Gerrard Winstanley, the experience of fraud', *Historical Journal*, 34, 4, 1991, 973–84; *Complete Works of Gerrard Winstanley*, I, 9; 'Saints Paradise', I, 344.

7. *Complete Works of Gerrard Winstanley*, I, 10; John Gurney, *Gerrard Winstanley: The Digger's Life and Legacy* (London, 2013), 19.

8. 'A Watch-Word to the City of London', *Complete Works of Gerrard Winstanley*, II, 80.

9. Gentles, *The New Model Army*, 45–7; 'A Watch-Word to the City of London', *Complete Works of Gerrard Winstanley*, II, 80; Charles Carlton, *Going to the Wars: The Experience of the British Civil Wars, 1638–1651* (London and New York, 1992).

10. *The Constitutional Documents of the Puritan Revolution*, S. R. Gardiner (ed.), 3rd edn (Oxford, 1908), 267–71; 'The True Levellers Standard Advanced', *Complete Works of Gerrard Winstanley*, II, 1–31; 'An Appeal to the House of Commons', 65–79; Davies and Saunders, *The History of the Merchant Taylors' Company*, ch. 12.

11. 'A Watch-Word to the City of London', *Complete Works of Gerrard Winstanley*, II, 80; 'The True Levellers Standard Advanced', ibid., 1–31; Whitelock, *Memorials of the English Affairs*, III, 19; Winstanley had lived in towns until coming to Cobham in 1643/4, his writings of 1648–50 are rich with reference to the countryside and seasons.

12. 'The New Law of Righteousness', *Complete Works of Gerrard Winstanley*, I, 472–568, 485; 'A Watch-Word to the City of London', II, 80–1.

13. *Clarke Papers*, II, 209–11; CSPD, 1649–50, 6.

14. 'The Agreement of the People, as presented to the Council of the Army', 1647, *Constitutional Documents of the Puritan Revolution*, 333–5; *A Short History of Parliament*, 7–11; John Hostettler and Brian Block, *Voting in Britain: A History of the Parliamentary Franchise* (Chichester, 2001), 27–9.

15. 'The Agreement of the People', 1649, *Constitutional Documents of the Puritan Revolution*, 359–71; Hutchinson, *Memoir of the Life of Colonel Hutchinson*, 191.

16. *Clarke Papers*, II, 209–12; CSPD, 1649–50, 93–5; Whitelock, *Memorials of the English Affairs*, III, 17.

17. CSPD, 1649–50, 172, 182; Simon Thurley, *Whitehall Palace: An Architectural History of the Royal Apartments 1260–1698* (London and New Haven, 1999), 96–8; Whitelock, *Memorials of the English Affairs*, II, 477; *State Trials*, V, 1147.

18. CSPD, 1649–50, 8, 83, 172; *Clarke Papers*, II, 211–12; *Commons Journal*, VI, 119; *The Diary of John Evelyn*, E. S. De Beer (ed.), 6 vols (Oxford, 1955), II, 551; Sidney J. Madge, *The Domesday of Crown Lands* (London, 1928); *The*

Late King's Goods: Collections, Possessions and Patronage of Charles I in the Light of the Commonwealth Sale Inventories, Arthur MacGregor (ed.) (London and Oxford, 1989).

19. *The Declaration and Standard of the Levellers of England delivered in a Speech to his Excellency the Lord Gen. Fairfax, on Friday last at White-Hall* (London, 1649); *The Complete Works of Gerrard Winstanley*, I, 31; Whitelock, *Memorials of the English Affairs*, III, 19; Andrew Hopper, *'Black Tom': Sir Thomas Fairfax and the English Revolution* (Manchester, 2010), ch. 6, 159; 'A Letter to the Lord Fairfax and his Councell of War', *Complete Works of Gerrard Winstanley*, II, 43.

20. 'The True Levellers Standard Advanced', *Complete Works of Gerrard Winstanley*, II, 1–31; Peter W. M. Blayney, *The Bookshops in Paul's Cross Churchyard*, Occasional Papers of the Bibliographical Society, 5 (1990); Ariel Hessayon, *'Gold Tried in the Fire': The Prophet TheaurauJohn Tany and the English Revolution* (Aldershot, 2007), 192.

4. THE EBBING TIDE

1. Whitelock, *Memorials of the English Affairs*, III, 24.

2. *CSPD*, 1649, 143; Whitelock, *Memorials of the English Affairs*, III, 26, 31; *Perfect Occurrences of Every Dayes Journall in Parliament*, 121, 20–27 April 1649, 987; Gentles, *The New Model Army*, 350–3; Ó Siochrú, *God's Executioner*.

3. 'A Declaration to the Powers of England (The True Levellers Standard Advanced)', in *Complete Works of Gerrard Winstanley*, II, 1; *Clarke Papers*, II, 209–11; *The Speeches of the Lord Generall Fairfax and the Officers of the Army to the Diggers at St George's Hill Surrey* (London, 1649).

4. Gurney, *Brave Community*, 128–34; John Platt would search in vain for evidence of the Diggers being put up to their actions by someone else, 'you ... that sat in counsel at the White Lion at Cobham to find out who are our backers', 78; 'Watch-Word to the City of London', *Complete Works of Gerrard Winstanley*, II, 98; John Gurney, 'Gerrard Winstanley and the Digger movement in Walton and Cobham', *Historical Journal*, 37, 4 (1994), 775–802.

5. *The Speeches of Lord Generall Fairfax* (London, 1649); 'A Letter to the Lord Fairfax and his Council of War', *Complete Works of Gerrard Winstanley*, II, 43–59.

6. Gurney, *Brave Community*, 77; 'An Ordinance for the punishing of Blasphemies and Heresies, with the several penalties therein expressed', May 1648, *Acts and Ordinances of the Interregnum*, 1133–6.

7. 'A Letter to the Lord Fairfax and his Council of War', *Complete Works of Gerrard Winstanley*, II, 44; *Speeches of the Lord Generall Fairfax*; John Gurney,

'"Furious divells"? the Diggers and their opponents', in Andrew Bradstock (ed.), *Winstanley and the Diggers 1649–1999* (London, 2000), 73–86.

8. *Speeches of the Lord Generall Fairfax; The Complete Works of Gerrard Winstanley*, I, 30–1; 'A New Yeers Gift for the Parliament and Armie'; ibid., II, 146–7; 'A Letter to the Lord Fairfax and his Council of War', ibid., II, 43–59.

9. 'A Watch-Word to the City of London', *Complete Works of Gerrard Winstanley*, II, 79–107; 'A New Yeers Gift', ibid., 107–61, 'One of the officers of the court told a friend of mine, that if the Diggers' cause was good, he would pick out such a jury as should overthrow him'.

10. 'Watch-Word to the City of London', *Complete Works of Gerrard Winstanley*, II, 81, 90.

11. Whitelock, *Memorials of the English Affairs*, III, 26, 67; 'So that old whores, and old laws, picks men's pockets and undoes them', 'A New Yeers Gift for Parliament and Armie', *Complete Works of Gerrard Winstanley*, II, 113.

12. Hopper, *Black Tom*, 110; Worden, *The Rump Parliament*, chs 9 and 10; HMC *Fifth Report*, 180.

13. 'A Watch-Word to the City of London', *Complete Works of Gerrard Winstanley*, II, 93, 98; Gurney, 'Gerrard Winstanley and the Digger Movement in Walton and Cobham'.

14. 'A Watch-Word to the City of London', *Complete Works of Gerrard Winstanley*, II, 92–3. I have modernized his language for clearer meaning here, Winstanley talks of 'Snapsack boys' and 'ammunition drabs' or 'sluts'. 'A New Yeers Gift', ibid., II, 117–120; BL, Egerton MS 2618, fol. 40r.

15. 'A New Yeers Gift', *Complete Works of Gerrard Winstanley*, II, 117, 123, 140, 146–7; CSPD, 1649–50, 335–6.

16. 'An Appeal to All Englishmen', *Complete Works of Gerrard Winstanley*, II, 243–55.

17. 'A New Yeers Gift', *Complete Works of Gerrard Winstanley*, II, 143.

18. 'An Humble Request', *Complete Works of Gerrard Winstanley*, II, 255–72; Introduction, ibid., 39.

19. 'A New Yeers Gift', *Complete Works of Gerrard Winstanley*, II, 144–5; 'An Appeal to the House of Commons', ibid., II, 72.

5. COUNTER-REVOLUTION

1. *The Lady of Latham: being the Life and Original Letters of Charlotte de la Trémoille*, Henriette Elizabeth Guizot de Witt (ed.) (London, 1869), 13; TNA, SP19/147, no. 40 for the furniture and furnishing of Castle Rushen during the Derbys' residence'; 'Unpublished documents in the Manx Museum. From the Castle Rushen Papers', *Journal of the Manx Museum*,

March 1931, II, 26, 9–14; 'Castle Rushen, Castletown, Isle of Man, Conservation Plan', Drury McPherson Partnership commissioned by Manx National Heritage, June 2012. I am grateful to Dr Paul Drury for kindly sharing with me his extensive work on Castle Rushen.

2. *The Stanley Papers*, William Ffarington, F. R. Raines et al. (eds) (*Chetham Society*, 29, 31, 66, 67, 70), 3 vols (Manchester, 1853–67), III, xii, xv; Mary Anne Everett Green, *The Lives of the Princesses*, 6 vols (London, 1849–55), V, 456–7; *The Lady of Latham*, 13; Barry Coward, *The Stanleys, Lords Stanley and Earls of Derby 1385–1672: The Origins, Wealth and Power of a Landowning Family* (Manchester, 1983).

3. *The Lady of Latham*, 145–6.

4. *A History of the Isle of Man written by William Blundell of Crosby Lancaster, 1648–1656*, William Harrison (ed.), 2 vols (Douglas, 1876–7), I, ch. XI; Clarendon, *History of the Rebellion*, V, 184–5; Elias Ashmole, *Order of the Garter* (London, 1672), 717; *Letters and Papers illustrating the relations between Charles the Second and Scotland in 1650*, S. R. Gardiner (ed.) (Edinburgh, 1894), 21, 41; Lord Derby wore the Garter insignia until he gave them to his son just before his execution, *State Trials*, V, 310.

5. *A Journal of the Siege of Lathom House in Lancashire Defended by Charlotte de la Tremouille Countess of Derby against Sir Thomas Fairfax Kt* (London, 1823), 14–15, 50–52; *Stanley Papers*, III, lxxxviii, c–ci; *Memorials of the Civil War Comprising the Correspondence of the Fairfax Family*, I, 87–8.

6. CSPD, 1635, 36–7.

7. *Stanley Papers*, III, xviii, xxxv, 106; Francis Peck, *Desiderata Curiosa* (London, 1779), 430; *The Lady of Latham*, 25–6; Clarendon, *History of the Rebellion*, II, 470–1; *Journal of the Siege of Lathom House*, 14; CSPD, 1635, 36–7.

8. Clarendon, *History of the Rebellion*, V, 184–5; CSPD, 1635, 36–7; Sandy Riley, *Charlotte de La Trémoïlle, the Notorious Countess of Derby* (Cambridge, 2017), 47–8.

9. For the flora and fauna of the Isle of Man, see Thomas Chaloner, *A Short Treatise of the Isle of Man* (London, 1656); TNA, SP19/147, fol. 79; *A History of the Isle of Man written by William Blundell*, I, chs viii and xi; TNA, SP19/147, fols 16–17, 78, 79; see also Katharine A. Walker, 'The military activities of Charlotte de la Trémoille, Countess of Derby, during the Civil War and Interregnum', *Northern History*, XXXVIII, 1, March 2001, 47–64; *Stanley Papers*, III, clxiv; *The Lady of Latham*, 143–4.

10. *The Lady of Latham*, 140–1.

11. *Harleian Miscellany*, V (London, 1810), 566–7; Gilbert Burton, *The Life of Sir Philip Musgrave, bart., of Hartley Castle, Co. Westmorland, and of Edenhall, Co. Cumberland. Governor of the City of Carlisle, &c* (Carlisle, 1840), 20–1;

Mona Miscellany: a Selection of Proverbs, Sayings, Ballads, Customs ... and Legends, Peculiar to the Isle of Man, William Harrison (ed.), Manx Society, XXI (Douglas, 1873), 258. For the Manx love of the violin see Chaloner, *A Short Treatise of the Isle of Man*, 5.

12. *The Lady of Latham*, 24, 25–6.

13. *Stanley Papers*, III, lxvii, ccxxv–vi; *Illiam Dhone and the Manx Rebellion, 1651*, W. Harrison (ed.), The Manx Society, XXVI (Douglas, 1877), 105–6; *Farington Papers: the Shrievalty of William Ffarington Esq*, Susan Maria Ffarington (ed.), Chetham Society (Manchester, 1856), 66, 67.

14. Clarendon, *History of the Rebellion*, II, 470–1; Peck, *Desiderata Curiosa*, 430; *Stanley Papers*, III, 30, 32–3, 38; 'Castle Rushen, Castletown, Isle of Man, Conservation Plan', Drury McPherson Partnership, 105.

15. *Stanley Papers*, III, 28; Riley, *Charlotte de La Trémoïlle*.

16. *The Lady of Latham*, 11, 13, 35, 36, 185–6; *Stanley Papers*, III, 38.

17. *The Lady of Latham*, 19, 30–31.

18. *The Lordship of Man under the Stanleys*, 15–26; TNA, SP19/147, Inventory of Peel Castle, 89–90.

19. TNA, SP20, Sequestration Committee: Books and Papers; Joan Thirsk (ed.), *The Agrarian History of England and Wales*, 8 vols (Cambridge, 1985), V(II), ch. 14; ibid., 'The sales of Royalist land during the Interregnum', *Economic History Review*, NS, V, no. 2 (1952), 188–207; H. J. Habakkuk, 'Landowners and the Civil War', *Economic History Review*, 18, 1 (1965), 130–51; Gardiner, *The History of the Great Civil War*, I, 231.

20. *The Lady of Latham*, 131; CSPD, 1649–50, 277; BL, Add MS 78238, fol. 8; Sonja Kmec, *Across the Channel: Noblewomen in Seventeenth Century France and England: a Study of the Lives of Marie de La Tour, 'Queen of the Huguenots', and Charlotte de la Trémoïlle, Countess of Derby* (Trier, 2010), 235; *The Calendar of the Committee for Compounding*, Mary Anne Everett Green (ed.), 5 vols (London, 1889–92), II, 1100ff.

21. *The Lady of Latham*, 127–8.

22. *The Lady of Latham*, 151.

23. CSPD, 1650, 5 June 1650, 188; *Letters and Papers illustrating the relations between Charles the Second and Scotland*, 'Second Report of Colonel Keane', 100.

24. Whitelocke, *Diary*, 260; Hutchinson, *Memoir of the Life of Colonel Hutchinson*, 193–6; *Memoirs of Edmund Ludlow*, I, 244–8; *Commons Journal*, VI, 26 June 1650, 432.

25. *The Lady of Latham*, 154–5; *Stanley Papers*, III, 3; TNA, SP19/147, no. 16.

26. *The Lady of Latham*, 162, 183–4; *Stanley Papers*, III, clxvi–clxviii; TNA, SP19/147, no. 17, fos 43–5; *Mercurius Politicus*, 63, 14–21 August 1651.

27. *Stanley Papers*, III, 6–7; *The Lady of Latham*, 132–4, 143–4; Clarendon, *History of the Rebellion*, V, 184–5.

28. *Illiam Dhone*, 105–6.

29. Chaloner, *A Short Treatise of the Isle of Man*; *Illiam Dhone*, 25–7.

30. TNA, SP19/147, fos 12–13; no. 17, fos 43–5, Fox 'saw the Picture of the said Scots King in her the said Countess hand, which shee said shee had sent her in the absence of the saide Earle'; *Stanley Papers*, III, clxxiv.

31. TNA, SP19/147, no. 17, fos 43–5, testimony of Major John Fox.

32. *Mercurius Politicus*, 64, 21–28 April 1651; 65, 28 August–4 September 1649; TNA, SP19/147, no. 17, fos 43–5, testimony of Major John Fox of Toxteth Park.

33. *Mercurius Politicus*, 55, 19–26 June 1651; 64, 21–28 August 1651.

34. *Stanley Papers*, III, cxciv; *Memoirs of Edmund Ludlow*, I, 280; CSPD, 1651, 395; *Mercurius Politicus*, 65, 28 August–4 September 1651.

6. VIRAGO

1. Hutchinson, *Memoir of the Life of Colonel Hutchinson*, 202.

2. *The Lady of Latham*, 162; Burton, *The Life of Sir Philip Musgrave*, 23; *Mercurius Politicus*, 63, 14–21 August 1651.

3. *The Lady of Latham*, 125.

4. *A Journal of the Siege of Lathom House*, 17.

5. *Charles II's Escape from Worcester*, William Matthews (ed.) (London, 1967), 88–9; *Stanley Papers*, III, v–cvii.

6. *Stanley Papers*, III, cxcvi; *The Lady of Latham*, 34, 171–4. Quarter being 'Exemption from being immediately put to death granted to a vanquished opponent by the victor in a battle or fight; clemency or mercy shown in sparing the life of a person who surrenders.' OED.

7. Whitelocke, *Diary*, 271; *Mercurius Politicus*, 67, 11–18 September 1651.

8. *CSPD*, 1651, 405, 421, 422–4; *Stanley Papers*, III, cc–cci.

9. TNA, SP25/96, fol. 545, 561; *Mercurius Politicus*, 69, 25 September–2 October 1649; 70, 2–9 October 1651.

10. *The Lady of Latham*, 184–6; *Stanley Papers*, III, cc–cci.

11. *Illiam Dhone*, 9, 23–4.

12. TNA, SP19/147, no. 17, 'the Countesse herself went & drew out some forces to man Derby ffort when Capt Young in the President ffrigate was shooting agt it'; *Perfect Account of the Daily Intelligence from the Armies*, 8–15 October 1651, 2; *Mercurius Politicus*, 70, 2–9 October 1651; Leo Miller, *John Milton and the Oldenburg Safeguard. Diaries and Letters of Herman Mylius* (New York, 1985), 71–2.

13. TNA, SP19/147, testimony of Thomas Birch, 7 May 1652; testimony of Colonel Robert Duckenfield, 8 May 1652; testimony of Major John Fox, no 17, fos 43–5.

14. *Illiam Dhone*, 9, 10–11, the examinations of Sir Robert Norris of Douglas and Hugh Moore of Douglas; TNA, SP19/147, testimony of Thomas Birch, 7 May 1652; testimony of Major John Fox, no. 17, fos 43–5; *Stanley Papers*, III, ccxliii.
15. CSPD, 1651, 459, 470; *State Trials*, V, 295–6; George Ormerod, *Tracts Relating to Military Proceedings in Lancashire during the Great Civil War* (Manchester, 1844), 311–24.
16. *State Trials*, V, 295; George Ormerod, *The History of the County Palatine and City of Chester*, 3 vols, III (London, 1819), 409–11; *Mercurius Politicus*, 72, 16–23 October 1651; CSPD, 1651, 473; Coward, *The Stanleys*, 172–5.
17. *Commons Journal*, VII, 27; *Stanley Papers*, III, ccxlv; ccxxvi–ccxxvii; *Mercurius Politicus*, 72, 16–23 October 1651; *The Lady of Latham*, 192–5; Woolrych, *Britain in Revolution*, 506.
18. *The Lordship of Man under the Stanleys*, 65; TNA, SP19/147, no. 24, evidence of Philip More of Man; testimony of Colonel Robert Duckenfield, 25–7. The use of this metaphor in the context of the Derbys was well established, a newspaper of 1645 describing Lady Derby, in her defence of Lathom House, as one who had 'stole the Earles breeches', *The Scotish Dove*, 112, 3–10 December 1645, 887.
19. *Illiam Dhone*, 9, 12–13, 16–17, 25–7.
20. TNA, SP19/147, 87–90, Inventory of Peel Castle, 3 November 1651; the 'countess had before sent the most part & best of her goods to Castle Peel', ibid., testimony of Major John Fox, no 17, fos 43–5.
21. *The Life of Sir Philip Musgrave*, 24; *Illiam Dhone*, 12–13, 27, 36–8; *Mercurius Politicus*, 75, 6–12 November 1651.
22. TNA, SP19/147, 64, examination of Walter Jones, 24 August 1652; *The Life of Sir Philip Musgrave*, 24–5.
23. *The Life of Sir Philip Musgrave*, 24–5; *Mercurius Politicus*, 75, 6–12 November 1651; TNA, SP19/147, testimony of Colonel Robert Duckenfield, 25–7.
24. *Mercurius Politicus*, 75, 6–12 November 1651; TNA, SP19/147, testimony of Thomas Birch 7 May 1652.
25. TNA, SP19/147, 25–7, testimony of Colonel Robert Duckenfield, 8 May 1652.
26. *Mercurius Politicus*, 75, 6–12 November 1651.
27. TNA, SP19/147, 25–7, testimony of Colonel Robert Duckenfield, 8 May 1652.
28. TNA, SP19/147, no. 40, Inventory of Castle Rushen, 9 November 1651.
29. *Mercurius Politicus*, 75, 6–12 November 1651; TNA, SP19/147, 25–7, testimony of Colonel Robert Duckenfield, 8 May 1652; *The Life of Sir Philip Musgrave*, 27.

30. *The Life of Sir Philip Musgrave*, 28; *Mercurius Politicus*, 75, 6–12 November 1651; TNA, SP19/147, 103. no. 44, 'surrendred that Castle ... wthout so much as reading them over'.

31. *Commons Journal*, VII, 1651–1660, 35.

32. *Perfect Diurnall of Some Passages and Proceedings*, 101, 10–17 November 1651, 1; *Commons Journal*, VII, 35.

33. *The Lady of Latham*, 209–10.

34. Lodewijck Huygens, *The English Journal 1651-2* (Leiden, 1982), 50–3. Charlotte and Constantijn Huygens corresponded warmly through the 1630s.

35. *Commons Journal*, VI, 604; *Acts and Ordinances of the Interregnum*, 520–45.

36. H. J. Habakkuk, 'Landowners and the Civil War', 130–51; Thirsk (ed.), *The Agrarian History of England and Wales*, 119–45; *Commons Journal*, VII, 24 February 1652, 95.

37. *The Lady of Latham*, 209–10, 218; CSPD, 1654, 253.

38. *The Lady of Latham*, 230.

39. *Calendar of the Committee for the Advance of Money*, 3, 1650–55, 1310; *Stanley Papers*, III, xxiv–xxv; *Commons Journal*, VII, 331–2; TNA, SP19/147, 103, no. 44; Schedule of silver, 11 April 1653; Kmec, *Across the Channel*, 238–40; Melanie Harrington, 'The earl of Derby and his tenants: sales of Royalist hand during the Interregnum revisited', *Economic History Review*, 64, 4 (2011), 1195–1217.

40. *The Lady of Latham*, 218.

41. *Calendar of the Committee of Compounding*, II, 1100; Brian Fairfax, *A Catalogue of the Curious Collection of Pictures ... with the Life of George Villiers, Duke of Buckingham* (London, 1758), 30; *Stanley Papers*, III, ccclxxxiv; BL, Add MS 71448, fol. 34r. When Lady Derby died decades later Fairfax's secretary John Rushworth was one of the two executors of her will.

7. THE INFAMOUS CASTLE OF MISERY

1. Stow, *A Survey of London*, I, 35–8; James Howell, *Londinopolis an historicall discourse or perlustration of the city of London* (London, 1657), 316–17; Caroline Barron, *London in the Later Middle Ages: Government and People 1200–1500* (Oxford, 2004), 165–6.

2. Margery Bassett, 'Newgate Prison in the Middle Ages', *Speculum* 18 (2) (1943), 233–46; Huygens, *English Journal*, 161; Ralph B. Pugh, *Imprisonment in Medieval England* (Cambridge, 1986), 103–9; Allan Brodie, Jane Croom and James O. Davies, *English Prisons: An Architectural History* (Swindon, 2002), 9–29.

3. Richard Overton, *The Commoners Complaint: or a Dreadful Warning from Newgate* (London, 1647); *The Oxinden and Peyton Letters, 1642–1670. Being*

*the correspondence of Henry Oxinden of Barham, Sir Thomas Peyton of
Knowlton, and their circle*, Dorothy Gardiner (ed.) (London, 1937), 146–50;
Mercurius Pragmaticus (for King Charles II), 2, 24 April–1 May 1649.

4. *Mercurius Pragmaticus (for King Charles II)*, 9, 12–19 June 1649.

5. *Mercurius Pragmaticus (for King Charles II)*, 1, 17–24 April 1649; 8, 5–12
June 1649.

6. Joseph Frank, *The Beginnings of the English Newspaper, 1620–1660*
(Cambridge, Mass., 1961), 162; Marcus Nevitt, *Women and the Pamphlet
Culture of Revolutionary England 1640–1660* (Aldershot, 2006), 93–112;
CSPD, 1651–2, 39–41; *Mercurius Pragmaticus*, 45, 13–20 February 1649;
CSPD, 1649–50, 537; Jason Peacey, *Politicians and Pamphleteers, Propaganda
During the Civil Wars and Interregnum* (Aldershot, 2004), 152–7; *The
Oxinden and Peyton Letters*, 144–5.

7. Bassett, 'Newgate Prison in the Middle Ages'; *Aulicus his Hue and Cry sent
forth after Britanicus* (London, 1645), 4, for the new corded bed and the
basket of capons that Newgate prisoners of means might expect; *Bloody
Newes from Enfield* (London, 1659); *A true and perfect list of the names of those
prisoners in Newgate ... February 18. 1651* (London, 1652); George Fidge,
The English Gusman; or The history of that unparallel'd thief James Hind
(London, 1652), 40–5; Overton, *The Commoners Complaint*, 14–15. As a
gentleman of some means, Nedham almost certainly lodged in such a
room. See, for instance, T. Connor, 'Malignant reading: John Squier's
Newgate prison library, 1642–46', *The Library*, 7th series, 7 (3), June 2006,
160–1; *Anna Trapnel's Report and Plea*, Hilary Hinds (ed.), Medieval and
Renaissance Texts and Studies, 503 (Toronto, 2006), 110–11.

8. Frank, *The Beginnings of the English Newspaper*, 3–13; Peacey, *Politicians and
Pamphleteers*.

9. Joad Raymond, *The Invention of the Newspaper: English Newsbooks 1641–
1649* (Oxford, 1996), 240–80; Roleand Harms, Joad Raymond and
Jeroen Salmans (eds), *Not Dead Things: The Dissemination of Popular Print
in England and Wales, Italy and the Low Countries 1500–1820* (Leiden,
2013); Joad Raymond, *Pamphlets and Pamphleteering in Early Modern
Britain* (Cambridge, 2003); *The Cambridge History of the Book in Britain*,
IV, 1557–1695, John Barnard and D. F. MacKenzie (eds) (Cambridge,
2002).

10. *Aulicus his Hue and Cry sent forth after Britanicus*, 1–2; *The Oxinden and
Peyton Letters*, 144–5, 161; *The Character of Mercurius Politicus* (London,
1650), 2; *The Second Character of Mercurius Politicus* (London, 1650), 5–7;
'An Hue and Cry after Mercurius Politicus'; *O. Cromwell's thankes to the Lord
Generall, faithfully presented by Hugh Peters in another conference* (London,
1660); TNA, SP46/95, fos 151–2; for the fashion for men's wigs in the
1640s and 1650s see Aileen Ribeiro, *Fashion and Fiction: Dress in Art and*

Literature in Stuart England (London and New Haven, 2005), 203–4;
Mercurius Pragmaticus (for King Charles II), 9, 12–19 June 1649.

11. The Character of Mercurius Politicus (London, 1650), 5; Joseph Frank,
Cromwell's Press Agent: A Critical Biography of Marchamont Nedham 1620–
1678 (Lanham, 1980); Anthony Wood, Athenae Oxonienses ... To which are
added the fasti or annals of the said university, Philip Bliss (ed.), 4 vols
(London, 1813–20), III, 1180–90; William Betham, The Baronetage of
England, III, 279, The Revd Christopher Glynn; M. N., A Discourse
Concerning Schools and School-Masters Offered to Publick Consideration
(London, 1663), 14.

12. Lords Journal, 8, 325–8; R. H. Gretton, The Burford Records: A Study in Minor
Town Government (Oxford, 1920), 123–4, 139; Mercurius Britanicus, 51,
23–30 September 1644; Blair Worden, '"Wit in a Roundhead": the
dilemma of Marchamont Nedham', in Susan Amusson and Mark A.
Kishlansky (eds), Political Culture in Early Modern England (Manchester,
1995), 301–37.

13. Mercurius Britanicus, 92, 28 July–4 August 1645; Lords Journal, VIII, 321–4,
325–8, 341–2, 354–8; HMC Fourth Report, I, 273.

14. Wood, Athenae Oxonienses, III, 1180–90; Mercurius Pragmaticus, 1, 14–21,
September 1647; A Rope for Pol or a Hue and Cry after Marchemont Nedham
The Late Scurrulous News-writer (London, 1660), 1–2.

15. Eikon Basilike: the Portraicture of His Sacred Majesty in his Solitudes and
Sufferings (London, 1648/9); CSPD, 1649–50, 43; The Life Records of
John Milton, J. Milton French (ed.), 5 vols (New Brunswick, 1949–58), II,
256.

16. Mercurius Pragmaticus, 1, 17–24 April 1649; Ó Siochrú, God's Executioner,
28–9, 62–3; James Cranford, The Teares of Ireland wherein is Lively Presented
as in a map a list of the Unheard off Cruelties and Perfidious Treacheries of
Blood-thirsty Jesuits and the Popish Faction (London, 1642); Woolrych,
Britain in Revolution, 196–8.

17. J. B. Williams, 'Fresh light on Cromwell at Drogheda', The Nineteenth
Century and After, 72 (1912), 471–90; Gentles, The New Model Army,
350–64; Ó Siochrú, God's Executioner, 82–96.

18. Marchamont Nedham, Certain Considerations Tendered in All Humility to an
Honourable Member of the Council of State (London, 1649); TNA, SP46/95,
fos 151–2; 190r–v; The Life Records of John Milton, II, 259.

19. Williams, 'Fresh light on Cromwell at Drogheda', 478–80; Nick Poyntz,
'"This day by letters severall from hands": News Networks and Oliver
Cromwell's letters from Drogheda', in Martyn Bennett, Raymond Gillespie
and Scott Spurlock (eds), Cromwell and Ireland: New Perspectives (Liverpool,
2021), ch. 10; Commons Journal, VI, 1648–51, 300–1; CSPD, 1649–50,
326–7.

20. Acts and Ordinances of the Interregnum, 245–54; Peacey, Politicians and Pamphleteers, 158–9; Frank, The Beginnings of the English Newspaper, 197–8; Raymond, The Invention of the Newspaper, 69–79.
21. Mercurius Elencticus, 24, 8–15 October 1649, 186–7; The Man in the Moon, 26, 17–24 October 1649, 212–18.
22. The Man in the Moon, 26, 17–24 October 1649, 212–18; Frank, The Beginnings of the English Newspaper, 1970–8; J. G. Muddiman, 'The licensed newsbooks, 1649 and 1650', Notes and Queries, CLXVII (1934), 113–16; Poyntz, "This day by letters severall from hands"', 272.
23. Wood, Athenae Oxonienses, III, 1182–3; Peter Heylyn, The Historical and Miscellaneous Tracts of Peter Heylyn (London, 1681), 'The Life of the most learned and reverend Dr Peter Heylyn', xix. It may be that Nedham's spell at Minster Lovell was earlier in the year (as Heylyn refers to his working on Mercurius Pragmaticus), but it is hard to see how he could easily have overseen a weekly London newspaper from a hiding place over 70 miles from the capital, while between August and November he was definitely out of London in hiding in the countryside.
24. The Oxinden and Peyton Letters, 149–50. The 'suburbs of hell' seems to refer to the area west of Newgate which were known as the suburb.
25. TNA, SP46/95, fos. 190–1; The Oxinden and Peyton Letters, 161.
26. Mercurius Elencticus, 25, 15–22 October 1649; Frank, The Beginnings of the English Newspaper, 197–9.
27. Mercurius Pragmaticus, 1, 17–24 April 1649; 3, 1–8 May 1649; 9, 12–19 June 1649.
28. CSPD, 1649–50, 204, 554; BL, Add MS 28,002, fol. 172r; Wood, Athenae Oxonienses, III, 1182–3.
29. John Milton, Eikonoklastes in answer to a book intitl'd Eikon Basilike (London, 1649); Kevin Sharpe, Image Wars: Promoting Kings and Commonwealths in England, 1603–1660 (London and New Haven, 2010), 391–403.
30. Marchamont Nedham, The Case of the Commonwealth of England, Stated: or the Equity, Utility, and Necessity of a Submission to the Present Government (London, 1650), 22; The Case of the Commonwealth of England Stated by Marchamont Nedham, Philip A. Knachel (ed.) (Charlottesville, Va., 1969).
31. The Oxinden and Peyton Letters, 149–50.

8. *MERCURIUS POLITICUS*

1. Mercurius Politicus, 1, 6–13 June 1650, 1; 2, 13–20 June 1650, 1; Nedham claimed Politicus was 'the only State-Almanack to tell what the weather is in the Commonwealth', Mercurius Politicus, 5, 4–11 July 1650, 69. Briefe Relation of Some Affaires and Transactions Civill and Military, 1, 2 October 1649, 1–2; The Character of Mercurius Politicus, 1–2.

2. TNA, SP45/95, fol. 409.

3. *Mercurius Politicus*, 13, 29 August–5 September 1650, 193; 16, 19–26 September 1650, 261.

4. *Mercurius Pragmaticus (for King Charles II)*, 1, 24 April–1 May 1649; *Mercurius Politicus*, 1, 6–13 June 1650, 3; 5, 4–11 July 1650, 72.

5. TNA, SP46/95, fol. 409.

6. *Mercurius Politicus*, 63, 14–21 August 1651; 67, 11–18 September 1651; 76, 13–20 November 1651; 89, 12–19 February 1652.

7. *Mercurius Politicus*, 12, 22–29 August 1650, 180.

8. *Mercurius Politicus*, 3, 20–27 June 1650; 5, 4–11 July 1650; 8, 25 July–1 August 1650.

9. *Mercurius Politicus*, 64–7, August–September 1651.

10. *Mercurius Politicus*, 31, 2–9 January 1651; 43, 27 March–3 April 1651; 53, 5–12 June 1651; 55, 19–26 June 1651.

11. Heylyn, *The Historical and Miscellaneous Tracts of Peter Heylyn*, 'The Life of the most learned and reverend Dr Peter Heylyn', xix; Wood, *Athenae Oxonienses*, III, 1182; *The Second Character of Mercurius Politics*, 4–5. Nedham's stepfather, Christopher Glyn, who had given him his remarkable education, and was buried with Nedham's mother Margery, pointedly omitted his stepson from his will, TNA, PROB11/329, 122.

12. Wood, *Athenae Oxonienses*, III, 1182–3; '... he was a very knave, and that his very good friends said so', HMC *Pepys*, 298; James Heath, *A Chronicle of the Late Intestine War* (London, 1675), 267; *The Oxinden and Peyton Letters*, 144–5.

13. Wood, *Athenae Oxonienses*, 484ff; CSPD, 1652–3, 176; *Life Records of John Milton*, III, 109; Blair Worden, *Literature and Politics in Cromwellian England: John Milton, Andrew Marvell and Marchamont Nedham*, ch. 2; Miller, *John Milton and the Oldenburg Safeguard*; Robert Thomas Fallon, *Milton in Government* (University Park, Pa., 1993).

14. *Mercurius Politicus*, 72, 16–23 October 1651; 89, 12–19 February 1652; 90, 19–26 February 1652; Frank, *Cromwell's Press Agent*, 87–90; *The Second Character of Mercurius Politicus*, 6; *The Character of Mercurius Politicus*, 1–2, 'the weekly comedy acted at White-hall by its Majesties Servant'.

15. *Mercurius Politicus*, 87, 29 January–5 February 1652; 91, 26 February–4 March 1456; 291, 3–10 January 1656; Frank, *Cromwell's Press Agent*, 104–6. Joseph Moxon, *Mechanick Exercises or the Doctrine of Hands-Work Applied to the Art of Printing* (London, 1683), passim, I have assumed the workings and layout of Newcomb's printing house was broadly consistent with Joseph Moxon's detailed description of the workings of a mid-seventeenth-century London printing house. Moxon, who published from the 1650s and had his own printing business on Ludgate Hill, must have known Nedham, Bryden, D., 'Moxon, Joseph (1627–1691), printer and globe maker', *Oxford Dictionary*

of National Biography. Philip Gaskell, *A New Introduction to Bibliography* (Winchester, 1995), 9–146. C. William Miller, 'Thomas Newcomb: a Restoration printer's ornament stock', *Studies in Bibliography*, 3 (1950–1), 155–70; *A Collection of the State Papers of John Thurloe*, 7 vols (London, 1742), VII, 470–1; Blayney, *The Bookshops in Paul's Cross Churchyard.*

16. Jason Peacey, '"Wandering with Pamphlets": the infrastructure of news circulation in civil war England', in *Not Dead Things* (Leiden, 2003), 95–114; Peacey, *Politicians and Pamphleteers*, 158–295; Frank, *Cromwell's Press Agent*, 104–17; Raymond, *The Invention of the Newspaper*, ch. 5, 246; Joad Raymond, 'International news and the Seventeenth-century English newspaper', in *Not Dead Things*, 229–53; *State Papers of John Thurloe*, 7, 37; Moxon, *Mechanick Exercises*, 344; Wood, *Athenae Oxonienses*, III, 1182; *A Rope for Pol or a Hue and Cry after Marchemont Nedham The Late Scurrulous News-writer* (London, 1660), 1–2; the earthquake in December 1650 that 'drowned' the island of Santorini, *Mercurius Politicus*, 31, 2–9 January 1651; 149, 14–21 April 1653; Gaskell, *A New Introduction to Bibliography*; Giles Mandebrote, 'From the warehouse to the counting-house: booksellers and bookshops in late 17th-century London', in *A Genius for Letters: Booksellers and Bookselling from the 16th to the 20th Century*, Robin Myers and Michael Harris (eds) (Winchester, 1995).

17. *Mercurius Politicus*, 3, 20–27 June 1650; 70, 2–9 October 1651; 71, 9–16 October 1651; 72, 16–23 October 1651; 79, 11–18 December 1651.

18. 'all Proceedings whatsoever in any Courts of Justice within this Commonwealth, and which concerns the Law, and Administration of Justice, shall be in the English Tongue onely, and not in Latine or French, or any other Language then English', *Acts and Ordinances of the Interregnum, 1642–1660*, 455–6; Worden, *The Rump Parliament*, ch. 6; Whitelocke, *Diary*, 265.

19. Worden, *The Rump Parliament*, 271; *Mercurius Politicus*, 85, 15–22 January 1652; 94, 18–25 March 1652; Mary Cotterell, 'Interregnum Law Reform: The Hale Commission of 1652', *English Historical Review*, 1 October 1968, 83 (329), 689–704.

20. Milton, 'Second Defence of the People of England'; *The Character of Mercurius Politicus*, 8; Earwaker, *East Cheshire Past and Present*, II, 76–7; *The Life Records of John Milton*, III, 109; *The Oxinden and Peyton Letters*, 142; Nedham described John Bradshaw as 'a name that shall live with Honor in our English Histories', *Mercurius Politicus*, 7, 18–25 July 1650.

21. *Memoirs of Edmund Ludlow*, I, 334; Miller, *John Milton and the Oldenburg Safeguard*, 108.

22. CSPD, 1650, xl–xli; 1651, cxxv; *Original Letters and Papers of State Addressed to Oliver Cromwell*, John Nickolls (ed.) (London, 1743), 50–1, 65; *Mercurius Politicus*, 77, 20–27 November 1651.

23. *Mercurius Politicus*, 70, 2–9 October 1651.

24. The several contemporary descriptions of this extraordinary episode are reprinted together in *The Writings and Speeches of Oliver Cromwell*, W. C. Abbott (ed.), 4 vols (Cambridge, Mass., 1937–47), II, 640–5; Austin Woolrych, *Commonwealth to Protectorate* (Oxford, 1982); Worden, *Rump Parliament*, ch. 15.

25. Ludlow, *Memoirs of Edmund Ludlow*, I, 357. Whether this meeting happened has been questioned, but there is no evidence that it did not happen, and the response that Edmund Ludlow ascribes to Bradshaw is consistent with the views he expressed on other occasions. Paul J. Pinckney, 'Bradshaw and Cromwell in 1656', *Huntington Library Quarterly*, 30 (3) (May 1967), 233–40.

26. *Mercurius Politicus*, 150, 21–28 April 1653.

9. TONGUES LIKE ANGELS

1. Anna Trapnel, after Richard Gaywood, line engraving, National Portrait Gallery, shows Anna Trapnel dressed exactly as would be expected of a Puritan woman of the 1650s. Ribeiro, *Fashion and Fiction*, ch. 3; *Severall Proceedings of State Affairs*, 12–19 January 1654; *A History of the County of Middlesex*, Victoria County History, 12 vols (London, 1969–2004), X, 10–14; Anna Trapnel, *A Legacy for Saints being several experiences of the dealings of God with Anna Trapnel, in, and after her conversion, (written some years since with her own hand)* (London, 1654), 2–3, 12, 'sometimes when I have gon along the street, my raptures hath been such that I minded not the ground I went upon but divers times have been ready to fall flat on the plain ground'; Anna Trapnel, *The Cry of a Stone, or a Relation of something spoken in Whitehall, by Anna Trapnel, being in the Visions of God* (London, 1654), 8–9, for commentary and context see also *The Cry of a Stone by Anna Trapnel*, Hilary Hinds (ed.), Medieval and Renaissance Texts and Studies, 220 (Arizona, 2000).

2. Trapnel, *The Cry of a Stone*, 8–9, 12, 30–1.

3. Trapnel, *The Cry of a Stone*, 9.

4. Trapnel, *A Legacy for Saints*, 37; *The Cry of a Stone by Anna Trapnel*, Introduction.

5. Trapnel, *A Legacy for Saints*, 1–3.

6. Trapnel, *A Legacy for Saints*, 10; Anna Trapnel, *A Lively Voice for the King of Saints and Nations &c.* (London, 1657), in which she speaks of Christ as 'my spouse'.

7. CSPD, 1641–3, 119–20, 372.

8. *History of the County of Middlesex*, IV, 87–95; Philip Taverner, *A Grand-father's Advice* (London, 1681); Edmund Calamy, *A Continuation of the*

Account of the Ministers, Lecturers, Masters and Fellows of Colleges ... Ejected and Silenced ... in 1660, 2 vols (London, 1727), II, 612–13; George Addleshaw and Frederick Etchells, *The Architectural Setting of Anglican Worship* (London, 1956), 108–48; Kenneth Fincham and Stephen Taylor, 'Episcopalian conformity and nonconformity, 1646–1660', in Jason McElligott and David L. Smith, *Royalists and Royalism during the Interregnum* (Manchester, 2010), 18–44.

9. Trapnel, *The Cry of a Stone*, 10.
10. *Acts and Ordinances of the Interregnum*, 954; Christopher Durston, 'Puritan rule and the failure of the cultural revolution 1645–1669', in Christopher Durston and Jackie Eales, *The Culture of English Puritanism* (Basingstoke, 1996); John Morrill, 'The church in England 1642–1649', in *The Nature of the English Revolution* (London and New York, 1993), 148–77.
11. J. C. Davis, *Fear, Myth and History: The Ranters and the Historians* (Cambridge University Press, 1986).
12. Bernard Capp, *The Fifth Monarchy Men: A Study in Seventeenth-Century Millenarianism* (London, 1972).
13. William Erbery, *The Bishop of London, the Welsh Curate and Common Prayers with Apocrypha in the End* (London, 1653), 1–5; one observer described 'my shoulders laden with a crowd of women riding over my head, upo the tops of the seats', *State Papers of John Thurloe*, V, 748–61; Christopher Feake, *A Beam of Light Shining in the Midst of Much Darkness and Confusion* (London, 1659), 40–5.
14. Trapnel, *A Legacy for Saints*, 8–9, 32; *Anna Trapnel's Report and Plea*, 14, 124; Richard L. Greaves, *Saints and Rebels: Seven Nonconformists in Stuart England* (Mercer, 1985), ch. 4.
15. Feake, *A Beam of Light Shining in the Midst of Much Darkness and Confusion*, 40–5; Keith Thomas, 'Women and the Civil War sects', *Past and Present*, 13, April 1958, 42–62; Capp, *The Fifth Monarchy Men*, 95–100; Andrew Bradstock, *Radical Religion in Cromwell's England: A Concise History from the English Civil War to the end of the Commonwealth* (London, 2010), 133; Phyllis Mack, *Visionary Women: Ecstatic Prophecy in Seventeenth-Century England* (Cambridge, 1992); BL, Harley MS 6395, Jests and Stories, n. 436; Trapnel, *A Legacy for Saints*, 51; when a delegation of Fifth Monarchists came to Whitehall in 1655, one of the yeomen of the guard remarked 'we wonder to see so many women and what they meant?', *The Faithful Narrative of the Late Testimony and Demand made to Oliver Cromwel* (London, 1655), 7; 'my delight is not nor ever was in men's company', *Anna Trapnel's Report and Plea*, 115; Trapnel, *A Legacy for Saints*, 557, sending her love to the All Hallows congregation including 'your brother, and to Betty and to my Stripling'.
16. Trapnel, *A Legacy for Saints*, 25–32; Trapnel, *The Cry of a Stone*, 4–8.

17. *The Letters and Speeches of Oliver Cromwell*, Thomas Carlyle, Sophia Crawford Lomas and C. H. Firth (eds) (London, 1904), III, 98; TNA, SP25/70, fol. 149; CSPD, 1653, 156.
18. *Letters and Speeches of Oliver Cromwell*, Lomas and Firth (eds), III, 98; *Commons Journal*, 7, 335.
19. Trapnel, *The Cry of a Stone*, 10.
20. Trapnel, *The Cry of a Stone*, 11–14.
21. Trapnel, *The Cry of a Stone*, 13.
22. *Letters and Speeches of Oliver Cromwell*, Lomas and Firth (eds), III, 98; *State Papers of John Thurloe*, I, 620–9; Capp, *Fifth Monarchy Men*, 65; Woolrych, *Commonwealth to Protectorate*.
23. Trapnel, *The Cry of a Stone*, 13–14; *The Protector, (so called,) in part unvailed: by whom the mystery of iniquity, is now working* (London, 1655), 17.
24. *Commons Journal*, 7, 363; CSPD, 1653–4, 297–8; Barry Coward, *The Cromwellian Protectorate* (Manchester, 2002), 12–13; 'Guibon Goddard's Journal', in *Diary of Thomas Burton*, I (London, 1828), xiv–xvi; *Anna Trapnel's Report and Plea*, 57; *Memoirs of Edmund Ludlow*, I, 366ff; Roger L'Estrange, *A memento, directed to all those that truly reverence the memory of King Charles the martyr* (London, 1662), 27.
25. John Bradshaw's Journal, *Trial of Charles I*, Muddiman (ed.), 201, for the court of chancery sitting at the high end of Westminster Hall; *Severall Proceedings of State Affaires* 221, 15–22 December 1653.
26. Thurley, *Whitehall Palace*, 73–4; *State Papers of John Thurloe*, I, 640–9; *The Grand Politique Post*, 127, 10–17 January 1654, 1.

10. CORNHELL IN THE WEST

1. *Strange and Wonderful Newes from White-Hall or the Mighty Visions Proceeding from Mistris Anna Trapnel* (London, 1654); Trapnel, *The Cry of a Stone*, 15; *Severall Proceedings of State Affairs*, 225, 12–19 January 1654; 'Anna Trapnel's Prophecies', *English History Review*, 26, 103, 533–4.
2. *The Cry of a Stone by Anna Trapnel*, 54; *Strange and Wonderful Newes from White-Hall*, 6; Trapnel, *The Cry of a Stone*, 2; *The Grand Politique Post*, 127, 10–17 January 1654, 1.
3. *Severall Proceedings of State Affairs*, 12–19 January 1654, 225; *The Grand Politique Post*, 127, 10–17 January 1654, 1; *Mercurius Politicus*, 188, 12–19 January 1654; 189, 19–26 January 1654.
4. *A True State of the Case of the Commonwealth* (London, 1654); CSPD, 1653–4, 393.
5. J. Morrill, 'Bennett, Robert (1605–1683), parliamentarian army officer and religious radical', *Oxford Dictionary of National Biography* (2004); *Anna Trapnel's Report and Plea*, 61–2.

6. *Anna Trapnel's Report and Plea*, 48–9.

7. *Anna Trapnel's Report and Plea*, 50–8.

8. *Anna Trapnel's Report and Plea*, 57–60; 'Roads', *A History of the County of Wiltshire*, Victoria County History, 16 vols (London, 1953–1999), IV, 254–71; the main seventeenth-century route from Exeter to Bodmin is illustrated in John Ogilby's map series of the 1670s; Mary Coate, 'An original diary of Colonel Robert Bennett of Hexworthy (1642–3)', *Devon and Cornwall Notes and Queries*, 18 (1934–5), 258. If they took the alternative northern route, the rocky landscape may have been Bodmin Moor; Mary Coate, *Cornwall in the Civil War 1642–1660* (Oxford, 1933).

9. *Anna Trapnel's Report and Plea*, 60–7.

10. 'Anna Trapnel's Prophecies', *English History Review*, 26, 103, 533–4; *Clarke Papers*, II, xxxiv.

11. *Acts and Ordinances of the Interregnum*, December 1653: The Government of the Commonwealth of England, Scotland and Ireland, and the Dominions thereunto belonging, 813–22.

12. Morrill, 'The church in England 1642–9', 160; Coate, *Cornwall in the Great Civil War*, 341.

13. *Anna Trapnel's Report and Plea*, 75; Coate, *Cornwall in the Great Civil War*, 336, 344; Trapnel, *A Legacy for Saints*, 50–2.

14. *Anna Trapnel's Report and Plea*, 80–1.

15. *Anna Trapnel's Report and Plea*, 82–92; Trapnel, *A Legacy for Saints*, 55–7; *Certain Passages of Every Dayes Intelligence from the Army and his Highness the Lord Protector*, 14, 14–21 April 1654; *Mercurius Politicus*, 201, 13–20 April 1654.

16. *Anna Trapnel's Report and Plea*, 93.

17. *Acts and Ordinances of the Interregnum*, 830–1013; Coate, *The Civil War in Cornwall*, 342.

18. *CSPD*, 1654, 86, 89, 134, 197, 436; Trapnel, *A Legacy for Saints*, 57–60, 61–3.

19. *Anna Trapnel's Report and Plea*, 109–20; Trapnel, *A Legacy for Saints*, 1–5; *A Perfect Account*, 179, 7–14 June 1654.

20. *Anna Trapnel's Report and Plea*, 120–1; *CSPD*, 1654, 436, 438.

21. *Anna Trapnel's Report and Plea*, 109, 134. Anna returned to Cornwall in 1656; *Mercurius Politicus*, 312, 29 May–5 June 1656; *Publick Intelligencer*, 13, 24–31 December 1656, 193–4. Her continuing travels, documentation and publishing of her visions is made evident by the 1,000-page printed book of her sayings and visions in the Bodleian Library, 'Anna Trapnel's Prophecies', *English Historical Review*, 26, 103 (July 1911), 526–35. In *A Lively Voice for the King of Saints and Nations &c.* Anna Trapnel spoke of herself as 'Christ's beloved wife', saying to God, 'many do strike at thee my spouse / But I will take thy part'.

22. The *Faithfull Narrative of the Late Testimony and Demand made to Oliver Cromwel* (London, 1651). Their detailed account of the meeting was in print within a month. *A Perfect Diurnall of some passages and proceedings*, 270, 5–12 February 1655, 4147–8.

11. PLOUGH AND GO TO MARKET

1. Peter Smith, 'Petitionary Negotiations in a Community in Conflict: King's Lynn and West Norfolk c1575–1662', University of East Anglia Ph.D., 2012, 211; *The Works of Sir Thomas Browne*, Simon Wilkin (ed.), 4 vols, (London, 1835–6), I, 369–70; BL, Sloane MS 1839, fos 50r–90r; Francis Blomefield, *An Essay towards a Topographical History of the County of Norfolk*, 11 vols (London, 1805–10), X, 312–2; 'Sir Hamon L'Estrange and his Sons', in R. W. Ketton Cremer, *A Norfolk Gallery* (London, 1948), 56–93.

2. Jane Whittle and Elizabeth Griffiths, *Consumption and Gender in the Early Seventeenth Century Household: The World of Alice Le Strange* (Oxford, 2012); Norfolk Record Office, LEST/P10, *passim*; *Her Price is Above Pearls: Family and Farming Records of Alice Le Strange 1617–1656*, Elizabeth Griffiths (ed.), Norfolk Record Society, LXXIX (Norwich, 2015).

3. Blomefield, *An Essay towards a Topographical History of the County of Norfolk*, X, 312–28.

4. Alice L'Estrange has been the subject of two recent books based on her fascinating household accounts: *Her Price is Above Pearls: Family and Farming Records of Alice Le Strange 1617–1656*, Elizabeth Griffiths (ed.); Whittle and Griffiths, *Consumption and Gender in the Early Seventeenth-Century Household: The World of Alice Le Strange*.

5. Vanessa Parker, *The Making of King's Lynn* (Phillimore, 1971).

6. *The History of Parliament: The House of Commons 1604–1629*, Andrew Thrush and John Ferris (eds) (Cambridge, 2010); Hamon L'Estrange, *Americans No Jews, or the Improbabilities that the Americans are of that Race* (London, 1652), 70; Octavia Beatrice Ramsay, 'A Study of King's Lynn in the English Civil War', M. Phil., Cambridge, 2011.

7. BL, Add MS 35,333; *Commons Journal*, III, 726–30; IV, 6–7; John Rushworth, *Historical Collections of Private Passages of State*, V, 748–87; Hamon L'Estrange, *The Charge Upon Sir Hamon L'Estrange together with his Vindication and Recharge* (London, 1649).

8. NRO, LEST/P10, 51–3; HMC, *11th Report, Appendix Part VII*, 102; Alfred Kingston, *East Anglia and the Great Civil War. The rising of Cromwell's Ironsides in the associated Counties of Cambridge, Huntingdon, Lincoln, Norfolk, Suffolk, Essex, and Hertford* (London, 1897), 295–6; Whittle and Griffiths, *Consumption and Gender*, fig. 6.2.

9. NRO, LEST/P11, fol. 23r-v, 43r, 46r; LEST/P10, 153r, 157–8; LEST/25/II/v; Whittle and Griffiths, *Consumption and Gender*, 97–101; LEST/P12, January 1653/4; TNA, PROB 11/238/248; Andrew Ashbee, '"My fiddle is a bass viol": music in the life of Roger L'Estrange', in *Roger L'Estrange and the Making of Restoration Culture*, Anne Dunan-Page and Beth Lynch (eds) (Aldershot, 2008), 149ff.

10. 'There is no day commanded in Scripture to be kept holy under the Gospel but the Lord's Day. Festival Days, vulgarly called Holy Days, having no warrant in the word of God, are not to be continued', *The Westminster Directory*, Thomas Leishman (ed.) (Edinburgh, 1901), 78; *The Vindication of Christmas* (London, 1653); Hutton, *The Rise and Fall of Merry England*, ch. 6; see also 'A Song in Defence of Christmass', Alexander Brome, *Rump, or, An exact collection of the choycest poems and songs relating to the late times by the most eminent wits from anno 1639 to anno 1661* (London, 1662), 144.

11. BL, Sloane MS 1839, fol. 54r, 67v, 71v; Thomas Browne, *Pseudodoxia Epidemica or Enquiries into very many received tenets and commonly presumed truths* (London, 1646); *The Works of Thomas Browne*, I, 369–70; NRO, LEST/ P20, 73.

12. Sir Hamon L'Estrange (1583–1654), of Hunstanton, Norf, *The History of Parliament: The House of Commons 1604–1629*; NRO, LEST /P10, 'for 3 sertificates for the Engagament', April 1650.

13. BL, Harley MS 6395, nos 261, 291, 493, 554; Bishop Challoner, *Memoirs of Missionary Priests and other Catholics* (Philadelphia, 1839), 65–8; Whittle and Griffiths, *Consumption and Gender*, 172.

14. HMC, *11th Report, Appendix VII*, 103; NRO, LEST/P20, no. 59; Cord Oestmann, *Lordship and Community: The Lestrange Family and the Village of Hunstanton, Norfolk in the First Half of the Sixteenth Century* (Woodbridge, 1994), 258; TNA, PROB11/301/650; Michael J. Braddick, *The Nerves of State: Taxation and the Financing of the English State 1558–1714* (Manchester, 1996), 91–7.

15. *Norfolk Quarter Sessions Order Book 1650–1657*, D. E. Howell James (ed.), Norfolk Records Society, 1955.

16. The clergy of the Church of England Database, www.theclergydatabase. org.uk; Kenneth Fincham and Stephen Taylor, 'Vital Statistics: Episcopal Ordination and Ordinands in England, 1646–60', *English Historical Review*, Vol. 126, No. 519 (April 2011), 319–44; Fincham and Taylor, 'Episcopalian conformity and nonconformity, 1646–1660', 18–44.

17. NRO, PD/698/2; NRO, PD/39/74, Church Wardens' Accounts St Margaret's church; King's Lynn Borough Archives, Hall Book, LK/C7/10, fol. 281v, Mr Tho Leech Minister; *Norfolk Quarter Sessions Order Book*, 63. See also Ramsay, 'A Study of King's Lynn in the Civil War', 60–1 for the continuation of communion on feast days and of the parish

perambulations which traditionally took place at Rogation (the week before Ascension) in King's Lynn during the 1650s.

18. Roger L'Estrange, *Truth and Loyalty Vindicated from the Reproches and Clamours of Mr Edward Bagshaw* (London, 1662), 48–50; *Acts and Ordinances of the Interregnum*, 565–77.

19. Roger L'Estrange, *To the Right Honourable Edward Earl of Clarendon The Humble Apology* (London, 1661), 3; *CSPD*, 1653, 225; *The Works of Thomas Browne*, I, 370; NRO, LEST/P20, nos 79, 81.

20. Roger L'Estrange, *Truth and Loyalty Vindicated*, 49; Roger L'Estrange, 38–41; *CSPD*, 1655, 225; NRO, LEST/P10, 171, 'Money for Roger's debt'; LEST/P10, fol. 153r; BL, Harley MS 6395, no. 409.

21. NRO, LEST/P10, 22, 78–9, 80–1, 157–8; LEST/NE/1, Catalogue of Hunstanton Library.

22. NRO, LEST/P11, *passim*; LEST/P10, 90.

23. '10s to Playford the Mountebanke', NRO, LEST/P10, 157–8; LEST/P20, nos 43, 50, 66, 68; Challoner, *Memoirs of Missionary Priests*, 65–8; TNA, PROB11/238/248.

24. NRO, ACC2005/8, Box 112, fol. 83; NRO, LEST/P10, 160–3.

25. BL, Harley MS 6395, nos 319, 388, 395, 436, 520, 538, 540, 606.

26. *The Diary of Thomas Burton*, III, 257.

27. King's Lynn Borough Archives, KL/C7/10, fol. 407v, 407v, 418r, 417v; NRO, PD39/74, Churchwardens' accounts, St Margaret's, King's Lynn, fol. 445; *CSPD*, 1654, 65; 1655–6, 5, 211.

28. NRO, LEST/P11, fol 20r, 38r, 39v; Sir William Spring, 2nd Bt (1642–84), of Pakenham, Suff. *The History of Parliament: The House of Commons 1660–1690*, B. D. Henning (ed.), 3 vols (London, 1983).

29. NRO, LEST/BN9 and 10; Whittle and Griffiths, *Consumption and Gender*, 163; TNA, PROB11/238/248.

30. *Writings and Speeches of Oliver Cromwell*, Abbott (ed.), III, 434–43.

31. *Memoirs of Edmund Ludlow*, I, 391–3; Whittle and Griffiths, *Consumption and Gender*, 232; 'Guibon Goddard's Journal', xvii–xliv; 'May 1649: An Act Declaring and Constituting the People of England to be a Commonwealth and Free-State', in *Acts and Ordinances of the Interregnum*, 122.

32. *The Last Speech of His Highnesse the Lord Protector to the Parliament on Tuesday in the Painted Chamber, being the 12. of this instant September* (London, 1654); 'Guibon Goddard's Journal', xvii–xx.

33. 'Guibon Goddard's Journal', cxxxiii; *Commons Journal*, 7, 421.

12. DECIMATION

1. TNA, PROB11/238/248.
2. NRO, LEST/KA6, Sir Nicholas L'Estrange's notebook of 'Dealing, diggings & buildings', 1; BL, Harley MS 6395; Pamela Willetts, 'Sir Nicholas Le Strange and John Jenkins', *Music & Letters*, 42, No. 1 (Jan., 1961), 30–43; Elizabeth Griffiths, 'Draining the coastal marshes of north-west Norfolk: the contribution of the Le Stranges at Hunstanton, 1605 to 1724', *Agricultural History Review*, 63, II, 221–42; BL, Harley MS 6395; '*Merry Passages and jeasts': Manuscript Jest Book of Sir Nicholas Le Strange*, H. F. Lippincott (ed.) (Salzburg, 1974).
3. Gordon Blackwood, 'The gentry of Norfolk during the civil war', in *An Historical Atlas of Norfolk*, Trevor Ashwin and Alan Davison (eds), 3rd edn (Chichester, 2005), 118–19; Ketton Cremer, *Norfolk in the Civil War*, 151.
4. NRO, LEST/P20, no. 83; LEST/KA6, *passim*; Griffiths, 'Draining the coastal marshes of north-west Norfolk', 221–42; Hamon L'Estrange, *God's Sabbath before under the law and under the Gospel* (Cambridge, 1641).
5. BL, Harley MS 6395, no. 180, 402. Only one anecdote from his wife, about a spelling mistake from her tailor, is recorded in Nicholas L'Estrange's jeast book of hundreds of funny stories; Hamon L'Estrange, *God's Sabbath*; LEST/P10, 47; *The Calendar of the Committee for Compounding*, part 4 (London, 1892), 2683–703.
6. Hamon L'Estrange, *An Answer to the Marquess of Worcester's Last Paper* (London, 1651). He would take up and develop this subject in his greatest work *The Alliance of Divine Offices* (London, 1659).
7. Gardiner, *Commonwealth and Protectorate*, III, 282–91; *The Perfect Diurnall of some passages and proceedings*, 275, 12–19 March 1655. *State Papers of John Thurloe*, III, 195–219; David Underdown, *Royalist Conspiracy in England 1649–1660* (Yale, 1960), ch. 7; *Mercurius Politicus*, 248, 8–15 March 1655; 249, 14–21 March 1655; 250, 22–29 March 1655.
8. *State Papers of John Thurloe*, I, xi–xx; Philip Aubrey, *Mr Secretary Thurloe: Cromwell's Secretary of State 1652–1660* (London, 1990); Alan Marshall, *Intelligence and Espionage in the Reign of Charles II, 1660–1685* (Cambridge, 1994).
9. Hilary McD. Beckles, 'The "Hub of Empire": the Caribbean and Britain in the seventeenth century', in *The Origins of Empire: British Overseas Enterprise to the Close of the Seventeenth Century*, Nicholas Canny (ed.) (Oxford, 1998), 218–41.
10. *State Papers of John Thurloe*, III, 195–213; *The Narrative of General Venables, with an appendix of papers relating to the expedition to the West Indies and the conquest of Jamaica, 1654–1655*, C. H. Firth (ed.) (London, 1900), 6–7; Bernard Capp, *Cromwell's Navy* (Oxford, 1989), 86–91; Carla Gardina

Pestana, *The English Conquest of Jamaica: Oliver Cromwell's Bid for Empire* (Cambridge, Mass., 2017).

11. NRO, PD/696/16, Parish Records of Ringstead St Andrew; John Rolfe, ODNB; L'Estrange, *Americans No Jews*, 72. England had long been engaged in the colonization of Ireland, of course, but the Hispaniola expedition was its first military-backed trans-oceanic colonial expedition.

12. *Mercurius Politicus*, 257, 10–17 May 1655; Nicole Greenspan, 'News and the politics of information in the mid seventeenth century: the Western Design and the conquest of Jamaica', *History Workshop Journal*, 69 (Spring 2010), 1–26; *The Narrative of General Venables*, 26; Pestana, *The English Conquest of Jamaica*, chs 1 and 2; Blair Worden, 'Oliver Cromwell and the sin of Achan', *History, Society and the Churches: Essays in Honour of Owen Chadwick* (Cambridge, 1985), 125–47. HMC *Fifth Report*, p. 176.

13. Christopher Durston, *Cromwell's Major Generals: Godly Government during the English Revolution* (Manchester, 2001), 128–9; *Mercurius Politicus*, 267, 19–26 July 1655; TNA, SP25/76, fos 318–19. *The Diary of Ralph Josselin*, Alan MacFarlane (ed.) (Oxford, 1976), 349; Hezekiah Haynes's men appeared at midnight one Sunday at one Suffolk gentry household, 'my Father's house was broke into by a Party of Horse-men sent from Yarmouth and the Cellars, and all suspected places of the House, were searched for Armys, but none found, but the Swords of me and my Brother, which hung up in the Hall; which they carried away, as well as my Father and Brother', Roger Coke, *A Detection of the Court and State of England during the four last reigns, and the inter–regnum*, III (London, 1694), 54.

14. *CSPD*, 1655, 296, 344–5; Durston, *Cromwell's Major Generals*, ch. 2.

15. Durston, *Cromwell's Major Generals*, 39.

16. W. L. F. Nuttall, 'Hezekiah Haynes: Oliver Cromwell's Major-General for the Eastern Counties', in *Transactions of the Essex Archaeological Society*, I (3), third series, (1964), 196–210; Durston, *Cromwell's Major Generals*; *CSPD*, 1655, 387.

17. *State Papers of John Thurloe*, IV, 170, 216; *Diary of Ralph Josselin*, 356; while the totals survive for the decimation tax collected in Norfolk, a detailed list of how much was paid by whom does not, *The Cromwellian Decimation Tax of 1655. The Assessment Lists*, J. T. Cliffe (ed.), Royal Historical Society Camden Fifth Series, 7, 1996, 403–92, 446–7; John T. Evans, *Seventeenth-Century Norwich: Politics, Religion and Government 1620–1690* (Oxford, 1979), chs 5 and 6.

18. Roger L'Estrange, *A Memento, Directed to all those that Truly Reverence the Memory of King Charles the Martyr* (London, 1662), 32–3.

19. Hamon L'Estrange, *The Reign of King Charles* (London, 1655); *A Transcript of the Registers of the Worshipful Company of Stationers*, G. E. Briscoe Eyre

(ed.), 3 vols (London, 1913–14), I, 45; *State Papers of John Thurloe*, III, 592; NRO, LEST/P12, fol. 55.

20. Whittle and Griffiths, *Consumption and Splendour*, 183; *Diary of John Evelyn*, III, 167–8; NRO, LEST/P11, fol. 27r; *The History of Hunstanton Parish Church* (2002), 27–9.

21. C. W. James, *Chief Justice Coke: His Family and Descendants at Holkham* (London, 1929), 102–3, 107; *The Norfolk Antiquarian Miscellany*, W. B. Rye (ed.), 3 vols (Norwich, 1873–7), II (i), 256–8; John Coke (1635–71), of Holkham, Norf., *The History of Parliament: The House of Commons 1660–1690*; NRO LEST/AA, 14, 15, 16. It seems likely that a marriage between Mary Coke and Nick's elder brother, Little Ham (Sir Hamon L'Estrange (1631–56)) was originally envisaged but on his early death was contracted with Nick instead.

22. BL, Add MS 34014, 'List of suspected persons in London and Westminster', 42, 45; Add MS 44016; Add MS 34,013; Durston, *Cromwell's Major Generals*, 135–6.

23. *Norfolk Quarter Sessions Order Book*, 86, 87, 88.

24. *State Papers of John Thurloe*, IV, 216.

25. Durston, *Cromwell's Major Generals*, ch. 9.

26. William Prynne, *A Summary Collection of the Principal Fundamental Rights, Liberties, Proprietaries of All English Freemen* (London, 1656), 63.

27. King's Lynn Borough Archives, KL/C7/10, 489v; CSPD, 1655–6, 211; 1656–7, 5; *Diary of Ralph Josselin 1616–1683*, 378.

28. *State Papers of John Thurloe*, 5, 311–12, 15 August 1656. For John Hobart of Norwich, see C. S. Egloff, 'John Hobart of Norwich', *Norfolk Archaeology*, XLII (1994–7), 38–56. I am grateful to Dr Andrew Barclay for information on John Hobart.

29. *Diary of Thomas Burton*, I, 228–43; Cliffe, 'The Cromwellian Decimation Tax', 407.

30. London Apprenticeship Abstracts, 1442–1850, Guildhall Library, accessed via findmypast.com, Edward L'Estrange 1656; LEST/AA/15. 1 December 1656; NRO, LEST/P12, fos 68–70; *The Norfolk Antiquarian Miscellany*, II (i), 259; *Minutes of the Parliament of the Middle Temple*, 4 vols, C. T. Martin (ed.) (London, 1904–5), III, 1088, 1098.

31. TNA, PROB11/301/650; *Diary of Thomas Burton*, I, 228–43.

32. George Kitchin, *Sir Roger L'Estrange: a Contribution to the History of the Press in the Seventeenth Century* (London, 1913); L'Estrange, *Truth and Loyalty Vindicated*, 45–50; *Diary of Thomas Burton*, III, 257.

13. INGENIOUS FRIENDS

1. *The Petty Papers: Some Unpublished Writings of Sir William Petty edited from the Bowood Papers of the Marquis of Lansdowne*, 2 vols (London, 1927), II, 157–67; Richard Watkins, *Newes from the Dead. Or a True and Exact Narration of the Miraculous Deliverance of Anne Green* (London, 1651); W. Burdet, *A Wonder of Wonders Being a Faithful Narrative and True Relation of one Anne Green* (London, 1651); M. Greengrass, Leslie and M. Hannon (eds), *The Hartlib Papers*, The Digital Humanities Institute, University of Sheffield, Hartlib Papers (2013), 8/23/1A–2B.

2. John Aubrey, *Brief Lives, Chiefly Contemporaries, set down by John Aubrey*, 2 vols, Andrew Clark (ed.) (Oxford, 1898), II, 144; Burdet, *A Wonder of Wonders*, 1.

3. Ian Roy and Dietrich Reinhart, 'Oxford and the civil wars', in Nicholas Tyacke (ed.), *The History of the University of Oxford: IV. Seventeenth Century Oxford* (Oxford, 1997), 715–17, 725–31; Robert G. Frank, *Harvey and the Oxford Physiologists: A Study of Scientific Ideas* (Berkeley, 1980), 45–50.

4. *Petty Papers*, 160–3; Watkins, *Newes from the Dead*, 3–4; Burdett, *Wonder of Wonders*.

5. *Mercurius Politicus*, 28, 12–19 December 1650; *The Petty Papers*, II, 164–5; Watkins, *Newes from the Dead*; *Diary of John Evelyn*, IV, 56–7.

6. *The Petty-Southwell Correspondence, 1676–1687. Edited from the Bowood papers by the Marquis of Lansdowne* (London, 1928), 284; Aubrey, *Brief Lives*, II, 139; Ted McCormick, *William Petty and the Ambitions of Political Arithmetic* (Oxford, 2009), ch. 1.

7. Maurice Duman, *Scientific Instruments of the 17th and 18th Centuries and their Makers* (London, 1972).

8. Frank, *Harvey and the Oxford Physiologists*, ch. 1.

9. McCormick, *William Petty*, 28–39.

10. Margery Purver, *The Royal Society: Concept and Creation* (London, 1967), 101–28; Aubrey, *Brief Lives*, II, 139–50; 'Dr Wallis's Account of some passages of his own life', *The Works of Thomas Hearne MA*, 4 vols (London, 1810), III, CLXII–CLXIV; *The Correspondence of John Wallis*, Philip Beeley and Christoph J. Scriba (eds), 4 vols (Oxford, 2003); J. A. Bennett, 'Christopher Wren. Astronomy, Architecture, and the Mathematical Sciences', *Journal for the History of Astronomy*, 6 (1974), 149–84; Thomas Sprat, *The History of the Royal Society for the Improving of Natural Knowledge* (London, 1667), 53–6.

11. Aubrey, *Brief Lives*, II,144; William Petty, *Reflections upon Some Persons and Things in Ireland* (London, 1660), 2–3; *The Correspondence of Robert Boyle*, Michael Hunter, Antonio Clericuzio and Lawrence M. Principe (eds), 6 vols (London, 2001), I, 142–4.

12. Aubrey, *Brief Lives*, II, 139–50; BL, Add MS 72,891, fol. 8, 228–230v; Petty, *Reflections Upon Some Persons and Things in Ireland*, 17; William Petty, *The Advice of WP to Mr Samuel Hartlib for the Advancement of some Particular Parts of Learning* (London, 1648), 1–15.
13. *Correspondence of Robert Boyle*, I, 72–3; *Lords Journal*, 10, 101.
14. Anthony Wood, *The History and Antiquities of the University of Oxford*, John Gutch (ed.), 2 vols (Oxford, 1796), II, 884; *Brasenose College Register* (Oxford, 1909), I, 187; Petty, *Reflections upon some Persons and Things in Ireland*, 2–3.
15. Aubrey, *Brief Lives*, II,142; Greengrass et al., *Hartlib Papers*, 8/23/1A–2B; *CSPD, 1651–2*, 236; *The History of the Survey of Ireland, commonly called the Down Survey, by Doctor William Petty, A.D. 1655–6*, Thomas Aiskew Larcom (ed.) (Dublin, 1851), 12.
16. Aubrey, *Brief Lives*, II, 142–5; *The Diary of John Evelyn*, IV, 59; *The Petty-Southwell Correspondence*, 86–9; Petty, *The Advice of WP to Mr. Samuel Hartlib*; *Ireland under the Commonwealth: being a selection of documents relating to the government of Ireland from 1651 to 1659*, Robert Dunlop, 2 vols (Manchester, 1913), I, 276–7; William Petty, *Tracts Chiefly relating to Ireland* (London, 1769), iv–v.
17. Gerard Boate, *Ireland's Natural History: Being a True and Ample Description of its Situation, Greatness, Shape and Nature of its Hills, Woods, Heaths, Bogs etc.* (London, 1652); McCormick, *William Petty*, 89; William Brereton, *Travels in Holland, the United Provinces, England, Scotland and Ireland 1634–5*, Edward Hawkes (ed.) (Manchester, 1844), 124–68.
18. William Petty, *The Political Anatomy of Ireland, with the establishment for that Kingdom, and Verbum sapienti*, facsimile of the first edition, John O'Donovan (ed.) (Shannon, 1970); Raymond Gillespie, 'The transformation of the Irish Economy 1550–1700', *Studies in Irish Economic and Social History*, 6, 1991. '… an cogadh do chriochnaigh Eire', *Five Seventeenth Century Political Poems*, Cecile Rahilly (ed.) (Dublin, 1952).
19. Brereton, *Travels in Holland, the United Provinces, England, Scotland and Ireland*, 376–83; Boate, *Ireland's Natural History*, 26, 160; Petty, *The Political Anatomy of Ireland*, 10–17; Colm Lennon, *The Irish Historic Towns Atlas, Dublin*, Part II: 1610–1756, Royal Irish Academy (2008); *Ireland under the Commonwealth*, Dunlop (ed.), I, 245; 'Commonwealth State Accounts Ireland, 1650–1656', Edward MacLysaght, *Analecta Hibernica*, no. 15, 1944, 227–321, 235.
20. Petty, *The History of the Survey of Ireland*, 1–2.
21. *Ireland under the Commonwealth*, Dunlop (ed.), I, 134, 138; Toby Barnard, *Cromwellian Ireland: English Government and Reform in Ireland 1649–1660* (Oxford, 1975, 2000 edn).
22. *Memoirs of Edmund Ludlow*, I, 338–9; *Acts and Ordinances of the Interregnum 1642–1660*, 598–603; HMC Portland: *The Manuscripts of His Grace the Duke*

of Portland, I, 621–5; John Cunningham, 'Oliver Cromwell and the
"Cromwellian" settlement of Ireland', *Historical Journal*, 53, 4 (2010),
919–93; John Cunningham, *Conquest and Land in Ireland: the
Transplantation to Connacht* (Woodbridge, 2011); *An Abstract of some few of
those barbarous, cruell massacres and murthers of the Protestants and English in
some parts of Ireland, committed since the 23 of October 1641* (London, 1652),
'Sent over to Parliament in a Letter from the Commissioners of
Parliament in Ireland and the Generall and Field Officers there and Read
in Parliament the 19 day of May 1652'.

23. *State Papers of John Thurloe*, II, 140–51; *Severall Proceedings of State Affairs*,
236, 31 March–6 April 1654.

24. 'An Act for the Speedy and Effectual Satisfaction of the Adventurers for
Lands in Ireland', *Acts and Ordinances of the Interregnum*, 722–53; *Memoirs of
Edmund Ludlow*, I, 359–60.

25. *Ireland under the Commonwealth*, Dunlop (ed.), I, 242; Petty, *Reflections upon
Some Persons and Things in Ireland*, 17–19.

26. R. E. W. Maddison, *The Life of the Honourable Robert Boyle* (London, 1969),
63–79; *Correspondence of Robert Boyle*, I, 167, 177.

27. 'Printed Declaration of the Council' A/84, 138, printed in John Patrick
Prendergast, *The Cromwellian Settlement in Ireland* (London, 1870), 307;
Correspondence of Robert Boyle, I, 152–3, 158; Patrick Little, *Lord Broghill
and the Cromwellian Union with Ireland and Scotland* (Woodbridge, 2004),
24–5; *History of the Down Survey by Dr William Petty 1655–6*, 81; *Diary of
Thomas Burton*, II, 207–12, in which the MP for Kildare and Wicklow
explained to the Commons the state of the Irish nation, 'Our churches,
bridges, sessions-house, and all houses are pulled down; not one
standing.' Roger Boyle, Lord Broghill published his four-volume romance
Parthenissa in 1654–5, C. William Miller, 'A Bibliographical Study of
"Parthenissa" by Roger Boyle Earl of Orrery', *Studies in Bibliography*
(Charlottesville, Va.), 2 (1949), 115–37.

28. *Writings and Speeches of Oliver Cromwell*, Abbott (ed.), III, 434–43; *Mercurius
Politicus*, 221, 31 August–7 September 1654; William J. Smyth,
*Map-making, Landscapes and Memory: a Geography of Colonial and Early-
Modern Ireland c1530–1750* (Cork, 2006), 172–3.

29. *History of the Down Survey by Dr William Petty*, 23–9, 311–12; Smyth,
Map-making, Landscapes and Memory, ch. 5.

14. THE END OF IRELAND

1. *History of the Down Survey by Dr William Petty*, 46, 119–20.

2. *History of the Down Survey by Dr William Petty*, xiii–xvii, 17–18, 20, 23–9,
120; Petty, *Reflections upon Some Persons and Things in Ireland*.

3. Smyth, *Map-making, Landscapes and Memory*, 178–9.

4. Smyth, *Map-making, Landscapes and Memory*, ch. 5; Cunningham, *Conquest and Land in Ireland*.

5. *Mercurius Politicus*, 239, 4–11 January 1655; 'Transplanters Certificates', Prendergast, *The Cromwellian Settlement of Ireland*, 363–8; Cunningham, *Conquest and Land in Ireland*, 74–5.

6. *The Great Case of Transplantation in Ireland Discussed* (London, 1655), 7, 13; Cunningham, 'Oliver Cromwell and the "Cromwellian" settlement of Ireland', 919–37.

7. *Mercurius Politicus*, 249, 15–22 March 1655; 251, 29 March–5 April 1655; *History of the Down Survey by Dr William Petty*, 120–7.

8. Madge, *The Domesday of Crown Lands*, 133–274; *Monarchs, Ministers and Maps: the Emergence of Cartography as a Tool of Modern Government in Early Modern Europe*, David Buisseret (ed.) (Chicago and London, 1992), 57–99. I am very grateful to Peter Barber, Visiting Fellow, King's College University of London, formerly Head of the Map Library at the British Library, for his advice on British and European cartography of the period.

9. Smyth, *Map-making, Landscapes and Memory*, 166–7; J. H. Andrews, *Plantation Acres: An Historical Study of the Irish Land Surveyor and his Maps*, Ulster Historical Foundation (Omagh, 1985), 61–71; E. Baigent, 'Swedish Cadastral Mapping 1628–1700: A Neglected Legacy', *The Geographical Journal*, Vol. 156, No. 1 (Mar., 1990), 62–9.

10. *History of the Down Survey by Dr William Petty*, 37–8, 49–51; *The Civil Survey 1654–6: County of Tipperary. I. Eastern and Southern Baronies*, Robert C Simington (ed.) (Dublin, 1931); Petty, *The Political Anatomy of Ireland*, 60–79; 'Commonwealth State Accounts', 227, 229–31, 241.

11. William Leybourn, *The Complete Surveyor* (London, 1653); *History of the Down Survey by Dr William Petty*, 52–3, 93–101. The Circumferentor was the forerunner of the theodolite. This small portable instrument comprised a compass set within a brass disc marked with degrees of orientation, which fitted onto a demountable tripod. The surveyor set up the Circumferentor at a good vantage point, usually one of the corners of the plot to be mapped, and had poles with flags planted at every other corner. With the Circumferentor orientated north–south, upright sights on the disc around the compass could be rotated until the view through them aligned precisely with a given flag. This enabled the surveyor to measure the angles between each of the poles in turn. The distances between them then were taken by the soldiers who strung 66-foot measuring chains out along the various field boundaries, hedges and ditches. Petty's men may also have used the 'Plane Table', a variant on the Circumferentor, as implied by reference to 'tables' being among the equipment moved about by the Down Survey teams. The Plane Table was

a demountable surveying board that stood on an adjustable tripod. Each table had an accompanying large magnetic compass that fixed to its side, allowing it, like the Circumferentor, to be orientated precisely north–south. A large piece of paper was held in place by a wooden frame that slotted over the table, marked with measurements and degrees of orientation. A ruler, with sights at each end, was laid across the table and aligned with the point from which an angle was to be measured allowing for a drawing to be made as the measurements were taken.

12. Petty, *Reflections upon Some Persons and Things in Ireland*, 104; *History of the Down Survey by Dr William Petty*, 43, 295–6; Smyth, *Map-making, Landscapes and Memories*, 174–5.

13. *The Correspondence of Henry Cromwell, 1655–1659: from the British Library Lansdowne manuscripts*, Peter Gaunt (ed.), Camden Fifth Series, 31 (Cambridge, 2007), 69, 77, 96; *Memoirs of Edmund Ludlow*, I, 373–4, 380–2.

14. *State Papers of John Thurloe*, IV, 72–3, 433; *Correspondence of Henry Cromwell*.

15. *Mercurius Politicus*, 276, 20–27 September 1655; *State Papers of John Thurloe*, III, 690, 697, 699; *Correspondence of Henry Cromwell*, 63–4; *Memoirs of the Protector, Oliver Cromwell, and of his sons Richard and Henry*, 2 vols (London, 1820–2), I, 397–8; 'Commonwealth state accounts', 284; Barnard, *Cromwellian Ireland*, 26–9.

16. *History of the Down Survey by Dr William Petty*, 106–9, 110–11; BL, Add MS 21,128, fol. 143r.

17. *History of the Down Survey by Dr William Petty*, 110–11.

18. *Mercurius Politicus*, 308, 1–8 May 1656; Mark Noble, *Memoirs of the Protectorate-house of Cromwell*, 2 vols (Birmingham, 1724), I, 286–7; *Correspondence of Henry Cromwell*, 132–3; Petty, *Reflections upon Some Persons and Things in Ireland*, 119–20.

19. *History of the Down Survey by Dr William Petty*, 16–17, 46, 60–1, 93–101.

20. *History of the Down Survey by Dr William Petty*, 125–78; 'Commonwealth State Accounts', 289; *Ireland under the Commonwealth*, Dunlop (ed.), II, 609; 'the Doctor was in such creditt with both [army and Council] to bee appointed a trustee for distributing the whole', *History of the Down Survey by Dr William Petty*, 102.

21. Petty, *Reflections upon Some Persons and Things in Ireland*, 104, 108.

22. *Correspondence of Henry Cromwell*, 523–4.

23. *Correspondence of Robert Boyle*, I, 254–5.

24. Petty, *Reflections upon Some Persons and Things in Ireland*, 37–41.

25. Petty, *Reflections upon Some Persons and Things in Ireland*, 50, 85, 109–20; *State Papers of John Thurloe*, VI, 481–92; BL, Add MS 21,128, fos 143r–45r.

26. Petty, *The Political Anatomy of Ireland*, 17; *Ireland under the Commonwealth*, Dunlop (ed.), II, 588; 'Commonwealth State Accounts', 277–8.

27. Petty, *Tracts Chiefly Relating to Ireland*, xiii; Aubrey, *Brief Lives*, II, 143; *Diary of John Evelyn*, IV, 56–61; *State Papers of John Thurloe*, 6, 788–90; Ó Siochrú, *God's Executioner*, 24–5.

28. *The Correspondence of Henry Cromwell*, 66, 194; *State Papers of John Thurloe*, III, 305; Barnard, *Cromwellian Ireland*, ch. 3; Raymond Gillespie, 'The transformation of the Irish economy 1550–1700', 1–55.

29. *History of the Down Survey by Dr William Petty*, 311–12; BL, Add MS 21,128, fol. 77v-87r.

30. *Petty Papers*, II, 61, I, 116–18; Petty, *The Political Anatomy of Ireland*, 'They are accused also of much Treachery, Falseness, and Thievery; none of all which, I conceive, is natural to them', 98–9; S. R. Gardiner, 'The transplantation to Connaught', *English Historical Review*, 1899, 700–34; Gardiner and Edmond Fitzmaurice, *Life of William Petty* (London, 1895) argued that Petty was a co-author of Gookin's pamphlet against transplantation.

31. Dunlop, *Ireland under the Commonwealth*, II, 553–6, 609; Cunningham, *Conquest and Land in Ireland*, 76–89; Robert C. Simington, *The Transplantation to Connacht 1654-8* (Dublin, 1970), xxiii-xxv.

32. Cunningham, *Conquest and Land in Ireland*, 89; Barnard, *Cromwellian Ireland*, 61–7; Patrick J. Cornish, 'The Cromwellian Regime, 1650-60', in *A New History of Ireland, III: Early Modern Ireland 1534–1691* (Oxford, 1976), 372–3; *Correspondence of Henry Cromwell*, 231, 315.

33. *Acts and Ordinances of the Interregnum*, 1250–62.

34. *History of the Down Survey by Dr William Petty*, xvii; *The Petty–Southwell Correspondence*, 48–9, 'having traded so little in the perishing Commoditie of friendshipp'.

35. *Correspondence of Robert Boyle*, I, 254–5; 286–7; BL, Add MS 21,128, fol. 87r.

36. Petty, *The Political Anatomy of Ireland*, 27, in a country with five times as many Irish as English and Scots.

37. Barnard, *Cromwellian Ireland*, preface and 298-36; see also John Morrill, 'Cromwell, Parliament, Ireland and a Commonwealth in Crisis: 1652 Revisited', *Parliamentary History*, June 2011, Vol. 30 (2), 193–214.

38. 'Commonwealth State Accounts', 284, 292, 308; *Mercurius Politicus*, 392, 26 November-3 December 1657; *Correspondence of Henry Cromwell*, 235–6, 272. Or 'Peace comes through war', Cromwell's motto derives from Vegetius's treatise on war, 'gitur qui desiderat pacem, praeparet bellum', 'Therefore let him who desires peace prepare for war'.

39. *Correspondence of Robert Boyle*, I, 286–7; *Diary of Thomas Burton*, I, 385–6; II, 531–43; *Ireland under the Commonwealth*, Dunlop (ed.), II, 622–4, 684; *State Papers of John Thurloe*, VI, 527, VII, 114–15, 282; Gillespie, 'The transformation of the Irish economy 1550–1700', 31–55; *Correspondence of*

Henry Cromwell, 236, n.149; *Clarke Papers*, II, 49–50; Albert J. Loomie, 'Oliver Cromwell's policy toward the English Catholics: the appraisal by diplomats, 1654–1658', *Catholic Historical Review*, 90, No. 1 (Jan., 2004), 29–44, 40.

15. A LIFE IN FIRE

1. Seven years earlier he had told his wife, 'I grow an old man and feel the infirmities of age marvellously steal upon me', *Writings and Speeches of Oliver Cromwell*, Abbott (ed.), II, 239; Oliver Cromwell's steward John Maidston described his master's physique in a letter to John Winthrop, Governor of Connecticut, printed in John Forster, *Eminent British Statesmen*, VII (London, 1839), Appendix A, 393–400; *Clarke Papers*, III, 51, 161; *Swedish Diplomats at Cromwell's court, 1655–1656: the Missions of Peter Julius Coyet and Christer Bonde*, Michael Roberts (ed.), Camden Fourth Series, 36 (London, 1988), 155, 251–2; *CSPVen*, 1656–7, 286; Cromwell had six apothecaries and surgeons and six physicians, *Diary of Thomas Burton*, I, 413–16, II, 516–30.

2. *Mercurius Politicus*, 345, 15–22 January 1657; *Diary of Thomas Burton*, I, 266.

3. *Clarke Papers*, III, 84; *Diary of Thomas Burton*, I, 370; Whitelocke, *Diary*, 464–5.

4. *The Letters and Speeches of Oliver Cromwell*, Lomas and Firth (eds), I, 246, 602; Hutchinson, *Memoir of the Life of Colonel Hutchinson*, 209; Jane Desbrow died in October 1656. The name is variously spelled Desbrow, Disbrowe and Desborough.

5. *Diary of Thomas Burton*, I, 382–5; *State Papers of John Thurloe*, III, 572; *The Writings and Speeches of Oliver Cromwell*, Abbott (ed.), IV, 274; Andrew Barclay, 'The Lord Protector and his Court', in Patrick Little (ed.), *Oliver Cromwell: New Perspectives* (Basingstoke, 2009), 195–215; Noble, *Memoirs of the Protectorate-house of Cromwell*, I, 414–16; Richard Cromwell's correspondence shows him looking to his younger brother for guidance and approval, see e.g. *Correspondence of Henry Cromwell*, 76.

6. *Diary of Thomas Burton*, I, 353; Ludlow, *Memoirs of Edmund Ludlow*, II, 20; *Memoirs of the Verney Family*, III, 219, 220–1; *A Second Narrative of the Late Parliament* (London, 1659), 21; *CSPVen*, 1657–9, 4/14 December 1657.

7. *Mercurius Politicus*, 345, 15–22 January 1657, 7541–4; Marshall, A., 'Sindercombe, Miles (d. 1657), parliamentarian soldier and conspirator', *Oxford Dictionary of National Biography*.

8. *Diary of Thomas Burton*, I, 360.

9. *The Court and Kitchen of Elizabeth Cromwell* (London, 1664), 42–3; *Mercurius Politicus*, 350, 19–26 February 1657; *CSPVen*, 1657–9, 21; Patrick Little,

'Music at the court of King Oliver', *The Court Historian*, 12:2, 173–91, 180; *The History of the King's Works*, H. M. Colvin (ed.) (London, 1962–82), IV, 335–6; Thurley, *Whitehall Palace*, 96–7.

10. Patrick Little, 'John Thurloe and the offer of the Crown to Oliver Cromwell', in Little (ed.), *Oliver Cromwell: New Perspectives*, 216–41; *State Papers of John Thurloe*, VI, 21; *The Court and Kitchen of Elizabeth Cromwell*, 42–3 ; Jonathan Fitzgibbons, *Cromwell's House of Lords: Politics, Parliaments and Constitutional Revolution 1642–1660* (Woodbridge, 2018).

11. Whitelocke, *Diary*, 281–2.

12. *Letters and Speeches of Oliver Cromwell*, Lomas and Firth (eds), II, 382; *The Oceana of James Harrington* (London, 1700), xix; *Correspondence of Henry Cromwell*, 216; C. H. Firth, 'Cromwell and the Crown', *English Historical Review*, January 1903, 18 (69), 52–80; *Swedish Diplomats at Cromwell's Court*, 75–6.

13. *State Papers of John Thurloe*, VI, 37–8; *Correspondence of Henry Cromwell*, 194.

14. *Correspondence of Henry Cromwell*, 206, 207; *Diary of Thomas Burton*, 378.

15. S. Carrington, *The History of the Life and Death of his Most Serene Highness Oliver* (London, 1659), 193, for the story of Cromwell's grief for the loss of his French manservant Duret; Duret's whole family was brought over from France and Mlle Duret was given her own apartment at Hampton Court, Ernest Law, *The History of Hampton Court Palace*, 3 vols (London, 1885–91), II, 290; CSPVen, 1655–6, 26 May 1656; *Correspondence of Henry Cromwell*, 184; Henry Fletcher, *The Perfect Politician or a Full View of the Life and Action of O Cromwell* (London, 1660), 348–50; *State Papers of John Thurloe*, VI, 37.

16. *Correspondence of Henry Cromwell*, 202–3, 206, 214, 216; *Diary of Thomas Burton*, I, 382–5; Carrington, *The History of the Life and Death of His Most Serene Highness Oliver*, 247, 'he was all as it were fire, that is, of a passionate constitution'; Winthrop's description of Cromwell, Forster, *Eminent British Statesmen*, VII, 393–400.

17. Robert Carruthers, *The History of Huntingdon: From the Earliest to the Present Times* (Huntingdon, 1824), 309–10; *A History of the County of Huntingdon*, Victoria County History, 4 vols (1926–1938), II, 121–39. James I stayed at Hinchingbrooke in 1603, 1604 (twice), 1605 (twice), 1608, 1610, 1614, 1617 (twice), 1618, 1619, 1622, 1623 (for over two weeks), Prince Charles certainly accompanied his father to Huntingdon in 1617 and was with him at Hinchingbrooke for some of his two-week stay in 1623, Emily V. Cole, 'The State Apartment in the Jacobean Country House 1603–1625', D. Phil., University of Sussex, 2010, Appendix 1, Itinerary of James I; Patrick Little, 'Uncovering a protectoral stud: horses and horse-breeding at the court of Oliver Cromwell, 1653–8', *Historical Research*, May 2009, 82 (216), 252–67. The specific story about a small Oliver Cromwell clouting a

small Prince Charles in a play fight at Hinchingbrooke in 1604 is probably apocryphal, but the premise that Sir Oliver's young kinsmen participated in these royal visits is likely to be correct, Noble, *The Protectorate House of Cromwell*, I, 110–11; *Letters and Speeches of Oliver Cromwell*, Lomas and Firth (eds), III, 313–14, for Oliver writing to John Newdigate in 1631 about the loss of a hawk bearing his badge; Whitelocke, *Diary*, 271; Marvell in his Poem *Upon the Death of his Late Highness*, refers to 'his delight / In horses fierce, wild deer, or armour bright …', line 244.

18. *Acts of the Privy Council*, 46, 1630–1, 128, 140; Sir Philip Warwick, *Memoirs of the Reign of King Charles the First* (Edinburgh, 1813), 275–6; see also *Original Letters Illustrative of English History*, Henry Ellis (ed.), 2nd ser. (4 vols, 1827), III, 248, although the 'Monsr Cromwell' being treated by Dr Mayerne for 'melancholicus' may be another member of the Cromwell family; CSPD, 1629–31, v–xxix Preface; John Morrill, 'The making of Oliver Cromwell', in John Morrill (ed.), *Oliver Cromwell and the English Revolution* (London and New York, 1990), 19–49.

19. *Edmund Pettis' Survey of St Ives, 1728*, Mary Carter (ed.), Cambridge Record Society, 2002; Caroline Clifford and Alan Akeroyd, *Risen from Obscurity? Oliver Cromwell and Huntingdonshire*, Huntingdonshire Local History Society, 2002, 33; *Letters and Speeches of Oliver Cromwell*, Lomas and Firth (eds), III, 313–14.

20. *Letters and Speeches of Oliver Cromwell*, Lomas and Firth (eds), I, 79, 88–9; *Reliquiae Baxterianae or Mr Richard Baxter's Narrative of the most Memorable Passages of his Life and Times* (London, 1696), 57; Noble, *Memoirs of the Protectorate-house of Cromwell*, I, 121–2.

21. *Writings and Speeches of Oliver Cromwell*, Abbott (ed.), II, 601–2.

22. The Lord Protector's Speech to Parliament, 20 January 1658, *Writings and Speeches of Oliver Cromwell*, Abbott (ed.), IV, 705; Andrew Barclay, 'Oliver Cromwell and the Cambridge elections of 1640', *Parliamentary History*, 29, 2 (2010); Andrew Barclay, *Electing Cromwell: The Making of a Politician* (Abingdon, 2011).

23. *Writings and Speeches of Oliver Cromwell*, Abbott (ed.), IV, 471–2; *Reliquiae Baxterianae*, 196.

24. 'his greatest delight was to read men rather then books', Carrington, *The History of Oliver, late Lord Protector*, 243; 'He seemed exceeding open hearted by a familiar rustick affected Carriage (especially to his soldiers in sporting with them)', *Reliquiae Baxterianae*, 70, 99; *Memoirs of Edmund Ludlow*, I, 185–6; James Heath, *Flagellum: or, the Life and death, birth and burial of Oliver Cromwell, the late usurper* (London, 1663), 174; Ian Gentles, *Oliver Cromwell: God's Warrior and the English Revolution* (Basingstoke, 2011), 111–15; Patrick Little, 'Oliver Cromwell's sense of humour', *Cromwelliana*, Series II, no. 4 (2007), 73–85.

25. *Writings and Speeches of Oliver Cromwell*, Abbott (ed.), I, 246; II, 198–9; 424–6; for Bridget's *froideur* see, for example, her letter to Henry Cromwell, *Correspondence of Henry Cromwell*, 521.

26. Joad Raymond, 'An eye-witness to King Cromwell', *History Today*, 47 (7), July 1997, 36; *Monarchy asserted to be the best, most ancient and legall form of government in a conference had at Whitehall* (London, 1660), 89; Worden, 'Cromwell and the Sin of Achan'.

27. C. H. Firth, 'Cromwell and the Crown', *English Historical Review*, 17 (67), July 1902, 429–42; 18 (69), January 1903, 52–80; Firth, *The Last Years of the Protectorate*, II, 128–64; *Correspondence of Henry Cromwell*, 214, 216, 222, 229–30, 235, 236; *State Papers of John Thurloe*, VI, 89–99; CSPD, 1656–7, 292, 307; *Clarke Papers*, III, 92–8; *Diary of Thomas Burton*, I, 380–93.

28. Little, *Lord Broghill and the Cromwellian Union with Ireland and Scotland*, ch. 5; *Correspondence of Henry Cromwell*, 236; *State Papers of John Thurloe*, VI, 152; *Diary of Thomas Burton*, I, 393–7; Little, 'John Thurloe and the offer of the Crown to Oliver Cromwell', in Little (ed.), *Oliver Cromwell: New Perspectives*, 216–41; Jonathan Fitzgibbons, 'Hereditary succession and the Cromwellian Protectorate: the offer of the crown reconsidered', *English Historical Review*, Vol. 128, No. 534 (October 2013), 1095–1128.

29. *Diary of Thomas Burton*, I, 397–413; *State Papers of John Thurloe*, I, 397; *Correspondence of Henry Cromwell*, 239.

30. CSPD, 1656–7, xxi.

31. CSPD, 1656–7, 31; *Diary of Thomas Burton*, I, 413–16; *Correspondence of Henry Cromwell*, 244; *Register of the Consultations of the Ministers of Edinburgh and Some other Brethren of the Ministry*, William Stephen (ed.), 2 vols (Edinburgh, 1921–30), II 1657–1660, 5–18; Little, 'Horses and horse-breeding at the court of Oliver Cromwell, 1653–8', 258.

32. *Correspondence of Henry Cromwell*, 273; *Swedish Diplomats at Cromwell's Court*, 75–6.

33. *Diary of Thomas Burton*, I, 419–20.

34. *State Papers of John Thurloe*, VI, 243; *Correspondence of Henry Cromwell*, 260.

35. *Correspondence of Henry Cromwell*, 267–8; *State Papers of John Thurloe*, VI, 243; Henry Walker, *A Collection of Several Passages Concerning his Late Highnesse Oliver Cromwell* (London, 1659), 20. Russell was the father of Henry Cromwell's wife, Elizabeth, and so a member of the wider Cromwell family.

36. Whitelocke, *Diary*, 462; *Correspondence of Henry Cromwell*, 257, 264, 266–8; *State Papers of John Thurloe*, VI, 43, 281.

37. As Lambert reportedly put it, 'it is a question of whether we will retrace our steps, or whether we will advance', reported by the French Ambassador Bordeaux to Cardinal Mazarin, quoted in Firth, 'Cromwell

and the Crown', EHR, 18, no. 96 (Jan., 1903), 52–80; Whitelocke, *Diary*, 464; Whitelock, *Memorials of the English Affairs*, IV, 289–91.

38. *Original Letters and Papers of State*, Nickolls (ed.), 141–2. *The Cromwell Association Online Directory of Parliamentarian Army Officers*, Stephen K. Roberts (ed.) (2017).

39. *Correspondence of Henry Cromwell*, 266–7.

40. *Commons Journal*, VII, 535, on the question of whether the change of the title from King to Lord Protector should proceed to a vote, 47 were in favour and 46 against; *Diary of Thomas Burton*, II, 118–19; *Correspondence of Henry Cromwell*, 273, 275. Cromwell's conduct in this kingship crisis has been interpreted differently by various scholars. For the argument that Oliver was managing and manipulating the two parties, clear he would never agree to take the title, see Austin Woolrych, *Britain in Revolution 1625–1660* (Oxford, 2002), ch. 22.

16. ON THE WATCH TOWER

1. *Diary of Thomas Burton*, II, 470–2; CSPD, 1657–8, 19–20; CSPVen, 1657–9, 77–91.

2. *Acts and Ordinances of the Interregnum*, 1170–80; *Diary of Thomas Burton*, II, 470; *Swedish Diplomats at Cromwell's Court*, 299; Heath, *Flagellum*, 174; *Original Letters and Papers of State*, Nickolls (ed.), 115; Whitelocke, *Diary*, 412; Simon Thurley, *Hampton Court: a Social and Architectural History* (London and New Haven, 2004), 71, 90–93, 125–8; the 1659 inventory of Hampton Court printed in Law, *The History of Hampton Court Palace*, II, Appendix C, 280, 302; Paul M. Hunneyball, 'Cromwellian style: the architectural trappings of the Protectorate regime', in Patrick Little (ed.), *The Cromwellian Protectorate*, 71–2; *The Picture of a New Courtier* (London, 1656), 13 refers to 'the new Rivers and Ponds at Hampton Court, whose making cost vast sums of money, and ... the game in the Hare warren that my dear Master hath inclosed for his own use.'

3. *State Papers of John Thurloe*, VI, 455; Howard Colvin, 'The Architect of Thorpe Hall', *Country Life*, 111, Issue 2890 (6 June 1952), 1732–5; John Cornforth, 'Thorpe Hall, Cambridgeshire: A Property of the Sue Ryder Foundation', *Country Life*, 185, 44 (31 October 1991), 70–3; Timothy Mowl and Brian Earnshaw, *Architecture without Kings: The Rise of Puritan Classicism under Cromwell* (Manchester, 1995); *A History of the County of Cambridge and the Isle of Ely*, IV, R. B. Pugh (ed.) (London, 2002), 254; David Farr, 'John Lambert and the roots of an early-modern art collection', *Cromwelliana*, 2002, 46–55.

4. *Diary of John Evelyn*, III, 193; *Commons Journal*, VII, 578; Thurley, *Hampton Court*, 225–8; Linda Levy Peck, *Consuming Splendor: Society and Culture in*

17th Century England (Cambridge, 2005), ch. 6; David Jacques, 'Garden design in the mid-seventeenth century', Architectural History, 44, 'Essays in Architectural History Presented to John Newman' (2001), 365–376; C. Litton Falkiner, Illustrations of Irish History and Topography Mainly of the Seventeenth Century (London, 1904), 51–2; Correspondence of Henry Cromwell, 57, 75–6, 284; Farr, 'John Lambert and the roots of an early-modern art collection', 46–55.

5. Severall Proceedings of State Affairs, 232, 2–9 March 1654; 243, 18–25 May 1654; State Papers of John Thurloe, II, 144–5; Memoirs of Edmund Ludlow, I, 379; The Court and Kitchen of Elizabeth Cromwell, 24; Whitelocke, Diary, 389; Roy Sherwood, The Court of Oliver Cromwell (Cambridge, 1989); the Cromwells moved into the former royal apartments at Whitehall in April 1654, almost four months after Oliver was created Lord Protector, on the arrival of the delegation of diplomats from the Dutch Republic, Severall Proceedings of State Affaires, 238, 13–20 April 1654.

6. CSPD, 1652–3, 22; The Inventories and Valuations of the King's Goods 1649–51, Oliver Millar (ed.), Walpole Society, 43 (Glasgow, 1972), 331–2. The tapestries have been identified by Wendy Hefford as a set of 'Horsemanship' by Jacob Jordaens, Koenraad Brosens (ed.), Flemish Tapestry in European and American Collections: Studies in Honour of Guy Delmarcel (Turnhout, 2003); The Faithful Narrative of the Late Testimony and Demand made to Oliver Cromwell, 6–8; Coke, A Detection of the Court and State of England, II, 58; Diary of John Evelyn, III, 166.

7. Clarke Papers, II, 118; CSPVen, 1657–9, 104; 'Inventory of Goods at Hampton Court, 1659', Law, Hampton Court, II, 303, 308; State Papers of John Thurloe, VI, 447.

8. Correspondence of Henry Cromwell, 85, 86, 103. When Elizabeth was ill in pregnancy in 1655 her doctor wrote to Henry Cromwell that 'I never saw 2 parents so affected (or more) than the Lord Protector and Her Highness'; The Oceana of James Harrington, xix; Calendar of the Clarendon State Papers preserved in the Bodleian Library, O. Ogle, W. H. Bliss and H. O. Coxe, et al., 5 vols (Oxford, 1872–1970), III, 245; Whitelocke, Diary, 281–2, 495; Richard Fleckno, Love's Dominion or a Dramatique Piece full of Excellent Moralitie (London, 1654); Carrington, The History of the Life and Death of Oliver Lord Protector, 219–22; State Papers of John Thurloe, VII, 94.

9. State Papers of John Thurloe, VI, 455; Raymond, 'An eye-witness to King Cromwell', 35–41; Correspondence of Henry Cromwell, 301; Clarke Papers, II, 118; III, 114; Andrew Marvell, 'A poem upon the death of his Late Highness the Lord Protector', lines 47–50.

10. Henry Walker, A Collection of Several Passages Concerning his late Highnesse Oliver Cromwell (London, 1659), 11; James Waylen, The House of Cromwell and the Story of Dunkirk (London, 1880), 7.

11. *Letters and Speeches of Oliver Cromwell*, Lomas and Firth (eds), I, 448–9; Noble, *The Protectorate House of Cromwell*, I, 423–6; 'My lord protector shewed a great deal of kindness to my wife and daughter in particular', *State Papers of John Thurloe*, II, 257; Noble, *The Protectorate House of Cromwell*, I, 405, 423–6; Fletcher, *The Perfect Politician*, 348–50.

12. CSPVen, 1657–9, 106; *The Diary of John Evelyn*, III, 197; Law, *History of Hampton Court*, II, 'Inventory of Cromwell's Goods (1659)', 281, 295.

13. *Diary of Sir Archibald Johnston of Wariston*, 3 vols (1911–40), III, 93–9; *Several Proceedings of State Affairs*, 242, 11–18 May 1654; *Diary of John Evelyn*, III, 109; 'Cromwell as music lover', in Percy A. Scholes, *The Puritans and Music in England and New England: A Contribution to the Cultural History of two Nations* (Oxford, 1934), 'Hingston ... had the Organ of Magd: Colledge in the Palace Hall of Hampton Court ... He had them [Latin songs] sung at the Cokepit at White Hall, where he had an organ ...', 142; 'Cromwell's death and funeral order', in *The Diary of Thomas Burton*, 2, 516–30; Law, *Hampton Court*, II, 295; *The Letters of Samuel Pepys*, Guy de la Bédoyère (ed.) (Woodbridge, 2006), 17–18; L'Estrange, *Truth and loyalty vindicated*, 50. When Frances Cromwell married Richard Rich '48 violins and 50 trumpets' played at Whitehall, an orchestra proper, as part of the entertainments including dancing which went on until 5 a.m., *HMC Fifth Report*, 177.

14. *Swedish Diplomats at Cromwell's Court*, 150–1; CSPVen, 1653–4, 273–80, 7 November 1654; Huygens, *English Journal*, 6.

15. *Diary of Sir Archibald Johnston of Wariston*, III, 93–9; Clarendon, *History of the Rebellion*, VI, 34; Jason Peacey, '"Fit for public services": the upbringing of Richard Cromwell', in Little (ed.), *Oliver Cromwell: New Perspectives*; Clarendon, *History of the Rebellion*, VI, 34.

16. *State Papers of John Thurloe*, VI, 455, 496; *Diary of Sir Archibald Johnston of Wariston*, III, 96–7.

17. *Mercurius Politicus*, 376, 13–20 August 1657; 378, 20–27 August 1657; CSPVen, 1657–9, 105; Whitelocke, *Diary*, 480; 'much lesse doe such thinges fall upon a person of his quality by chance. This rod hath a voyce', *State Papers of John Thurloe*, VI, 493; CSPD, 1657–8, 84. Richard Cromwell had sustained another serious injury earlier in 1657 when the timber stair leading to the Banqueting House had collapsed as he and a crowd of MPs mounted it.

18. *Mercurius Politicus*, 382, 17–24 September 1657; 383, 24 September–1 October; 385, 8–15 October 1657; 388, 29 October–5 November 1657.

19. Levy Peck, *Consuming Splendor*, 273–4; *Oxford History of the British Empire. 1: The Origins of Empire*, Nicholas Canny (ed.) (Oxford, 1998), chs 10, 11, 12; John Keay, *The Honourable Company: A History of the East India Company* (London, 1991), ch. 6; *The Court and Kitchen of Elizabeth*

Cromwell, 16; *The Oceana of James Harrington*, xix; Ribeiro, *Fashion and Fiction*, 296–9; Whittle and Griffiths, *Consumption and Gender*, 120–2; Law, *Hampton Court*, II, 278–80, 292, 299; *Historical Manuscripts Commission, Second Report*, 148. Whitehall and Hampton Court were furnished for the Cromwells with a combination of unsold pieces from Charles I's collection and new items purchased by Clement Kinnersley, and were handsomely funded – over £6,000 was spent on purchases and reupholstery for Whitehall alone in 1654. Kinnersley was to undertake this work 'according to instructions from her highness Lady Cromwell', *CSPD*, 1654, 394, 402; *Memoirs of the Verney Family*, III, 130; Millar (ed.), *The Inventories and Valuations of the King's Goods 1649–1651*, *passim* for the numerous items retained for Oliver Cromwell's use (marked 'in His Highness's service').

20. *Acts and Ordinances of the Interregnum*, 26–7; *Diary of John Evelyn*, III, 197–8, 229; C. H. Firth, 'Sir William Davenant and the revival of the drama during the Protectorate', *English Historical Review*, Vol. 18, No. 70 (Apr., 1903), 319–21; Hotson, *The Commonwealth and Restoration Stage* (London, 1928), ch. 3; *The Diurnal of Thomas Rugg*, William L. Sachse (ed.) (London, 1961), 10; *The Diary of Samuel Pepys*, Robert Latham and William Matthews (eds) (London, 1970–83), X, 70–1. Steve Pincus, '"Coffee Politicians Does Create": coffeehouses and Restoration political culture', *Journal of Modern History*, Vol. 67, No. 4 (Dec., 1995), 807–34; William Davenant, *The Cruelty of the Spaniards in Peru* (London, 1658). The closest thing the British Isles had hitherto known to public opera were the court 'masques' beloved of Charles I and Henrietta Maria which featured royal or aristocratic amateur singers and dancers, for which Inigo Jones had adapted the Tudor cockpit at Whitehall.

21. *Diary of John Evelyn*, III, 97; Edmund Waller, *A Panegyric to my Lord Protector* (London, 1655); *Severall Proceedings of State Affairs*, 240, 27 April–4 May 1654; *CSPVen*, 1653–4, 264–73, 19 October 1654; 1657–9, 123–35, 23/13 November 1657; *Writings and Speeches of Oliver Cromwell*, Abbott (ed.), IV, 390; *HMC Fifth Report*, 177; BL, Harl MS 991, fol. 23; Heath, *Flagellum*, 204–5.

22. *Mercurius Politicus*, 304, 3–10 April 1656; *Ireland under the Commonwealth*, II, 416–21, 456; *Writings and Speeches of Oliver Cromwell*, Abbott (ed.), III, 805; Wilfred S. Samuel and M. N. Castello, 'The first London synagogue of the resettlement', *Transactions of the Jewish Historical Society of England*, Vol. 10 (1921–1923), 1–48, i–ii, 49–147; Lucien Wolf, 'Crypto-Jews under the Commonwealth', *Transactions of the Jewish Historical Society of England*, Vol. 1 (1893–94), 55–88; D. Katz, 'Menasseh ben Israel (1604–1657), rabbi and campaigner for the readmission of Jews to England.' *Oxford Dictionary of National Biography*; Christopher Durston, 'Puritan rule and

the failure of cultural revolution 1645–1669', in Durston and Eales, *The Culture of English Puritanism*, 210–33; Bradstock, *Radical Religion in Cromwell's England*.

23. *Letters of Samuel Pepys*, 21–2; *Clarke Papers*, III, 129; *CSPVen*, 1657–9, 11/21 December 1657, 135–48; *Swedish Diplomats at Cromwell's Court*, 68; *Acts and Ordinances of the Interregnum*, 1170–80, for the oath to be sworn by Catholics, including denying the authority of the Pope, the real presence in the mass, the existence of purgatory and salvation through good works. Cromwell was an adept diplomat when it came to dealing with his French Catholic allies, hanging Whitehall with paintings of French sovereigns and professing sympathy with their plight. *The Inventories and Valuations of the Late King's Goods*, Millar (ed.).

24. Whitelocke, *Diary*, 482.

25. Edward Holberton, *Poetry and the Cromwellian Protectorate: Culture, Politics and Institutions* (Oxford, 2011), 143–63; *CSPVen*, 1653–4, 264–73, 19 October 1654; C. H. Firth, 'Letters concerning the dissolution of Cromwell's last parliament, 1658', *EHR*, 7, no. 25 (Jan. 1892), 102–10; Fitzgibbons, *Cromwell's House of Lords*, 122–55.

26. *Writings and Speeches of Oliver Cromwell*, Abbott (ed.), VI, 709; Whitelocke, *Diary*, 483; *Diary of Thomas Burton*, II, 316–30; *Clarke Papers*, III, 133.

27. *Diary of Thomas Burton*, II, 346–71; *CSPD*, 1657–8, 273; *State Papers of John Thurloe*, VI, 648; VII, 115; *Memoirs of Edmund Ludlow*, II, 31–2; C. H. Firth, 'A letter from Lord Saye and Sele to Lord Wharton, 29 December 1657', *EHR*, 10, 37, January 1895, 106–7; *Clarke Papers*, III, 133.

28. Whitelocke, *Diary*, 485; Firth, 'Letters concerning the dissolution of Cromwell's last parliament', 102–10; *Writings and Speeches of Oliver Cromwell*, Abbott (ed.), IV, 735; *Commons Journal*, VII, 1651–1660, 592.

29. Firth, 'Letters concerning the dissolution of Cromwell's last parliament', 102–10; *HMC Fifth Report*, 166; *Writings and Speeches of Oliver Cromwell*, Abbott (ed.), IV, 737; *Clarke Papers*, III, 140–1.

30. *State Papers of John Thurloe*, VII, 218.

31. *CSPVen*, 1657–9, 168–9, 269; *Writings and Speeches of Oliver Cromwell*, Abbott (ed.), IV, 744–6; *HMC Fifth Report*, 161, 166; John Maidston's character of Oliver Cromwell, printed in Forster, *Eminent British Statesmen*, VII, 393–400; *Clarke Papers*, III, 141; *State Papers of John Thurloe*, VII, 340; Firth, 'Letters concerning the dissolution of Cromwell's last Parliament', 110; 'February 1657[/8] ... One night in bed he could not sleep & rose & of a sudden struck his bedchamber man & called him Presbiterean rascall. He went out to his fellow servants & when they came in they found O. crying and howling', BL, Harley MS 991, fol. 13r.

32. *Reliquae Baxterianiae*, 57; Clarendon, *History of the Rebellion*, VI, 97; Peter Gaunt, '"The single person's confidants and dependants"? Oliver

Cromwell and his Protectoral councillors', *Historical Journal*, Vol. 32, No. 3 (Sept., 1989), 537–60.

33. *State Papers of John Thurloe*, VII, 72, 85, 171–2, 218; Firth, *The Last Years of the Protectorate* II, 278; *Memoirs of Edmund Ludlow*, II, 41; Heath, *Flagellum*, 204–5; Carrington, *The History of the Life and Death of Oliver Lord Protector*, 219.

34. *State Papers of John Thurloe*, VII, 115, 269; Andrew Marvell, 'A Poem upon the Death of the Late Highness the Lord Protector', lines 55–60, 'Each groan he doubled and each sigh he sighed / Repeated over to the restless night'; *Correspondence of Henry Cromwell*, 396; Whitelocke, *Diary*, 495.

35. *State Papers of John Thurloe*, VII, 320, 340; *Correspondence of Henry Cromwell*, 399–401, the first 135 lines of Andrew Marvell's 320-line 'Poem on the Death of his Late Highness the Lord Protector' are devoted to the death of Elizabeth Claypole and its effect on Oliver; Walker, *A Collection of Severall Passages Concerning his late Highnesse Oliver Cromwell*, 1; *The Memoirs of Edmund Ludlow*, 43; *Clarke Papers*, III, 161; Carrington, *The History of the Life and Death of Oliver Lord Protector*, 218–20; Cromwell's new son-in-law Viscount Fauconberg confirmed to Henry Cromwell on 31 August, three days before Oliver's death, that 'A successor there is none named', *State Papers of John Thurloe*, VII, 365.

36. *State Papers of John Thurloe*, VII, 362–5.

37. *State Papers of John Thurloe*, VII, 372–5. The Cromwell family were beside themselves with grief, Mary Fauconberg wept for days with a 'passion that tears her very hart in peeces ...', but Oliver's mind was elsewhere in his last hours 'he seems to forget even his own family', Walker, *A Collection of Severall Passages Concerning his late Highnesse Oliver Cromwell*, 2–12; Whitelocke, *Diary*, 496; Edward Nichols reported that even among the army officers 'some say Henry Cromwell is fitter for that charge then Richard', BL, Add MS 78,195, fol. 139r. Cromwell had written in his letter to his cousin Elizabeth of his spiritual rebirth as the dawning certainly that God would 'bring me to his tabernacle, to His resting place', see ch. 15. For the argument that Oliver Cromwell never named a successor and the choice of Richard Cromwell was a speedy stitch-up by the Council of State see Jonathan Fitzgibbons, '"Not in any doubtful dispute"? Reassessing the nomination of Richard Cromwell', *Historical Research*, 83, 220 (May 2010), 281–300. The events of the Protector's final hours are murky, but if Richard had not in fact been named it seems strange it was not referenced at the time of, or after, his fall.

17. THIS LYON ROUZED

1. E. Dennison and Russel Coleman, *Historic Dalkeith: the Scottish Burgh Survey* (Historic Scotland, 1998), 20–9; William Fraser, *The Douglas Book*, 4 vols (Edinburgh, 1885), IV, 378; *The Register of the Privy Council of Scotland*, V, 1592–1599, 507; *Calendar of State Papers, Scotland*, 4, 1571–74, 677, 680.

2. For Monck's character see Thomas Gumble, *The Life of General Monck, Duke of Albemarle, etc. with Remarks upon his Actions* (London, 1671), 465–75; for Anne's character and appearance see John Price, *The Mystery and Method of His Majesty's Happy Restauration laid open to Publick View* (London, 1683), 11–32; Pepys, *Diary*, VI, 324; VII, 56–7.

3. Aubrey, *Brief Lives*, II, 72–3; *Extracts from the Records of the Burgh of Edinburgh*, 1655–65, 48; Thomas Skinner, *The Life of General Monk, Duke of Albemarle* (London, 1724), 24, 70; Gumble, *Life of General Monck*, 470, 475, 'never father took the loss of a child with more tears and grief'.

4. Lawrence Stone, 'Inigo Jones and the New Exchange', *Archaeological Journal*, 114 (1957), 106–121; Ann Saunders (ed.), *The Royal Exchange*, London Topographical Society, 152 (1997), ch. VIII; John Stow, *Annales, or, a generall chronicle of england. begun by iohn stow: Continued … vnto the end of this present yeere, 1631. by edmund howes, gent London* (London, 1632), 868–9. I have assumed Anne Clarges was born in 1619, based on the assertion in 1670 that the 53 women mourners at her funeral represented the years of her life, *HMC Twelfth Report, Le Fleming MSS* (London, 1890), 69. Anne Clarges daughter of John Clarges, farrier, married Thomas Radford at St Lawrence Pountney on 28 February 1632/3, 'Marriage Register of St Laurence Pountney', www.ancestry.com; Radford, of Fosson, Derbyshire, had served his apprenticeship as a Haberdasher from 1624 to 1632, Worshipful Company of Haberdashers, 'Register of apprentice bindings 1610–1630' and 'Register of freedom admissions 1526–1613', London Metropolitan Archives. Thomas and Anne Radford were parents to an apparently short-lived daughter, Mary, baptized in 1634 in St Martin in the Fields, *The Register of St Martin-in-the-Fields London*, II, 1619–1636, J. V. Kitto (ed.) (London, 1939), 11. Hatfield House, Accounts 161/4, register of leases granted by the second Earl of Salisbury 1632–7, fol. 34; Box N/9, fol 9; Box R/5; Accounts 38/7, in which an Anne Redford was renting a small shop in the upper part of the Exchange in 1641; I am indebted to Robin Harcourt Williams for his generous assistance and for these references from the Hatfield collection.

5. In 1649 Anne was an executor with her brother Thomas of their father's estate, TNA, PROB11/207/11, in which she received a bequest of £30 and some furniture. Her marriage to George Monck on 23 January 1653, 'The

---

Rejester Book for Marriages, for Christenings and Burials for St Georges in Southwark from 1602', fol. 68v, www.ancestry.com; *State Papers of John Thurloe*, I, 740. A shopkeeper named Thomas Radford was operating in Chesterfield, Derbyshire in the 1660s and (like many others) issued tokens; his bore the arms of London's Worshipful Company of Haberdashers. No one else named Thomas Radford became a freeman of the Haberdashers' Company in this era, making it likely this was indeed Anne Clarges/Monck's missing first husband. British Museum, Alloy Token issued in Chesterfield bearing the name 'Thomas Radford', Registration number T.338. In 1669 the Grand Duke of Tuscany was told Anne had once been 'employed in one of the mercers' shops in the Exchange', *Travels of Cosmo the Third Grand Duke of Tuscany through England* (London, 1821), 469–70; *Gentlemen's Magazine*, 1793, 63 (II), 886–7; Pepys, *Diary*, VII, 536; *The Case of the Heirs at Law to George Monke Late Duke of Albemarle* (London, 1709); Josiah Brown, *Reports of Cases upon Appeals and Writs of Error in the High Court of Parliament 1701–1779*, (Dublin, 1784), 256–70.

6. '... he remembred an Apothegm of Mr Nye, That he had rather be devoured by a Lion, than eaten up by Rats, Mice or Lice', Gumble, *Life of General Monck*, 259.

7. *Letters and Speeches of Oliver Cromwell*, Lomas and Firth (eds), II, 116–18.

8. *Scotland and the Protectorate: Letters and Papers Relating to the Military Government of Scotland from January 1654 to June 1659*, C. H. Firth (ed.) (Edinburgh, 1899), 149–53; John Nicholl, *A Diary of Public Transactions and other Occurrences Chiefly in Scotland* (Edinburgh, 1836), 137; F. D. Dow, *Cromwellian Scotland 1651–1660* (Edinburgh, 1979), 12–42; Gumble, *Life of General Monck*, 81–5.

9. Nicholl, *A Diary of Public Transactions*, 183. *Scotland and the Protectorate*, xxx–xlvii; *State Papers of John Thurloe*, IV, 161, 221; VI, 863; CSPD, 1657–8, 372; Price, *The Mystery and Method*, 8; Dow, *Cromwellian Scotland*, 166ff, 188; R. Scott Spurlock, *Cromwell and Scotland: Conquest and Religion 1650–1660* (Edinburgh, 2007).

10. *State Papers of John Thurloe*, VI, 863; 'my deare friend', *Correspondence of Henry Cromwell*, 357, 407; Skinner, *Life of General Monk*, 10–12; Gumble, *Life of General Monck*, 3; Price, *The Mystery and Method*, 15; Mark Stoyle, 'An early incident in the life of George Monck', *Devon & Cornwall Notes and Queries*, 37, 1992–6, 7–14.

11. *Diary of Sir Archibald Johnston of Wariston*, David Hay Fleming (ed.), 3 vols (Edinburgh, 1911–40), II, 240; Gumble, *Life of General Monck*, 90–1; *Clarke Papers*, IV, 152–3; Price, *The Mystery and Method*, 31–2; Aubrey, *Brief Lives*, II, 72. For religion in Scotland during the Protectorate see Spurlock, *Cromwell and Scotland*.

12. Gumble, *Life of General Monck*, 93, 183; *State Papers of John Thurloe*, VII, 387–8.
13. François Guizot, *History of Richard Cromwell and the Restoration of Charles II*, A. R. Scoble, trans., 2 vols (London, 1856), I, 268–9, 380; Richard Baker, *A Chronicle of the Kings of England from the Time of the Romans Government unto the Death of King James ... Whereunto is Added the Reign of King Charles the First and the first Thirteen Years of His Sacred Majesty King Charles the Second* (London, 1670), 654–5, which C. H. Firth established was closely based on the papers of Thomas Clarges for its account of the restoration.
14. *State Papers of John Thurloe*, VII, 654–5.
15. *State Papers of John Thurloe*, VII, 488–500.
16. *Mercurius Politicus*, 564, 21–28 April 1659; Guizot, *Richard Cromwell*, I, 374–5; *Clarke Papers*, IV, 20–1.
17. *Clarke Papers*, IV, 3, 6–7, 8–9; CSPD, 1658–9, 340; *Mercurius Politicus*, 566, 5–12 May 1659.
18. *Clarke Papers*, IV, 280–1.
19. Guizot, *Richard Cromwell*, I, 374–6, 381–2, 392; *State Papers of John Thurloe*, VII, 654–5; CSPD, 1658–9, 340.
20. *Correspondence of Henry Cromwell*, 344, 407, 425; Price, *The Mystery and Method*, preface; Baker, *A Chronicle of the Kings of England*, 654–5.
21. Baker, *A Chronicle of the Kings of England*, 669–70; Gumble, *Life of General Monck*, 97; *State Papers of John Thurloe*, VII, 669–70; *Correspondence of Henry Cromwell*, 516–17.
22. *Correspondence of Henry Cromwell*, 515–16, 516–17; *State Papers of John Thurloe*, VII, 666–78, 'I am glad at least that our dear father went off in that glory which was due to his actings', 683–5; *Clarke Papers*, IV, 23; Pepys, *Diary*, I, 21.
23. Nicholl, *A Diary of Public Transactions*, 227–43; Spurlock, *Cromwell and Scotland*; R. Scott Spurlock, 'Cromwell's Edinburgh press and the development of print culture in Scotland', *Scottish Historical Review*, 90, 230, pt 2 (October 2011), 179–203.
24. Clarendon, *History of the Rebellion*, VI, 54–7.
25. *Clarke Papers*, IV, 28–9, 38–9, 48. Monck's chaplain Gumble claimed that the General was preparing to join Booth's rebellion when the news of the rebels' defeat arrived. It is unclear whether this was in fact the case, or whether he was backdating Monck's support for the restoration, Maurice Ashley, *General Monck* (London, 1977), 164–5; Godfrey Davies, *The Restoration of Charles II 1658–1660* (Oxford, 1955), 140; Gumble, *Life of General Monck*, 107–8; Price, *The Mystery and Method*, 27–8, 67.
26. *A Collection of Letters written by His Excellency General George Monk afterwards Duke of Albemarle relating to the Restoration of the Royal Family* (London,

1714), 78; Clarendon, *History of the Rebellion*, VI, 154–6; Price, *The Mystery and Method*, 5–31, 38; Gumble, *Life of General Monck*, 103–7.

27. Gumble, *Life of General Monck*, 107; Aubrey, *Brief Lives*, II, 74; Baker, *A Chronicle of the Kings of England*, 688; Price, *The Mystery and Method*, preface, 13; *Clarke Papers*, II, 242; Spurlock, 'Cromwell's Edinburgh Press', 179–203; *Extracts from the Records of the Burgh of Edinburgh*, 1655–65, 18, 32.

28. *State Papers of John Thurloe*, VII, 241; *Clarke Papers*, IV, 25–8, 41, 152–3.

29. Price, *The Mystery and Method*, 11–15, 19–20, Monck would have the consequences of not acting pressed on him by Anne after they got into bed: 'in the Night, [he would be] quickned with a Curtain-Lecture of Damnation; a Text that his Lady oft Preached upon to him, and sometime he would complain of it, where he safely might'; Guizot, *Richard Cromwell*, II, 423; *Parliamentary or Constitutional History of England*, XXII (London, 1763), 5.

30. TNAS, GD224/940/3; GD157/3094; Gumble, *Life of General Monck*, 87; Skinner, *The Life of General Monk*, 63, the General 'much delighted in Planting and husbandry'; Price, *The Mystery and Method*, 11–12, 44–5; Baker, *A Chronicle of the Kings of England*, 675–6.

31. Davies, *The Restoration of Charles II*, 144–54; *A True Narrative of the Proceedings in Parliament, Councell of State, Generall Councell of the Army, and Committee of Safetie* (London, 1659), 1–9, referring to rumours that 'there were intentions to violate the Parliament, to set up a single person or another General'.

32. Baker, *A Chronicle of the Kings of England*, 682; *A True Narrative of the Proceeding in Parliament*, 22–3. In his letter of support to Fleetwood he had added some words of advice, including a reminder that 'you are the free-borne people of England, and nott mercenaries', and must work with this reassembled parliament – warning that there could 'be noe more dashing in pieces nor dissolvings of them, but such as are regular and according to the established forme of government', *State Papers of John Thurloe*, VII, 241.

18. MARS AND MINERVA

1. *Commons Journal*, VII, 796–7; *A True Narrative of the Proceedings in Parliament*, 19–20; *Clarke Papers*, IV, 60–3, 298–9; Rugg, *Diurnal*, 7–8; *Mercurius Politicus*, 591, 13–20 October 1659.

2. Price, *The Mystery and Method*, 44–5; Gumble, *Life of General Monck*, 133; *A Letter from a Person of Quality in Edenburgh to an Officer of the Army* (London, 1659).

3. *The Parliamentary or Constitutional History of England*, XXII 4–7; Baker, *A Chronicle of the Kings of England*, 685; Gumble, *Life of General Monck*, 137–8.

4. The Parliamentary or Constitutional History of England, XXII, 4–7; The Memoirs of Edmund Ludlow, II, 100–1, 132–3; Clarke Papers, IV, 22–3, 90–1; Gumble, Life of General Monck, 137–8; A Letter from a Person of Quality in Edenburgh; David Farr, John Lambert, Parliamentary Soldier and Cromwellian Major-General, 1619–1684 (Woodbridge, 2003), 190–4.

5. Baker, A Chronicle of the Kings of England, 690; Price, The Mystery and Method, preface, 31; Gumble, Life of General Monck, 116–17; Pepys, Diary, I, 22.

6. Price, The Mystery and Method, 14–16; 27–8; The Parliamentary or Constitutional History of England, XXII, 68–70; Clarke Papers, IV, 114–15. There remains debate about when precisely Monck decided he was for the restoration of the monarchy. It was clearly in the interests of many writing after May 1660 to contend that this was his intention all along. My own reading is that he did not become convinced of this until after his arrival in London in February 1660, Woolrych, Britain in Revolution, 743–4; Ronald Hutton, Restoration: A Political and Religious History of England and Wales, 1658–1667 (Oxford, 1986), pt 2; F. M. S. McDonald, 'The timing of General George Monck's march into England, 1 January 1660', EHR, April 1990, 363–76; for another interpretation see Ashley, General Monck.

7. Price, The Mystery and Method, 43–4; Heath, A Chronicle of the Late Intestine War, 763, dedicated to George Monck, now Duke of Albemarle.

8. Davies, The Restoration of Charles II, 167–8.

9. Gumble, Life of General Monck, 136, 155; Price, The Mystery and Method, 61–3; A Letter from a Person of Quality in Edenburgh; Davies, The Restoration of Charles II, 162–3, 167; Clarke Papers, IV, 166.

10. BL, Add MS 4197, no. 19; CSPD, 1659–60, xxiii–xxv; Pinckney, 'Bradshaw and Cromwell in 1656', 233–40; Memoirs of Edmund Ludlow, II, 140–1; Calendar of Clarendon State Papers, IV, 317–18; Guizot, Richard Cromwell, II, 73; Mercurius Politicus, 593, 27 October–3 November 1659; Roger L'Estrange, No fool, to the old fool (London, 1660).

11. Clarke Papers, IV, 119–20; Dunlop, Ireland under the Commonwealth, II, 697; Baker, A Chronicle of the Kings of England, 688; Davies, The Restoration of Charles II, 172; McDonald, 'The timing of General Monck's march into England', 363–76.

12. Gumble, Life of General Monck, 143–4; Baker, A Chronicle of the Kings of England, 690; Pepys, Diary, VII, 354; A. Woolrych, 'Yorkshire and the Restoration', Yorkshire Archaeological Journal (1958), XXXIX, 483–507; B. Morgan, 'Morgan, Sir Thomas, first baronet (1604–1679), army officer', Oxford Dictionary of National Biography (2004)

13. Gumble, Life of General Monck, 143–5; Baker, A Chronicle of the Kings of England, 690; The Monckton Papers, Edward Peacock (ed.) (London, 1884), 23–4; Memoirs of Edmund Ludlow, II, 268; Fairfax, A Catalogue of the curious collection of pictures, 32–3.

14. TNA, PROB11/296/457; Heath, *A Chronicle of the Late Intestine War*, 430; *The Last Will and Testament of John Bradshaw, President of the High Court of Justice* (London, 1659); *The Arraignment of the Divel for Stealing Away President Bradshaw* (London, 1659); *Clarke Papers*, IV, 133–4, 140–1, 187–8.

15. *Clarke Papers*, IV, 179, 181–2, 183; Gumble, *Life of General Monck*, 161–2; Price, *The Mystery and Method*, 67–8.

16. Price, *The Mystery and Method*, 61; Gumble, *Life of General Monck*, 162ff., 177–8.

17. Baker, *A Chronicle of the Kings of England*, 690; Bell, *Memorials of the Civil War*, II, 152.

18. Bell, *Memorials of the Civil War*, II, 152–70; *The Monckton Papers*, 29.

19. Baker, *A Chronicle of the Kings of England*, 692, 699; Price, *The Mystery and Method*, 68; *A Perfect Narrative of the Grounds and Reasons moving some Officers of the Army in Ireland to the Securing of Dublin Castle* (London, 1660); *The Faithful Intelligencer*, 1, 29 November–3 December 1659.

20. Whitelocke, *Diary*, 552–4; *Clarke Papers*, IV, 220.

21. Bell, *Memoirs of the Civil War*, II, 166–7; Woolrych, 'Yorkshire and the Restoration', 483–507; *The Monckton Papers*, 30–43.

22. Even Monck's chaplain Thomas Gumble expressed his admiration of the courage and character of John Lambert, 'he was a Person of great Parts and good Courage, and as fit for a Protectorship as Oliver, and some think fitter (but that foolish comedy was not to be acted again)', Gumble, *Life of General Monck*, 186.

23. *A Letter and Declaration of the Gentry of the Country of Norfolk* (London, 1660); *An Address from the Gentry of Norfolk and Norwich to General Monck in 1660* (Norwich, 1913); Gumble, *Life of General Monck*, 223; Rugg, *Diurnal*, 32; *Mercurius Politicus*, 605, 26 January–2 February 1660; *The Parliamentary or Constitutional History of England*, XXII, 68–70; *Clarke Papers*, IV, 258–9; BL, Egerton MS 2618, fol 60r, Fairfax and co. to Monck.

24. *Mercurius Politicus*, 605, 26 January–2 February 1660; Rugg, *Diurnal*, 31; *HMC Manuscripts of F. W. Leyborne-Popham* (London, 1899), 211–12; *Memoirs of Edmund Ludlow*, II, 216–17.

25. *The Faithful Intelligencer from the Parliaments Army in Scotland, written by an Officer of the Army there* (Edinburgh, 1659), it became *Mercurius Britanicus*; Gumble, *Life of General Monck*, 159–60.

26. Aubrey, *Brief Lives*, I, 289–90, II, 148; Guizot, *Richard Cromwell*, II, 298–9; *Clarke Papers*, IV, 112, 187–8; Rugg, *Diurnal*, 27–30; Pepys, *Diary*, I, 45.

27. Geoff Kemp, 'The Works of Roger L'Estrange: an Annotated Bibliography', in Anne Dunan-Page and Beth Lynch (eds), *Roger L'Estrange and the Making of Restoration Culture* (Aldershot, 2008), 181–225; Roger L'Estrange, *To His Excellency, General Monck a Letter from the Gentlemen of Devon in answer to his Lordships of January 23. to them directed from Leicester* (London, 1660).

28. Baker, *A Chronicle of the Kings of England*, 706; Christie, *Shaftesbury*, I, 205–8; *The Memoirs of Edmund Ludlow*, II, 219–22; Price, *The Mystery and Method*, preface; HMC *Manuscripts of F. W. Leyborne-Popham*, 215–16; *Commons Journal*, VII, 1651–1660, 837–8.

29. W. D. Christie, *A Life of Anthony Ashley Cooper, First Earl of Shaftesbury*, 2 vols (London, 1871), I, 205–8, 211; Gumble, *Life of General Monck*, 239, 240–3, 244–5; Baker, *A Chronicle of the Kings of England*, 704–6, 707–8; Rugg, *Diurnal*, 38–40; Price, *The Mystery and Method*, 96–7, 102–4; *A Collection of Letters written by His Excellency General George Monk*, 61–5; *The Memoirs of Edmund Ludlow*, II, 219–20.

30. Rugg, *Diurnal*, 38–40; Pepys, *Diary*, I, 51–3; *Diary of John Evelyn*, III, 242; Price, *The Mystery and Method*, 106–7; HMC *Manuscripts of F. W. Leyborne-Popham*, 219–20; Rugg, *Diurnal*, 38–40; that Monck did not expect his ultimatum to be ignored and lead to the readmission of secluded members is clear from his letter to Lord Fairfax of 18 February explaining why the secluded members were not being readmitted and that the 'filling up' of the empty seats was about to start, Bell, *Memorials of the Civil War*, II, 208.

31. Guizot, *Richard Cromwell*, II, 359, 362–5; Pepys, *Diary*, I, 63; *Commons Journal*, VII, 1651–1660, 880–1; Price, *The Mystery and Method*, 117.

32. Price, *The Mystery and Method*, 27–8, 43–4; Guizot, *Richard Cromwell*, II, 42–3; Pepys, *Diary*, I, 74–5; in his letter to the Devon gentry in January 1660 Monck had been clear that the readmission of the secluded MPs (which he then opposed) would lead to constitutional change, 'in that very many of those Members assert the Monarchical Interest', *The Parliamentary or Constitutional History of England*, XXII, 69.

33. Price, *The Mystery and Method*, 137; in addressing the secluded MPs Monck again stated his support for a republic, *A Collection of General Monk's Letters*, 68–70; on 4 March the French Ambassador reported that 'Monk intends to maintain the establishment of the republic ... he will have some difficulty to maintain himself against the general desire and bent of the whole nation', Guizot, *Richard Cromwell*, II, 362–5; Andrew Barclay, 'George Monck's role in the drafting of the declaration of Breda', *Archives: The Journal of the British Records Association* (2010), 35 (123), 63–7; Paul H. Hardacre, 'The Genesis of the Declaration of Breda, 1657–1660', *Journal of Church and State*, 15, No. 1 (Winter 1973), 65–82.

34. Baker, *A Chronicle of the Kings of England*, 717–18; Gumble, *Life of General Monck*, 116, 271–9; Price, *The Mystery and Method*, 135–7; Barclay, 'George Monck's role in the drafting of the declaration of Breda', 63–7; Hardacre, 'The Genesis of the Declaration of Breda, 1657–1660', 65–82.

35. Rugg, *Diurnal*, 60, 84; Pepys, *Diary*, I, 89, 113; CSPD, 1659–60, 394; Guizot, *Richard Cromwell*, II, 382.

36. Marchamont Nedham, *News from Brussels* (London, 1660); *Calendar of Clarendon State Papers*, IV, 71; *The Letter-book of John Viscount Mordaunt 1658-1660*, Mary Coate (ed.) (London, 1945), 174.

37. *Letter-book of John Viscount Mordaunt*, 166; *Commons Journal*, VIII, 1660-1667, 4-5; Guizot, *Richard Cromwell*, II, 418; Rugg, *Diurnal*, 9-80; *Relation in form of Journal of the Voiage and Residence which the most Excellent and Most Mighty Prince Charls the II King of Britain &c hath made in Holland* (The Hague, 1660), 51.

38. John Price, *A letter written from Dover to the Commissioners for the Customs, London, May 26, relating certain passages of His Majesties arrival and reception there* (London, 1660); Pepys, *Diary*, I, 157-8; HMC Ormonde, III, 1; Baker, *A Chronicle of the Kings of England*, 729-33; *Mercurius Publicus*, 22, 24-31 May 1660; *The Memoirs of Ann Lady Fanshawe*, 94-5; Fleming Papers, HMC 12th Report, VII, 25-6.

39. Price, *The Mystery and Method*, 161-2.

40. *Calendar of Clarendon State Papers*, IV, 71, 665; V, 18; Christie, *Shaftesbury*, I, 204, 'his lady ... did not spare to declare her passion for the King's cause (which was most real and sincere in her)'; Guizot, *Richard Cromwell*, II, 423, 'the General's wife ... her inclination have undoubtedly contributed to the revolution in government'; *A Chronicle of the Late Intestine War*, 763, dedicated to General Monck: 'the Lady Monck arrived at White-hall, the Minerva and great Patroness of this grand design'; 'the influence of her tongue' in the restoration, *On the Death of her Illustrious Grace Anne Dutchess Dowager of Albemarle* (London, 1669); BL, Egerton MS 2618, fol. 79r; *A Letter from an Anti-Phanatique to the most Illustrious and Truly Virtuous Lady Monk. By a Lover of his Country* (London, 1660).

41. Clarendon, *The Life of Edward, Earl of Clarendon*, I, 326-7; Rugg, *Diurnal*, 98-9; *Diary of John Evelyn*, III, 246; Hutchinson, *Memoir of the Life of Colonel Hutchinson*, 227

EPILOGUE

1. Rugg, *Diurnal*, 142-3, 146; Samuel Butler, *Hudibras. A poem in three cantos*, 3 vols (London, 1793), III, 379-80; *The Diary of John Evelyn*, III, 268-9; *Mercurius Publicus*, 5, 31 January-7 February 1660; *The Kingdomes Intelligencer of the Affairs now in Agitation in England, Scotland, and Ireland*, 5, 28 January-4 February 1661; Pepys, *Diary*, I, 309; Alfred Marks, *Tyburn Tree: its History and Annals* (London, 1908), 190-3; Abraham Miles, *The last farewel of three bould traytors* (London, 1661); Stanley Papers, III, 2, cclxxx; Jonathan Fitzgibbons, *Cromwell's Head* (London, 2008), 37-8; Lorna Clymer, 'Cromwell's head and Milton's hair: corpse theory in spectacular bodies of the Interregnum', *The Eighteenth Century*, 40, No. 2 (Summer 1999), 91-112.

2. *Commons Journal*, VIII, 202; *The Parliamentary or Constitutional History of England*, XXIII, 37; 'An Act of Free and Generall Pardon Indemnity and Oblivion', *Statutes of the Realm*, 5, 1628–80, 226–34. See Hutton, *Restoration* for a brilliant blow-by-blow account of the restoration.

3. *The Memoirs of Edmund Ludlow*, II, 26; Bell, *Memorials of the Civil War*, 172; Brian Fairfax, *Short Memorials of Thomas Lord Fairfax written by himself* (London, 1699); see the ODNB for the fate of each significant figure at the restoration.

4. 'Act of Free and Generall Pardon', clause XLII; HMC *Fifth Report*, 208.

5. BL, Egerton MS 2618, fol. 58r–v; Clarendon, *History of the Rebellion*, VI, 106–7; Wood, *Athenae Oxonienses*, II, 768; BL, Add MS 72,850, fol. 116; Baker, *A Chronicle of the Kings of England*, 669–70; Arthur Stanley, *Historical Memorials of Westminster Abbey*, 2 vols (London, 1911), 505.

6. *The Lady of Latham*, 247, 270–2, 275; *Stanley Papers*, III, 2, cclxxxiv; Joan Thirsk, 'The Restoration Land Settlement', *Journal of Modern History*, 26, No. 4 (Dec., 1954), 315–28; *Stanley Papers*, 3, ccclxxvii–ccclxxxv; Harrison, *Illiam Dhone*.

7. See, for instance, Roger L'Estrange, *A Caveat to the Cavaliers* (London, 1661). Geoff Kemp, 'The Works of Roger L'Estrange: An Annotated Bibliography', in Anne Dunan-Page and Beth Lynch (eds), *Roger L'Estrange and the Making of Restoration Culture* (Aldershot, 2008), 181–225. L'Estrange relentlessly pursued Marchamont Nedham, publishing *A Rope for Pol or a Hue and Cry after Marchemont Nedham the Late Scurrulous News-Writer* in 1660, which reprinted his most virulent journalism against the monarchy.

8. *Notes which passed at meetings of the Privy Council between Charles II and the Earl of Clarendon, 1660–1667*, W. D. Macray (ed.) (London, 1896), 29; Robert W. Ramsey, *Henry Cromwell* (London, 1933), 363–4; 'Anna Trapnel's Prophecies', EHR, 26, 103 (July 1911), 526–35; G. Rogers, *The Fifth Monarchy Men* (Oxford, 1966), 110–122.

9. George Fox, *A Declaration from the harmles & innocent people of God called Quakers against all plotters and fighters in the world, for the removing of the ground of jealousie and suspition from both magistrates and people in the kingdoms concerning wars and fightings* (London, 1660/1).

10. Verses 'Upon the Horse that his Majesty rode upon at his Coronation' by Thomas Fairfax, M. A. Gibb, *The Lord General: A Life of Thomas Fairfax* (London, 1938), 280–1. Gibb asserts that the chestnut mare which bore the horse was that ridden by Fairfax at Naseby, but does not give a source for this statement.

11. 'Charles II, 1662: An Act for the Uniformity of Publique Prayers and Administrac[i]on of Sacraments', in *Statutes of the Realm*, 5, 1628–80, 364–70; Calamy, *A Continuation of the Account of the Ministers ... Ejected and*

Silenced in 1660, II, 612–13; William Taverner, *The Quakers rounds, or, A Faithful account of a large discourse between a party of them called Quakers viz. William Fisher and Edward Burroughs, &c with Mr. Philip Taverner, Mr. Richard Goodgroom, and Mr. M. Hall, ministers of the Gospel* (London, 1658).

12. Charles Patin, *Relations historiques et curieuses de voyages, en Allemagne, Angleterre* (Amsterdam, 1695), 169.

13. Alsop, 'Gerrard Winstanley: What do we know of his life?', 19–36; a print of Anna Trapnel entitled 'A Quaker' appeared in a publication in the 1670s, with the words 'With face of brass this woman that you see / most impudently doth afirm that shee / The mind of God, in all poynts more doth know / then from the Sacred Scriptures ere could flow / Presumptious wretch it were more fitt that shee / at home showld keepe, and mind hir housewifery ...' Richard Gaywood, British Museum, print, number 1870,0514.305.

14. BL, Add MS 72,850, fol. 26; Sprat, *The History of the Royal Society for the Improving of Natural Knowledge*; McCormick, *William Petty*; Gianni Vaggi and Peter Groenewegen, *A Concise History of Economic Thought* (Basingstoke, 2003), 29.

15. Nedham, *Discourse concerning schools and school-masters offered to publick consideration, by M. N.*; *The Life Records of John Milton*, II, 168–9; see Jonathan Scott, *England's Troubles: seventeenth-century English political instability in European context* (Cambridge, 2000) for a brilliant exploration of the English revolution as a play in three acts, the civil war and Interregnum, the Exclusion Crisis and the Glorious Revolution.

16. Pepys, *Diary*, VII, 56–7, 354, 536, 'some of the Duke of Albemarle's family did say that the Earl of Torrington [their son] was a bastard'; VIII, 147–8; Gumble, *Life of General Monck*, 471–2; *Travels of Cosmo the Third Grand Duke of Tuscany*, 468–70; *Directions to a Painter for Describing our Naval Business* (London, 1667).

17. TNA, LC2/10/1, fol. 46v; Seth Ward, *The Christians victory over death a sermon at the funeral of the Most Honourable George Duke of Albemarle, &c.: in the Collegiate Church of S. Peter, Westminster, on the XXXth of April M.DC.LXX* (London, 1670); *A Letter from an Anti-Phanatique to the most Illustrious and Truly Vertuous lady, the Lady Monk*; Melanie Unwin, 'J'y Suis, J'y Reste': The Parliamentary Statue of Oliver Cromwell by Hamo Thornycroft, *Parliamentary History*, 28, Issue 3, October 2009, 413–25.

ILLUSTRATIONS

PLATES

John Bradshaw (Buxton Museum and Art Gallery)

Charles I at his trial, painted by Edward Bower (IanDagnall Computing / Alamy)

Charlotte Stanley, Countess of Derby with her husband James and eldest daughter, painted by Anthony van Dyck (Frick Collection)

Charlotte Stanley in widowhood, painted by Peter Lely (ART Collection / Alamy)

Sir Hamon L'Estrange, painted by John Hoskins (© KSH Conservation Ltd with permission of the Le Strange Collection)

Lady Alice L'Estrange, painted by John Hoskins (© KSH Conservation Ltd with permission of the Le Strange Collection)

Sir Nicholas L'Estrange (© KSH Conservation Ltd with permission of the Le Strange Collection)

Wisbech Castle (The National Trust, by permission of the Wisbech Society and the Diocese of Ely)

Dr William Petty, painted by Isaac Fuller (© National Portrait Gallery)

Charles Fleetwood, painted by Robert Walker (The History Collection / Alamy)

Henry Cromwell, painted by Samuel Cooper (Buccleuch Heritage Trust)

College Green, Dublin (Alamy)

The parish of Glenarm (sic) in Ulster (courtesy of the Public Record Office of Northern Ireland)

William Petty's survey of Ireland (Boston Public Library)

Oliver Cromwell, painted by Samuel Cooper (Buccleuch Heritage Trust)

Hampton Court, painted by Hendrick Danckerts (Royal Collection Trust /
© Her Majesty Queen Elizabeth II 2021)
Elizabeth Claypole, painted by Samuel Cooper (Buccleuch Heritage Trust)
Richard Cromwell (© National Portrait Gallery)
The Paston Treasure (Norwich Castle Museum)
Oliver Cromwell (Courtesy of the Cromwell Museum, Huntingdon)
George Monck, painted by Samuel Cooper (Royal Collection Trust / © Her
Majesty Queen Elizabeth II 2021)
Anne Monck (née Clarges) (Chronicle / Alamy)
Oliver Cromwell's funeral banner (Bonhams)
General Monck's army arriving into London (© The Trustees of the British
Museum)

INTEGRATED IMAGES

New Palace Yard and the entrance to Westminster Hall (Look and Learn /
Illustrated Papers Collection / Bridgeman Images)
Thomas Fairfax (© The Trustees of the British Museum)
The Great Seal of the Commonwealth (Chronicle / Alamy)
The Trial of Charles I (World History Archive / Alamy)
Map of Cobham (Topographical Collection / Alamy)
The houses of Cheapside (Chronicle / Alamy)
Pillaging soldier carrying chicken and cooking pot (© British Library Board /
Bridgeman)
William Everard addressing Lord Fairfax (Pictoral Press Ltd / Alamy)
Rushen Castle (© British Library / Bridgeman)
The execution of the Earl of Derby (© The Trustees of the British Museum)
Newgate Prison (Signal Photos / Alamy)
Catholics attacking Protestants during the Irish uprising of 1641–2 (© British
Library Board / Bridgeman)
The first issue of Mercurius Politicus (Public domain)
An almanac seller (Heritage Image Partnership Ltd / Alamy)
Oliver Cromwell expelling the Rump Parliament (Alamy)
Anna Trapnel (Chronicle / Alamy)
A Catalogue of the Severall Sects (Bridgeman)
A print depicting Oliver Cromwell leading Puritan congregation (Alamy)
Hunstanton Hall (Author's collection)
The Vindication of Christmas (Bridgeman)
Anne Green's hanging (Public domain)
Extract from The Complete Surveyor (Royal Astronomical Society / Science
Photo Library)
The South-East Prospect of Ballicar Castle (Public domain)

Hinchingbrooke House (Topographical Collection / Alamy)

John Lambert (Public domain)

Wimbledon Palace (Historic Images / Alamy)

The Castle of Dalkeith (Canmore)

Charles Stuart (Royal Collection Trust / © Her Majesty Queen Elizabeth II 2021)

The 'roasting of the Rump' (Public domain)

Charles Stuart dining at The Hague (Archive PL / Alamy)

Charles II landing at Dover (Atlas en Kaart)

BIBLIOGRAPHY

MSS COLLECTIONS

Bodleian Library
British Library
Cheshire Record Office
Hatfield House
King's Lynn Borough Archives
London Metropolitan Archives
National Archives
Norfolk Record Office
Westminster Abbey Muniments

NEWSPAPERS

A Perfect Account
Certain Passages of Every Dayes Intelligence from the Army and his Highness the Lord Protector
The Faithful Intelligencer
Gentlemen's Magazine
The Grand Politique Post
The Kingdomes Intelligencer
The Man in the Moon
Mercurius Britanicus
Mercurius Elencticus
Mercurius Politicus
Mercurius Pragmaticus

Mercurius Pragmaticus (for King Charles II)
The Moderate Intelligencer
Perfect Diurnall of Some Passages and Proceedings
Perfect Occurrences of Every Dayes Journall in Parliament
Publick Intelligencer
Severall Proceedings of State Affairs

PRIMARY

An Abstract of some few of those Barbarous, Cruell Massacres and Murthers of the Protestants and English in some parts of Ireland, committed since the 23 of October 1641 (London, 1652)

Acts and Ordinances of the Interregnum 1642–1660, C. H. Firth and R. S. Rait (eds) (London, 1911)

Acts of the Privy Council of England, 46, 1630–1631, P. A. Penfold (ed.) (London, 1964)

An Address from the Gentry of Norfolk and Norwich to General Monck in 1660 (Norwich, 1913)

Anna Trapnel's Report and Plea, Hilary Hinds (ed.), Medieval and Renaissance Texts and Studies, 503 (Toronto, 2006)

'Anna Trapnel's Prophecies', *English Historical Review*, 26, 103, July 1911, 533–4

The Arraignment of the Divel for Stealing Away President Bradshaw (London, 1659)

Aubrey, John, *Brief Lives, Chiefly Contemporaries, set down by John Aubrey*, 2 vols, Andrew Clark (ed.) (Oxford, 1898)

Aulicus his Hue and Cry sent forth after Britanicus (London, 1645)

Baker, Richard, *A Chronicle of the Kings of England from the Time of the Romans Government unto the Death of King James ... Whereunto is Added the Reign of King Charles the First and the first Thirteen Years of His Sacred Majesty King Charles the Second* (London, 1670)

Bloody Newes from Enfield (London, 1659)

Brasenose College Register 1509–1909 (Oxford, 1909)

Brereton, William, *Travels in Holland, the United Provinces, England, Scotland and Ireland 1634–5*, Edward Hawkes (ed.) (Manchester, 1844)

Brome, Alexander, *Rump, or, An exact Collection of the Choycest Poems and Songs relating to the late times by the most Eminent Wits from anno 1639 to anno 1661* (London, 1662)

Brown, Josiah, *Reports of Cases upon Appeals and Writs of Error in the High Court of Parliament 1701–1779* (Dublin, 1784)

Browne, Thomas, *Pseudodoxia Epidemica or Enquiries into very many received tenets and commonly presumed truths* (London, 1646)

Burdet, W., *A Wonder of Wonders Being a Faithful Narrative and True Relation of one Anne Green* (London, 1651)

Calamy, Edmund, *A Continuation of the Account of the Ministers, Lecturers, Masters and Fellows of Colleges, and Schoolmasters, Who Were Ejected and Silenced After the Restoration in 1660, By or Before the Act for Uniformity*, 2 vols (London, 1727)

Calendar of the Clarendon State Papers preserved in the Bodleian Library, O. Ogle, W. H. Bliss and H. O. Coxe et al., 5 vols (Oxford, 1872–1970)

The Calendar of the Committee for Compounding, Mary Anne Everett Green (ed.), 5 vols (London, 1889–92)

Calendar of the Proceedings of the Committee for Advance of Money, 1642–1656, Mary A. E. Green (ed.), 3 vols (London, 1888)

The Calendar of State Papers, Domestic: Interregnum, Mary Anne Everett Green (ed.), 13 vols (London, 1875–86)

Calendar of State Papers and Manuscripts, Relating to English Affairs, Existing in the Archives And Collections of Venice, and in other Libraries of Northern Italy, Rawdon Brown (ed.), 38 vols (London, 1864–1947)

Calendar of State Papers, Scotland, 1547–1595, Joseph Bain et al. (eds), 11 vols (1898–1936)

The Case of the Commonwealth of England States by Marchamont Nedham, Philip A. Knachel (ed.) (Charlottesville, Va., 1969).

The Case of the Heirs at Law to George Monke Late Duke of Albemarle (London, 1709)

Ceremonies of Charles I: The Note Books of John Finet. Master of Ceremonies, 1628–1616 (New York, 1987)

Challoner, Bishop, *Memoirs of Missionary Priests and other Catholics* (Philadelphia, 1839)

Chaloner, Thomas, *A Short Treatise of the Isle of Man* (London, 1656)

The Character of Mercurius Politicus (London, 1650)

Charles II's Escape from Worcester, William Matthews (ed.) (London, 1967)

The Civil Survey 1654–6: County of Tipperary. I. Eastern and Southern Baronies, Robert C. Simington (ed.) (Dublin, 1931)

Clarendon, Edward Hyde, Earl of, *The History of the Rebellion and Civil Wars in England*, W. Dunn Macray (ed.), 6 vols (Oxford, 1888)

The Clarke Papers: Selections from the Papers of William Clarke, C. H. Firth (ed.), 4 vols (London, 1901)

Coke, Roger, *A Detection of the Court and State of England during the four last reigns, and the inter-regnum*, III (London, 1694)

A Collection of Letters written by His Excellency General George Monk afterwards Duke of Albemarle relating to the Restoration of the Royal Family (London, 1714)

A Collection of the State Papers of John Thurloe, Thomas Birch (ed.), 7 vols (London, 1742)

Commons Journal

'Commonwealth State Accounts Ireland, 1650–1656', Edward MacLysaght, *Analecta Hibernica*, no. 15, 1944, 227–321

A Complete Collection of State Trials, T. B. Howell (ed.), 21 vols (London, 1816–28)

The Complete Works of Gerrard Winstanley, Thomas N. Corns, Ann Hughes and David Loewenstein (eds), 2 vols (Oxford, 2009)

The Constitutional Documents of the Puritan Revolution, S. R. Gardiner (ed.), 3rd edn (Oxford, 1908)

The Correspondence of Henry Cromwell, 1655–1659: from the British Library Lansdowne manuscripts, Peter Gaunt (ed.), Camden Fifth Series, 31, (Cambridge, 2007)

The Correspondence of John Wallis, Philip Beeley and Christoph J. Scriba (eds), 4 vols (Oxford, 2003)

The Correspondence of Robert Boyle, Michael Hunter, Antonio Clericuzio and Lawrence M. Principe (eds), 6 vols (London, 2001)

The Court and Kitchen of Elizabeth Cromwell (London, 1664)

Cranford, James, *The Teares of Ireland wherein is Lively Presented as in a map a list of the Unheard off Cruelties and Perfidious Treacheries of Blood-thirsty Jesuits and the Popish Faction* (London, 1642)

The Cromwellian Decimation Tax of 1655. The Assessment Lists, J. T. Cliffe (ed.), Royal Historical Society Camden Fifth Series, 7, 1996, 403–92

The Cry of a Stone by Anna Trapnel, Hilary Hinds (ed.), Medieval and Renaissance Texts and Studies, 220 (Arizona, 2000)

Davenant, William, *The Cruelty of the Spaniards in Peru* (London, 1658)

A Declaration and Ordinance of the Lords and Commons assembled in Parliament for the seizing and Sequestring of the estates ... of Notorious Delinquents (London, 1643)

The Declaration and Standard of the Levellers of England (London, 1649)

Defoe, Daniel, *The Complete English Tradesman* (London, 1726)

Diary of Sir Archibald Johnston of Wariston, David Hay Fleming (ed.), 3 vols (Edinburgh, 1911–40)

The Diary of John Evelyn, E. S. De Beer (ed.), 6 vols (Oxford, 1955)

The Diary of Ralph Josselin, Alan MacFarlane (ed.) (Oxford, 1976)

The Diary of Samuel Pepys, Robert Latham and William Matthews (eds), 11 vols (London, 1970–83)

Directions to a Painter for Describing our Naval Business (London, 1667)

The Diurnal of Thomas Rugg 1659–1661, William L. Sachse (ed.) (London, 1961)

'Dr Wallis's Account of some passages of his own life', *The Works of Thomas Hearne MA*, 4 vols (London, 1810), III

Edmund Pettis' Survey of St Ives, 1728, Mary Carter (ed.), Cambridge Record Society, 2002

Eikon Basilike: the Portraicture of His Sacred Majesty in his Solitudes and Sufferings (London, 1648/9)

Erbery, William, *The Bishop of London, the Welsh Curate and Common Prayers with Apocrypha in the End* (London, 1653)

Extracts from the Records of the Burgh of Edinburgh, 10, 1655–65 (Edinburgh, 1940)

Fairfax, Brian, *A Catalogue of the Curious Collection of Pictures ... with the Life of George Villiers, Duke of Buckingham* (London, 1758)

Fairfax, Brian, *Short Memorials of Thomas Lord Fairfax written by himself* (London, 1699)

The Faithfull Narrative of the Late Testimony and Demand made to Oliver Cromwel, and his powers, on the behalf of the Lords prisoners, in the name of the Lord Jehovah (Jesus Christ,) King of Saints and Nations (London, 1655)

Farington Papers: the Shrievalty of William Ffarington Esq, Susan Maria Ffarington (ed.), Chetham Society (Manchester, 1856)

Feake, Christopher, *A Beam of Light Shining in the Midst of Much Darkness and Confusion* (London, 1659)

Fidge, George, *The English Gusman; or The History of that unparallel'd thief James Hind* (London, 1652)

Fisher, Payne, *Veni, Vidi, Vici: the Triumph of the most Execellent and Illustrious Oliver Cromwell* (London, 1652).

Five Seventeenth Century Political Poems, Cecile Rahilly (ed.) (Dublin, 1952)

Fleckno, Richard, *Love's Dominion or a Dramatique Piece full of Excellent Moralitie* (London, 1654)

Fox, George, *A Declaration from the Harmles & Innocent people of God called Quakers against all plotters and fighters in the world, for the removing of the ground of jealousie and suspition from both magistrates and people in the kingdoms concerning wars and fightings* (London, 1660/1)

'Guibon Goddard's Journal', in *Diary of Thomas Burton*, I (London, 1828)

Gumble, Thomas, *The Life of General Monck, Duke of Albemarle, etc. with Remarks upon his Actions* (London, 1671)

The Harleian Miscellany: a Collection of Scarce, Curious, and Entertaining Pamphlets and Tracts ... found in the late Earl of Oxford's Library, 12 vols (London, 1808–11)

Heath, James, *A Chronicle of the Late Intestine War* (London, 1675)

Her Price is Above Pearls: Family and Farming Records of Alice Le Strange 1617–1656, Elizabeth Griffiths (ed.), Norfolk Record Society, LXXIX (Norwich, 2015)

Heylyn, Peter, *The Historical and Miscellaneous Tracts of Peter Heylyn* (London, 1681)

Historical Manuscripts Commission: The Manuscripts of the Marquis of Ormonde, 3 vols (London, 1895–1909)

Historical Manuscripts Commission: Second Report (London, 1874)

Historical Manuscripts Commission: Fourth Report (London, 1874)

Historical Manuscripts Commission: Fifth Report (London, 1876)

Historical Manuscripts Commission: Eleventh Report, Appendix Part VII (London, 1888)

Historical Manuscripts Commission: Twelfth Report, The Manuscripts of S. H. Le Fleming (London, 1890)

Historical Manuscripts Commission: The Manuscripts of the Duke of Portland, 10 vols (London, 1891–1931)

Historical Manuscripts Commission: Manuscripts of F. W. Leyborne-Popham (London, 1899)

The History of the Survey of Ireland, commonly called the Down Survey, by Doctor William Petty, A.D. 1655–6, Thomas Aiskew Larcom (ed.) (Dublin, 1851)

Howell, James, Londinopolis an Historicall Discourse or Perlustration of the City of London (London, 1657)

Hutchinson, Lucy, Memoir of the Life of Colonel Hutchinson with the Fragment of an Autobiography of Mrs. Hutchinson, James Sutherland (ed.) (London, 1973)

Illiam Dhone and the Manx Rebellion, 1651, W. Harrison (ed.), The Manx Society, XXVI (Douglas, 1877)

Ireland under the Commonwealth: being a Selection of Documents relating to the Government of Ireland from 1651 to 1659, Robert Dunlop, 2 vols (Manchester, 1913)

The Inventories and Valuations of the Late King's Goods 1649–51, Oliver Millar (ed.), Walpole Society, 43 (Glasgow, 1972)

A Journal of the Siege of Lathom House in Lancashire Defended by Charlotte de la Tremouille Countess of Derby against Sir Thomas Fairfax Kt (London, 1823)

The Journal of Thomas Juxon, 1644–1647, Keith Lindley and David Scott (eds) (Cambridge, 1999)

The Lady of Latham: being the Life and Original Letters of Charlotte de la Trémoille, Henriette Elizabeth Guizot de Witt (ed.) (London, 1869)

The Last Speech of His Highnesse the Lord Protector to the Parliament on Tuesday in the Painted Chamber, being the 12. of this instant September (London, 1654)

The Last Will and Testament of John Bradshaw, President of the High Court of Justice (London, 1659)

L'Estrange, Hamon, God's Sabbath before under the law and under the Gospel (Cambridge, 1641)

L'Estrange, Hamon, The Charge Upon Sir Hamon L'Estrange together with his Vindication and Recharge (London, 1649)

L'Estrange, Hamon, An Answer to the Marquess of Worcester's Last Paper (London, 1651)

L'Estrange, Hamon, Americans No Jews, or the Improbabilities that the Americans are of that Race (London, 1652)

L'Estrange, Hamon, The Reign of King Charles (London, 1655)

L'Estrange, Hamon, The Alliance of Divine Offices (London, 1659)

L'Estrange, Roger, *No Fool, to the Old Fool* (London, 1660)

L'Estrange, Roger, *To His Excellency, General Monck a Letter from the Gentlemen of Devon in answer to his Lordships of January 23. to them directed from Leicester* (London, 1660)

L'Estrange, Roger, *A Caveat to the Cavaliers* (London, 1661)

L'Estrange, Roger, *To the Right Honourable Edward Earl of Clarendon The Humble Apology* (London, 1661)

L'Estrange, Roger, *A Memento, Directed to all those that Truly Reverence the Memory of King Charles the Martyr* (London, 1662)

L'Estrange, Roger, *Truth and Loyalty Vindicated from the Reproches and Clamours of Mr Edward Bagshaw* (London, 1662)

A Letter from an Anti-phanatique, to the most Illustrious and Truly Vertuous Lady, the Lady Monk. By a true lover of his country (London, 1660)

A Letter and Declaration of the Gentry of the Country of Norfolk (London, 1660)

'A Letter from John Bradshawe of Gray's Inn to Sir Peter Legh of Lyme', *Chetham Miscellanies*, II, Chetham Society (Manchester, 1855)

A Letter from an Anti-Phanatique to the most Illustrious and Truly Virtuous Lady Monk (London, 1660

A Letter from a Person of Quality in Edenburgh to an Officer of the Army (London, 1659)

Letter Book of John Viscount Mordaunt 1658–1660, Mary Coate (ed.) (London, 1945)

Letter Books of Sir William Brereton, R. N. Dore (ed.), 2 vols (1984, 1990)

The Letters of Samuel Pepys, Guy de la Bédoyère (ed.) (Woodbridge, 2006)

Letters and Papers illustrating the relations between Charles the Second and Scotland in 1650, S. R. Gardiner (ed.) (Edinburgh, 1894)

The Letters and Speeches of Oliver Cromwell, Thomas Carlyle, Sophia Crawford Lomas and C. H. Firth (eds), 3 vols (London, 1904)

Leybourn, William, *The Complete Surveyor* (London, 1653)

The Life Records of John Milton, J. Milton French (ed.), 5 vols (New Brunswick, 1949–58)

Lodewijck Huygens, The English Journal 1651–2, A. G. H. Bachrach and R. G. Collmer (ed. and trans.) (Leiden, 1982)

Lords Journal

Ludlow, Edmund, *A Voyce from the Watch Tower*, A. B. Worden (ed.) (London, 1978)

The Memoirs of Ann Lady Fanshawe Wife of the Right Hon:ble Sir Richard Fanshawe Bart 1600–72 (London, 1907)

The Memoirs of Edmund Ludlow, C. H. Firth (ed.), 2 vols (Oxford, 1894)

Memoirs of the Verney Family, F. P. Verney (ed.), 4 vols (London, 1892–9)

Memorials of the Civil War comprising the Correspondence of the Fairfax Family, Robert Bell (ed.), 2 vols (London, 1849)

Memorials of the Civil War in Cheshire and the Adjacent Counties ... and Providence Improved by Edward Burghall, James Hall (ed.), The Record Society for the Publication of Original Documents relating to Lancashire and Cheshire, XIX (1889)

Merry Passages and Jeasts: A Manuscript Jestbook of Sir Nicholas Le Strange, H. F. Lippincott (Salzburg, 1974)

Mabbot, Gilbert, 'A perfect narrative of the whole proceedings of the High Court of Justice in the tryal of the King in Westminster Hall', *State Trials*, T. B. Howell (ed.), IV, 1640–1649 (London, 1816)

Miles, Abraham, *The Last Farewel of Three Bould Traytors* (London, 1661)

Milton, John, *Eikonoklastes in answer to a book intitl'd Eikon Basilike* (London, 1649)

Milton, John, *Milton: Poetical Works*, Douglas Bush (ed.) (London, 1966)

Milton, John, *The Complete Works of John Milton*, Thomas N. Corns and Gordon Campbell (eds), 11 vols (Oxford, 2008–19)

Minutes of the Parliament of the Middle Temple, C. T. Martin (ed.), III (London, 1905)

Mona Miscellany: a Selection of Proverbs, Sayings, Ballads, Customs ... and Legends, Peculiar to the Isle of Man, Harrison, William (ed.), Manx Society, XXI (Douglas, 1873)

Monarchy Asserted to be the best, most ancient and legall Form of Government in a Conference had at Whitehall (London, 1660)

The Monckton Papers, Edward Peacock (ed.) (London, 1884)

Moxon, Joseph, *Mechanick Exercises or the Doctrine of Hands-Work Applied to the Art of Printing* (London, 1683)

Nalson, J., *A True Copy of the Journal of the High Court of Justice for the Trial of K. Charles I* (London, 1684)

Nalson, J., 'A Journal of the High-Court of Justice, for the Trial of King Charles', *State Trials*, IV, 1054–8

The Narrative of General Venables, with an appendix of papers relating to the expedition to the West Indies and the conquest of Jamaica, 1654–1655, C. H. Firth (ed.) (London, 1900)

Nedham, Marchamont, *Certain Considerations Tendered in All Humility to an Honourable Member of the Council of State* (London, 1649)

Nedham, Marchamont, *The Case of the Commonwealth of England, Stated: or the Equity, Utility, and Necessity of a Submission to the Present Government* (London, 1650)

Nedham, Marchamont, *News from Brussels* (London, 1660)

Nedham, Marchamont, *A Discourse Concerning Schools and School-Masters Offered to Publick Consideration* (London, 1663)

Nicholl, John, *A Diary of Public Transactions and other Occurrences Chiefly in Scotland from January 1650 to June 1667* (Edinburgh, 1836)

The Norfolk Antiquarian Miscellany, W. B. Rye (ed.), 3 vols (Norwich, 1873–7)

Norfolk Quarter Sessions Order Book 1650–1657, D. E. Howell James (ed.), Norfolk Records Society, 1955

Notes which passed at meetings of the Privy Council between Charles II and the Earl of Clarendon, 1660–1667, W. D. Macray (ed.) (London, 1896)

The Oceana of James Harrington (London, 1700)

O. Cromwell's thankes to the Lord Generall, faithfully presented by Hugh Peters in another conference (London, 1660)

On the Death of her Illustrious Grace Anne Dutchess Dowager of Albemarle (London, 1669)

'Original correspondence of the Lord President Bradshaw', Gibson, A. C. (ed.), *Transactions of the Historic Society of Lancashire and Cheshire*, new ser., 2 (1861–2)

'An original diary of Colonel Robert Bennett of Hexworthy (1642–3)', Mary Coate (ed.), *Devon and Cornwall Notes and Queries*, 18 (1934–5)

Original Letters Illustrative of English History, Henry Ellis, ed., 2nd ser. (4 vols, 1827)

Original Letters and Papers of State Addressed to Oliver Cromwell, John Nickolls (ed.) (London, 1743)

Overton, Richard, *The Commoners Complaint: or a Dreadful Warning from Newgate* (London, 1647)

The Oxinden and Peyton Letters, 1642–1670. Being the correspondence of Henry Oxinden of Barham, Sir Thomas Peyton of Knowlton, and their circle, Dorothy Gardiner (ed.) (London, 1937)

The Parliamentary or Constitutional History of England, being a Faithful Account of all the most Remarkable Transactions in Parliament from the earliest times (to the Dissolution of the Convention Parliament that Restored King Charles II, 24 vols (London, 1751–63)

Patin, Charles, *Relations Historiques et Curieuses de Voyages, en Allemagne, Angleterre* (Amsterdam, 1695)

Peck, Francis, *Desiderata Curiosa: or, a Collection of Divers Scarce and Curious Pieces relating chiefly to matters of English History* (London, 1779)

A Perfect Narrative of the Grounds and Reasons moving some Officers of the Army in Ireland to the Securing of Dublin Castle (London, 1660)

Petty, William, *The Advice of WP to Mr Samuel Hartlib for the Advancement of some Particular Parts of Learning* (London, 1648)

Petty, William, *Reflections upon Some Persons and Things in Ireland* (London, 1660)

Petty, William, *Tracts Chiefly relating to Ireland* (London, 1769)

Petty, William, *The Political Anatomy of Ireland, with the establishment for that Kingdom, and Verbum sapienti*, facsimile of the first edition, John O'Donovan (ed.) (Shannon, 1970)

The Petty Papers: Some Unpublished Writings of Sir William Petty edited from the Bowood Papers of the Marquis of Lansdowne, 2 vols (London, 1927)

The Petty–Southwell Correspondence, 1676–1687. Edited from the Bowood papers by the Marquis of Lansdowne (London, 1928)

The Picture of a New Courtier (London, 1656)

Price, John, *A Letter written from Dover to the Commissioners for the Customs, London, May 26, relating certain passages of His Majesties Arrival and Reception there* (London, 1660)

Price, John, *The Mystery and Method of His Majesty's Happy Restauration laid open to Publick View* (London, 1683)

The Prose Works of John Milton, Charles Symmons (ed.) 7 vols (London, 1806) VI, 413–14

The Protector, (so called,) in Part Unvailed: by whom the Mystery of Iniquity, is now Working (London, 1655)

The Register of Admissions to Gray's Inn, 1521–1889, together with the Register of Marriages in Gray's Inn Chapel, 1695–1754, Joseph Foster (ed.) (London, 1889)

Register of the Consultations of the Ministers of Edinburgh and Some other Brethren of the Ministry, William Stephen (ed.), 2 vols (Edinburgh, 1921–30)

The Register of the Privy Council of Scotland, J. H. Burton and others (eds), 16 vols (Edinburgh, 1877–1970)

The Register of St Martin-in-the-Fields London, II, 1619–1636, J. V. Kitto (ed.) (London, 1939)

Relation in form of Journal of the Voiage and Residence which the most Excellent and Most Mighty Prince Charls the II King of Britain &c hath made in Holland (The Hague, 1660)

Reliquiae Baxterianae or Mr Richard Baxter's Narrative of the most Memorable Passages of his Life and Times (London, 1696)

A Rope for Pol or a Hue and Cry after Marchemont Nedham The Late Scurrulous News-writer (London, 1660)

Scotland and the Protectorate: Letters and Papers Relating to the Military Government of Scotland from January 1654 to June 1659, C. H. Firth (ed.) (Edinburgh, 1899)

The Second Character of Mercurius Politicus (London, 1650)

The Speeches of the Lord Generall Fairfax and the Officers of the Army (London, 1649)

Sprat, Thomas, *The History of the Royal Society for the Improving of Natural Knowledge* (London, 1667)

The Stanley Papers, William Ffarington, F. R. Raines et al. (eds) (Chetham Society, 29, 31, 66, 67, 70), 3 vols (Manchester, 1853–67)

Stow, John, *A Survey of London. Reprinted From the Text of 1603*, C. L. Kingsford (ed.), 2 vols (Oxford, 1908)

Strange and Wonderful Newes from White-Hall or the Mighty Visions Proceeding from Mistris Anna Trapnel (London, 1654)

Swedish Diplomats at Cromwell's Court, 1655–1656: the Missions of Peter Julius Coyet and Christer Bonde, Michael Roberts (ed.), Camden 4th series, 36 (London, 1988)

Taverner, Philip, *A Grand-father's Advice* (London, 1681)

Taverner, William, *The Quakers rounds, or, A Faithful account of a large discourse between a party of them called Quakers viz. William Fisher and Edward Burroughs, &c with Mr. Philip Taverner, Mr. Richard Goodgroom, and Mr. M. Hall, ministers of the Gospel* (London, 1658)

A Transcript of the Registers of the Worshipful Company of Stationers, G. E. Briscoe Eyre (ed.), 3 vols (London, 1913–14)

Trapnel, Anna, *The Cry of a Stone, or a Relation of something spoken in Whitehall, by Anna Trapnel, being in the Visions of God* (London, 1654)

Trapnel, Anna, *A Legacy for Saints being several experiences of the dealings of God with Anna Trapnel, in, and after her Conversion, (written some years since with her own hand)* (London, 1654)

Trapnel, Anna, *A Lively Voice for the King of Saints and Nations &c.* (London, 1657)

Travels of Cosmo the Third Grand Duke of Tuscany through England (London, 1821)

Trial of King Charles I, J. G. Muddiman (ed.) (Edinburgh and London, 1928)

A True Narrative of the Proceedings in Parliament, Councell of State, Generall Councell of the Army, and Committee of Safetie (London, 1659)

A True and Perfect list of the Names of those in Newgate … February 18. 1651 (London, 1652)

A True State of the Case of the Commonwealth (London, 1654)

'Unpublished documents in the Manx Museum. From the Castle Rushen Papers', *Journal of the Manx Museum*, March 1931, II, 26, 9–14

The Vindication of Christmas (London, 1653)

Walker, Henry, *A Collection of Several Passages Concerning his late Highnesse Oliver Cromwell* (London, 1659)

Waller, Edmund, *A Panegyric to my Lord Protector* (London, 1655)

Ward, Seth, *The Christians Victory over Death a Sermon at the Funeral of the Most Honourable George Duke of Albemarle, &c.: in the Collegiate Church of S. Peter, Westminster, on the XXXth of April M.DC.LXX* (London, 1670)

Warwick, Sir Philip, *Memoirs of the Reign of King Charles the First* (Edinburgh, 1813)

Watkins, Richard, *Newes from the Dead. Or a True and Exact Narration of the Miraculous Deliverance of Anne Green* (London, 1651)

The Westminster Directory, Thomas Leishman (ed.) (Edinburgh, 1901)

Whitelock, Bulstrode, *Memorials of the English Affairs from the Beginning of the Reign of Charles the First to the Happy Restoration of Charles II*, 4 vols (Oxford, 1853)

Whitelocke, Bulstrode, *The Diary of Bulstrode Whitelocke*, Ruth Spalding (ed.) (Oxford, 1990)

The Works of Sir Thomas Browne, Simon Wilkin (ed.), 4 vols (London, 1835–6)

The Writings and Speeches of Oliver Cromwell, Wilbur Cortez Abbott (ed.), 4 vols (Cambridge Mass., 1937–47)

SECONDARY

Addleshaw, George, and Frederick Etchells, *The Architectural Setting of Anglican Worship* (London, 1956)

The Agrarian History of England and Wales, Joan Thirsk (ed.), V (II) (London, 1972)

Alsop, James D., 'Gerrard Winstanley: What do we know of his life', in Andrew Bradstock (ed.), *Winstanley and the Diggers*, Prose Studies, 22, 2, August 1999, 1936

Alsop, J. D., 'Ethics in the Marketplace: Gerrard Winstanley's London Bankruptcy, 1643', *Journal of British Studies*, 28 (April 1989), 97–119

Andrews, J. H., *Plantation Acres: An Historical Study of the Irish Land Surveyor and his Maps*, Ulster Historical Foundation (Omagh, 1985)

Ashbee, Andrew, '"My fiddle is a bass viol": music in the life of Roger L'Estrange', in *Roger L'Estrange and the Making of Restoration Culture*, Anne Dunan-Page and Beth Lynch (eds) (Aldershot, 2008)

Ashley, Maurice, *General Monck* (London, 1977)

Aubrey, Philip, *Mr Secretary Thurloe: Cromwell's Secretary of State 1652–1660* (London, 1990)

Baigent, E., 'Swedish Cadastral Mapping 1628–1700: A Neglected Legacy', *Geographical Journal*, Vol. 156, No. 1 (Mar., 1990)

Barclay, Andrew, 'The Lord Protector and his Court', in Patrick Little (ed.), *Oliver Cromwell: New Perspectives* (Basingstoke, 2009)

Barclay, Andrew, 'George Monck's role in the drafting of the declaration of Breda', *Archives: The Journal of the British Records Association*, 35, 123 (2010), 63–7

Barclay, Andrew, 'Oliver Cromwell and the Cambridge elections of 1640', *Parliamentary History*, 29, 2 (2010)

Barclay, Andrew, *Electing Cromwell: The Making of a Politician* (Abingdon, 2011)

Barnard, Toby, *Cromwellian Ireland: English Government and Reform in Ireland 1649–1660* (Oxford, 1975, 2000 edn)

Barron, Caroline, *London in the Later Middle Ages: Government and People 1200–1500* (Oxford, 2004)

Bassett, Margery, 'Newgate Prison in the Middle Ages', *Speculum* 18 (2) (1943), 233–46

Beckles, Hilary McD, 'The "Hub of Empire": the Caribbean and Britain in the
    seventeenth century', in *The Origins of Empire: British Overseas Enterprise to
    the Close of the Seventeenth Century*, Nicholas Canny (ed.) (Oxford, 1998),
    218–41

Bennett, J. A., 'Christopher Wren. Astronomy, architecture, and the
    mathematical sciences', *Journal for the History of Astronomy*, 6 (1974), 149–84

Betham, William, *The Baronetage of England, or the History of the English
    baronets and such baronets of Scotland, as are of English families*, 5 vols
    (London, 1801–5)

Birch, Thomas, *The Court and Times of Charles I*, 2 vols (London, 1848)

Blackwood, Gordon, 'The gentry of Norfolk during the civil war', in *An
    Historical Atlas of Norfolk*, Trevor Ashwin and Alan Davison (eds), 3rd edn
    (Chichester, 2005)

Blayney, Peter W. M., *The Bookshops in Paul's Cross Churchyard*, Occasional
    Papers of the Bibliographical Society, 5 (1990)

Blomefield, Francis, *An Essay towards a Topographical History of the County of
    Norfolk*, 11 vols (London, 1805–10)

Boate, Gerard, *Ireland's Natural History: Being a True and Ample Description of its
    Situation, Greatness, Shape and Nature of its Hills, Woods, Heaths, Bogs etc.*
    (London, 1652)

Braddick, Michael J., *The Nerves of State: Taxation and the Financing of the
    English State 1558–1714* (Manchester, 1996)

Bradshaw, Richard Lee, *God's Battleaxe: The Life of Lord President John Bradshawe
    (1603–1659)* (Manhattan Beach, Ca., 2010)

Bradstock, Andrew (ed.), *Winstanley and the Diggers 1649–1999* (London, 2000)

Bradstock, Andrew, *Radical Religion in Cromwell's England: A Concise History
    from the English Civil War to the end of the Commonwealth* (London, 2010)

Brodie, Allan, Jane Croom and James O. Davies, *English Prisons: An Architectural
    History* (Swindon, 2002)

Brosens, Koenraad (ed.), *Flemish Tapestry in European and American Collections:
    Studies in Honour of Guy Delmarcel* (Turnhout, 2003)

Burton, Gilbert, *The Life of Sir Philip Musgrave, bart., of Hartley Castle, Co.
    Westmorland, and of Edenhall, Co. Cumberland. Governor of the City of Carlisle,
    &c* (Carlisle, 1840)

Butler, Samuel, *Hudibras. A Poem in Three Cantos*, 3 vols (London, 1793)

The Cambridge History of the Book in Britain, IV, 1557–1695, John Barnard and
    D. F. MacKenzie (eds) (Cambridge, 2002)

Capp, Bernard, *The Fifth Monarchy Men: A Study in Seventeenth-Century
    Millenarianism* (London, 1972)

Capp, Bernard, *Cromwell's Navy* (Oxford, 1989)

Carlton, Charles, *Going to the Wars: The Experience of the British Civil Wars,
    1638–1651* (London and New York, 1992)

Carrington, S., *The History of the Life and Death of his Most Serene Highness Oliver* (London, 1659)

Carruthers, Robert, *The History of Huntingdon: From the Earliest to the Present Times* (Huntingdon, 1824)

Chambers, E. K., *The Elizabethan Stage*, 4 vols (London, 1923)

Christie, W. D., *A Life of Anthony Ashley Cooper, First Earl of Shaftesbury*, 2 vols (London, 1871)

Clifford, Caroline, and Alan Akeroyd, *Risen from Obscurity? Oliver Cromwell and Huntingdonshire*, Huntingdonshire Local History Society, 2002

Clymer, Lorna, 'Cromwell's head and Milton's hair: corpse theory in spectacular bodies of the Interregnum', *The Eighteenth Century*, 40, No. 2 (Summer 1999), 91–112

Coate, Mary, *Cornwall in the Civil War 1642–1660* (Oxford, 1933)

Colvin, Howard, 'The Architect of Thorpe Hall', *Country Life*, 111, Issue 2890 (6 June 1952), 1732–5

Connor, T, 'Malignant reading: John Squier's Newgate prison library, 1642–46', *The Library*, 7th series, 7 (3), June 2006, 160–1

Cornforth, John, 'Thorpe Hall, Cambridgeshire: A Property of the Sue Ryder Foundation', *Country Life*, 185, 44 (31 October 1991), 70–3

Cornish, Patrick J., 'The Cromwellian Regime, 1650–60', in *A New History of Ireland, III: Early Modern Ireland 1534–1691* (Oxford, 1976)

Coward, Barry, *The Stanleys, Lords Stanley and Earls of Derby 1385–1672: The Origins, Wealth and Power of a Landowning Family* (Manchester, 1983)

Coward, Barry, *The Cromwellian Protectorate* (Manchester, 2002)

Cunningham, John, 'Oliver Cromwell and the "Cromwellian" settlement of Ireland', *The Historical Journal*, 53, 4 (2010), 919–93

Cunningham, John, *Conquest and Land in Ireland: The Transplantation to Connacht* (Woodbridge, 2011)

Cressy, David, *Charles I and the People of England* (Oxford, 2015)

Dalton, R. J., 'Gerrard Winstanley, the experience of fraud', *Historical Journal*, 34, 4 (1991), 973–84

Davies, Godfrey, *The Restoration of Charles II 1658–1660* (Oxford, 1955)

Davies, Matthew, and Ann Saunders, *The History of the Merchant Taylors' Company* (Leeds, 2004)

Davis, J. C., *Fear, Myth and History: The Ranters and the Historians* (Cambridge University Press, 1986)

Dennison, E., and Russel Coleman, *Historic Dalkeith: the Scottish Burgh Survey* (Historic Scotland, 1998), 20–9

Dore, R. N., *The Civil Wars in Cheshire* (Chester, 1966)

Dow, F. D., *Cromwellian Scotland 1651–1660* (Edinburgh, 1979)

Duman, Maurice, *Scientific Instruments of the 17th and 18th Centuries and their Makers* (London, 1972)

Durston, Christopher, 'Puritan rule and the failure of the cultural revolution 1645–1669', in Christopher Durston and Jackie Eales, *The Culture of English Puritanism* (Basingstoke, 1996)

Durston, Christopher, *Cromwell's Major Generals: Godly Government during the English Revolution* (Manchester, 2001)

Earwaker, J., *East Cheshire: Past and Present; or a History of the Hundred of Macclesfield ... From original records*, 2 vols (London, 1877)

Egloff, C. S., 'John Hobart of Norwich', *Norfolk Archaeology*, XLII (1994–7), 38–56

Evans, John T., *Seventeenth-Century Norwich: Politics, Religion and Government 1620–1690* (Oxford, 1979)

Fallon, Robert Thomas, *Milton in Government* (University Park, Pennsylvania, 1993)

Farr, David, 'John Lambert and the roots of an early-modern art collection', *Cromwelliana*, 2002, 46–55

Farr, David, *John Lambert, Parliamentary Soldier and Cromwellian Major-General, 1619–1684* (Woodbridge, 2003)

Fincham, Kenneth, and Stephen Taylor, 'Episcopalian conformity and nonconformity, 1646–1660', in Jason McElligott and David L. Smith, *Royalists and Royalism during the Interregnum* (Manchester, 2010), 18–44

Fincham, Kenneth, and Stephen Taylor, 'Vital statistics: episcopal ordination and ordinands in England, 1646–60', *English Historical Review*, Vol. 126, No. 519 (April 2011), 319–44

Firth, C. H., 'Letters concerning the dissolution of Cromwell's last parliament, 1658', *English Historical Review*, 7, No. 25 (Jan. 1892), 102–10

Firth, C. H., 'A letter from Lord Saye and Sele to Lord Wharton, 29 December 1657', *English Historical Review*, 10, 37 (Jan. 1895), 106–7

Firth, C. H., 'Cromwell and the Crown', *English Historical Review*, 17 (67), (July 1902) 429–42; 18 (69), 52–80

Firth, C. H., 'Sir William Davenant and the revival of the drama during the Protectorate', *English Historical Review*, 18, No. 70 (Apr., 1903), 319–21

Firth, C. H., *The Last Years of the Protectorate 1656–8*, 2 vols (London, 1909)

Fitzgibbons, Jonathan, '"Not in any doubtful dispute"? Reassessing the nomination of Richard Cromwell', *Historical Research*, 83, 220 (May 2010), 281–300

Fitzgibbons, Jonathan, *Cromwell's Head* (London, 2008)

Fitzgibbons, Jonathan, 'Hereditary succession and the Cromwellian Protectorate: the offer of the crown reconsidered', *English Historical Review*, Vol. 128, No. 534 (October 2013), 1095–1128

Fitzgibbons, Jonathan, *Cromwell's House of Lords: Politics, Parliaments and Constitutional Revolution 1642–1660* (Woodbridge, 2018)

Fitzmaurice, Edmond, *Life of William Petty* (London, 1895)

Fletcher, Henry, *The Perfect Politician or a Full View of the Life and Action of O Cromwell* (London, 1660)

Forster, John, *Eminent British Statesmen*, VII (London, 1839), Appendix A, 393–400

Frank, Joseph, *The Beginnings of the English Newspaper, 1620–1660* (Cambridge, Mass., 1961)

Frank, Joseph, *Cromwell's Press Agent: A Critical Biography of Marchamont Nedham 1620–1678* (Lanham, 1980)

Frank, Robert G., *Harvey and the Oxford Physiologists: A Study of Scientific Ideas* (Berkeley, 1980)

Fraser, William, *The Douglas Book*, 4 vols (Edinburgh, 1885)

Gardiner, Samuel Rawson, *History of the Commonwealth and Protectorate*, 4 vols (London, 1894–1903)

Gardiner, Samuel Rawson, 'The transplantation to Connaught', *English Historical Review*, XIV, Issue LVI (October 1899), 700–34

Gaskell, Philip, *A New Introduction to Bibliography* (Winchester, 1995)

Gaunt, Peter, '"The single person's confidants and dependants"? Oliver Cromwell and his Protectoral councillors', *Historical Journal*, Vol. 32, No. 3 (Sept., 1989), 537–60

Gaunt, Peter, *Oliver Cromwell* (Oxford, 1996)

Gentles, Ian, *The New Model Army* (Oxford, 1992)

Gentles, Ian, *Oliver Cromwell: God's Warrior and the English Revolution* (Basingstoke, 2011)

Gibb, A., *The Lord General: A Life of Thomas Fairfax* (London, 1938)

Gillespie, Raymond, 'The transformation of the Irish Economy 1550–1700', *Studies in Irish Economic and Social History*, 6, 1991

Greaves, Richard L., *Saints and Rebels: Seven Nonconformists in Stuart England* (Mercer, 1985)

Green, Mary Anne Everett, *The Lives of the Princesses*, 6 vols (London, 1849–55)

Greenspan, Nicole, 'News and the politics of information in the mid seventeenth century: the Western Design and the conquest of Jamaica', *History Workshop Journal*, 69 (Spring 2010), 1–26

Gretton, R. H., *The Burford Records: A Study in Minor Town Government* (Oxford, 1920)

Griffiths, Elizabeth, 'Draining the coastal marshes of north-west Norfolk: the contribution of the Le Stranges at Hunstanton, 1605 to 1724', *Agricultural History Review*, 63, II, 221–42

Guizot, François, *History of Richard Cromwell and the Restoration of Charles II*, A. R. Scoble, trans., 2 vols (London, 1856)

Gurney, John, *Brave Community: The Digger Movement in the English Revolution* (Manchester, 2007)

Gurney, John, *Gerrard Winstanley: The Digger's Life and Legacy* (London, 2013)

Habakkuk, H. J., 'Landowners and the Civil War', *Economic History Review*, NS, 18 (1), 1965, 130–51

Hardacre, Paul H., 'The genesis of the Declaration of Breda, 1657–1660', *Journal of Church and State*, 15, No. 1 (Winter 1973), 65–82

Harms, Roleand, Joad Raymond and Jeroen Salmans (eds), *Not Dead Things: The Dissemination of Popular Print in England and Wales, Italy and the Low Countries 1500–1820* (Leiden, 2013)

Harrington, Melanie, 'The earl of Derby and his tenants: sales of Royalist land during the Interregnum revisited', *Economic History Review*, 64, 4 (2011), 1195–1217

Head, Robert, *Congleton Past and Present* (Congleton, 1887)

Heath, James, *Flagellum: or, the Life and death, birth and burial of Oliver Cromwell, the late usurper* (London, 1663)

Herbert, William, *The History of the Twelve Great Livery Companies*, 2 vols (London, 1834)

Hessayon, Ariel, *'Gold Tried in the Fire': The Prophet TheaurauJohn Tany and the English Revolution* (Aldershot, 2007)

Hindle, Steve, 'Dearth and the English Revolution: the harvest crisis of 1647–50', *Economic History Review*, New Series, 61, S1, 2008, 64–98

The History of Hunstanton Parish Church (2002)

A History of the County of Cambridge and the Isle of Ely, Victoria County History, 10 vols (1938–2002)

A History of the County of Chester, Victoria County History, 5 vols (1979–2005)

A History of the County of Huntingdon, Victoria County History, 4 vols (1926–1938)

A History of the County of Middlesex, Victoria County History, 12 vols (London, 1969–2004)

A History of the County of Surrey, Victoria County History, 5 vols (1902–14)

A History of the County of Wiltshire, Victoria County History, 16 vols (London, 1953–1999)

A History of the Isle of Man written by William Blundell of Crosby Lancaster, 1648–1656, William Harrison (ed.), 2 vols (Douglas, 1876–7)

The History of the King's Works, H. M. Colvin (ed.), 6 vols (London, 1962–82)

The History of Parliament: The House of Commons 1604–1629, Andrew Thrush and John Ferris (eds) (Cambridge, 2010)

The History of Parliament: The House of Commons 1660–1690, B. D. Henning (ed.), 3 vols (London, 1983)

Holberton, Edward, *Poetry and the Cromwellian Protectorate: Culture, Politics and Institutions* (Oxford, 2011)

Holmes, Clive, 'The Trial and Execution of Charles I', *Historical Journal*, 53, 2 (2010), 289–316

Hostettler, John, and Brian Block, *Voting in Britain: A History of the Parliamentary Franchise* (Chichester, 2001)

Hotson, Leslie, *The Commonwealth and Restoration Stage* (London, 1928)

Hunneyball, Paul M., 'Cromwellian style: the architectural trappings of the Protectorate regime', in Patrick Little (ed.), *The Cromwellian Protectorate* (Woodbridge, 2007)

Hutton, Ronald, *Restoration: A Political and Religious History of England and Wales, 1658–1667* (Oxford, 1986)

Hutton, Ronald, *The Rise and Fall of Merry England: The Ritual Year 1400–1700* (Oxford, 1994)

Jacques, David, 'Garden design in the mid-seventeenth century', *Architectural History*, 44, 'Essays in Architectural History Presented to John Newman' (2001), 365–76

James, C. W., *Chief Justice Coke: His Family and Descendants at Holkham* (London, 1929)

Keay, John, *The Honourable Company: A History of the East India Company* (London, 1991)

Kelsey, Sean, 'Staging the trial of Charles I', in Jason Peacey (ed.), *The Regicides and the Execution of Charles I* (Basingstoke, 2001), 71–93

Kelsey, Sean, 'The death of Charles I', *Historical Journal*, 45, 4 (2002), 727–54

Kelsey, Sean, 'Constructing the Council of State', *Parliamentary History*, Vol. 22, pt 3 (2003), 217–41

Kelsey, Sean, 'Politics and procedure in the trial of Charles I', *Law and History Review*, 22 (1), Spring 2004, 1–25

Ketton Cremer, R. W., *A Norfolk Gallery* (London, 1948)

Kingston, Alfred, *East Anglia and the Great Civil War. The rising of Cromwell's Ironsides in the associated Counties of Cambridge, Huntingdon, Lincoln, Norfolk, Suffolk, Essex, and Hertford* (London, 1897)

Kitchin, George, *Sir Roger L'Estrange: a Contribution to the History of the Press in the Seventeenth Century* (London, 1913)

Kmec, Sonja, *Across the Channel: Noblewomen in Seventeenth Century France and England. A Study of the Lives of Marie de La Tour, 'Queen of the Huguenots', and Charlotte de la Trémoïlle, Countess of Derby* (Trier, 2010)

The Late King's Goods: Collections, Possessions and Patronage of Charles I in the Light of the Commonwealth Sale Inventories, Arthur MacGregor (ed.) (London and Oxford, 1989)

Law, Ernest, *The History of Hampton Court Palace*, 3 vols (London, 1885–91)

Lennon, Colm, *The Irish Historic Towns Atlas, Dublin, Part II: 1610–1756*, Royal Irish Academy (2008)

Little, Patrick, *Lord Broghill and the Cromwellian Union with Ireland and Scotland* (Woodbridge, 2004)

Little, Patrick, 'Music at the court of King Oliver', *The Court Historian*, 12:2 (Dec. 2007), 173–91

Little, Patrick, 'Oliver Cromwell's sense of humour', *Cromwelliana*, Series II, no. 4 (2007), 73–85

Little, Patrick, 'John Thurloe and the offer of the Crown to Oliver Cromwell', in Patrick Little (ed.), *Oliver Cromwell: New Perspectives* (Basingstoke, 2009), 216–41

Little, Patrick, 'Uncovering a protectoral stud: horses and horse-breeding at the court of Oliver Cromwell, 1653–8', *Historical Research*, 82 (216), May 2009 252–67

Litton Falkiner, C., *Illustrations of Irish History and Topography Mainly of the Seventeenth Century* (London, 1904)

Loomie, Albert J., 'Oliver Cromwell's policy toward the English Catholics: the appraisal by diplomats, 1654–1658', *Catholic Historical Review*, 90, No. 1 (Jan., 2004), 29–44

Mack, Phyllis, *Visionary Women: Ecstatic Prophecy in Seventeenth-Century England* (Cambridge, 1992)

Madge, Sidney J., *The Domesday of Crown Lands: A Study of the Legislation, Surveys, and Sales of Royal Estates under the Commonwealth* (London, 1938)

Maddison, R. E. W., *The Life of the Honourable Robert Boyle* (London, 1969)

Mandebrote, Giles, 'From the warehouse to the counting-house: booksellers and bookshops in late 17th-century London', in *A Genius for Letters: Booksellers and Bookselling from the 16th to the 20th Century*, Robin Myers and Michael Harris (eds) (Winchester, 1995)

Manley, Roger, *The History of the Rebellions in England, Scotland and Ireland* (London, 1691)

Marks, Alfred, *Tyburn Tree: its History and Annals* (London, 1908)

Marshall, Alan, *Intelligence and Espionage in the Reign of Charles II, 1660–1685* (Cambridge, 1994)

McCormick, Ted, *William Petty and the Ambitions of Political Arithmetic* (Oxford, 2009)

McDonald, F. M. S., 'The timing of General George Monck's march into England, 1 January 1660', *English Historical Review*, April 1990, 363–76

Memoirs of the Protector, Oliver Cromwell, and of his sons Richard and Henry, 2 vols (London, 1820–2)

Miller, C. William, 'Thomas Newcomb: a Restoration printer's ornament stock', *Studies in Bibliography*, 3 (1950–1), 155–70

Miller, C. William, 'A Bibliographical Study of "Parthenissa" by Roger Boyle Earl of Orrery', *Studies in Bibliography*, 2 (1949), 115–37

Miller, Leo, *John Milton and the Oldenburg Safeguard. Diaries and Letters of Herman Mylius* (New York, 1985)

Monarchs, Ministers and Maps: the Emergence of Cartography as a Tool of Modern Government in Early Modern Europe, David Buisseret (ed.) (Chicago and London, 1992)

Morrill, John, Cheshire 1630–1660: County Government and Society during the 'English Revolution' (Oxford, 1974)

Morrill, John, 'Sir William Brereton and England's Wars of Religion', Journal of British Studies, 24, 3 (Jul., 1985), 311–12

Morrill, John, 'The making of Oliver Cromwell', in John Morrill (ed.), Oliver Cromwell and the English Revolution (London and New York, 1990)

Morrill, John, 'The church in England 1642–1649', in The Nature of the English Revolution (London and New York, 1993), 148–77

Morrill, John, 'Cromwell, Parliament, Ireland and a Commonwealth in Crisis: 1652 Revisited', Parliamentary History, Vol. 30 (2), 2011, 06, 193–214

Mowl, Timothy, and Brian Earnshaw, Architecture without Kings: The Rise of Puritan Classicism under Cromwell (Manchester, 1995)

Muddiman, J. G., 'The licensed newsbooks, 1649 and 1650', Notes and Queries, CLXVII (1934)

Noble, Mark, Memoirs of the Protectorate-house of Cromwell, 2 vols (Birmingham, 1724)

Nevitt, Marcus, Women and the Pamphlet Culture of Revolutionary England 1640–1660 (Aldershot, 2006)

Nuttall, W. L. F., 'Hezekiah Haynes: Oliver Cromwell's Major-General for the Eastern Counties', in Transactions of the Essex Archaeological Society, I (3), third series (1964), 196–210

Oestmann, Cord, Lordship and Community: The Lestrange Family and the Village of Hunstanton, Norfolk in the First Half of the Sixteenth Century (Woodbridge, 1994)

Ormerod, George, The History of the County Palatine and City of Chester, 3 vols (London, 1819)

Ormerod, George, Tracts Relating to Military Proceedings in Lancashire during the Great Civil War (Manchester, 1844)

Ó Siochrú, Micheál, God's Executioner: Oliver Cromwell and the Conquest of Ireland (London, 2008)

Parker, Vanessa, The Making of King's Lynn (Phillimore, 1971)

Peacey, Jason, Politicians and Pamphleteers, Propaganda During the Civil Wars and Interregnum (Aldershot, 2004)

Peacey, Jason, '"Fit for public services": the upbringing of Richard Cromwell', in Patrick Little (ed.), Oliver Cromwell: New Perspectives (Basingstoke, 2009)

Peacey, Jason, '"Wandering with Pamphlets": the infrastructure of news circulation in civil war England', in Roleand Harms, Joad Raymond and Jeroen Salmans (eds), Not Dead Things: The Dissemination of Popular Print in

England and Wales, Italy and the Low Countries 1500–1820 (Leiden, 2013), 95–114

Peck, Linda Levy, *Consuming Splendor: Society and Culture in 17th Century England* (Cambridge, 2005)

Pestana, Carla Gardina, *The English Conquest of Jamaica: Oliver Cromwell's Bid for Empire* (Cambridge, Mass., 2017)

Pinckney, Paul J., 'Bradshaw and Cromwell in 1656', *Huntington Library Quarterly*, 30 (3) (May 1967), 233–40

Pincus, Steve, '"Coffee Politicians Does Create": coffeehouses and Restoration political culture', *Journal of Modern History*, Vol. 67, No. 4 (Dec., 1995)

Porter, Stephen, *Destruction in the English Civil Wars* (Stroud, 1994)

Poyntz, Nick, '"This day by letters severall from hands": News Networks and Oliver Cromwell's letters from Drogheda', in Martyn Bennett, Raymond Gillespie and Scott Spurlock (eds), *Cromwell and Ireland: New Perspectives* (Liverpool, 2021), ch. 10

Prendergast, John Patrick, *The Cromwellian Settlement in Ireland* (London, 1870)

Prynne, William, *A Summary Collection of the Principal Fundamental Rights, Liberties, Proprietaries of All English Freemen* (London, 1656)

Pugh, Ralph B., *Imprisonment in Medieval England* (Cambridge, 1986)

Purver, Margery, *The Royal Society: Concept and Creation* (London, 1967)

Ramsey, Robert W., *Henry Cromwell* (London, 1933)

Raymond, Joad, *The Invention of the Newspaper: English Newsbooks 1641–1649* (Oxford, 1996)

Raymond, Joad, 'An eye-witness to King Cromwell', *History Today*, 47 (7), July 1997, 36

Raymond, Joad, *Pamphlets and Pampleteering in Early Modern Britain* (Cambridge, 2003)

Raymond, Joad, 'International news and the Seventeenth-century English newspaper', in Roleand Harms, Joad Raymond and Jeroen Salmans (eds), *Not Dead Things: The Dissemination of Popular Print in England and Wales, Italy and the Low Countries 1500–1820* (Leiden, 2013)

Ribeiro, Aileen, *Fashion and Fiction: Dress in Art and Literature in Stuart England* (London and New Haven, 2005)

Riley, Sandy, *Charlotte de La Trémoïlle, the Notorious Countess of Derby* (Cambridge, 2017)

Roger L'Estrange and the Making of Restoration Culture, Anne Dunan-Page and Beth Lynch (eds) (Aldershot, 2008)

Rogers, G., *The Fifth Monarchy Men* (Oxford, 1966)

Roy, Ian, and Dietrich Reinhart, 'Oxford and the civil wars', in Nicholas Tyacke (ed.), *The History of the University of Oxford: IV. Seventeenth Century Oxford* (Oxford, 1997)

Rutter, Peter, *The Haberdashers' Oldest School: A History of the Aldersey School, Bunbury 1594–1994* (Cambridge, 1993)

Samuel, Wilfred S., and M. N. Castello, 'The first London synagogue of the resettlement', *Transactions of the Jewish Historical Society of England*, Vol. 10 (1921–1923), 1–48

Saunders, Ann (ed.), *The Royal Exchange*, London Topographical Society, 152 (1997)

Saunders, Ann, and John Schofield, *Tudor London: A Map and a Plan* (London, 2001)

Scholes, Percy A., *The Puritans and Music in England and New England: A Contribution to the Cultural History of two Nations* (Oxford, 1934)

Scott, Jonathan, *England's Troubles: Seventeenth-century English Political Instability in a European Context* (Cambridge, 2000)

Sharpe, Kevin, *Sir Robert Cotton, 1586–1631: History and Politics in Early Modern England* (Oxford, 1979)

Sharpe, Kevin, *Image Wars: Promoting Kings and Commonwealths in England, 1603–1660* (London and New Haven, 2010)

A Short History of Parliament: England, Great Britain, the United Kingdom, Ireland and Scotland, Clyve Jones (ed.) (Woodbridge, 2009)

Simington, Robert C., *The Transplantation to Connacht 1654–8* (Dublin, 1970)

Skinner, Thomas, *The Life of General Monk, Duke of Albemarle* (London, 1724)

Smyth, William J., *Map-making, Landscapes and Memory: a Geography of Colonial and Early-Modern Ireland c1530–1750* (Cork, 2006)

Spurlock, R. Scott, *Cromwell and Scotland: Conquest and Religion 1650–1660* (Edinburgh, 2007)

Spurlock, R. Scott, 'Cromwell's Edinburgh press and the development of print culture in Scotland', *Scottish Historical Review*, 90, 230, pt 2 (October 2011), 179–203

Stanley, Arthur, *Historical Memorials of Westminster Abbey*, 2 vols (London, 1911)

Stone, Lawrence, 'Inigo Jones and the New Exchange', *Archaeological Journal*, 114 (1957), 106–21

Stoyle, Mark, 'An early incident in the life of George Monck', *Devon & Cornwall Notes and Queries*, 37, 1992–6, 7–14

The Surrey Diggers Trail: Sites Associated with the Movement 1649–50, printed pamphlet, the Elmbridge Diggers Heritage Group

Thirsk, Joan, 'The Restoration Land Settlement', *Journal of Modern History*, 26, No. 4 (Dec., 1954), 315–28

Thomas, Keith, 'Women and the Civil War sects', *Past and Present*, 13, April 1958, 42–62

Thurley, Simon, *Whitehall Palace: An Architectural History of the Royal Apartments 1260–1698* (London and New Haven, 1999)

Thurley, Simon, *Hampton Court: a Social and Architectural History* (London and New Haven, 2004)

Tite, C. G. C., *The Manuscript Library of Sir Robert Cotton*, The Panizzi Lecture, 1993 (London, 1994)

Underdown, David, *Royalist Conspiracy in England 1649–1660* (Yale, 1960)

Unwin, Melanie, '"J'y Suis, J'y Reste": The Parliamentary Statue of Oliver Cromwell by Hamo Thornycroft', *Parliamentary History*, 28, 3, October 2009, 413–25.

Urwick, William, *Historical Sketches of Nonconformity in Cheshire* (London and Manchester, 1864)

Vaggi, Gianni, and Peter Groenewegen, *A Concise History of Economic Thought* (Basingstoke, 2003)

Walker, Katharine A., 'The military activities of Charlotte de la Trémoille, Countess of Derby, during the Civil War and Interregnum', *Northern History*, XXXVIII, 1, March 2001, 47–64

Waylen, James, *The House of Cromwell and the Story of Dunkirk* (London, 1880)

Whittle, Jane, and Elizabeth Griffiths, *Consumption and Gender in the Early Seventeenth Century Household: The World of Alice Le Strange* (Oxford, 2012)

Willetts, Pamela, 'Sir Nicholas Le Strange and John Jenkins', *Music & Letters*, 42, No. 1 (Jan., 1961), 30–43

Williams, J. B., 'Fresh light on Cromwell at Drogheda', *The Nineteenth Century and After*, 72 (1912), 471–90

Wilson, Christopher, 'Henry III's Palace at Westminster', in Warwick Rodwell and Tim Tatton-Brown (eds), *Westminster. II. The Art, Architecture and Archaeology of the Royal Palace*, BAA Transactions, XXXIX, part II (Leeds, 2015)

Wolf, Lucien, 'Crypto-Jews under the Commonwealth', *Transactions of the Jewish Historical Society of England*, Vol. 1 (1893–94), 55–88

Wood, Anthony, *The History and Antiquities of the University of Oxford*, John Gutch (ed.), 2 vols (Oxford, 1796)

Wood, Anthony, *Athenae Oxonienses: an Exact History of all the Writers and Bishops who have had their Education in the University of Oxford ... To which are added the fasti or annals of the said university*, Philip Bliss (ed.), 4 vols (London, 1813–20)

Woolrych, Austin, 'Yorkshire and the Restoration', *Yorkshire Archaeological Journal* (1958), XXXIX, 483–507

Woolrych, Austin, *Commonwealth to Protectorate* (Oxford, 1982)

Woolrych, Austin, *Britain in Revolution 1625–1660* (Oxford, 2002)

Worden, Blair, *The Rump Parliament* (Cambridge, 1974)

Worden, Blair, 'Oliver Cromwell and the sin of Achan', *History, Society and the Churches: Essays in Honour of Owen Chadwick* (Cambridge, 1985), 125–47

Worden, Blair, '"Wit in a Roundhead": the dilemma of Marchamont Nedham', in Susan D. Amussen and Mark A. Kishlansky (eds), *Political Culture and*

Cultural Politics in Early Modern England: Essays Presented to David Underdown (Manchester, 1995), 301–37

Worden, Blair, 'Whig history and puritan politics: The Memoirs of Edmund Ludlow revisited', *Historical Research*, 75/188 (2002), 209–37

Worden, Blair, *Literature and Politics in Cromwellian England: John Milton, Andrew Marvell, Marchamont Nedham* (Oxford, 2009)

Wren Society, XI, 'Designs by Sir Chr Wren for Westminster Abbey, the new dormitory Westminster School, works at Westminster Palace for the Houses of Parliament etc' (Oxford, 1934)

Yates, Samuel, *A History of the Ancient Town and Borough of Congleton* (Congleton, 1820)

UNPUBLISHED

'Castle Rushen, Castletown, Isle of Man, Conservation Plan', Drury McPherson Partnership commissioned by Manx National Heritage, June 2012

Cheshire Historic Towns Survey. Bunbury. Archaeological Assessment. English Heritage, 2003

Cole, Emily V., 'The State Apartment in the Jacobean Country House 1603–1625', D.Phil., University of Sussex, 2010

Peacey, Jason, 'Henry Parker and parliamentary propaganda in the English Civil Wars', Ph.D., Cambridge University, 1994

Ramsay, Octavia Beatrice, 'A Study of King's Lynn in the English Civil War', M. Phil., Cambridge, 2011

Smith, Peter, 'Petitionary Negotiations in a Community in Conflict: King's Lynn and West Norfolk c1575–1662', Ph.D., University of East Anglia, 2012

OTHER

The clergy of the Church of England Database, www.theclergydatabase.org.uk

London Apprenticeship Abstracts, 1442–1850, Guildhall Library, accessed via www.findmypast.com

Marriage Register of St Laurence Pountney, 'The Rejester Book for Marriages, for Christenings and Burials for St Georges in Southwark from 1602', www.ancestry.com

The Hartlib Papers, M. Greengrass, Leslie and M. Hannon (eds), The Digital Humanities Institute, University of Sheffield, Hartlib Papers (2013)

The Cromwell Association Online Directory of Parliamentarian Army Officers, Stephen K. Roberts (ed.) (2017)

INDEX